Multimedia Systems and Applications

Series Editor

Borko Furht

More information about this series at http://www.springer.com/series/6298

Paisarn Muneesawang • Ning Zhang • Ling Guan

Multimedia Database Retrieval

Technology and Applications

 Springer

Paisarn Muneesawang
Department of Electrical
  and Computer Engineering
Naresuan University
Muang, Phitsanulok, Thailand

Ning Zhang
Department of Electrical
  and Computing Engineering
Ryerson University
Toronto, ON, Canada

Ling Guan
Department of Electrical
  and Computer Engineering
Ryerson University
Toronto, ON, Canada

ISBN 978-3-319-35414-9   ISBN 978-3-319-11782-9 (eBook)
DOI 10.1007/978-3-319-11782-9
Springer Cham Heidelberg New York Dordrecht London

Printed on acid-free paper

Springer is part of Springer Science+Business Media (www.springer.com)

Acknowledgements

This book is dedicated to all the members of the former Sydney Multimedia Processing (SMP) Lab, University of Sydney; and to the members, past and present, of Ryerson Multimedia Processing Lab (RML), Ryerson University, Toronto.

In addition, the authors would like to thank Professor Sujin Jinahyon, President of Naresuan University; Dr. Tao Mei and Dr. Xian-Sheng Hua, Microsoft Research Asia (MSRA); Dr. Ling-Yu Duan and Dr. Wen Gao, Peking University.

Contents

Chapter 1
Introduction

1.1 Objectives

The ever-increasing volume of multimedia data being generated in the world has led to much research interest in multimedia database retrieval since the early years of the twentieth century. Computer vision and machine learning technologies have been developed, forming a solid research foundation for the creation of stage-of-the-art applications, such as MPEG-7, interactive multimedia retrieval, multimodal fusion, annotation, and database re-ranking. The time has come to explore the consequences of these multimedia applications. *Multimedia Database Retrieval: Technology and Application* is an application-oriented book, borne out of established researchers in this emerging field. It covers the latest developments and important applications in multimedia database technology, and offers a glimpse of future technologies. With a strong focus on industrial applications along with an overview of research topics, *Multimedia Database Retrieval: Technology and Application* is an indispensable guide for all engineers and researchers involved in the development and use of state-of-the-art systems in the multimedia industry. It serves as an invaluable reference for multimedia database technologies involving large scale image and video databases; interactive search and recognition technologies on mobile and on distributed and cloud databases; news video, sports video, and film; forensic image databases; and gesture databases of advanced motion training in virtual reality systems.

© Springer International Publishing Switzerland 2014
P. Muneesawang et al., *Multimedia Database Retrieval: Technology and Applications*,
Multimedia Systems and Applications, DOI 10.1007/978-3-319-11782-9_1

1.2   Multimedia Database Retrieval

1.2.1   Background

Living in the information era, we are surrounded by an enormous amount of digital content. According to Bohn and Short [1], the estimated size of newly created digital data in 2011 was about 1,800 exabytes (1 exabyte = 1 billion gigabytes), roughly 700 times more than the production in 2002 (2–3 exabytes). This number is equivalent to a ten-fold average annual growth rate. In terms of image and video content, according to the latest released statistics, YouTube hosts more than 120 million copyright claimed videos and serves four billion video requests per day [2]. Facebook, on the other hand, hosts about 50 billion photos (2010), 15 billion of which are tagged [3]. Another statistic shows that Facebook had 845 million monthly active users and 483 million daily active users on average in December 2011 [4]. Undoubtedly, digital content, including images and videos, are deeply rooted in our daily life, served on a wide range of devices, from desktops and laptops to mobile phones and tablets. Large-scale content-based multimedia data organization and analysis not only helps to retrieve users' desired information, but also serves as the basis for multimedia applications such as classification and retrieval of images/videos, forensic images, film, motion data, as well as the recent boom of cross-platform mobile visual search and recommendations.

1.2.2   Challenges

As a result of the recent explosion in the quantity of digital media, there is an urgent need for new and better techniques for accessing data. Indexing and retrieval are at the heart of multimedia system design—large amounts of multimedia data may not be useful if there are no effective tools for easy and fast access to the collected information. Once collected, the data must be organized efficiently, so that a query search via a search engine will yield a limited, yet useful, number of results. The retrieval process is designed to obtain limited information which satisfies a user at a particular time and within a particular domain application; however, this does not often work as efficiently as intended. A significant challenge, therefore, is to develop techniques that can "interpret" the multimedia content in large data collections to obtain all the information items relevant to the user query, while retrieving as few non-relevant ones as possible.

The analysis and retrieval of multimedia content in large-scale image and video databases faces more challenges than in small scale content-based multimedia analysis. Some of the unique challenges of large-scale multimedia analysis include:

- *Automatic classification and retrieval, with minimum human labeling and inter-vention.* According to a recent study, among web-based image and video consortia, only 5–10 % of the data are labeled [5]. The majority of multimedia data cannot be retrieved using current text-based search engines.

- *Multimedia retrieval, including efficient database index, compact storage, and quick and accurate retrieval performance.* Since large-scale databases consist of millions of images, the computational efficiency of both off-line and on-line retrieval processes is crucial.
- *Integration with cross platform-based applications.* With the emerging technologies of mobile devices and cloud computing, a lot of desktop-based multimedia applications need to be migrated to cloud and must find suitable positions in the mobile domain.

Multimedia database retrieval has attracted researchers from the fields of computer vision, machine learning, database technology, and multimedia for almost two decades. It still remains a popular research direction, especially when considering how to cope with the vast size and increasing growth of multimedia data. In the beginning of this millennium, Rui, Huang, and Chang stated that there are two major difficulties with large-scale image datasets [6]. One is the vast amount of labor required in manual image annotation. The other is how to understand different human perceptions towards the same image content. Moreover, the question of how to efficiently index large-scale image archives for fast retrieval was also raised as a fundamental consideration in designing large-scale image retrieval systems [6, 7].

1.2.3 The Development of Multimedia Database Retrieval Technology

This book presents the development of multimedia database retrieval technology from two perspectives. The first perspective presents up-to-date methods and appealing topics in multimedia retrieval. It shows the state-of-the art technology used for small, medium, and large-scale databases. The second perspective provides an application-oriented view of multimedia technology. This will inspire the reader towards innovation in developing new applications, and towards the practice of multimedia technology.

1.3 Technology Perspective

1.3.1 Human Centered Search and Retrieval

Visual seeking is the process of communication between a user and a computer system, and requires a decision-making method for both sides. This visual seeking involves interpretations of visual content by both the user and the computer. For successful retrieval, it is necessary that the user and the computer system use the same interpretation criteria.

However, human beings are complex creatures, and their motivations and behaviors are difficult to measure and characterize. As a result, the interpretation criteria utilized by human users are not fixed. Human beings are capable of interpreting and understanding visual contents—to simultaneously synthesize context, form and content—which is beyond the capability of any current computer method. Human interpretation depends on individual subjectivity and the information needed at a particular time and for a particular event. In addition, users learn from the available information (search results) to recognize their needs and refine their visual information requests (refine the queries) [8]. In other words, the interpretation of visual content by a human user is non-stationary, or fuzzy, and is very difficult to describe with fixed rules. A human user is an adaptive-learning component in the decision-making system.

In order to build a computer system to simulate and understand the decision making processes of human beings, the above-mentioned characteristics of adaptability should be taken into account. Learning to adapt and to optimize decision-making is primary to the goal of creating a better computer-based retrieval system.

1.3.1.1 User-Controlled Relevance Feedback

Chapter 1 of this book, therefore, explores the development of an adaptive machine that can learn from its environment, from both user advice as well as self-adaptation. Specifically, the adaptive machine requires two important properties to achieve this purpose: nonlinear decision-making ability, and the ability to learn from different sources of information (i.e., multi-modeling recognition). By embedding these two properties into the computer, the system can potentially learn what humans regard as significant. Through a human–computer interactive process, the system will develop the ability to mimic non-stationary human decision-making in visual-seeking environments. The relevant topics include: Content-based similarity measurement, using linear functions and nonlinear functions, Relevance feedback (RF), Linear/non-linear kernel-based adaptive retrieval, Single-class Radial basis function (RBF) network, RBF networks with adaptive learning, gradient-descent learning, fuzzy-RBF with soft decision, and a Bayesian framework for fusion of short-term relevance feedback (content information) and long-term relevance feedback (context information).

1.3.1.2 Machine-Controlled Relevance Feedback

Chapter 2 introduces the automation process to optimize the learning system by incorporating self-organizing adaptation into relevance feedback. This process is referred to as pseudo relevance feedback (RF). Optimization is the process of reducing the user's direct input, as well as adjusting the learning system architecture for flexibility in practical use in multimedia retrieval. While user interaction results in a valuable information exchange between the user and the computer, programming the computer system to be self-learning is highly desirable.

Consequently, the interactive retrieval system of Fig. 1.1a is generalized to include a self-learning component, as shown in Fig. 1.1b. The interaction and relevance feedback modules are implemented in the form of specialized neural networks. In these fully automatic models, the learning capability associated with the networks and their ability to perform general function approximations offers improved flexibility in modeling the user's preferences according to the submitted query.

Pseudo RF offers multimedia retrieval in fully automatic and semi-automatic modes, which allow: (1) avoidance of errors caused by excessive human involvement, (2) utilization of unlabeled data to enlarge training sets, and (3) minimization of iterations in RF. These properties are highly desirable for multimedia retrieval in a cloud-data center.

The relevant topics include: Pseudo-RF method, implemented by the self-organizing tree map, Compressed domain features, Energy histograms of discrete cosine transformation (DCT), Multi-resolution histograms of wavelet transformation, Re-ranking of images based on knowledge of region-of-interest, and Re-ranking of videos using the adaptive cosine network.

1.3.2   Internet Scale Multimedia Analysis and Retrieval

In order to cope with large scale multimedia classification and retrieval, this book presents the adoption of the bag-of-words (BoW) model for the analysis of images and videos. A BoW model can effectively combine the locally extracted feature vectors of either an image or a video frame. It focuses on the characteristics of the local feature ensemble, and treats individual local descriptors uniformly. The merits of the BoW model include the homogenous process in which it compactly represents images or video frames for classification, as well as its usability for large-scale image retrieval due to its success in text retrieval. The relevant topics this book will be presented as follows.

1.3.2.1   BoW in Unsupervised Classification and Video Analysis

The first topic describes the BoW model for unsupervised classification in video analysis. A distinguishing yet compact representation of the video clip is constructed using the BoW model. Candidate videos are indexed and represented as a histogram-based interpretation using the learned BoW model. The advantage of using the BoW model is that labeled data is not required. Therefore, video analysis can be realized for large-scale applications.

Chapter 8 of this book presents a systematic and generic approach by using the BoW based video representation. The system aims at event detection in

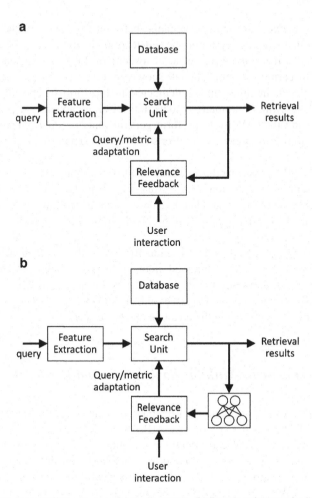

Fig. 1.1 (**a**) User-controlled relevance feedback system. (**b**) Pseudo-relevance feedback system

an input video via an orderly sequential process. Initially, domain knowledge independent local descriptors are extracted homogeneously from the input video sequence. The video's genre is identified by applying k-nearest neighbor (k-NN) classifiers onto the obtained video representation, with various dissimilarity measures assessed and evaluated analytically. Subsequently, an unsupervised probabilistic latent semantic analysis (PLSA) based algorithm is employed on the same histogram-based video representation to characterize each frame of video sequence into one of the representative view groups. Finally, a hidden conditional random field (HCRF) structured prediction model is utilized for detecting events of interest. In a trial evaluation, sports videos were used.

1.3.2.2 BoW in Retrieval and Mobile Image Search

Chapter 4 of this book explores the merits of using BoW in mobile visual search by effectively incorporating user interaction. Efficient and scalable indexing and non-linear fast retrieval algorithms are adopted in handling large-scale images. Human interaction is included in the loop. Therefore, specific user perception and distinguishing requests are used to lead the system into achieving a customized search result.

Based on the above idea, an interactive mobile visual search application aimed at social activity suggestion is developed using a coined term "visual intent", which can be naturally expressed through a visual query incorporating human specification. To accomplish the discovery of visual intent on the phone, Tap Tell was developed, as an exemplary real application. This prototype takes advantage of user interaction and rich context to enable interactive visual search and contextual recommendation. Through the *Tap Tell* system, a mobile user can take a photo and indicate an object-of interest within the photo via a *circle* gesture. Then, the system performs search-based recognition by retrieving similar images based on both the object-of-interest and surrounding image context. Finally, the contextually relevant entities (i.e. local businesses) are recommended to complete social tasks.

1.3.3 Mobile Visual Search

The widespread availability of networks has enabled portable multimedia devices, particularly mobile phones, to capture, share, and access vast amount of multimedia content. This has led to the emergence of technologies providing improved multimedia data management in mobile environments. Among others, *mobile visual search* technology has been at the center of mobile applications. Mobile phones are equipped with camera and imaging functionality, which enable a visual query that can be naturally expressed in a visual form instead of by text or voice. The user can capture the objects/scenes that he or she is interested in, and obtain relevant information about the captured objects/scenes [9].

In an advanced system for mobile visual search, instead of sending the whole query image over the network, a compact signature is used, achieving a low-bit-rate for the search. Figure 1.2 shows the vocabulary coding process of obtaining a compact signature for mobile visual search. The utilization of a compact signature overcomes the significant limitation of the battery power of mobile terminals, and achieves better uplink bandwidth at the servers and latency network access. To date, BoW models with scalable vocabulary tree (SVT) form the basis for research into the development of compact signatures [10]. However, the BoW model is limited by its homogenous process in treating all paths/regions without distinction. Features are extracted homogeneously, and local features are treated without emphasis. Therefore, a query image with unprioritized information can mislead a computer

Fig. 1.2 Mobile visual search via vocabulary coding through a wireless upstream query transmission pipeline. The scale invariance feature transform (SIFT) is applied to the captured landmark for feature extraction and the resulting features are encoded to obtain a compact signature for the recognition of the landmark image at the server end

visual recognition algorithm. Recognition requires discriminative BoW, to give a more distinctive representation for local descriptors through discriminative learning of image patches or saliency mapping.

Chapter 4 presents a soft-BoW method for mobile visual search based on the discriminative learning of image patches. Specifically, a multi-touch screen and the user's interaction on a mobile device are utilized by a user to select regions-of-interest (ROIs) as prioritized information, and the surrounding context is used as secondary information. Along with the BoW model, a context-embedded vocabulary tree (CVT) for soft weighting is adopted by using both the ROI and its surrounding image context to allow the mining of mobile visual intents. A system is built upon an initial visual query input to obtain the recognition results. Once the context metadata is associated with the intent, the system takes advantage of more reliable contextual text and Global Positioning System (GPS) features in searching and re-ranking. Ultimately, interesting and relevant social activities are recommended to the users. The discriminative BoW presented in this work not only enables mobile access to large multimedia repositories, but also provides more effective user interaction.

Chapter 5 focuses on mobile visual search systems, which can identify landmarks in a user's surroundings from the images captured by the camera on the user's devices, and retrieve interesting information related to those landmarks. In particular, saliency information is used with a re-ranking approach and incorporated at various stages of recognition: saliency-aware local descriptor, saliency-aware SVT, saliency-aware BoW, and discriminative learning via re-ranking. An important novelty of this work is that, instead of relying on a plain structure of a compact database of image signatures, the saliency information and re-ranking method are used for increasing discriminating power and improving recognition accuracy.

1.3.4   Multimedia Retrieval in a Cloud Datacenter

In today's multimedia network systems, multimedia files are distributed over the nodes in an overlay network as a cloud datacenter. Apparently, the searching of

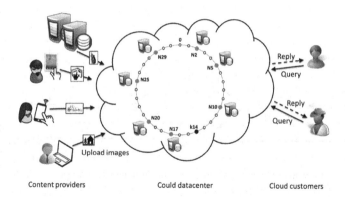

Fig. 1.3 A structured P2P network system utilizing a DHT to link nodes so that a query can be effectively and efficiently resolved. The nodes are clustered by the application of a self-organizing method in a cluster-identification search system

multimedia objects requires a large number of query transactions to be sent from nodes to nodes in the network. In comparison to a centralized datacenter, a retrieval task requires an initial search of the relevant nodes owning multimedia objects potentially relevant to the query, before it can perform similarity matching. In this regard, the *automatic clustering* of multimedia objects on the network is desirable for organizing the owner nodes in order to process the initial node search quickly.

Chapter 8 looks into an automatic clustering method for the organization of nodes in a distributed hash table (DHT) for effective node searching and retrieval of multimedia objects. A cluster-identification search system (CCS) is developed to organize nodes as a structured peer-to-peer network. A structured Peer-to-Peer (P2P) network, as shown in Fig. 1.3, uses a DHT to link nodes so that a query can be effectively and efficiently resolved. The automatic clustering allows the partition of nodes on the network in the DHT and Chord layers, according to the cluster identification. This indexing stage facilitates online search by pinpointing the relevant nodes without traversing all the participating nodes.

While the automatic indexing of nodes is one important requirement for retrieval systems in the cloud datacenter, increasing retrieval accuracy is another requirement. In this regard, the pseudo-relevance feedback presented in Chap. 8 can be applied to achieve sufficient improvement in retrieval accuracy without user supervision. In this scenario, the relevant node performs pseudo-RF and forwards the modified query to its neighbors. This offers continuously improving retrieval without transferring training samples over the network during adaptive searching.

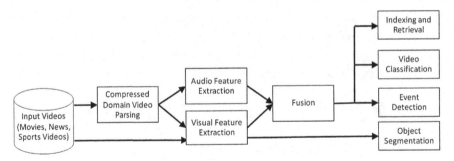

Fig. 1.4 Flow diagram of video processing in multimedia database retrieval

1.3.5   Technologies of 2-D Video and 3-D Motion Database Retrieval

Figure 1.4 summarizes the technologies of 2-D video database retrieval. This composts of various modules described in the following sections.

1.3.5.1   Video Indexing Beyond the Shot Level

Effective video retrieval requires a representation which is specifically applicable to the time-varying nature of video, rather than simply applying still-image techniques. The book presents a video representation based on Template-Frequency Mode (TFM) that is specific to video database applications. TFM is applied for video characterization at various levels, specifically, shot, group of shots, or story. Compared with traditional techniques, which use either a representative key-frame or a group of frames, TFM provides a new approach to video descriptors: it can organize and differentiate the importance of the visual contents in various frames, and it describes the contents of the entire video within a shot, group of shots, and a story. This provides multi-level access to video collections. Unlike previous querying methods that were limited to video shots or key-frames, TFM offers, to users who wish to retrieve a video group or story, the potential of sending queries using video clips that contain more accurate narratives.

Chapter 3 presents the development of TFM, while Chap. 7 presents its application in video retrieval systems that facilitate multi-level access to video databases. Chapter 10 then provides a more comprehensive evaluation of TFM and compares it to other video indexing methods.

1.3.5.2 Adaptive Video Retrieval with Human in the Loop

While many RF models have been successfully developed for still-image applications, they have not yet been widely implemented for video databases. This is because effective content-analysis through RF learning must also capture the temporal information in a video, and not just spatial information, as required for a single image. The fundamental requirement is a representation that allows RF processes to capture sequential information on a video file.

In this book, the efficiency of TFM-based video indexing in capturing user perception is demonstrated for video retrieval in the RF process as well as semi-automatic process. The technology developments along this line are presented in Chaps. 3, 7, 8, and 10.

1.3.5.3 Video Retrieval with Pseudo-Relevance Feedback

There is a difficulty faced in the practical application of RF learning in the domain of video databases. Compared to images, the interactive retrieval of video samples can be a time-consuming task, since video files are usually large. The user has to play a sufficient amount of videos to train the retrieval process to make a better judgment of relevance. Furthermore, on a network-based database, this RF learning process requires high-bandwidth transmissions during the user interaction.

The video retrieval strategy presented in this book combines the video indexing structure based on TFM with pseudo RF to overcome the above challenges. The integration of TFM with an (unsupervised) adaptive cosine network is presented to adaptively capture different degrees of visual importance in a video sequence. This network structure implements an pseudo RF process through its signal propagation with no user input to achieve higher accuracy in retrieval. Hence, this technique can avoid the time-consuming task of user-interaction, and allows suitable implementation of video retrieval on the network-based database. This pseudo-RF is presented in Chaps. 3 and 8.

1.3.5.4 Multi-Modal Fusion

Tasks involving the analysis of video content, such as detection of complex events, are intrinsically multimodal problems, since audio, textual, and visual information all provide important clues to identify content. The fusion of these modalities offer a more completed description of video and hence facilitate effective video retrieval.

Chapter 7 explores the multiple modalities in video with the MPEG-7 standard descriptors. Video segmentation is performed by characterizing events with motion activity descriptors. Then, the events are classified by multimodal analysis using motion, audio, and Mel Frequency Cepstrum Coefficients (MFCC) features.

Chapter 10 presents an audio-visual fusion that combines TFM-visual features with Laplacian-Mixture Model (LMM)-audio features. The multimodal signals of video are used to extract high-level descriptors via a support-vector machine decision fusion. This increases the system's capability to retrieve videos via concept-based queries. For example, the concepts "dancing" and "gun shooting" are utilized for retrieving relevant video clips.

1.3.5.5   Event Detection and Video Classification

Video classification explores audio, textual, and visual information to classify videos into categories according to semantics such as events. Examples of such events are the "Touchdowns" and "Field goals" in American football. The video classification method based on high-level concepts is presented in Chap. 7. The method classifies recurring events of the games without using any domain knowledge, utilizing MPEG-7 standard descriptors. The specific events are "Run play", "Field goal" and "Pass play". In addition, Chap. 9 presents the method for video genre classification. This method employs domain-knowledge independent descriptors, and an unsupervised clustering technique to identify video genres. Moreover, a systematic scheme is employed for detection of events of interest, by taking the video sequence as a query. After the video genre is identified, the query video is evaluated by a semantic view assignment as the second stage, using the unsupervised probabilistic latent semantic analysis (PLSA) model. Both genre identification and video classification tasks utilize the initially processed video representation as input, and unsupervised algorithm classifiers. Finally in the third task, the event of interest is detected by feeding the view labels into a hidden conditional random field (HCRF)-structured prediction model.

1.3.5.6   Video Object Segmentation

Video segmentation is done to allow the selection of some portions of video that contain meaningful video structure based on the user's goal. If the goal is to obtain video portions based on a single camera shot, a video parsing method is employed. However, if the goal is to segment the video according to the object of interest, a method for detection and tracking of video objects is needed. Chapter 7 discusses video object segmentation for both scenarios.

Video parsing will look into an algorithm to detect shot transitions from the compressed video, using the energy histogram of the discrete cosine transformation (DCT) coefficients. The transition regions are amplified by using a two-sliding window strategy for attenuation of the low-pass filtered frame distance. This achieves high detection rates at low computational complexity on the compressed video database.

The method for object-based video segmentation produces a video structure, which is more descriptive than the full portion of video sequence. The video objects are automatically detected and tracked from the input video according to the user preference. The segmentation method incorporates *shape prior* to implement

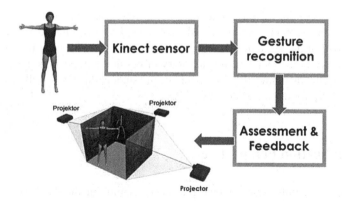

Fig. 1.5 3D motion database retrieval in a virtual reality dance training system

graph cut for video object segmentation. It is particularly effective when applied to video objects appearing at weak edges, with poor lamination distribution, and having backgrounds of similar color and movement. In addition, human faces are also interesting video objects. Detection algorithms have to cope with inconsistent performance due to sensitivity to lamination variations such as local shadowing, noise, and occlusion. The face detection method overcomes these problems by the incorporation of the local histogram and optimal adaptive correlation methods.

1.3.5.7 3D Motion Database Retrieval

3D motion data is acquired by the sensors in a process which is different from the acquisition of image and video data. The 3D motion data of human movement is represented by a time series of the body's joint positions. It can be captured by Microsoft Kinect in terms of the skeleton tracking of joint positions, as well as by the full motion capture system using optical-reflective markers. The usefulness of 3D motion database applications can be seen in the recent trend towards more immersive and interactive computing. This application requires tools to analyze, understand, and interpret human motion, in particular human gestural input. Human gestures include movement of the hands, arms, head, face or body with the intention of conveying meaningful information or interacting with the environment.

Figure 1.5 show the application of 3D motion database retrieval in a dance training system. In a virtual reality dance training system, dance gesture recognition is the key issue in the comparison of captured dance motion taken in real time from the trainee against the trainer data. The recognition result will enable the execution of subsequent tasks, such as automatic dance performance assessment, and synthesizing virtual dance characters and dance partners in the VR settings.

In Chap. 11, a dance training system is presented for automatic dance gesture recognition. The system adopts the spherical self-organizing map (SSOM) for the unsupervised parsing of dance movement into a structured posture space, which allows the description of the uniqueness of gestures for recognition, in terms of trajectories on the map. The hidden Markov model is then utilized for trajectory analysis. Within the system, the dance sequence of the student can be segmented online and cross-referenced against a library of gestural components performed by the teacher. This facilitates the assessment of the student dance, as well as provides visual feedback for effective training.

1.4 Application Perspective

This book is an application-oriented reference for multimedia database technologies. It reports the progress in the area that has led to a range of innovative applications and served in a number of different user scenarios, such as:

- *Search and retrieval of multimedia objects*, where a user from the local or remote terminals submits a query (in the form of audio, photos, texture, video files) to a search engine containing a large collection of multimedia repositories.
- *Mobile social network*, where users exchanges multimedia information among friends or people located in a certain area, possibly enriched with recommendation data related to points of interest. The users use the multi-touch screen to focus on the visual intent, and the visual recognition system recommends interesting restaurants, which may be incorporated with contextual information, such as geo-location, for location-based recommendations.
- *Landmark recognition*, whereby a user captures the landmarks/scenes that he or she is interested in, and obtains relevant information about the captured landmarks/scenes.
- *Movie/sports-video-on demand*, where a single long duration video is retrieved from a pool of servers, each of which retrieves disjoint portions of a movie in a particular sequence to form one complete continuous stream for the user. The book presents the indexing, retrieval, and classification methods for movie databases, which can be potentially adopted for the movie-on-demand application.
- *Interactive television news service*, where a user employs a news headline, which represents the subset of story, to retrieve full new stories, and find further relevant stories in newscasts.
- *Digital forensic investigation support*, where an investigator utilizes digital image (i.e., cartridge-based case image) taken at the crime scenes to query a forensic reference database to search for digital evidence, which can allow conclusions to be drawn for further physical investigation.
- *Virtual reality motion/dance training*, where a student dance is automatically captured and used as a query to retrieve similar teacher motion data in a database for the student's assessment; or where a user submits a short query motion clip, and the task is to retrieve all clips in the database containing parts or aspects similar to the query for data-driven computer animations.

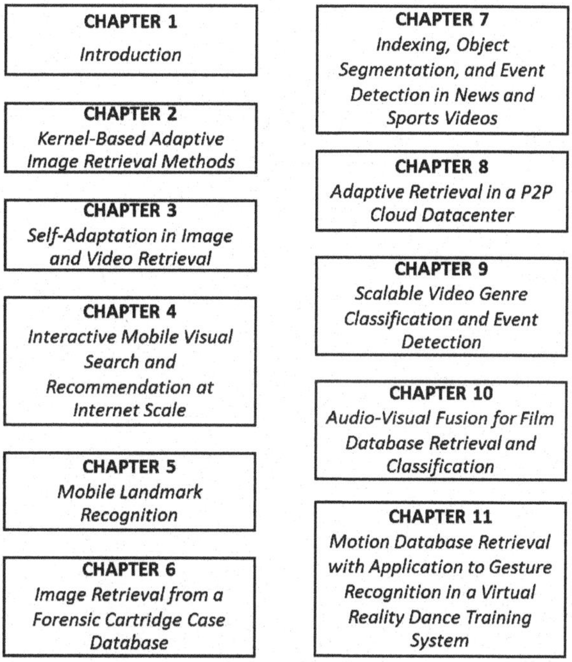

Fig. 1.6 Chapter outline of the book

CHAPTER 1 *Introduction*	**CHAPTER 7** *Indexing, Object Segmentation, and Event Detection in News and Sports Videos*
CHAPTER 2 *Kernel-Based Adaptive Image Retrieval Methods*	**CHAPTER 8** *Adaptive Retrieval in a P2P Cloud Datacenter*
CHAPTER 3 *Self-Adaptation in Image and Video Retrieval*	**CHAPTER 9** *Scalable Video Genre Classification and Event Detection*
CHAPTER 4 *Interactive Mobile Visual Search and Recommendation at Internet Scale*	**CHAPTER 10** *Audio-Visual Fusion for Film Database Retrieval and Classification*
CHAPTER 5 *Mobile Landmark Recognition*	**CHAPTER 11** *Motion Database Retrieval with Application to Gesture Recognition in a Virtual Reality Dance Training System*
CHAPTER 6 *Image Retrieval from a Forensic Cartridge Case Database*	

1.5   Organization of the Book

This book focuses primarily on the aspects of technologies and applications for the retrieval of image and video. Our prime goal is to describe how meaningful information can be extracted from multimedia signals, and how multimedia data can be efficiently described, compared and classified, as well as the relevant applications. Figure 1.6 provides an overview of the book's chapters.

Chapter 2
Kernel-Based Adaptive Image Retrieval Methods

Abstract This chapter presents machine learning methods for adaptive image retrieval. In a retrieval session, a nonlinear kernel is applied to measure image relevancy. Various new learning procedures are covered and applied specifically for adaptive image retrieval applications. These include the adaptive radial basis function (RBF) network, short term learning with the gradient-decent method, and the fuzzy RBF network. These methods constitute the likelihood estimation corresponding to visual content in a short-term relevance feedback (STRF). The STRF component can be further incorporated in a fusion module with contextual information in long-term relevance feedback (LTRF) using the Bayesian framework. This substantially increases retrieval accuracy.

2.1 Introduction

Adaptation of the traditional similarity function plays a vital role in enhancing the capability of image retrieval and broadening the domain of applications for machine learning. In particular, it is often necessary to adapt the traditional Euclidean inner-product to the more flexible and nonlinear inner products characterized by relevance feedback parameters. The new inner products lead to a new similarity metric. As a result, the image retrieval has to be necessarily conducted in a new space that is adaptively re-defined in accordance with different user preferences. This implies a greater flexibility for image retrieval. The topics addressed in this chapter are as follows:

Section 2.2 will look into the *linear kernel* that is implemented through the query adaptation method, metric adaptation method, and a combination of these methods. In a linear-based adaptive retrieval system, the similarity score of a pair of vectors may be represented by their inner product or Mahalanobis inner product.

Depending on the data cluster structure, either linear or nonlinear inner products may be used to characterize the similarity metric between two vectors. The linear metric would be adequate if the data distribution is relatively simple. To handle more complex data distributions, it is often necessary to adopt nonlinear inner products prescribed by nonlinear kernel functions, e.g., the *Gaussian radial basis function* (RBF). Section 2.3 introduce a single-class RBF method for adaptive retrieval.

© Springer International Publishing Switzerland 2014

P. Muneesawang et al., *Multimedia Database Retrieval: Technology and Applications*, Multimedia Systems and Applications, DOI 10.1007/978-3-319-11782-9_2

To cope with the small size of training sample sets and convergence speed, new learning methods are required for the construction of the RBF network, instead of the direct application of traditional learning procedures. Section 2.4 introduces an adaptive RBF network to exploit the local context defied by query sessions, and aids in improving retrieval accuracy. This section follows by the optimization of network parameters by the gradient-descent-based learning procedure, then introducing fuzzy RBF network which offers a soft-decision choice to the users.

Section 2.5 establishes the fusion of content and context information, by the application of Bayesian theory. The content component is gathered from a short-term relevance feedback (STRF), which is the estimation of the likelihood of a specific query model. The context information is obtained by a long-term relevance feedback (LTRF), representing a user history or the *a priori* information.

2.2   Kernel Methods in Adaptive Image Retrieval

2.2.1   Adaptive Retrieval Framework

The most important part in the adaptive process is the analysis of the role of the user in perceiving image similarity according to preferred image selections. This is implemented by a mapping function, $f_q : \mathbb{R}^P \to \mathbb{R}$, which is given by:

$$y_q = f_q(\mathbf{x}) \tag{2.1}$$

where $\mathbf{x} = [x_1, \ldots, x_P]^t$ is called a feature vector in a P-dimensional Euclidean space $\mathbb{R}^P$, corresponding to an image in the database. The main procedure is to obtain the mapping function f_q (for the query class q) from a small set of training images, $\mathscr{T} = \{(\mathbf{x}_1, l_1), (\mathbf{x}_2, l_2), \ldots, (\mathbf{x}_N, l_N)\}$, where the class label l_i can be in binary or non-binary form. In the binary form, the training samples contains a set of positive samples, $\mathscr{X}^+$ and a set of negative samples, $\mathscr{X}^-$:

$$\mathscr{T} = \mathscr{X}^+ \cup \mathscr{X}^- \tag{2.2}$$

$$\mathscr{X}^+ = \left\{ \mathbf{x}'_i | l_i = 1 \right\}, \quad i = 1, \ldots, N_p \tag{2.3}$$

$$\mathscr{X}^- = \left\{ \mathbf{x}''_j | l_j = 0 \right\}, \quad j = 1, \ldots, N_n \tag{2.4}$$

where N_p and N_n are the numbers of positive and negative samples, respectively.

The adaptive process for constructing the mapping function for retrieval is summarized in Table 2.1.

Table 2.1 Summary of the adaptive retrieval algorithm

Input:	Query vector $= \mathbf{x}_q$
	Set of vectors to be searched in the database $= \mathbf{x}_n, n = 1, \cdots, T$
Output:	The final retrieval set, containing k-relevant samples $= S_k(\mathbf{x}_q)$
Computation:	$$d(\mathbf{x}_q, \mathbf{x}_n) = \left[\sum_i^P |x_{qi} - x_{ni}|^2 \right]^{\frac{1}{2}}, n = 1, 2, \ldots, T,$$ $$S_k(\mathbf{x}_q) = \{\mathbf{x} | d(\mathbf{x}_q, \mathbf{x}) \leq d(\mathbf{x}_q, \mathbf{x}_k)\}$$ where $S_k(\mathbf{x}_q)$ is the set of nearest neighbors, and $\mathbf{x}_k$ is the k-th nearest neighbor of $\mathbf{x}_q$.
Repeat:	Obtain training sample: $\{\mathbf{x}_i\}_{i=1}^N \leftarrow S_k(\mathbf{x}_q)$
	User selects class label: l_i
	Calculate model parameters of the mapping function f_q
	Calculate $f_q(\mathbf{x}_n)$, for $n = 1, 2, \ldots, T$, and obtain $$S_k(\mathbf{x}_q) = \{\mathbf{x} | f_q(\mathbf{x}) \geq f_q(\mathbf{x}_k)\}$$
Until:	User is satisfied with the retrieval result.

2.2.2 Query Adaptation Method

Among the early attempts to conduct adaptive retrieval, Rui et al. [11, 12] implemented the query modification strategy, and the mapping function takes the form of the following linear function:

$$f_q(\mathbf{x}) = \frac{\mathbf{x} \cdot \mathbf{x}_{\hat{q}}}{\|\mathbf{x}\| \|\mathbf{x}_{\hat{q}}\|} \tag{2.5}$$

$$\propto K(\mathbf{x}, \mathbf{x}_{\hat{q}}) \tag{2.6}$$

where K is the linear kernel function:

$$K(\mathbf{x}, \mathbf{x}_{\hat{q}}) \equiv \langle \mathbf{x}, \mathbf{x}_{\hat{q}} \rangle \equiv \mathbf{x} \cdot \mathbf{x}_{\hat{q}} \tag{2.7}$$

and $\mathbf{x} \cdot \mathbf{x}_{\hat{q}}$ denotes the Euclidean inner product, $\mathbf{x}_{\hat{q}} = [x_{\hat{q}1}, \ldots, x_{\hat{q}P}]^t$ is the modified query vector, and $\|\cdot\|$ is the Euclidean norm. The linear kernel function represents the similarity metric for a pair of vectors, $\mathbf{x}$ and $\mathbf{x}_{\hat{q}}$. The two vectors, $\mathbf{x}$ and $\mathbf{x}_{\hat{q}}$

are called orthogonal if $\langle \mathbf{x}, \mathbf{x}_{\hat{q}} \rangle = 0$ in which case we write $\mathbf{x} \perp \mathbf{x}_{\hat{q}}$, i.e. they are geometrically perpendicular. Given two vectors, the smaller the magnitude of their inner-product, the less similar they are.

The modified query vector $\mathbf{x}_{\hat{q}}$ discussed in Eq. (2.7), is obtained by the training samples as:

$$\mathbf{x}_{\hat{q}} = \alpha \mathbf{x}_q + \beta \left(\frac{\sum_{i=1}^{N_p} \mathbf{x}'_i}{N_p} \right) - \varepsilon \left(\frac{\sum_{i=1}^{N_n} \mathbf{x}''_i}{N_n} \right) \tag{2.8}$$

where $\mathbf{x}_q = \left[x_{q1}, \ldots, x_{qP} \right]^t$ denotes the original query vector, and $(\alpha, \beta, \varepsilon)$ are suitable parameters [13]. The new query is obtained by adjusting the positive and negative *terms* of the original query. When adding the positive terms to the query, the modified query is close to the mean of the positive samples (i.e., $\mathbf{x}_{\hat{q}} \cong \bar{\mathbf{x}}'$), and the inner product $\langle \mathbf{x}', \mathbf{x}_{\hat{q}} \rangle \cong 1$. On the other hand, subtracting the negative terms from the query will make the modified query more dissimilar to the negative samples.

The query modification method has been widely used for information retrieval [13, 107] and image retrieval systems [14, 103]. However, one disadvantage of this model is the requirement of an indexing structure to follow term-weighting model, as in text retrieval for greater effectiveness. The models assume that the query index terms are sparse and are usually of a binary vector representation. However, as compared to text indexing, image feature vectors are mostly real vectors. Thus, a large number of terms can be applied for characterization of images in order to overcome this problem [103]. This also increases computational complexity.

2.2.3   Metric Adaptation Method

The Euclidean inner-product may be extended as the Mahalanobis inner product

$$K(\mathbf{x}, \mathbf{x}_q) = \langle \mathbf{x}, \mathbf{x}_q \rangle_{\mathbf{M}} = \mathbf{x}^t \mathbf{M} \mathbf{x}_q \tag{2.9}$$

with a weight matrix $\mathbf{M}$. The Euclidean inner product is a special case of the Mahalanobis inner product with $\mathbf{M} = \mathbf{I}$. In this case, we assume that all the features are equally weighted in their importance, and there exists no inter-feature dependence. However, when the features are mutually independent, but not isotropic, the Mahalanobis matrix takes the following form

$$\mathbf{M} = Diag\{w_i\}, \ i = 1, \cdots, P \tag{2.10}$$

where the weights $\{w_i, i = 1, \cdots, P\}$ reflect the importance of the respective features.

The Mahalonobis inner product leads to the following Mahalonobis distance between $\mathbf{x}$ and $\mathbf{x}_q$, which is associated as the mapping function as in [17, 19–24, 103],

$$f_q(\mathbf{x}) = \|\mathbf{x} - \mathbf{x}_q\|_{\mathbf{M}} \equiv \sqrt{(\mathbf{x} - \mathbf{x}_q)^t \mathbf{M}(\mathbf{x} - \mathbf{x}_q)} \qquad (2.11)$$

$$= \left(\sum_{i=1}^{P} w_i (x_i - x_{qi})^2 \right)^{\frac{1}{2}} \qquad (2.12)$$

$$\equiv \left(\sum_{i=1}^{P} h(d_i) \right)^{\frac{1}{2}} \qquad (2.13)$$

where $\mathbf{x}_q = [x_{q1}, \ldots, x_{qP}]^t$ is the feature vector of the query image, and $h(d_i)$ denotes a transfer function of distance $d_i = |x_i - x_{qi}|$. The weight parameters $\{w_i, i = 1, \cdots, P\}$ are called relevance weights, and $\sum_i w_i = 1$. The weight parameters can be calculated by the standard deviation criterion [17, 20, 21] or a probabilistic feature relevance method [16].

Different types of distance function have also been exploited. These include the selection of Minkowski distance metrics according to a minimum distance within the positive class [23], the selection of metrics based on reinforcement learning [22] and on the interdependencies between feature elements [25].

2.2.4   Query and Metric Adaptive Method

In order to reduce time for convergence, the adaptive systems have been designed to combine the query reformulation model with the adaptive similarity function [26–30]. Apart from Eq. (2.8), the query modification model can be obtained by a linear discrimination analysis [30], and a probabilistic distribution analysis methods applied to the training samples [28].

The optimum solutions for query model and similarity function can be obtained by the optimal learning relevance feedback (OPT-RF) method [26]. The optimum solution for a query model, obtained by Lagrange multiplier, is given by the weighted average of the training samples:

$$\mathbf{x}_{\hat{q}}^t = \frac{\mathbf{v}^t \mathbf{X}}{\sum_{i=1}^{N} v_i} \qquad (2.14)$$

where $\mathbf{x}_{\hat{q}} = [x_{\hat{q}1}, \ldots, x_{\hat{q}P}]^t$ denotes the new query, $\mathbf{v} = [v_1, v_2, \ldots, v_N]^t$, v_i is the degree of relevance for the i-th training sample given by the user, $\mathbf{X}$ is the training sample matrix, obtained by stacking the N training vectors into a matrix, i.e., $\mathbf{X} = [\mathbf{x}_1 \ldots \mathbf{x}_N]^t$. The optimum solution for the weight matrix $\mathbf{M}$ is obtained by:

$$\mathbf{M} = \begin{cases} (\det(C))^{\frac{1}{k}} C^{-1} & \text{if } \det(C) \neq 0 \\ Diag\left\{\frac{1}{C_{11}}, \frac{1}{C_{22}}, \ldots, \frac{1}{C_{PP}}\right\} & \text{Otherwise} \end{cases} \tag{2.15}$$

where C denotes the weight covariance matrix, given by:

$$C_{rs} = \frac{\sum_{i=1}^{N} v_i \left(x_{ir} - x_{\hat{q}r}\right) \left(x_{is} - x_{\hat{q}s}\right)}{\sum_{i=1}^{N} v_i}, \quad r, s = 1, \ldots, P \tag{2.16}$$

Based on Eq. (2.15), the weight matrix is switched between a full matrix and a diagonal matrix. This overcomes possible singularities when the number of training samples, N, is smaller than the dimensionality of the feature space, P.

Table 2.2 gives a summary of the OPT-RF method, where the relevance feedback process is conducted after the initial search.

Table 2.2 Summary of the optimal learning relevance feedback algorithm

Input:	Query vector $= \mathbf{x}_q$
	Set of vectors to be searched in the database $= \mathbf{x}_n, n = 1, \ldots, T$
	The training samples $= \{\mathbf{x}_i\}_{i=1}^{N}$
Output:	The final retrieval set, containing k-relevant samples $= S_k\left(\mathbf{x}_{\hat{q}}\right)$
Repeat:	User provides relevance scores of training samples, $v_1, v_2, \ldots, v_N$ Calculate new query: $\mathbf{x}_{\hat{q}}^t = \frac{v^t \mathbf{X}}{\sum_{i=1}^{N} v_i}$ Calculate weight parameter: $$\mathbf{M} = \begin{cases} (\det(C))^{\frac{1}{k}} C^{-1} & \text{if } \det(C) \neq 0 \\ Diag\left\{\frac{1}{C_{11}}, \frac{1}{C_{22}}, \ldots, \frac{1}{C_{PP}}\right\} & \text{Otherwise} \end{cases}$$ Calculate $f_{\hat{q}}(\mathbf{x}_n) = \left(\left(\mathbf{x}_n - \mathbf{x}_{\hat{q}}\right)^t \mathbf{M} \left(\mathbf{x}_n - \mathbf{x}_{\hat{q}}\right)\right)^{\frac{1}{2}}$, for $n = 1, 2, \ldots, T$, and obtain $$S_k\left(\mathbf{x}_{\hat{q}}\right) = \left\{\mathbf{x} | f_{\hat{q}}(\mathbf{x}) \leq f_{\hat{q}}(\mathbf{x}_k)\right\}$$ where $S_k\left(\mathbf{x}_{\hat{q}}\right)$ is the set of nearest neighbors and $\mathbf{x}_k$ is the k-th nearest neighbor of $\mathbf{x}_{\hat{q}}$. $$\{\mathbf{x}_i\}_{i=1}^{N} \leftarrow S_k\left(\mathbf{x}_{\hat{q}}\right)$$
Until:	User is satisfied with the retrieval result.

2.2.5   Nonlinear Model-Based Adaptive Method

The methods outlined above are referred to as linear-based learning and this restricts
the mapping function to quadratic form, which cannot cope with a complex decision
boundary. For example, the one-dimensional distance mapping function $h(d_i)$ in
Eq. (2.13) may take the following form:

$$h(d_i) = w_i d_i^2 \qquad (2.17)$$

where $d_i = |x_i - x_{qi}|$. This function has a small degree of nonlinear behaviour, i.e.,

$$\frac{\partial f_q(\mathbf{x})}{\partial d_i} = 2w_i d_i \qquad (2.18)$$

where w_i is *fixed* to a numerical constant for the respective feature dimension.

To simulate human perception, a radial basis function (RBF) network [31, 45]
is employed in this chapter. The input–output mapping function, $f(\mathbf{x})$, is employed
on the basis of a method called *regularization* [32]. In the context of a mapping
problem, the idea of regularization is based on the *a priori* assumption about the
form of the solution (i.e., the input–output mapping function $f(\mathbf{x})$). In its most
common solution, the input–output mapping function is *smooth*, in the sense that
similar inputs correspond to similar outputs. In particular, the solution function
that satisfies this regularization problem is given by the expansion of the radial basis
function [33]. In this case, a new inner product is expressed as a nonlinear kernel
function $K(\mathbf{x}, \mathbf{z})$:

$$\langle \mathbf{x}, \mathbf{z} \rangle = K(\mathbf{x}, \mathbf{z}) \qquad (2.19)$$

The Gaussian-shaped redial basis function is utilized:

$$K(\mathbf{x}, \mathbf{z}) = \exp\left(-\frac{\|\mathbf{x} - \mathbf{z}\|^2}{2\sigma^2}\right) \qquad (2.20)$$

where $\mathbf{z}$ denotes the center of the function and σ denotes its width. The activity of
function $K(\mathbf{x}, \mathbf{z})$ is to perform a Gaussian transformation of the distance $\|\mathbf{x} - \mathbf{z}\|$,
which describes the degree of similarity between the input $\mathbf{x}$ and center of the
function. Under Gaussian distribution, this function reflects the likelihood that a
vector $\mathbf{x}$ may be mistaken to be another vector $\mathbf{z}$.

To estimate the input–output mapping function $f(\mathbf{x})$, the Gaussian RBF is
expanded through both its center and width, yielding different RBFs which are then
formed as an RBF network. Its expansion is implemented via a learning process,
where the expanded RBFs can modify weighting, to capture user perception.

2.3 Single-Class Radial Basis Function Based Relevance Feedback

Whist in the later sections in this chapter, the P-dimensional RBF function is explored, in this section, a one-dimensional Gaussian-shaped RBF applied for the distance function $h(d_i)$ in Eq. (2.13), i.e.,

$$f_q(\mathbf{x}) = \sum_{i=1}^{P} G(x_i, z_i) \tag{2.21}$$

$$= \sum_{i=1}^{P} \exp\left(-\frac{(x_i - z_i)^2}{2\sigma_i^2}\right) \tag{2.22}$$

where $\mathbf{z} = [z_1, z_2, \ldots z_P]^t$ is the center of the RBF, $\sigma = [\sigma_1, \sigma_2, \ldots, \sigma_P]^t$ is the tuning parameter in the form of RBF width. Each RBF unit implements a Gaussian transformation which constructs a local approximation to a nonlinear input–output mapping. The magnitude of $f_q(\mathbf{x})$ represents the similarity between the input vector $\mathbf{x}$ and the center $\mathbf{z}$, where the highest similarity is attained when $\mathbf{x} = \mathbf{z}$.

Each RBF function is characterized by two adjustable parameters, the tuning parameters and the adjustable center:

$$\{\sigma_i, z_i\}_{i=1}^{P} \tag{2.23}$$

This results in a set of P basis functions,

$$\{G_i(\sigma_i, z_i)\}_{i=1}^{P} \tag{2.24}$$

The parameters are estimated and updated via learning algorithms. For a given query class, some pictorial features exhibit greater importance or *relevance* than others in the proximity evaluation [16, 30]. Thus, the expanded set of tuning parameters, $\sigma = [\sigma_1, \sigma_2, \ldots, \sigma_P]^t$ controlled the weighting process according to the relevance of individual features. If the i-th feature is highly relevant, the value of σ_i should be small to allow greater sensitivity to any change of the distance $d_i = |x_i - z_i|$. In contrast, a large value of σ_i is assigned to the non-relevant features. Thus, the magnitude of the corresponding function G_i is approximately equal to unity regardless of the distance d_i.

2.3.1 Center Selection

The selection of query location is done by a modified version of the learning quantization (LVQ) method [31]. In the LVQ process, the initial vectors (in a codebook), referred to as Voronoi vectors, are modified in such a way that all points partitioned in the same Voronoi cells have the minimum (overall) encoding distortion. The movement of the Voronoi vectors is based on the class labels provided in a training set, so as to improve the accuracy of classification. Let $\{\mathbf{z}_j\}_{j=1}^{J}$ denote the set of Voronoi vectors. Also, let $\{\mathbf{x}_i\}_{i=1}^{N}$ denote the set of training samples. First, for the input vector $\mathbf{x}_i[t]$ at iteration index t, the class index $c(\mathbf{x}_i)$ of the best-matching Voronoi vector $\mathbf{z}_c$ is identified by:

$$c = \arg\min_{j}\{\|\mathbf{x}_i - \mathbf{z}_j\|\} \tag{2.25}$$

The Voronoi vector $\mathbf{z}_c$ is modified by the *reinforced learning* rule if the class indexes of $\mathbf{z}_c$ and $\mathbf{x}_i$ are in agreement,

$$\mathbf{z}_c[t+1] = \mathbf{z}_c[t] + \alpha[t](\,\mathbf{x}_i[t] - \mathbf{z}_c[t]) \tag{2.26}$$

Otherwise, the modification is obtained by the *anti-reinforced learning* rule:

$$\mathbf{z}_c[t+1] = \mathbf{z}_c[t] - \alpha[t](\,\mathbf{x}_i[t] - \mathbf{z}_c[t]) \tag{2.27}$$

where $\alpha[t]$ is the leaning constant, which decreases monotonically with the number of iterations. All other Voronoi vectors remain unchanged, except the best-matching Voronoi vector.

In the adaptive image retrieval process, we have the training samples with two-class labels, $\{\mathbf{x}_i, l_i\}_{i=1}^{N}, l_i \in \{0, 1\}$, associated with the query vector, $\mathbf{x}_q$. This training set represents the set of points closest to the query, according to the distance calculation in the previous search operation. Consequently, each data point can be regarded as the vector that is *closest* to the Voronoi vector. Therefore, following the LVQ algorithm, it is observed that all points in this training set are used to modify only the best-matching Voronoi vector, that is, $\mathbf{z}_c \equiv \mathbf{x}_q$.

Center shifting model 1: The first model approximates the Voronoi vector (after the convergence) by the position that is close to the data points that are in the positive class ($l_i = 1$), and away from those points that are in the negative class ($l_i = 0$):

$$\mathbf{z}_c^{new} = \mathbf{z}_c^{old} + \alpha_R\left(\bar{\mathbf{x}}' - \mathbf{z}_c^{old}\right) - \alpha_N\left(\bar{\mathbf{x}}'' - \mathbf{z}_c^{old}\right) \tag{2.28}$$

$$\bar{\mathbf{x}}' = \frac{\sum_{i=1}^{N_p}\mathbf{x}_i'}{N_p} \tag{2.29}$$

$$\bar{\mathbf{x}}'' = \frac{\sum_{i=1}^{N_n}\mathbf{x}_i''}{N_n} \tag{2.30}$$

where $\mathbf{z}_c^{old}$ is the previous RBF center, $\mathbf{x}_i', i = 1, \ldots N_p$ are the positive samples, $\mathbf{x}_i'', i = 1, \ldots N_n$ are the negative samples, α_R and α_N are suitable positive constants.

Center shifting model 2: We may reduce the procedural parameters and provide a direct movement of the RBF center towards the positive class. Equation (2.28) is reduced to:

$$\mathbf{z}_c^{new} = \bar{\mathbf{x}}' - \alpha_N \left(\bar{\mathbf{x}}'' - \mathbf{z}_c^{old} \right) \tag{2.31}$$

Since the positive class indicates the user's preferred images, the presentation of $\bar{\mathbf{x}}'$ for the new RBF center will give a reasonable representation of the desired images. In particular, the mean value, $\bar{x}' = \frac{1}{N_p} \times \sum_{i=1}^{N_p} x_i'$, is a statistical measure providing a good representation of the i-th feature component since this is the value which minimizes the average distance $\frac{1}{N_p} \times \sum_{i=1}^{N_p} (x_i' - \bar{x}')$.

2.3.2   Width Selection

The RBFs are adjusted in accordance with different user preferences and different types of images. Through the proximity evaluation, differential biases are assigned to each feature, while features with higher relevance degrees are emphasized, and those with lower degrees are de-emphasized. To estimate the relevance of individual features, the training vectors associated with the set of positive images are used to form an $N_p \times P$ feature matrix $\mathbf{R}$,

$$\mathbf{R} = \left[\bar{\mathbf{x}}_1' \dots \bar{\mathbf{x}}_m' \dots \bar{\mathbf{x}}_{N_p}' \right]^t \tag{2.32}$$

$$= [x_{mi}'], \quad m = 1, \dots, N_p, \quad i = 1, \dots, P \tag{2.33}$$

where x_{mi}' is the i-th component of the m-th feature vector $\bar{\mathbf{x}}_m'$, P is the total number of features, and N_p is the number of positive samples. As the previous discussion, the tuning parameter σ_i should reflect the relevance of individual features. It was demonstrated, in [16,34], that given a particular numerical value z_i for a component of the query vector, the length of the interval which complexly encloses z_i and a pre-determined number L of the set of values x_{mi}' in the positive set which falls into its vicinity, is a good indication of the relevancy of the feature. In other words, the relevancy of the i-th feature is related to the density of x_{mi}' around z_i, which is inversely proportional to the length of the interval. A large density usually indicates high relevancy for a particular feature, while a low density implies that the corresponding feature is not critical to the similarity characterization. Setting $L = N_p$, the set of turning parameters is thus estimated as follows:
RBF width model 1:

$$\sigma = [\sigma_1, \dots, \sigma_i, \dots \sigma_P]^t \tag{2.34}$$

$$\sigma_i = \eta \cdot \max_m \left(|x_{mi}' - z_i| \right) \tag{2.35}$$

The factor η guarantees a reasonably large output $G(x_i, z_i)$ for the RBF unit, which indicates the degree of similarity, e.g., $\eta = 3$.

RBF width model 2: The feature relevancy is also related to sample variance in the positive set $\{x'_{mi}\}_{m=1}^{N_p}$, and thus, the RBF width can also be obtained by

$$\sigma_i = \exp\left((\beta)\,Std_i\right) \tag{2.36}$$

$$Std_i = \left(\frac{1}{N_p - 1}\sum_{m=1}^{N_p}\left(x'_{mi} - \bar{x}'\right)^2\right)^{\frac{1}{2}} \tag{2.37}$$

where Std_i is the standard deviation of the members in set $\{x'_{mi}\}_{m=1}^{N_p}$ which is inversely proportional to their density (Gaussian distribution), and β is a positive constant. The parameter β can be chosen to maximize or minimize the influence of Std_i on the RBF width. For example, when β is large, a change in Std_i will be exponentially reflected in the RBF width σ_i.

Both models provide a small value of σ_i if the i-th feature is highly relevant. This allows higher sensitivity to any change in the distance $d_i = |x_i - z_i|$. In contrast, a high value of σ_i is assigned to the non-relevant feature, so that the corresponding vector component can be disregarded when determining the similarity. Table 2.3 summarizes the RBF-based relevance feedback algorithm using RBF center model 1 and RBF width model 1.

2.3.3 Experimental Result

This section reports the experimental results [35, 329] of the nonlinear RBF approach in comparison with linear-based adaptive retrieval methods. Table 2.4 describes the database and feature extraction methods used in the experiment. The Laplacian mixture model (LMM) demonstrated in [35] is applied to the texture images for feature characterization. Table 2.5 summarizes the learning procedure of all methods of comparison, which comprise of the RBF method, the query adaption method (QAM), and the metric adaption method (MAM). Table 2.6 summarizes the retrieval results in terms of average precision. The initial precision of 76.7 %, averaged over all queries, was obtained. The precision was significantly improved by updating weighting functions. During relevance feedback, most of the performance enhancement was achieved after the first iterations. A slight improvement was achieved after the second iteration. A significant improvement in the retrieval efficiency was observed by employing a nonlinear RBF method. The final results, after learning, show that RBF-1 gave the best performance with 88.12 % correct retrievals, followed by RBF-2 (87.37 %), and MAM (80.74 %) at a distant third. The QAM is also given for benchmarking purposes.

Figure 2.1 illustrates retrieval examples with and without learning similarity. It shows some of the difficult patterns analyzed, which clearly illustrates the superiority of the RBF method.

Table 2.3 Summary of the single-RBF based relevance feedback algorithm

Input:	Query vector $= \mathbf{x}_q$
	The training samples $= \{\mathbf{x}_i\}_{i=1}^N$
Output:	The final retrieval set, containing k-relevant samples $= S_k(\mathbf{x}_q)$
Initialization:	RBF center $\mathbf{z}_c \equiv \mathbf{x}_q$
Repeat:	User labels training samples, i.e., $l_i, i = 1,\dots,N, l_i \in \{0,1\}$
	Calculate RBF center: $\mathbf{z}_c^{new} = \mathbf{z}_c^{old} + \alpha_R\left(\bar{\mathbf{x}}' - \mathbf{z}_c^{old}\right) - \alpha_N\left(\bar{\mathbf{x}}'' - \mathbf{z}_c^{old}\right)$
	Calculate RBF widths:
	$$\sigma_i = \eta \max_m \left|x'_{mi} - z_i\right|, \ i = 1,\dots,P$$
	Calculate $f_q(\mathbf{x}_n) = \sum_{i=1}^P G(x_{ni}, z_i)$, for $n = 1,2,\dots,T$, and obtain
	$$S_k(\mathbf{x}_q) = \left\{\mathbf{x} \mid f_q(\mathbf{x}) \geq f_q(\mathbf{x}_k)\right\}$$
	where $S_k(\mathbf{x}_q)$ is the set of nearest neighbors and $\mathbf{x}_k$ is the k-th nearest neighbor of $\mathbf{x}_q$.
	$$\{\mathbf{x}_i\}_{i=1}^N \leftarrow S_k(\mathbf{x}_q)$$
Until:	User is satisfied with the retrieval result.

Table 2.4 Database and feature extraction methods

Item	Description
Brodatz texture database	The database contains 1,856 texture images divided into 116 classes. Every class has 16 images
Laplacian mixture model (LMM) [35]	The images are decomposed to three levels using Daubechies wavelet filters (db4). The wavelet coefficients in each of high-frequency subbands are modeled as a mixture of two Laplacians. The parameters of the model are used as the features. The feature set composes of (1) the mean and standard deviation of the wavelet coefficients in the approximation subbands and (2) the variances of the two Laplacians in each of the nine high-frequency subbands. This results in 20-dimensional feature vector

In the second experiment, the adaptive retrieval methods are applied in photograph collection. Table 2.7 gives details of the database and the multiple types of visual descriptors, including color, texture, and shape. Table 2.8 gives details of the methods being compared. The average precision rates and CPU times required are summarized in Table 2.9. Evidently, the nonlinear RBF method exhibits significant retrieval effectiveness, while offering more flexibility than MAM and OPT-RF. With the large, heterogeneous image collection, an initial result obtained by the non-adaptive method had less than 50 % precision. With the application of the RBF learning method, the performance could be improved to greater than 90 % precision. Due to limitations in the degree of adaptability, MAM provides the

Table 2.5 Comparison of adaptive retrieval methods

Method	Learning algorithm
RBF-1	RBF center model 1 ($\alpha_R = 1.2$, $\alpha_N = 0.08$)
	RBF width model 1 ($\eta = 12$)
RBF-2	RBF center model 2 ($\alpha_R = 1.2$)
	BRF width model 1 ($\eta = 12$)
QAM [12, 14, 18, 36, 51, 103]	Query modification in Eq. (2.8), Cosine similarity metric in Eq. (2.6) ($\alpha = 1$, $\beta = 4$, $\gamma = 0.8$)
MAM [17, 20, 21]	City-block distance is used for similarity metric. The feature weighting is obtained by the standard deviation criterion

Table 2.6 Average
precision (%)

Method	Iter. 0	Iter. 1	Iter. 2	Iter. 3
MAM	76.70	80.43	80.71	80.74
RBF-1	76.70	85.02	86.90	88.12
RBF-2	76.70	85.32	86.80	87.37
QAM	67.10	75.12	76.42	76.95

lowest performance gains and converges at about 62 % precision. It is observed that the learning capability of RBF is more robust than that of OPT-RF, not only in retrieval capability, but also learning speed. As presented in Table 2.9, results after one round of the RBF method are similar to results after three rounds of the OPT-RF method. This quick learning is highly desirable, since the user workload can be minimized. This robustness follows from imposing nonlinear discriminant capability in combination with positive and negative learning strategies.

Typical retrieval sessions are shown in Fig. 2.2, for the Yacht query. Figure 2.2a show the 16 best-matches images before applying any feedback, with query image display in the top-left corner. It was observed that some retrieved images were similar to the query image in terms of color composition. In this set, three retrieved images were marked as relevant subjects to the ground truth classes. Figure 2.2b shows the improvement in retrieval after three rounds of using the RBF learning method. This is superior to the results obtained by MAM (cf. Fig. 2.2c) and OPT-RF (cf. Fig. 2.2d). This query may be regarded as a "hard" query, which requires a high degree of nonlinear discrimination analysis. There are some quires that are relatively easier to retrieve, which are shown in Fig. 2.3. Those queries have prominent features, such as a shape in the Rose query, and a combination of texture and color in the Polo query. In each case, it is observed that the MAM and OPT-RF methods show better performance than in the previous results. In these cases, however, the retrieval results obtained by RBF approached 100 % precision.

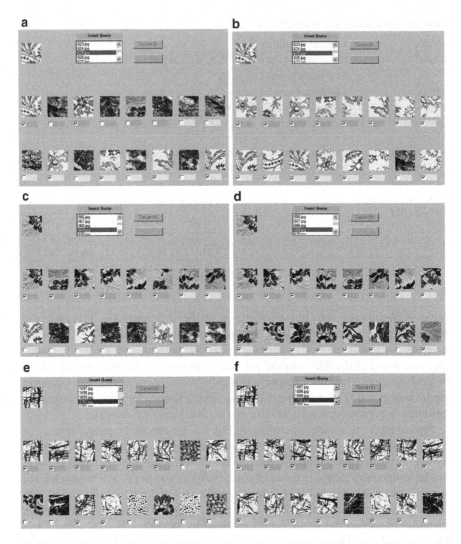

Fig. 2.1 Top 16 retrievals obtained by retrieving textures D625, D669, and D1700 from the Brodatz database, using RBF-1. Images on the *left*, (**a**), (**c**), and (**e**) show results before learning, and images on the right, (**b**), (**d**), and (**f**), show results after learning

2.4   Multi-Class Radial Basis Function Method

In image retrieval, particularly in general image collections, the relevancy of images to a specific query is most appropriately characterized by a multi-class modeling approach. For example, when a user has a query for a plane, she or he may wish to have any image containing planes. The semantics of a plane is usually described by a variety of models, which are correlated, but each of which has its

Table 2.7 Database and feature extraction methods

Item	Description
Corel database [73]	The database contains 40,000 real-life images divided into 400 classes. Every class has 100 images
Color histogram [38] and color moments	The first descriptor is a 48-bin color histogram in HSV color space. The second descriptor is a nine-dimensional vector, conducted from the mean, standard deviation, and skew of the three RGB-color channels
Gabor wavelet descriptor [91]	The 48-dimensional descriptor contains the mean and standard deviations of the Gabor wavelet coefficients from the filtering in four scales and six orientations
Fourier descriptor [37]	The nine-dimensional descriptor contains the Fast Fourier transform coefficients (at low frequency) of the edge information of an input image

Table 2.8 Comparison of adaptive retrieval methods

Method	Learning algorithm
RBF	RBF center model 2, RBF width model 2
OPT-RF [26]	Optimum query adaptation model Eq. (2.14), optimum weighting metric Eq. (2.15), Mahalanobis distance Eq. (2.11) as similarity function
MAM [17,20,21]	Mahalanobis distance Eq. (2.11) as similarity function, weight parameters Eq. (2.10) are obtained by the standard deviation criterion

Table 2.9 Average precision rate (%) obtained by retrieving 35 queries selected from different categories, using the Corel database (columns 2–5)

Method	Iter. 0	Iter. 1	Iter. 2	Iter. 3	CPU time (Sec./Iter.)
RBF	44.82	79.82	88.75	91.76	2.34
MAM	44.82	60.18	61.61	61.96	1.26
OPT-RF	44.82	72.14	79.64	80.84	1.27
Non-adaptive method	44.82	–	–	–	0.90

Average CPU time obtained by retrieving a single query, not including the time to display the retrieved images, measured from a 1.8 GHz Pentium IV processor and a MATLAB implementation

own local characteristics. The difficulty in characterizing image relevancy, then, is identifying the local context associated with each of the sub-classes within the class plane. Human beings utilize multiple types of modeling information to acquire and develop their understanding about image similarity. To obtain more accurate, robust, and natural characterizations, a computer must generate a fuller definition of what humans regard as significant features. Through user feedback, computers do acquire knowledge of novel features which are significant but have not been explicitly specified in the training data. This implicit information constitutes subclasses within the query, permitting better generalization. In this case, a mixture of Gaussian models is used, via the RBF network, to represent multiple types of model information for the recognition and presentation of images by machines.

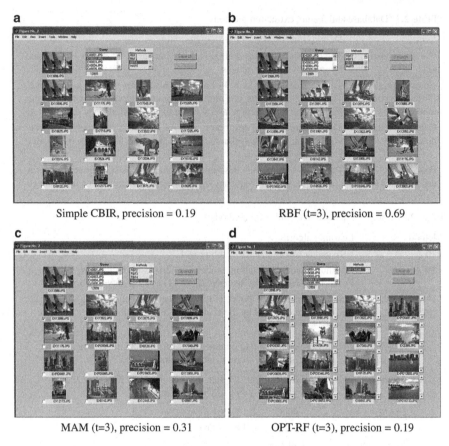

a Simple CBIR, precision = 0.19   **b** RBF (t=3), precision = 0.69

c MAM (t=3), precision = 0.31   **d** OPT-RF (t=3), precision = 0.19

Fig. 2.2 Top 16 retrieved images obtained by the Yacht query, using the Corel Database, (**a**) before RF learning, (**b**) after RF learning with the RBF method, (**c**) MAM, and (**d**) OPT-RF

Previously, Sect. 2.3 introduced a nonlinear input–output mapping function based on a single-RBF model. As discussed by most other works [15–17], this has been concerned with *global* modeling, in which a query image is described by one model, which is then associated with only a particular location in the input space. Furthermore, the similarity function is based on a single metric. This combination gives rise to a single model function $f(\mathbf{x})$, which cannot fully exploit the local data information. This section introduces a mixture of Gaussian models for adaptive retrieval that enables the learning system to take advantage of the information from multiple sub-classes. The learning system utilizes a highly local characterization of image relevancy in the form of a superposition of different local models, as $\sum_i f_i(\mathbf{x})$, to obtain the input–output mapping function.

The learning methods for constructing the RBF network include the adaptive RBF method [61], gradient-descent method [40], and fuzzy RBF method [39].

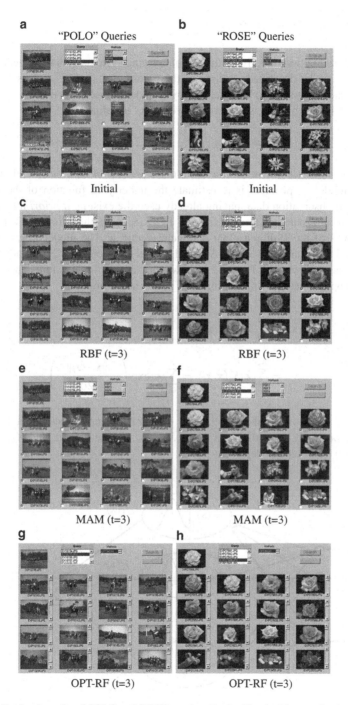

Fig. 2.3 Retrieval results of POLO and ROSE queries, obtained by (**a, b**) non-adaptive retrieval method, (**c, d**) RBF, (**e, f**) MAM, and (**g, h**) OPT-RF

2.4.1 Local Model Network

The basic assumption underlying the use of learning systems is that the behavior of the system can be described in terms of the training set $\{\mathbf{x}_i, y_i\}_{i=1}^N$. It is therefore assumed that the system to be described by a model whose observable output y_i, at the time of step i, in response to an input vector $\mathbf{x}_i$, is defined by:

$$y_i = f(\mathbf{x}_i) + \varepsilon_i, \quad i = 1, 2, \dots, N \tag{2.38}$$

where ε_i is a sample drawn from a white noise process of zero mean and variance σ^2. The modeling problem is to estimate the underlying function of the model, $f(\mathbf{x}_i)$, from observation data, having already used the existing *a priori* information to structure and parameterize the model. Let $\hat{f}(\mathbf{x}, \mathbf{z})$ be the estimate of $f(\mathbf{x})$ for some values of the P-dimensional parameter vector $\mathbf{z}$. The model $\hat{f}(\mathbf{x}, \mathbf{z})$ can be estimated in a number of ways. A Local Model Network (LMN), is adopted to achieve this purpose [41]. Figure 2.4 shows the network architecture. This type of network approximates the model function $\hat{f}(\mathbf{x}, \mathbf{z})$ according to:

$$\hat{f}(\mathbf{x}) = \sum_{i=1}^{N_m} \lambda_i \hat{f}_i(\mathbf{x}, \mathbf{z}_i) \tag{2.39}$$

$$= \sum_{i=1}^{N_m} \lambda_i K_i(\mathbf{x}, \mathbf{z}_i) = \sum_{i=1}^{N_m} \lambda_i \exp\left(-\frac{\|\mathbf{x} - \mathbf{z}_i\|^2}{2\sigma_i^2}\right) \tag{2.40}$$

where $\mathbf{x} = [x_1, \dots, x_P]^t$ and $\mathbf{z} = [z_1, \dots, z_P]^t$ are the input vector and the RBF center, respectively. In addition, $\lambda_i, i = 1, \dots, N_m$ are the weight, and $K(\mathbf{x}, \mathbf{z})$ is a nonlinearity of hidden nodes.

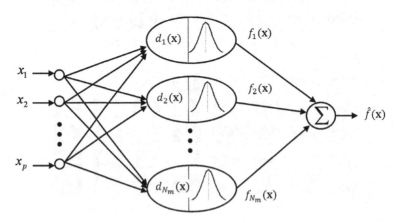

Fig. 2.4 RBF network architecture

The advantage of this network's use in the current application is that it finds the input-to-output map using local approximators; consequently, the underlying basis function responds only to a small region of the input space where the function is centered, e.g., a Gaussian response, $K_i = \exp\left(-\frac{d^2}{2}\right)$, where:

$$d\left(\mathbf{x}, \mathbf{z}_i, \sigma_i\right) = \sqrt{\left(\mathbf{x} - \mathbf{z}\right)^t \sigma_i^{-2} \left(\mathbf{x} - \mathbf{z}_i\right)} \qquad (2.41)$$

This allows local evaluation for image similarity matching.

The parameters to learn for the LMN are the set of linear weight λ_i, the center $\mathbf{z}_i$, and the width σ_i for each local approximator $K_i, i = 1, \ldots, N_m$. The linear weights are usually estimated by the least-squared (LS) method [43]. When using the Gaussian function as the nonlinearity of hidden nodes, it has been observed that the same width of σ_i is sufficient for the RBF network to obtain universal approximation [42]. However, more recent theoretical investigations and practical results indicate that the choice of center $\mathbf{z}_i$ is most significant in the performance of the RBF network [44]. As we shall see, this suggestion plays a central role in overcoming the variation in the performance of the network in the adaptive retrieval application.

2.4.2 Learning Methods for the RBF Network

Various learning strategies have been proposed to structure and parameterize the RBF network [41, 43–45]. This section will consider two of these beside the new learning strategy for adaptive image retrieval. For a given training set $\{\mathbf{x}_i, y_i\}_{i=1}^{N}$, the initial approaches [41], constructed the RBF network by associating all available training samples to the hidden units, using one-to-one correspondence. A radial-basis function centered at $\mathbf{z}_i$ is defined as:

$$K\left(\mathbf{x}, \mathbf{z}_i\right) = \exp\left(-\frac{\|\mathbf{x} - \mathbf{z}_i\|^2}{2\sigma_i^2}\right), \quad i = 1, \ldots, N_m \qquad (2.42)$$

where

$$\{\mathbf{z}_i\}_{i=1}^{N_m} = \{\mathbf{x}_i\}_{i=1}^{N}, \quad N_m = N \qquad (2.43)$$

This solution may be expensive, in terms of computational complexity, when N is large. Thus, we may arbitrarily choose some data points as centers [43]. This gives an approximation to the original RBF network, while providing a more suitable basis for practical applications. In this case, the approximated solution is expanded on a finite basis:

$$\hat{f}\left(\mathbf{x}\right) = \sum_{i=1}^{N_m} \lambda_i K\left(\mathbf{x}, \mathbf{z}_i\right) \qquad (2.44)$$

where

$$\{\mathbf{z}_i\}_{i=1}^{N_m} \subset \{\mathbf{x}_i\}_{i=1}^{N}, \quad N_m < N \tag{2.45}$$

The linear weights λ_i, $i = 1, \ldots, N_m$ are determined by minimizing the following cost function, $\xi(f)$:

$$\xi\left(\hat{f}\right) = \sum_{i=1}^{N} \left(y_i - \sum_{j=1}^{N_m} \lambda_j K\left(\mathbf{x}_i, \mathbf{z}_j\right) \right)^2 + \gamma \left\| \mathbf{D}\hat{f} \right\|^2 \tag{2.46}$$

where γ is the regularization parameter, and $\mathbf{D}$ is a differential operator. Based on the *pseudoinverse* method [43], the minimization of Eq. (2.46) with respect to the weight vector $\lambda = [\lambda_1, \ldots, \lambda_{N_m}]^t$, yields:

$$\lambda = \mathbf{G}^+ \mathbf{y} \tag{2.47}$$

$$= \left(\mathbf{G}^t \mathbf{G}\right)^{-1} \mathbf{y} \tag{2.48}$$

where

$$\mathbf{y} = [y_1, y_2, \ldots, y_N]^t \tag{2.49}$$

The matrix $\mathbf{G} \in \mathcal{M}_{N \times N_m}$ is defined as:

$$\mathbf{G} = \left\{ K_{ij} \right\} \tag{2.50}$$

$$K_{ij} = \exp\left(-\frac{\left\| \mathbf{x}_i - \mathbf{z}_j \right\|^2}{2\sigma_j^2} \right), \quad i = 1, \ldots, N; \ j = 1, \ldots, N_m \tag{2.51}$$

where $\mathbf{x}_i$ is the i-th training sample.

Table 2.10 summarizes the RBF network learning with randomly selected centers, applied to image retrieval. The main problem with this method is that it cannot guarantee desired performance, because it may not satisfy the requirement that the centers should suitably sample the input domain. To overcome this problem, the orthogonal least squares (OLS) learning algorithm [44] is designed to select a suitable set of centers so that adequate RBF networks can be obtained. The OLS algorithm chooses centers one by one from the training data; that is, at each iteration the vector that results in the largest reduction in network errors is used to create the center. When the sum-squared error of the network computed is higher than a specified level, the next center is added to the network. The iteration process stops when the error falls beneath an error goal, or when the maximum number of centers is reached. This provides a simple and efficient means for fitting RBF networks.

Table 2.10 Summary of the RBF network learning with randomly selected centers, applied to image retrieval

Input:	The training samples $= \{\mathbf{x}_i\}_{i=1}^{N}$ for a given query $\mathbf{x}_q$
Output:	The final retrieval set, containing k-relevant samples $= S_k$
Initialization:	Number of RBF centers $= N_m$
	Setting RBF width to a positive constant, $\sigma_i \leq 1,\ i = 1,\ldots,N_m$
Repeat:	User provides class label $l_i, i = 1,\cdots,N,\ l_i \in \{0,1\}$
	Select RBF center $\{\mathbf{z}_i\}_{i=1}^{N_M} \subset \{\mathbf{x}_i\}_{i=1}^{N}$
	Calculate weights $\lambda = [\lambda_1,\ldots,\lambda_{N_m}]^t$:
	$$\lambda = \left(\mathbf{G}^t\mathbf{G}\right)^{-1}\mathbf{y}$$
	where $$\mathbf{G} = \left\{K_{ij}\right\}$$
	$$K_{ij} = \exp\left(-\frac{\|\mathbf{x}_i - \mathbf{z}_j\|^2}{2\sigma_j^2}\right),\quad i = 1,\ldots,N;\ j = 1,\ldots,N_m$$
	$$\mathbf{y} = [y_1,\ldots,y_i,\ldots,y_N]^t,\ y_i \leftarrow l_i$$
	For $n = 1,2,\ldots,T$, calculate $\hat{f}(\mathbf{x}_n) = \sum_{i=1}^{N_m} \lambda_i K(\mathbf{x}_n, \mathbf{z}_i)$
	Obtain k-nearest neighbor:
	$$S_k(\mathbf{x}_q) = \left\{\mathbf{x} \mid \hat{f}(\mathbf{x}) \geq \hat{f}(\mathbf{x}_k)\right\}$$
	where S_k is the set of top k ranked samples.
	$$\{\mathbf{x}_i\}_{i=1}^{N} \leftarrow S_k(\mathbf{x}_q)$$
Until:	User is satisfied with the retrieval result.

2.4.3   Adaptive Radial-Basis Function Network

Problems in adaptive image retrieval are considered as a special case for function approximation. The characteristics of learning are quite different. First, the training data size for image retrieval is very small compared to the general approximation strategy. Second, the training samples available for image retrieval are highly correlated, i.e., each sample is selected from a specific area of the input space and is near to the next, in the Euclidean sense. When the training samples are highly correlated, the choice of centers is the most important factor. The BRF network will be ill-conditioned, owing to the near-linear dependency caused by some centers being too close together [44].

In order to circumvent the environmental restrictions in image retrieval, an adaptive learning strategy for the RBF network is introduced and referred to as adaptive RBF network (ARBFN). This is a special network for learning in image retrieval where there is a small set of samples with a high level of correlation between the samples. This new strategy is based on the following points:

- The learning method formulates and solves the local approximator $K(\mathbf{x}, \mathbf{z})$ from available positive samples.
- In order to obtain a dynamic weighting scheme, the Euclidean norm in $\|\mathbf{x} - \mathbf{z}\|$ is replaced with the weighted Euclidean, $\|\mathbf{x} - \mathbf{z}\|_M$.
- In order to take advantage of negative samples to improve the decision boundary, a method of shifting centers is obtained, instead of employing linear weights.

The learning strategy for the ARBFN consists of two parts. First, the local approximators $K(\mathbf{x}, \mathbf{z})$ are constructed using *positive* samples. Second, in order to improve the decision boundary, *negative* samples are used for shifting the centers, based on anti-reinforced learning [331].

2.4.3.1 Construction of Local Approximators

Given the set of positive samples, $\mathscr{X}^+ = \{\mathbf{x}_i'\}_{i=1}^{N_p}$, each positive sample is assigned to the local approximator $K(\mathbf{x}, \mathbf{z}_i)$, so that the shape of each relevant cluster can be described by:

$$K(\mathbf{x}, \mathbf{z}_i) = \exp\left(-\frac{\|\mathbf{x} - \mathbf{z}_i\|^2}{2\sigma_i^2}\right), \tag{2.52}$$

$$\mathbf{z}_i = \mathbf{x}_i', \quad \forall i \in \{1, \ldots, N_m\}, \quad N_m = N_p \tag{2.53}$$

$$\sigma_i = \delta \cdot \min\left(\|\mathbf{z}_i - \mathbf{z}_j\|\right), \forall j \in \{1, 2, \ldots, N_p\}, \quad i \neq j \tag{2.54}$$

where $\delta = 0.5$ is an overlapping factor.

Here, only the positive samples are assigned as the centers of the RBF functions. Hence, the estimated model function $f(\mathbf{x})$ is given by:

$$\hat{f}(\mathbf{x}) = \sum_{i=1}^{N_m} \lambda_i K(\mathbf{x}, \mathbf{z}_i) \tag{2.55}$$

$$\lambda_i = 1, \forall i \in \{1, \ldots, N_m\} \tag{2.56}$$

The linear weights are set to constant, indicating that all the centers (or the positive samples) are taken into consideration. However, the degree of importance of $K(\mathbf{x}, \mathbf{z}_i)$ is indicated by the natural responses of the Gaussian-shaped RBF functions and their superposition. For instance, if centers $\mathbf{z}_a$ and $\mathbf{z}_b$ are highly correlated (i.e., $\mathbf{z}_a \approx \mathbf{z}_b$), the magnitude of $\hat{f}(\mathbf{x})$ will be biased for any input vector $\mathbf{x}$ located near $\mathbf{z}_a$ or $\mathbf{z}_b$, i.e., $\hat{f}(\mathbf{x}) \approx 2K(\mathbf{x}, \mathbf{z}_a) \approx 2K(\mathbf{x}, \mathbf{z}_b)$.

2.4.3.2   Integrating Elliptic Basis Function

The basic RBF version of the ARBFN discussed in Eq. (2.52) is based on the assumption that the feature space is uniformly weighted in all directions. However, image feature variables tend to exhibit different degrees of importance which heavily depend on the nature of the query and the relevant images defined [16]. This leads to the adoption of an elliptic basis function (EBF):

$$\|\mathbf{x} - \mathbf{z}_i\|_{\mathbf{M}} = (\mathbf{x} - \mathbf{z}_i)^t \mathbf{M} (\mathbf{x} - \mathbf{z}_i) \tag{2.57}$$

where

$$\mathbf{M} = Diag[\alpha_1, \ldots, \alpha_j, \ldots, \alpha_P] \tag{2.58}$$

So, the parameter $\alpha_j, j = 1, \ldots, P$ represents the relevance weights which are derived from the variance of the positive samples in $\{\mathbf{x}'_i\}_{i=1}^{N_p}$, $\mathbf{x}'_i \in \mathbb{R}^P$ as follows:

$$\alpha_j = \begin{cases} 1, & \zeta_p = 0 \\ \frac{1}{\zeta_j}, & \text{Otherwise} \end{cases} \tag{2.59}$$

where

$$\zeta_j = \left(\frac{1}{N_p - 1} \sum_{i=1}^{N_p} (x'_{ij} - \bar{x}'_j)^2 \right)^{\frac{1}{2}} \tag{2.60}$$

$$\bar{x}'_j = \frac{1}{N_p} \sum_{i=1}^{N_p} x'_{ij} \tag{2.61}$$

The matrix $\mathbf{M}$ is a symmetrical $\mathbf{M}_{P \times P}$, whose diagonal elements α_j assign a specific weight to each input coordinate, determining the degree of the relevance of the features. The weight α_j is inversely proportional to ζ_j, the standard deviation of the j-th feature component of the positive samples, $\{x'_{ij}\}_{i=1}^{N_p}$. If a particular feature is relevant, then all positive samples should have a very similar value to this feature, i.e., the sample variance in the positive set is small [17].

2.4.3.3   Shifting RBF Centers

The possibility of moving the expansion centers is useful for improving the representativeness of the centers. Recall that, in a given training set, both positive and negative samples are presented, which are ranked results from the previous search operation. For all negative samples in this set, the similarity scores from the previous search indicate that their clusters are close to the positive samples retrieved.

Here, the use of negative samples becomes essential, as the RBF centers should be moved slightly away from these clusters. Shifting the centers reduces the similarity scores for those negative samples, and thus more favorable similarity scores can be obtained for any positive samples that are in the same neighborhood area, in the next round of retrieval.

Recall that the set of negative samples is denoted by $\mathcal{X}^- = \{\mathbf{x}_i''\}_{i=1}^{N_n}$, and N_n is the number of these samples. At the n-th iteration, let the input vector $\mathbf{x}''$ (randomly selected from the negative set) be the closest point to $\mathbf{z}_{i^*}$, such that:

$$i^* = \arg\min_i (\|\mathbf{x}'' - \mathbf{z}_i\|_{\mathbf{M}}), \quad i \in \{1, \ldots, N_m\} \tag{2.62}$$

Then, the center $\mathbf{z}_{i^*}$ is modified by the anti-reinforce learning rule:

$$\mathbf{z}_{i^*}(n+1) = \mathbf{z}_{i^*}(n) - \eta(n)[\mathbf{x}'' - \mathbf{z}_{i^*}(n)] \tag{2.63}$$

where η is a learning constant which decreases monotonically with the number of iteration, and $0 < \eta < 1$. The algorithm is repeated by selecting a new sample from the set of input samples, $\{\mathbf{x}_i''\}_{i=1}^{N_n}$, and stops after a maximum number of iterations is reached.

Table 2.11 summarizes the learning procedure of the ABRF network for image retrieval. This includes learning steps explained in Sects. 2.4.3.1–2.4.3.3.

2.4.4 Gradient-Descent Procedure

Apart from the ARBFN model, the procedural parameters for RBF can be obtained by a gradient-descent procedure [39, 40]. This procedure is employed to optimize all three parameters, $\mathbf{z}_i$, σ_i, and λ_i for each RBF unit. Here, all training samples (both positive and negative) are assigned to the RBF centers, and the linear weights are used to control the output of each RBF unit. Thus, the mapping function becomes:

$$\hat{f}(\mathbf{x}) = \sum_{i=1}^{N} \lambda_i K(\mathbf{x}, \mathbf{z}_i) = \sum_{i=1}^{N} \lambda_i \exp\left(-\frac{\|\mathbf{x} - \mathbf{z}_i\|_{\mathbf{M}}^2}{2\sigma_i^2}\right) \tag{2.64}$$

where $\{\mathbf{z}_i\}_{i=1}^{N} = \mathcal{X}^+ \cup \mathcal{X}^-$. During relevance feedback learning, the network attempts to minimize the following error function:

$$\xi(\hat{f}) = \frac{1}{2}\sum_{j=1}^{N} e_j^2 = \frac{1}{2}\sum_{j=1}^{N}\left(y_j - \sum_{i=1}^{N}\lambda_i K(\mathbf{x}_j, \mathbf{z}_i)\right)^2 \tag{2.65}$$

where e_j is the error signal for the training sample $\mathbf{x}_j$, and y_j represents the desired output of the j-th training sample. The network parameters can be obtained by the

Table 2.11 Summary of the learning algorithm of the ARBF network for adaptive retrieval

Input:	The training samples $= \{\mathbf{x}_i\}_{i=1}^{N}$ for a given query $\mathbf{x}_q$
Output:	The final retrieval set, containing k-relevant samples $= S_k(\mathbf{x}_q)$
Initialization:	Setting smoothing parameter $\delta = 0.5$
	Maximum number of iterations $= N_{max}$
	Setting anti-reinforce learning parameter η
Repeat:	User provides labels for training vectors, $l_i, i = 1, \cdots N, l_i \in \{0,1\}$
	Construct $\mathscr{X}^+$ and $\mathscr{X}^-$
	Assigning RBF center $\mathbf{z}_i \leftarrow \mathbf{x}_i', \quad \forall i \in \{1, \ldots, N_p\}$
	Obtain weight matrix $\mathbf{M}$
	For $n = 1 : N_{max}$, adjust RBF centers
	1. Randomly select the input vector $\mathbf{x}''$ from $\mathscr{X}^-$
	2. Select winning node $\mathbf{z}_{i^*}$, such that:
	$$i^* = \arg\min_{i}(\|\mathbf{x}'' - \mathbf{z}_i\|_{\mathbf{M}}), \quad i \in \{1, \ldots, N_m\}$$
	3. Update
	$$\mathbf{z}_{i^*}(n+1) \leftarrow \mathbf{z}_{i^*}(n) - \eta(n)[\mathbf{x}'' - \mathbf{z}_{i^*}(n)]$$
	End for-loop
	For $i = 1, 2, \ldots, N_p$, calculate RBF width
	$$\sigma_i = \delta \min \|\mathbf{z}_i - \mathbf{z}_j\|, \; \forall_j \in \{1, 2, \ldots, N_p\}, \quad i \neq j$$
	For $j = 1, 2, \ldots, T$, calculate $\hat{f}(\mathbf{x}_j) = \sum_{i=1}^{N_m} \exp\left(-\frac{\|\mathbf{x}_j - \mathbf{z}_i\|_{\mathbf{M}}^2}{2\sigma_i^2}\right)$
	Obtain k-nearest neighbor:
	$$S_k(\mathbf{x}_q) = \{\mathbf{x} | \hat{f}(\mathbf{x}) \geq \hat{f}(\mathbf{x}_k)\}$$
	where $S_k(\mathbf{x}_q)$ is the set of top k ranked samples.
	$$\{\mathbf{x}_i\}_{i=1}^{N} \leftarrow S_k(\mathbf{x}_q)$$
Until:	User is satisfied with the retrieval result.

gradient-descent method to minimize the cost function, i.e.,

$$\{\mathbf{z}_i, \ \sigma_i, \lambda_i\}_{i=1}^N = \arg\min\left(\xi\right) \qquad (2.66)$$

The learning procedure starts with the initialization of the linear weights:

$$\lambda_i = \begin{cases} 1, & \text{if } \mathbf{z}_i \text{ is conducted from positive sample} \\ -0.5, & \text{if } \mathbf{z}_i \text{ is conducted from negative sample} \end{cases} \qquad (2.67)$$

and the RBF widths:

$$\sigma_i = \delta \min\left(\left\|\mathbf{z}_i - \mathbf{z}_j\right\|_{\mathbf{M}}\right), \ j \in \{1, 2, \ldots, N\} \ \ i \neq j \qquad (2.68)$$

Based on the gradient-descent method, the parameters for the i-th RBF unit are updated in the iterative process, as follows:

1. For $t = 1, 2, \ldots, N_{max}$:
2. Update

$$\lambda_i(t+1) \leftarrow \lambda_i(t) - \eta_1 \frac{\partial \xi(t)}{\partial \lambda_i(t)} \qquad (2.69)$$

where $\frac{\partial \xi(t)}{\partial \lambda_i(t)} = -\sum_{j=1}^N e_j(t) K(\mathbf{x}_j, \mathbf{z}_i)$
3. Update

$$\mathbf{z}_i(t+1) \leftarrow \mathbf{z}(t) - \eta_2 \frac{\partial \xi(t)}{\partial \mathbf{z}_i(t)} \qquad (2.70)$$

where $\frac{\partial \xi(t)}{\partial \mathbf{z}_i(t)} = -\lambda_i(t) \sum_{j=1}^N e_j(t) K(\mathbf{x}_j, \mathbf{z}_i) \frac{\mathbf{M}(\mathbf{x}_j - \mathbf{z}_i(t))}{\sigma_i^2(t)}$
4. Update

$$\sigma_i^2(t+1) \leftarrow \sigma_i^2(t) - \eta_3 \frac{\partial \xi(t)}{\partial \sigma_i(t)} \qquad (2.71)$$

where $\frac{\partial \xi(t)}{\partial \sigma_i(t)} = -\lambda_i(t) \sum_{j=1}^N e_j(t) K(\mathbf{x}_j, \mathbf{z}_i) \frac{(\mathbf{x}_j - \mathbf{z}_i(t))' \mathbf{M}(\mathbf{x}_j - \mathbf{z}_i(t))}{\sigma_i^2(t)}$
5. Return

where N_{max} is the maximum iteration count, and η_1, η_2, and η_3 are the step sizes.

The adjustment of the RBF models proceeds along many relevance feedback sessions. The training samples are gathered from the first to the last retrieval sessions, and only selective samples are used to retrain the network. In each feedback session, newly retrieved samples which have not been found in the previous retrieval are inserted into the existing RBF network. In the next iteration, the updating procedure is performed on the newly inserted RBF units, thus improving training speed.

2.4.5   *Fuzzy RBF Network with Soft Constraint*

The error function $\xi\left(\hat{f}\right)$ defined in Eq. (2.65) is based on the binary labeling or hard-decision. The desired network output y_j is equal to 1 for positive samples, and zero for negative samples. For a soft-decision, a third option, "fuzzy" is used to characterize a vague description of the retrieved (image) samples [39]. Thus, in a retrieval session, users have three choices for relevance feedback: relevant, irrelevant, and fuzzy. The error function is then calculated by:

$$\xi\left(\hat{f}\right) = \frac{1}{2}\sum_{j=1}^{N}\left(y_j - \sum_{i=1}^{N}\lambda_i K(\mathbf{x}_j, \mathbf{z}_i)\right)^2 \tag{2.72}$$

$$y_j = \begin{cases} 1, & \mathbf{x}_j \text{ is relevant} \\ 0, & \mathbf{x}_j \text{ is irrelevant} \\ P(\mathscr{X}^+|\mathbf{x}_j), & \mathbf{x}_j \text{ is fuzzy} \end{cases} \tag{2.73}$$

where $P(\mathscr{X}^+|\mathbf{x}_j)$ is the probability that a fuzzy sample $\mathbf{x}_j$ belongs to the relevant class $\mathscr{X}^+$. This represents the degree of relevancy for the corresponding fuzzy sample. The learning problem is the problem in estimating the desired output $y_j = P(\mathscr{X}^+|\mathbf{x}_j)$ of the fuzzy sample $\mathbf{x}_j$ by the *a posteriori* probability estimator. Let $\mathbf{x}_j$ be defined by feature vector that is concatenated from M sub-vector, i.e., $\mathbf{x}_j \equiv [\mathbf{v}_{j1}, \dots, \mathbf{v}_{ji}, \dots, \mathbf{v}_{jM}]$, where $\mathbf{v}_{ji}$ is a d_i-dimensional feature sub-vector such as a color histogram, a set of wavelet moments or others. To deal with the uncertainly, the probability estimator takes into account the multiple features, by using the following estimation principle:

$$P\left(\mathscr{X}^+|\mathbf{x}_j\right) = \frac{1}{M}\sum_{i=1}^{M}P\left(\mathscr{X}^+|\mathbf{v}_{ji}\right) \tag{2.74}$$

where $P(\mathscr{X}^+|\mathbf{v}_{ji})$ is the *a posteriori* probability for the i-th feature vector $\mathbf{v}_{ji}$ of the fuzzy sample $\mathbf{x}_j$. the Bayesian theory is applied to $P(\mathscr{X}^+|\mathbf{v}_{ji})$,

$$P\left(\mathscr{X}^+|\mathbf{v}_{ji}\right) = \frac{P(\mathbf{v}_{ji}|\mathscr{X}^+)P(\mathscr{X}^+)}{P(\mathbf{v}_{ji}|\mathscr{X}^+)P(\mathscr{X}^+) + P(\mathbf{v}_{ji}|\mathscr{X}^-)P(\mathscr{X}^-)} \tag{2.75}$$

where $P(\mathscr{X}^+)$ and $P(\mathscr{X}^-)$ are, respectively, the prior probabilities of the positive and negative classes, which can be estimated from the feedback samples; $P(\mathbf{v}_{ji}|\mathscr{X}^+)$ and $P(\mathbf{v}_{ji}|\mathscr{X}^-)$ are the class conditional probability density functions of $\mathbf{v}_{ji}$ for the positive and negative classes, respectively. Assuming the Gaussian distribution, the probability density function for the positive class is given by:

$$P\left(\mathbf{v}_{ji}|\mathscr{X}^+\right) = \frac{1}{(2\pi)^{\frac{d_i}{2}}|\Sigma_i'|^{\frac{1}{2}}}\exp\left[-\frac{1}{2}(\mathbf{v}_{ji} - \mu_i')^t {\Sigma_i'}^{-1}(\mathbf{v}_{ji} - \mu_i')\right] \tag{2.76}$$

where μ'_i is the d_i-component mean vector and $\sum'_i$ is the d_i-by-d_i covariance matrix for the i-th feature vector, and $|\sum'_i|$ and $\sum'_i{}^{-1}$ are its determinant and inverse, respectively. These variables can be estimated using the positive training vectors in the positive class $\mathcal{X}^+$,

$$\mu'_i = \frac{1}{N_p} \sum_{j=1}^{N_p} \mathbf{v}'_{ji} \tag{2.77}$$

$$\sum{}'_i = \frac{1}{(N_p - 1)} \sum_{j=1}^{N_p} \left(\mathbf{v}'_{ji} - \mu_i\right)\left(\mathbf{v}'_{ji} - \mu_i\right)^t \tag{2.78}$$

where $\mathbf{v}'_{ji}$ is the i-th sub-vector of j-th positive sample, and N_p is the number of positive samples. For simplicity we abbreviate Eq. (2.76) as $P(\mathbf{v}_{ji}|\mathcal{X}^+) \sim N(\mu'_i, \sum'_i)$. Similarly, the probability density function for the negative class is given by: $P(\mathbf{v}_{ji}|\mathcal{X}^-) \sim N(\mu''_i, \sum''_i)$ where μ''_i is the mean vector and $\sum''_i$ is the covariance matrix for the i-th feature vector, which can be estimated using the negative training vectors in the negative class $\mathcal{X}^-$.

After the desired output y_j of the fuzzy sample is estimated, the gradient-descent procedure of Eqs. (2.69)–(2.71) are applied to construct the learning parameters of the RBF network.

2.4.6 Experimental Result

The Corel database was used in the experiments reported in Sect. 2.3.3. All 40,000 images in the database were used, each of which was characterized by a multi-feature representation (explained in Table 2.7). This section begins by implementing the RBF network using the ARBFN leaning method and comparing its performance with two other learning strategies. This is followed by examining the ARBFN and the single-class learning methods discussed in Sects. 2.2–2.3.

The first objective is to verify that the ARBFN is able to meet the demands of adaptive retrieval applications; in particular, where there is a small set of training samples with a high level of correlation between the samples. A learning session with this condition may be observed in Fig. 2.3d, where the top sixteen retrieved images are returned to the user who provides relevance feedback. It is seen that at later iterations the learning system can improve the result sets, which means that the more times the interactive retrieval is implemented, the higher the level of correlation retrieved images.

The ARBFN method was compared with two learning strategies that have been successfully used in other situations to construct the RBF network. Table 2.12 summarizes the methods being compared. The first learning method, the orthogonal least square (OLS) learning procedure described in [44], was used to identify a RBF network model. In the second learning method [43], each vector in a

Table 2.12 Comparison of RBF learning methods

Method	Learning algorithm
ARBFN	Table 2.11, RBF centers: using positive samples in $\mathscr{X}^+ = \{\mathbf{x}'_i\}_{i=1}^{N_p}$; RBF width: Eq. (2.54)
EDLS [43]	The weight and bias of the second layers were calculated by the least squares criterion; RBF centers: using all samples in $\{\mathbf{x}'_i\}_{i=1}^{N_p} \cup \{\mathbf{x}''_i\}_{i=1}^{N_n}$; RBF width: $\sigma = 0.8$ for all RBF units
OLS [44]	RBF centers: selecting from $\{\mathbf{x}'_i\}_{i=1}^{N_p} \cup \{\mathbf{x}''_i\}_{i=1}^{N_n}$ using the orthogonal least square method. The RBF center selection starts zero centers, and new centers were iteratively picked in the subsequent selection procedure. Each time, the network's mean square error was checked and compared to the pre-defined tolerance set at 0.0001; RBF width: $\sigma = 0.8$ for all RBF units

Table 2.13 Average precision rate (%) as a function of iteration, $\bar{P}r(Iter.)$, obtained by retrieving 35 queries, using Corel dataset

Method	Iter. 0	Iter. 1	Iter. 2	Iter. 3
ARBFN	44.82	80.72	90.36	92.50
EDLS	44.82	50.18	43.39	43.04
OLS	44.82	66.07	73.21	76.61

retrieved set was associated with the RBF centers [Eq. (2.43)], using a one-to-one correspondence. This is named as EDLS (exact design network using the least squares criterion). For both methods, the final RBF network model can be written as:

$$\hat{f}(\mathbf{x}_j) = \lambda_0 + \sum_{i=1}^{N_m} \lambda_i \exp\left(-\frac{\|\mathbf{x} - \mathbf{z}_i\|^2}{2\sigma_i^2}\right) \qquad (2.79)$$

where $N_m = 16$ for the EDLS method, and $N_m \leq 16$ for the OLS learning method, since the size of retrieved samples is set to 16 at each feedback iteration.

The query image set used here is identical to the experiments reported in Sect. 2.3.3. Precision (Pr) was recorded after each query iteration. Table 2.13 summarizes the average precision results, $\bar{P}r(Iter.)$, as a function of iteration, taken over the 35 test queries. It can be seen from the results that the ARBFN significantly improved the retrieval accuracy (up to 92 % precision). The first iteration showed an improvement of 35.9 %. The ARBFN outperformed the OLS (76.61 %) and the EDLS. This result confirms that the ARBFN learning strategy offers a better solution for the construction of an RBF network for adaptive image retrieval, compared to the two standard learning strategies.

Both the OLS and the EDLS strategies usually perform well under the opposite condition, where the training samples are sufficiently large [46], and where the data samples may not correlate closely to each other. In this experiment, it was observed that the EDLS achieved improvement after the first iteration (i.e., $\bar{P}r(Iter. = 1) = 50.2\%$), because the retrieved data at $Iter. = 0$ usually has a low degree of correlation. Its performance, however, was reduced after two iterations as the retrieved samples became correlated more strongly. This suggests that the EDLS may not be suitable for constructing the RBF network under this learning condition. Using the same RBF widths, the OLS learning strategy was more stable and much better than the EDLS.

It was observed that the RBF centers critically influenced the performance of the RBF classifier, and that the RBF classifier constructed by matching all retrieved samples exactly to the RBF centers degraded the retrieval performance. The OLS algorithm was fairly successful at resolving this problem, by choosing the subset of the retrieved samples for the RBF centers. However, the OLS provided a less adequate RBF network, compared to the ARBFN. In ARBFN learning, each available positive sample was considered as important. Also, the centers were shifted by negative samples with the weighted norm parameters being updated during adaptive cycles. The ARBFN also managed well with the small set of samples encountered. The ARBFN is thus the most adequate model for the current application.

The retrieval performance of the ARBFN was next compared to the single-class model discussed in Sects. 2.2–2.3, using a new query set, which contained 59 images randomly selected from different categories. The methods compared include ARBFN, single-RBF, OPT-RF, and MAM. Two criteria were employed for performance measures: precision Pr measured from the top N_c images, where N_c was set to 10, 16, 25, and 50; and second, a precision versus recall graph. However, the relevance feedback was done only on the *top 16* retrieved images.

Table 2.14 summarizes the precision results averaged over all queries, measured from the top 10, 16, 25, and 50 retrieved images. It can be seen that the learning methods provided a significant improvement in each of the first three iterations. The ARBFN achieved the best precision results in all conditions, compared to the other methods discussed. At $N_c = 10$, ARBFN reached a near-perfect precision of 100 % after three iterations. This means that all the top ten retrieved images were relevant. The results also show that, at $N_c = 16$, more than 14 relevant images were presented in the top 16 ranking set. The most important precision results are perhaps those after the first iteration, since users would likely provide only one round of relevance feedback. It was observed that the ARBFN provided a better improvement than the other methods for this requirement.

Figure 2.5a–c illustrates the average precision versus recall figures after one, two, and three iterations, respectively. The behavior of the system without learning and the strong improvements with adaptive learning can easily be seen. In all cases, the precision at 100 % recall drops close to 0. This fact indicates that it was not possible to retrieve all the relevant images in the database, which had been pre-classified by the Corel Professionals. It is observed from Fig. 2.5a that the ARBFN was superior to the single-RBF at the higher recall levels, while both provided similar precision at the lower recall levels. Also, the ARBFN achieved better improvements than the single-RBF by up to 8.6 %, 7.3 % and 6.5 %, at one, two and three iterations, respectively.

Table 2.14 Average precisions, $\bar{P}r$, compared at four settings of top matches (N_c), obtained by retrieving 59 queries, using the Corel Database

N_c	Method	Average precision (%), $\bar{P}r(N_c)$			
		t = 0	t = 1	t = 2	t = 3
10	ARBFN	55.93	+32.03	+42.03	+43.56
	Single-RBF	55.93	+27.97	+39.15	+42.03
	MAM	55.93	+17.12	+19.32	+19.66
	OPT-RF	55.93	+24.07	+30.51	+32.37
16	ARBFN	47.67	+30.83	+39.30	+41.21
	Single-RBF	47.67	+26.48	+34.64	+38.45
	MAM	47.67	+13.88	+16.00	+16.21
	OPT-RF	47.67	+20.97	+23.83	+25.00
25	ARBFN	39.93	+26.44	+30.44	+31.19
	Single-RBF	39.93	+21.36	+26.58	+28.14
	MAM	39.93	+11.46	+12.47	+12.07
	OPT-RF	39.93	+17.02	+19.73	+20.00
50	ARBFN	30.03	+19.08	+20.58	+20.75
	Single-RBF	30.03	+15.29	+17.76	+18.44
	MAM	30.03	+8.24	+8.31	+8.17
	OPT-RF	30.03	+11.86	+12.17	+12.51

Interactive results are quoted relative to the $\bar{P}r$ observed with the initial retrieval

2.5   Bayesian Method for Fusion of Content and Context in Adaptive Retrieval

Adaptive retrieval method can be implemented to integrate visual content and contextual information through relevance feedback [47,48]. Contextual information refers to the statistical correlation across multiple images. In this section, a Bayesian framework is developed for fusion of content and context components. Specifically, the visual content analysis is associated with the likelihood evaluation, whereas the contextual information is represented by the *a priori* probability, learned through a maximum entropy algorithm.

2.5.1   Fusion of Content and Context

Let C represent the set of class labels and $C = \{1, 2, \ldots, C\}$, where C is the number of classes. The class label of a particular image in a database is denoted c, where $c \in C$. Based on the *maximum a posteriori* probability (MAP) criterion which minimizes the classification error, the true class label is estimated with:

$$\hat{c} = \arg\max_{c \in C} P(c|\mathbf{x}, \boldsymbol{I}) \tag{2.80}$$

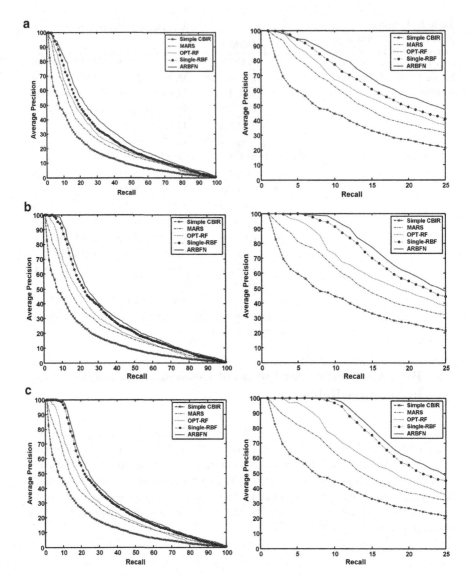

Fig. 2.5 Average precision versus recall figures, obtained by retrieving 59 queries, using the Corel database. Figures on the right are the zoom versions of the figures on the left. Note that, in each case, results obtained by the non-adaptive retrieval method are fixed, and used as a benchmark for other adaptive retrieval methods. (**a**) Results after first RF. (**b**) Results after second RF. (**c**) Results after third RF

where $\hat{c}$ is the estimate of c, $\boldsymbol{I}$ is the background information, which exists with a well-formulated problem. In the context of the subsequent description, it represents a set of indexes of query images. Therefore, $\boldsymbol{I}$ can be defined as $\boldsymbol{I} = \{I_i | i =$

$1, 2, \ldots, |I|\}$, where $|I|$ is the number of query images, $I_i \in C$, $i = 1, 2, \ldots, |I|$. Using Bayes' theorem, the *a posteriori* probability can be written as

$$P(c|\mathbf{x}, I) \propto p(\mathbf{x}|c, I) P(c|I), \qquad (2.81)$$

with the equality replaced by the proportionality due to the unimportance of the probability density function (PDF) of an observation, i.e. $p(\mathbf{x}|I)$, when the theorem is employed to solve a classification problem. Based on the meaning of the background information I, we can assume the conditional independence between the observation $\mathbf{x}$ and I given the class label of the observation, i.e. $\mathbf{x} \perp I|c$. Therefore, the *a posteriori* probability in Eq. (2.81) can be calculated through

$$P(c|\mathbf{x}, I) \propto p(\mathbf{x}|c) P(c|I) \qquad (2.82)$$

The first term on the right-hand side of Eq. (2.82) is the PDF of the feature vector of the class c, which is considered as the content model characterizing the visual properties of that class. The second term is essentially a distribution of one class or candidate image, say c, conditional on a set of other classes or query images, collectively represented by I. This is exactly the contextual information that characterizes the statistical relation between different classes or images. It will be shown that such contextual information can be learned from past user feedback for image retrieval. According to Eq. (2.82), the content and contextual information are integrated through the decision-level fusion in a multiplicative fashion.

The Bayesian framework is applied to tackle the semantic gap of image retrieval by integrating short-term relevance feedback (STRF) and long-term relevance feedback (LTRF). STRF refers to the user interaction during a retrieval session consisting of a number of feedback iterations, such as query shifting and feature re-weighting. On the other hand, LTRF is the estimation of a user history model from past retrieval results approved by previous users. LTRF plays a key role in refining the degree of relevance of the candidate images in a database to a query. The STRF and LTRF play the roles of refining the likelihood and the *a priori* information, respectively, and the images are ranked according to the *a posteriori* probability. By exploiting past retrieval results, it can be considered as a retrieval system with memory, which incrementally learns the high level knowledge provided by users.

The underlying rationale of applying the Bayesian framework to image retrieval can be illustrated using Fig. 2.6, of which the gist is to boost the retrieval performance using some information extracted from the retrieval history. The two types of similarity measure are complementary to each other. Specifically, the similarity measure by the content-based component illustrated by the low-level feature space in Fig. 2.6a suffers from the semantic gap which can be alleviated using the contextual information. The links between relevant images in Fig. 2.6b are estimated by utilizing the co-occurrence of relevant images in the past retrieval results. At the same time, the contextual information can only be acquired by learning from the knowledge accumulated through the content-based component. The retrieval system, illustrated in Fig. 2.7, seamlessly integrates the content-based

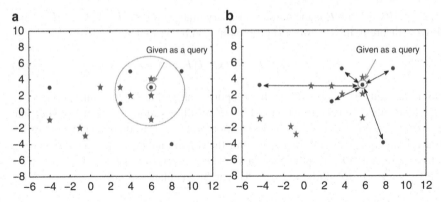

Fig. 2.6 The similarity measure in the content and context domains. (**a**) Semantic gap exists in the content domain. (**b**) There might not be sufficient data to extract accurate contextual information

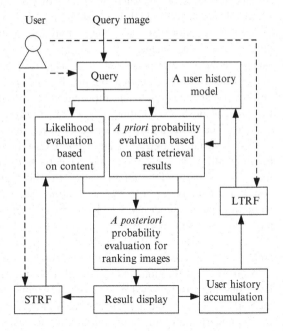

Fig. 2.7 Block diagram of the integration of STRF and LTRF in an adaptive retrieval system. The *solid and dashed directed lines* indicate the information flow and the user-controlled components, respectively

and the context-based methods into a mathematically justifiable framework. In the beginning, there is no available retrieval history from which to learn the context model but the system can still work using the content-based component and incrementally accumulate the retrieval results. When past retrieval results are available, the context component of the system performs LTRF by extracting information from the data gradually, which can be considered as a knowledge accumulation process. When a user presents a query, the content component of the system learns the user's information needs from the query through similarity measures and STRF. If the context component has been trained by the time a user queries the database, the system is capable of integrating the useful information predicted using the context component and that learned using the content component. The *a posteriori* probability evaluated by the system is used to rank the images in the database.

2.5.2 Content-Based Likelihood Evaluation in Short-Term Learning

The visual content model of a certain semantic class, e.g. c, is the parametric form of the distribution of the visual features of that class. The parameters of the model are adapted to a given set of training data of class c through a supervised learning procedure. A visual content model plays the role of evaluating the likelihood of a visual feature with respect to a certain class. The support vector machine (SVM) is selected as the key component of the content model to evaluate the likelihood. L1 norm is also employed in addition to SVM for calculating the likelihood using the content model. At the same time, it should be noted that the formulation of the Bayesian framework requires that the output of the visual content model comply with the definition of a PDF. To this end, the exponential function is employed, i.e. $h(s) = \exp(s)$, $s \in \mathbb{R}$, to convert the discriminant function of SVM into a PDF. The selection of the above exponential function is based on the following consideration. First, it is monotonically increasing, resulting in the preservation of the physical interpretation of the algebraic distance between a sample and the decision boundary. Second, it is positive. Since the total integral of a function must be equal to unity, appropriate normalization is necessary. Finally, representing the discriminant function of SVM corresponding to the c-th class as $f_c(\mathbf{x})$ and substituting it for the variable s in the exponential function followed by normalization, we obtain

$$p(\mathbf{x}|c) = \frac{1}{A} \exp(f_c(\mathbf{x})) \tag{2.83}$$

where $A = \int \exp(f_c(\mathbf{x})) dx$.

2.5.2.1 Using the Nearest Neighbor (NN) Method

The nearest neighbor (NN) method returns the top K images on the list, which is ranked based on the similarity measure between the feature of the query and that of each of the candidate images, where $K \ll C$. The L1-norm is used as the distance function for the NN method. In adaptive retrieval, the query is refined using the method of query point movement [i.e., Eq. (2.8)]. To calculate the likelihood, the exponential function in Eq. (2.83) converts the L1-Norm into a similarity function, i.e.

$$p(\mathbf{x}_q|c) = \frac{1}{A} \exp(f_c(\mathbf{x}_q)) = \frac{1}{A} \exp\left(-|\mathbf{x}_q - \mathbf{x}_c|\right) \tag{2.84}$$

where $A = \int \exp(-|\mathbf{x}_q - \mathbf{x}_c|)$, is the normalization constant, $\mathbf{x}_q$ denotes the feature vector of a query, and $\mathbf{x}_c$ denotes a candidate image. When the likelihood is calculated using the L1 norm, the corresponding negative distance function should be substituted into the exponential function because the similarity is a decreasing function of the distance between features.

2.5.2.2 Using the Support Vector Machine Active Learning (SVMAL) Method

SVM is a powerful tool for pattern recognition because it maximizes the minimum distance between the decision hyperplane and the training samples so as to minimize the generalization error. Given training samples $\{(\mathbf{x}_i, y_i)\}_{i=1}^{N}$, where $\mathbf{x}_i \in \mathbb{R}^P$, $y_i \in \{-1, 1\}$ is the ground-truth label of $\mathbf{x}_i$, the optimal hyperplane can be represented as $f(\mathbf{x}) = \sum_{i=1}^{N} \alpha_i y_i K(\mathbf{x}_i, \mathbf{x}) + b$ where $K(\mathbf{x}_i, \mathbf{x})$ is the kernel function, α_i is the Lagrangian multiplier, and b is the bias. Due to the sparse sample problem of the relevance feedback leaning, the active learning method was introduced into the learning process, whereby the most informative images are shown to request user-provided labeling, resulting in the support vector machine active learning (SVMAL)-CBIR [49]. Since the output of an SVM with respect to a sample is the oriented distance from the sample to the hyperplane, the value could be either positive or negative. Therefore, the exponential function is employed again to convert the value of the discriminant function. When selecting radial basis functions as the kernel, we obtain

$$p(\mathbf{x}_q|c) = \frac{1}{A} \exp(f_c(\mathbf{x}_q)) = \frac{1}{A} \exp\left(\sum_{i=1}^{N} \alpha_i y_i K(\mathbf{x}_i, \mathbf{x}_q) + b\right) \qquad (2.85)$$

where $A = \int \exp(\sum_{i=1}^{N} \alpha_i y_i K(\mathbf{x}_i, \mathbf{x}_q) + b)$ is the normalization constant.

2.5.3 Context Model in Long-Term Learning

This part aims at calculating the $P(c|I)$ in Eq. (2.82), which is the contextual information about c inferred based on the I. Without I, the probability mass of c is uniformly distributed over the class ensemble C without I. Due to the statistical dependence across different classes, however, the distribution of c conditional on I will deviate from the uniform distribution once I is available. As a result, the classes that are more strongly correlated with I have higher probabilities than the others do. Since the problem is essentially the estimation of a conditional probability mass function (PMF), a typical train of thought leads to the conventional approach that calculates the conditional probability through $P(c|I) = P(c, I)/P(I)$, for which we need a set of training samples belonging to the Cartesian product of $|I| + 1$ C's.

Regardless of the approach to estimating $P(c, I)$ and $P(I)$, there are two problems with above estimation of $P(c|I)$. First, the background information I may include different numbers of indexes, which requires separate estimations of the model for different sizes of I. Second, when collecting training data, we cannot guarantee enough or even available samples for a certain configuration of c and I, where the configuration refers to a particular instantiation of the number of random variables of $c \cup I$ and their values.

To deal with the estimation of the context model efficiently, the $P(c|I)$ is approximated using a distribution of a set of binary random variables estimated based on the maximum entropy (ME) principle. In this approach, an image is represented using a C-dimensional vector of binary random variables, denoted $Y = (Y_1, Y_2, \ldots, Y_C)^t$, where the value of each variable Y_c is defined by

$$Y_c = \begin{cases} 1 & \text{if the } c\text{-th image is relevant to a query} \\ 0 & \text{otherwise} \end{cases} \tag{2.86}$$

Instead of being from the Cartesian product of $|I| + 1$ C's, the data utilized by the context modeling procedure belong to the set of vertices of a C-dimensional hypercube. Given a set of N training samples, denoted $Y_1, Y_2, \ldots, Y_N$, we can estimate the $P(Y)$ and then calculate the conditional probability $P\left(Y_c | Y_{I_1}, Y_{I_2}, \ldots, Y_{I_{|I|}}\right)$, which is represented as $P(Y_c | Y_I)$ in what follows. To approximate the $P(c|I)$ in Eq. (2.82), the following formula is utilized

$$P(c|I) = \frac{P(Y_c | Y_I)}{\sum_{v=1}^{C} P(Y_v | Y_I)} \tag{2.87}$$

As the size of the concept ensemble, i.e. C, grows, the computational intensity of the calculation of $P(Y_c | Y_I)$ increases exponentially. Therefore, it would be more efficient if we can directly estimate $P(Y_c | Y_I)$ based on a set of training samples. To this end, the ME approach demonstrated in [50] is employed, which estimates a conditional distribution by maximizing its Rényi entropy. Essentially, the ME principle states that the optimal model should only respect a certain set of statistics induced from a given training set and otherwise be as uniform as possible. The ME approach searches for the conditional distribution $P(Y_c | Y_I)$, with the maximum entropy, among all the distributions which are consistent with a set of statistics extracted from the training samples. Therefore, it can be considered as constrained optimization, which is formulated as

$$\max_{P(Y_c | Y_I) \in [0,1]} - \sum_{y_c, y_I} \hat{P}(Y_I = y_I) P(Y_c = y_c | Y_I = y_I)^2, \tag{2.88}$$

subject to:

$$\frac{\sum_{y_I} \hat{P}(Y_I = y_I) P(Y_c = y_c | Y_I = y_I) f_k}{\hat{P}(f_k)} = \hat{P}(f_c | f_k), k \in \{0\} \cup I, \qquad (2.89)$$

where $c \in C$ and $c \notin I$ because $P(Y_c = 1 | Y_I = 1) \equiv 1$ for $c \in I$. In addition, $\hat{P}(\cdot)$ represents the empirical probabilities directly estimated from the training samples, $f_c = Y_c$ and $f_k = Y_k$ when $k \neq 0$ and $f_k = 1$ otherwise. Using a matrix-based representation, solving the above optimization leads to the result that

$$P = M \times N^{-1} \times f \qquad (2.90)$$

where

$$P = \left[P(Y_{a1} | Y_I), P(Y_{a2} | Y_I), \ldots, P\left(Ya_{|C/I|} Y_I\right) \right]^t \qquad (2.91)$$

$$M = \begin{bmatrix} \hat{P}(f_{a1}|f_0) & \hat{P}(f_{a1}|f_{l_1}) & \cdots & \hat{P}\left(f_{a1}|f_{l_{|I|}}\right) \\ \hat{P}(f_{a2}|f_0) & \hat{P}(f_{a2}|f_{l_1}) & \cdots & \hat{P}\left(f_{a2}|f_{l_{|I|}}\right) \\ \vdots & \vdots & \ddots & \vdots \\ \hat{P}\left(f_{a|C/I|}f_0\right) & \hat{P}\left(f_{a|C/I|}f_{l_1}\right) & \cdots & \hat{P}\left(f_{a|C/I|}f_{l_{|I|}}\right) \end{bmatrix} \qquad (2.92)$$

$$N = \begin{bmatrix} 1 & 1 & \cdots & 1 \\ \hat{P}(f_{l_1}|f_0) & 1 & \cdots & \hat{P}\left(f_{l_1}|f_{l_{|I|}}\right) \\ \vdots & \vdots & \ddots & \vdots \\ \hat{P}\left(f_{l_{|I|}}f_0\right) & \hat{P}\left(f_{l_{|I|}}f_{l_1}\right) & \cdots & 1 \end{bmatrix} \qquad (2.93)$$

$$f = \left[f_0, f_1, \ldots, f_{l_{|I|}} \right]^t \qquad (2.94)$$

and $|C/I| = \{a_1, a_2, \ldots, a_{|C/I|}\}$.

2.5.4   Experimental Result

In the experiment, four methods summarized in Table 2.15 were compared. A total of 200 classes of images was selected from the COREL image collection, with 50 images in each class. The resulting 10,000 images and the vendor-defined categories were used as the database and the ground truth for evaluating the performance. From the database, 10 queries are selected from each of the 200 classes, resulting in 2,000 queries being selected, each of which is composed of two different images. Under

Table 2.15 Comparison of learning methods

Method	Learning criterion	STRF	LTRF
NN-CBIR	Adaptive image retrieval method, using *nearest neighbor* (NN) criterion, where L1-norm is employed as the distance function and Eq. (2.8) is employed for a query modification	✓	×
SVMAL-CBIR	Adaptive image retrieval method using *support vector machine active learning* (SVMAL)	✓	×
NN-CLBIR	Collaborative Bayesian Image Retrieval (CLBIR), using Eq. (2.84) for estimation of $p(\mathbf{x}_q|c)$ and Eq. (2.87) for estimation of $P(c|I)$	✓	✓
SVMAL-CLBIR	Collaborative Bayesian Image Retrieval (CLBIR), using Eq. (2.85) for estimation of $p(\mathbf{x}_q|c)$ and Eq. (2.87) for estimation of $P(c|I)$	✓	✓

the query-by-example retrieval paradigm, the average of the features of the two images is used as the feature of an exemplar image.

To facilitate the subsequent elaboration, the query subsets which consist of the first five queries, the sixth through the eighth, and the ninth and the tenth in each class, are denoted T_A, $T_{B,1}$, and $T_{B,2}$, where $|T_A| = 1,000$, $|T_{B,1}| = 400$, and $|T_{B,2}| = 600$. Such a query set selection guarantees that the system trained using the LTRF will be tested based on previously unseen samples. T_A was used when there is no accumulated high-level knowledge, i.e. before LTRF happens. In such a case, only STRF is involved, and the "nearest neighbor collaborative Bayesian image retrieval" (NN-CLBIR) and the "support vector machine active learning collaborative Bayesian image retrieval" (SVMAL-CLBIR) are essentially the same as the NN-CBIR and SVMAL-CBIR because the *a priori* distribution of the candidate images is uniform. After the initial LTRF, the CLBIR systems are expected to present better performance in general thanks to the accumulated knowledge, while the STRF still improves the results with respect to each specific query. $T_{B,1} \cup T_{B,2}$, comprising 1,000 images, was used to verify the improvement after the initial LTRF. During the operation of the CLBIR systems, the new retrieval results after the initial LTRF are gradually accumulated, and a second LTRF can be carried out upon a certain point. The retrieval results corresponding to $T_{B,1}$ were used to perform an incremental update of the system, i.e. the second LTRF, after which the performance was evaluated using $T_{B,2}$.

To capture various visual properties of the images, three types of low-level descriptors are selected, including global color histogram in Hue-Saturation-Value (HSV) space, color layout in YCbCr space [92], as well as Gabor wavelet [91].

Shown in Fig. 2.8a is the comparison between NN-CBIR and NN-CLBIR in terms of the average precision $\bar{Pr}$ as a function of the number of iterations of STRF. The precision is given by $Pr = N_C/N_R$, where N_C and N_R are the numbers of relevant images and retrieved images, respectively. The precision is measured in the top $N_R = 48$ in this case. Using the query set $T_{B,1}$, the improvement due to LTRF based on past retrieval results with respect to the query set T_A is obvious, and the effect of STRF can also be observed. After the second LTRF, the performance of NN-CLBIR using query set $T_{B,2}$ is further enhanced due to more accumulated

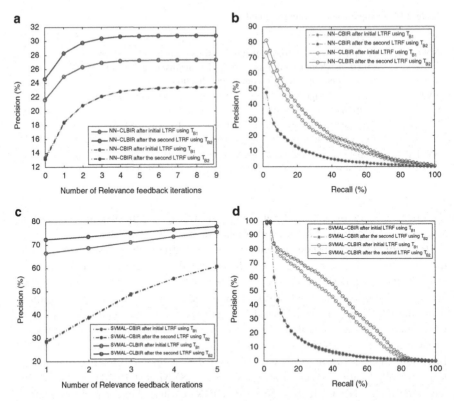

Fig. 2.8 (**a**) Comparison between the performance of NN-CBIR and NN-CLBIR in terms of the average precision versus the number of relevance feedback iterations; (**b**) comparison between the performance of NN-CBIR and NN-CLBIR in terms of the precision versus recall after the first retrieval iteration; (**c**) comparison between the performance of SVMAL-CBIR and SVMAL-CLBIR in terms of the average precision versus the number of relevance feedback iterations; (**d**) comparison between the performance of SVMAL-CBIR and SVMAL-CBIR in terms of the precision versus recall after the first retrieval iteration

knowledge through the LTRF. Based on the same query set, the performance of NN-CBIR remains unchanged. To test the performance in terms of ranking ability, the precision-versus-recall curve (PRC) is employed. The recall is defined as $R = N_C/N_G$, where N_G is the number of images in the same classes as that of the query. The precision is averaged over all queries at each different recall value. The PRC after the initial retrieval is shown in Fig. 2.8b. Higher precision values at a certain recall indicates more relevant images being ranked ahead of irrelevant ones, i.e. to reach the recall value, a smaller set of retrieved images has to be processed. Based on this fact, the advantage of the integration of user history as high-level knowledge with the content analysis can be demonstrated based on the comparison in Fig. 2.8b.

Fig. 2.9 Retrieval results for the subjective evaluation of the performance improvement resulting from extended user history; (**a**) based on the user history model trained using 2,000 past retrieval results; (**b**) based on the user history model trained using 3,200 past retrieval results

The comparison shown in Fig. 2.8c, d is for the same purpose of performance evaluation as that described above, and the difference lies with the approach to the content analysis for the likelihood computation, which is based on the output of the SVM employed for the active learning-based STRF. In this case, $N_R = 20$ was adopted for the evaluation of precision as a function of the number of STRF iterations, and $N_C = 50$ for the evaluation of PRC. Since the initial retrieval is just random ranking, the precision was evaluated starting from the first STRF iteration. Still, we can observe the improvement resulting from the integration through the Bayesian framework.

An interface with the NN-CLBIR enabled has been implemented to demonstrate the effectiveness of the system in terms of performance improvement by the accumulation of user history. Illustrated in Fig. 2.9a, b are the top 20 images retrieved using NN-CLBIR. Shown in the figure on the left is the result obtained using a system whose *a priori* knowledge was extracted from 1,000 user data, while on the right, the result is based on the *a priori* knowledge learned from 1,400 user data. The query is selected from the semantic class of the theme soldier, and the last four images do not belong to this class in Fig. 2.9a. Nonetheless, all of the top 20 images are relevant to the query.

2.6 Summary

The kernel approach makes use of a nonlinear kernel-induced inner product, instead of the traditional Euclidean inner product, to measure the similarity metrics of two vectors. In a relevance feedback session, the nonlinear kernel approach implements the nonlinear mapping function to analyze the role of the users in perceiving image similarity. This results in a high performance machine that can cope with the small size of the training sample set and the convergence speed. The new learning algorithms for the nonlinear kernel-based RF can be categorized into two groups. The first group includes the single-class RBF, the adaptive RBF, the gradient-descent-based learning, where hard constraints are used to force a clear separation on the RF samples. Then, in the second group, soft constraints are used to allow more support vectors to be included in the so-called fuzzy RBF formulations. Much of the chapter is meant to build the theoretical footing for the machine learning models in the subsequent chapters.

In addition, the nonlinear-kernel approach in a STRF is extended to a Bayesian fusion model. The STRF represents a content component that can be incorporated with a context component in a LTRF, through a Bayesian framework. This can be considered as a retrieval system with a memory, which can incrementally accumulate high-level semantic knowledge, assisting in bridging the semantic gap in future retrieval performed by prospective users.

Chapter 3
Self-adaptation in Image and Video Retrieval

Abstract This chapter explores the automatic methods for implementing pseudo-relevance feedback for retrieval of images and videos. The automation is based on dynamic self-organization, the self-organizing tree map that is capable of identification of relevance in place of human users. The automation process leads to the avoidance of errors in excessive human involvement, and enlarging the size of training set, as compared to traditional relevance feedback. The automatic retrieval system applies for image retrieval in compressed domains (i.e., JPEG and wavelet based coders). In addition, the system incorporates knowledge-based learning to acquire a suitable weighting scheme for unsupervised relevance identification. In the video domain, the pseudo-relevance feedback is implemented by an adaptive cosine network than enhances retrieval accuracy through the network's forward–backward signal propagation, without user input.

3.1 Introduction

In order to handle the large volumes of multimedia information that are becoming readily accessible in the consumer and the industrial world, some level of automation is desirable. Automation requires intelligence systems, to formulate its own models of the data in question with little or no user intervention. The system is able to make decisions about what information is actually important and what is not. In effect, like a human user, the system must be able to discover characteristic properties of data in some appropriate manner, without a teacher. This process is known as *unsupervised learning,* and in this chapter we explore its use in performing relevance identification in place of human users in relevance feedback based multimedia retrieval.

This chapter introduces self-adaptation methods for the automation of adaptive retrieval systems in image and video database applications. This aims to achieve the following advantages in overcoming the difficulties faced in traditional relevance feedback,

- Avoiding errors caused by excessive human involvement in relevance feedback loops, thus, offering a more-user friendly environment.

© Springer International Publishing Switzerland 2014
P. Muneesawang et al., *Multimedia Database Retrieval: Technology and Applications,*
Multimedia Systems and Applications, DOI 10.1007/978-3-319-11782-9_3

- Utilizing unlabeled data to enlarge training sets, in the same spirit as *active leaning*, for relevance feedback to increase learning capability and fast convergence.
- Minimizing relevance feedback iterations so that there is no requirement of transmitting *training* images and video files over the distributed multimedia database (i.e., internet, cloud, and peer-to-peer databases), reducing the required transmission bandwidth.

The topics addressed in this chapter are as follows:

Section 3.2 presents a framework of *pseudo relevance feedback* and a relatively new approach to the problem of unsupervised learning, the *self-organizing tree map* (SOTM). These are the essential tools for the implementation of the automation. The SOTM is a new member within the family of generative, self-organizing maps. Its architecture is based on *dynamic* self-organization and is suitable for data clustering in the current application.

In most of the centralized and distributed database systems, multimedia files are stored in the compressed formats (e.g., JPEG and JPEG2000). Thus, real-time indexing and retrieval of these files requires algorithms that can process the compressed data without full decompression of files. It is necessary to adopt compressed domain indexing to accomplish the low computational complexity at run time. Section 3.3 applies the pseudo relevance feedback method to the energy histogram features in the compressed domain of the JPEG coder, as well as other types of compressed domain features extracted from the wavelet-based coders.

Section 3.4 explores the automatic retrieval framework by incorporating the use of knowledge to produce some levels of the equivalent classification performance used in human vision. The *region of interest* characterizes perceptually important features, and offers a weighting scheme for the unsupervised data classification.

Finally, the automation for video retrieval will be presented in Sect. 3.5 The spatial–temporal information of videos needs be properly captured in the indexing stage. Then, an *adaptive cosine network* is applied to implement pseudo-relevance feedback, as the network's forward–backward signal propagation, to increase retrieval accuracy.

3.2 Pseudo Relevance Feedback Methods

3.2.1 Re-ranking Domain

Pseudo-relevance feedback is referred to as *blind* relevance feedback. The philosophy behind this method is that the retrieval system is able to make use of unlabeled data to improve the retrieval performance from the initial search results. The essential task is to obtain a set of pseudo labels (i.e., the label of samples that have been evaluated by a machine, not human users) for training relevance feedback algorithms. Obtaining meaningful and effective sets of pseudo labels is challenging and has been researched extensively.

Traditionally, the evaluation of pseudo labels is carried out on the feature space in a (single) domain similar to the feature space used for image ranking. Given the feature space $\mathbb{F}_1$, an initial ranking set is obtained for retrieval. Then, the system assumes that a small number of top-ranked objects in the initial set are the pseudo positive samples, and the latest-ranked objects are given the pseudo negative samples [52, 53]. This rule for labeling data uses the query sample (labeled data) to explore unlabeled data in order to increase the size of training set. This can be viewed as the transductive learning problem, which has been studied to handle small numbers of labeled data [54–57]. The pseudo-labels are inferred using the nearest-neighbor rule applied to the unlabeled samples in the dataset. This method enlarges training sample sets, and has been used to improve effectiveness of the support vector machine (SVM)-based adaptive retrieval [52, 58, 59, 307].

There is a difficulty in making assumptions about the class assigned to unlabeled data. The nearest-neighbor rule applied on the feature space $\mathbb{F}_1$, which is the same as the feature space for obtaining initial ranking, can lead to imprecision in class information. The top-ranked samples are not always the relevant, correct answers that meet the user's information needs, due to the limited accuracy of current multimedia retrieval systems [60]. Alternatively, instead of using ranking scores on a single domain for the assignment of pseudo labeling, the self-organization methods [61] can be adopted for this task on a different feature space $\mathbb{F}_2$. The systems label the unlabeled points according to the clusters to which they naturally belong. An advantage of the self-organizing method is that it may be able to make better predictions, with fewer labeled points than standard pseudo-RF, because it uses the natural breaks found in the unlabeled points.

Figure 3.1 illustrates the process for assignment of pseudo labeling using two feature sets in $\mathbb{F}_1$ and $\mathbb{F}_2$, which is used for the adaptation of image/video retrieval system. The feature set in $\mathbb{F}_1$ is a standard feature used for ranking image/video database, whereas the feature set in $\mathbb{F}_2$ has high quality features to be used for relevant judgment (the assignment of pseudo labels) by the self-organization methods. Both sets can be characterized by visual descriptor, text, and other modalities of multimedia files in the database. For instance, previous works [56, 62–65] have used pseudo-positive samples in the visual domain for query expansion in the text domain. This is possible due to the availability of metadata associated with images, especially for web image retrieval applications [66, 67].

In order to perform the assignment of pseudo labeling on the feature set $\mathbb{F}_2$, the self-organization method SOTM is adopted. The motivation is that this method is suitable for clustering *sparsely* distributed data in the current application. The feature space $\mathbb{F}_2$ is usually of high dimension and only a small number of training samples is considered for the assignment of pseudo labels. The efficiency and flexibility of the SOTM in adapting to, and its implicit awareness of topology of input space, make it an appropriate candidate for implementing this idea.

The SOTM [68] attempts to partition a feature space description of input data, by locating clusters of high density within this feature space. Competitive learning is used to locate clusters such that the final representation maintains the general topology of the feature space, yet doing so in a flexible and efficient manner by

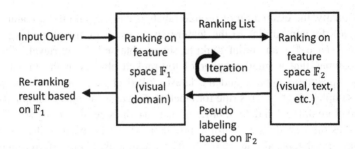

Fig. 3.1 Automation in an adaptive image/video retrieval system. The pseudo labeling is obtained by feature space $\mathbb{F}_2$, which is used to guide the adaptation of the retrieval system applied to the feature space $\mathbb{F}_1$

dynamically generating a model of this topology as it parses the input space. This results in a representation that tends not to suffer from nodes being trapped in regions of low density [69, 70].

3.2.2   Self-organizing Tree Map

In order to construct a suitable map, the SOTM offers two levels of adaptation: weight and structure. Weight adaptation is the process of adjusting the weight vector of the winning nodes. Structure adaptation is the process of adjusting the structure of the network by changing the number of nodes and the structural relationships between them. Given a training data set $\mathscr{T} = \{\mathbf{v}_i\}_{i=1}^{N}$, $\mathbf{v}_i \in \mathbb{F}_2$, the adaptation map using the SOTM algorithm is summarized as follows:

Step 1. Initialization

- Choose the root node $\{\mathbf{w}_j\}_{j=1}^{N_c}$ with a randomly selected training vector from $\mathscr{T}$, where N_c is the total number of nodes currently allocated.
- Initialize learning parameters: $H(0)$ and $\alpha(0)$.

Step 2. Similarity matching

- Randomly select a new feature vector $\mathbf{v}$, and compute the Euclidean distance, d to all currently existing nodes $\mathbf{w}_j$, $j = 1, 2, \cdots, N_c$:

$$d(\mathbf{v}, \mathbf{w}_j) = \|\mathbf{v} - \mathbf{w}_j\| \tag{3.1}$$

Step 3. Updating

- Select the winning node, j^*, with minimum distance,

$$d_{j^*} = \min_j d(\mathbf{v}, \mathbf{w}_j) \tag{3.2}$$

- If $d_{j^*} \leq H(t)$, assign $\mathbf{v}$ to the j^*-th cluster, and update the weight vector according to the reinforced learning rule:

$$\mathbf{w}_{j^*}(t+1) = \mathbf{w}_{j^*}(t) + \alpha(t)[\mathbf{v} - \mathbf{w}_{j^*}] \qquad (3.3)$$

where $H(t)$ is a hierarchy control function, and $\alpha(t)$ is the learning rate.
- Alternatively, if $d_{j^*} > H(t)$, spawn a new node from $\mathbf{w}_{j^*}$ at the position $\mathbf{v}$.

Step 4. Update network parameters

- Decay $\alpha(t)$ with time
- Decay $H(t)$ monotonically, controlling the leafs of the tree

Step 5. Continue from step 2 until either

- There is no significant change in the SOTM
- All nodes are allocated AND there is no significant change in the SOTM
- A maximum number of epochs is reached

Scanning the input data in a random manner is essential for convergence in the algorithm [70, 71]. Consider that the data is scanned in such a way that the i-th component of feature vector $\mathbf{v}$ is monotonically increasing, then the i-th component of the weight vector $\mathbf{w}_j$ will also monotonically increase (according to step 3). Thus all of the nodes will have a monotonically increasing component in the i-th position of the weight vector.

3.2.2.1 Hierarchical Control Function and Learning Parameters

In Step 3, if there is no significant similarity (i.e., $d_{j^*} > H(t)$), then the network figures that it needs to allocate a new node to the network topology. This node then becomes a child of the node it was found to be closest to. The hierarchical control function decays, allowing for nodes to be allocated as leaf nodes of their closest nodes from previous states of the network. Thus the SOTM forms a flexible tree structure that spreads and twists across the feature space. The decay can be implemented by linear and exponential functions:

$$H(t) = H(0) - \left[\left(1 - e^{-\frac{\xi}{\tau_H}}\right)H(0)/\xi\right] \cdot t \qquad (3.4)$$

$$H(t) = H(0)e^{-\frac{t}{\tau_H}} \qquad (3.5)$$

where the time constant τ_H is bound to the project size of the input data $\mathscr{T}$; $H(0)$ is the initial value; t is the number of iterations; and ξ is the number of iterations over which the linear version of $H(t)$ would decay to the same level as the exponential version of $H(t)$.

If $H(t)$ is allowed to decay indefinitely, and there is no limitation on the number of nodes that may be allocated to the network, then it follows that the network will continue to grow indefinitely. Intuitively, this growth should be limited by the smallest resolution of the feature points (i.e., the Euclidean sum of the smallest resolutions of all feature sets included in the feature space). At this limit, the purpose of clustering to provide a compact representation of the dominant patterns or redundancies in the data also becomes meaningless, since the network will continue to grow until the number of classes equals the number of feature data points (or greater).

The adaptation parameter $\alpha(t)$ controls the learning rate, which decreases with time as the weight vectors approach the cluster centers. It is given by either a linear function:

$$\alpha(t) = (1 - \frac{t}{\tau_1}) \tag{3.6}$$

or an exponential function:

$$\alpha(t) = e^{-\frac{t}{\tau_2}} \tag{3.7}$$

where τ_1 and τ_2 are constants which determine the decreasing rate. During the locating phase, global topological adjustment of the weight vectors $\mathbf{w}_j$ takes place. $\alpha(t)$ stays relatively large during this phase. Initially, $\alpha(t)$ can be set as 0.8 and it decreases with time. After the locating phase, a small $\alpha(t)$ for the convergence phase is needed for the fine turning of the map.

3.2.2.2   Visual Experiments on Synthetic 2D Data

As a means of understanding the important properties of the SOTM, the ability of SOTM to cluster synthetic data is demonstrated. A comparison is made between the self-organizing feature map (SOFM) [72] and the SOTM, highlighting the results for clustering the same synthetic dataset at various node capacities. In the SOFM, maps of sizes 2×2, 3×3, 4×4, and 5×5 are considered. As a direct comparison, the SOTM is run a single time without any stop criteria, pausing at the equivalent number of nodes (4, 9, 16, and 25) for comparison with SOFM.

There are two primary factors evident in this simulation (Fig. 3.2). Firstly, the SOFM is more constrained by the natural rigidity of its imposed grid topology. Since this is not a natural fit to the underlying topology, some distortion ensues: In the 2×2 case, the SOTM is shown with five nodes (however this is at the point of insertion of the fifth node, thus the positions of the other 4 may be compared), and has already distinguished between the most separated regions in the underlying density. In the SOFM 3×3 case, some distortion becomes evident, as partitioning has favored the subdivision of dense clusters, over locating other quite clearly distinct regions. As a result of this and the imposed topology, some nodes have become trapped in low or zero density regions, which is undesired. The SOTM by contrast has located all clusters efficiently at this point.

In the SOFM 4×4 case, sufficient nodes have resulted in the mapping across the entire dataspace, however the distortion and zero density nodes still remain. The SOTM, in allocating nodes to outlying regions of low density, does exhibit some limitations in the 16 node case, although with minimal impact on the integrity of the main clusters. The SOTM becomes more sensitive to outliers, once all the natural clusters have been located (see node 10). Generally these nodes will *track back* to flesh out and subdivide larger, more dense clusters, however as competition increases over already limited space, this becomes more difficult: one might imagine a situation in which data has more noisy clusters.

3.2.3 Pseudo Labeling

Figure 3.3 summarizes the application of SOTM for pseudo labeling in an adaptive retrieval system. The retrieval process occurs in the following steps. First, the system obtains the retrieved samples, $\mathbf{x}_1, \mathbf{x}_2, \ldots, \mathbf{x}_N$ that are most similar to the query $\mathbf{x}_q$ based on feature space $\mathbb{F}_1$. Second, these samples are associated with the corresponding feature vectors, $\mathbf{v}_1, \mathbf{v}_2, \ldots, \mathbf{v}_N$, $\mathbf{v}_i \in \mathbb{F}_2$. These are input to the SOTM for unsupervised learning. Third, after convergence, the output of SOTM is used for labeling each $\mathbf{v}_1, \mathbf{v}_2, \ldots, \mathbf{v}_N$, resulting in the label set $\{y_i\}_{i=1}^{N}$. Finally, the labels are associated with the retrieved samples, $\mathbf{x}_1, \mathbf{x}_2, \ldots, \mathbf{x}_N$, and used for the adaptation of the relevance feedback module (i.e., the RBF-based relevance feedback).

Let $\mathbf{w}_j$, $j = 1, 2, \cdots, L$ denote the weight vectors of the SOTM algorithm after the convergence, where L is the total number of nodes. Also, let $\mathbf{v}_q \in \mathbb{F}_2$ be the feature vector associated with a given query image in the current retrieval session. Thus, the distance between the query to all nodes can be obtained by:

$$d\left(\mathbf{v}_q, \mathbf{w}_j\right) = \left\|\mathbf{v}_q - \mathbf{w}_j\right\|, \; j = 1, 2, \cdots, L \tag{3.8}$$

It follows that the K-nearest neighbors of the query is obtained by:

$$S_k\left(\mathbf{v}_q\right) = \left\{\mathbf{w} \middle| d\left(\mathbf{v}_q, \mathbf{w}_j\right) \le d\left(\mathbf{v}_q, \mathbf{w}_k\right)\right\} \tag{3.9}$$

where $S_k\left(\mathbf{v}_q\right)$ is the set of nearest neighbors, and $\mathbf{w}_k$ is the k-th nearest neighbor of $\mathbf{v}_q$. All nodes in this set are relevant to the query vector. The assignment of labeling to the retrieved sample, $\mathbf{v}_i, i \in \{1, N\}$ is firstly conducted by calculating the Euclidean distance between the sample and all nodes $\mathbf{w}_j$, $j = 1, 2, \cdots, L$.

$$d\left(\mathbf{v}_i, \mathbf{w}_j\right) = \left\|\mathbf{v}_i - \mathbf{w}_j\right\|, \; j = 1, 2, \cdots, L \tag{3.10}$$

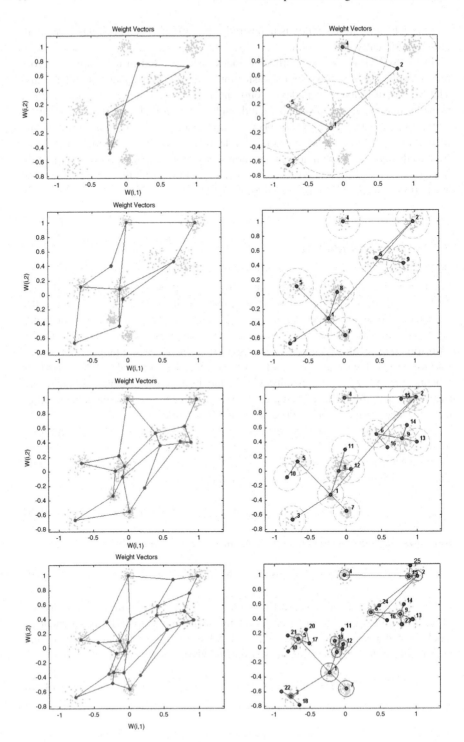

Fig. 3.2 (continued)

Then, the winning node is obtained:

$$j^* = \arg\min_{j} d(\mathbf{v}_i, \mathbf{w}_j) \tag{3.11}$$

The input vector $\mathbf{v}_i$ is assigned with the label, y_i according to the following assignment,

$$y_i = \begin{cases} 1 & \mathbf{w}_j^* \in S_k(\mathbf{v}_q) \\ 0 & \text{Otherwise} \end{cases} \tag{3.12}$$

The application of Eqs. (3.10)–(3.12) to all samples $\mathbf{v}_1, \mathbf{v}_2, \ldots, \mathbf{v}_N$, results in the set of labels $\{y_i\}_{i=1}^{N}$, $y_i \in \{0, 1\}$. This constitutes the label set for the corresponding samples $\mathbf{x}_1, \mathbf{x}_2, \ldots, \mathbf{x}_N$, which forms the training set $\{\mathbf{x}_i, y_i\}_{i=1}^{N}$ for the relevance feedback modules for the next retrieval step.

3.2.4   Experimental Result

The experiment was conducted to compare the performance of SOTM with SOM for obtaining pseudo-RF in the adaptive retrieval process. This was carried out using a subset of the Corel image database [73] consisting of nearly 12,000 images, covering a wide range of real-life photos, from 120 different categories, each containing 100 images. Three set of query images were constructed for testing and evaluation: Set A, Set B, and Set C. In each set, one random sample was selected from each class; thus, one set of tests quires included an example for every class (120 in total). For feature space $\mathbb{F}_1$, color histograms, color moments, wavelet moments, and Fourier descriptors were used, while Hu's event moment [74] and Gabor descriptors accompanied with color histograms and color moments were used for feature space $\mathbb{F}_2$.

The system architecture of pseudo-RF discussed in Fig. 3.3 was implemented. In the SOM and SOTM algorithms, the maximum number of allowed clusters was set to eight. A 4×2 grid topology was used in the SOM structure to locate the eight possible cluster centers (fixed topology). Table 3.1 shows the retrieval result obtained by the pseudo-RF as compared to the initial retrieval result (at first search

---

Fig. 3.2 (continued) Comparison of SOFM vs. SOTM. SOFM (*left*) was run to completion with 4 different grid lattices (*top* to *bottom*: 2×2, 3×3, 4×4, 5×5); SOTM (*right*) is the result of a single run, shown at equivalent stages of node generation (*top* to *bottom*: 4 nodes + trigger site for next node, 9 nodes, 16 nodes, and 25 nodes). SOTM shows efficient allocation of nodes to regions in which data exists. The *broken circles* indicate the hierarchical control function (threshold about each node beyond which data spawns new nodes). The circles in the final plot indicate cluster densities

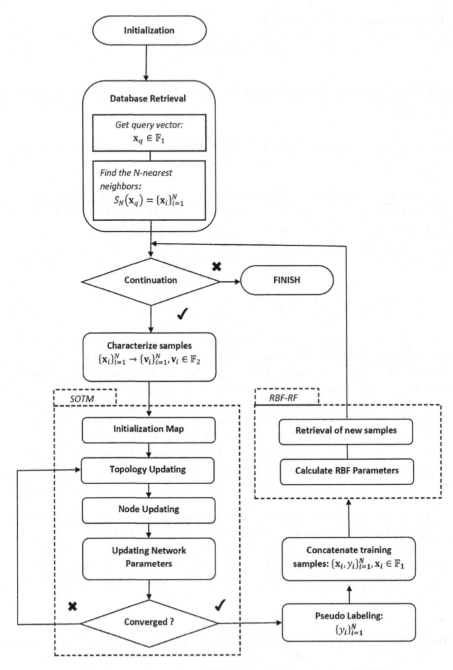

Fig. 3.3 Flowchart of the adaptive retrieval process using SOTM for pseudo labeling

Table 3.1 Retrieval results, obtained by the automatic retrieval system using pseudo-RF and self-organization methods

Classifier	Query Set A	Query Set B	Query Set C
Initial retrieval	37.8	39.2	39.8
SOM	51.2	49.1	52.3
SOTM	52.1	50.6	54.4
SOM with GA weighting	61.2	59.9	63.6
SOTM with GA weighting	66.8	65.7	63.3

operation), for all three sets of queries. It can be observed that the application of pseudo-RF employing the two self-organizing methods improves retrieval accuracy significantly. This result also shows that the map obtained by SOTM is more suitable for pseudo-labeling, as compared to that of SOM.

In addition, the feature maps obtained by SOTM and SOM can be further improved by incorporating feature weighting algorithm [75]. In this case, the Genetic Algorithm (GA) was applied to the feature set in $\mathbb{F}_2$ to automatically assign different weights to the color, shape, and texture features, during the construction of the maps. The experimental results are illustrated in the last two rows of Table 3.1. The self-organizing methods offer even higher accuracy with the application of the GA feature weighting algorithm.

3.3   Re-ranking in Compressed Domains

Compressed domain descriptors are widely used in image retrieval [76–79]. The main reason for this is that feature extraction algorithms can be applied to image and video databases without full decompression. This provides fast and efficient tools that are appropriate for real-time applications. In this section, the compressed domain features are considered as feature space $\mathbb{F}_1$ for database retrieval. The characteristics of discrete cosine transform (DCT) in the Joint Photographic Experts Group (JPEG) standard and discrete wavelet transform (DWT) in image compressions are investigated for adaptive retrieval in compressed domains.

3.3.1   Descriptor in Discrete Cosine Transformation

Largely due to its energy packing property, DCT has been widely used in JPEG and many other popular image and video compression standards. When a typical 8×8 block of data undergoes DCT transformation, most of the significant coefficients are concentrated in the upper-left (low frequency) region of the transform block, thus allowing the storage and transmission of a small number of coefficients.

Figure 3.4 shows the block diagram of JPEG compression and decompression. The feature extraction is performed before the inverse transformation in the decompression process. The energy histogram of the DCT coefficients demonstrated in [76] is utilized as the image feature. An energy histogram of DCT coefficients is obtained by counting the number of times a particular coefficient value appears in an 8×8 block. Formally, the value of the histogram in the m-th bin can be written as:

$$h[m] = \sum_{u=0}^{7} \sum_{v=0}^{7} I(Q(F[u,v]) = m) \tag{3.13}$$

where $Q(F[u,v])$ denotes the value of the dequantized coefficient at the location (u,v), and m is the index of the current histogram bin. The function I is equal to 1 if the argument is true, and 0 otherwise.

For a chrominance DCT block, the DC coefficient is proportional to the average of the chrominance values in the block. As a result, the histogram of DC coefficients can be used as an approximation of the color histogram of the original image. On the other hand, the histogram of the AC coefficients can be used to characterize the frequency composition of the image. This carries texture and edge information, which are contributory to the similarity measure. It has been proven that this feature extraction method is translation and rotational invariance.

In Fig. 3.4, the 9 DCT coefficients in the upper left corner of the block are partitioned into three sets, according to the frequency range. These are:

$$F1D = \{DC\} \tag{3.14}$$

$$F1A = \{AC_{10}, AC_{11}, AC_{01}\} \tag{3.15}$$

$$F2A = \{AC_{20}, AC_{21}, AC_{22}, AC_{12}, AC_{21}\} \tag{3.16}$$

For effectiveness, the energy histogram features can be obtained from the coefficients in two of these collections:

$$F = F1D \cup F1A = \{DC, AC_{10}, AC_{11}, AC_{01}\} \tag{3.17}$$

In addition, separate energy histograms can be constructed for the DC and AC coefficients for each of the color channels, as in the YCbCr color space.

3.3.2   Descriptor in Wavelet Based Coders

Recent multimedia compression standards employ state-of-the art compression technologies by discrete wavelet transform (DWT), including MPEG-4 Visual Texture Coding (VTC) [80], JPEG2000 [81], and set partitioning in hierarchical trees (SPIHT) [82]. This trend has caused much of the latest work on indexing and

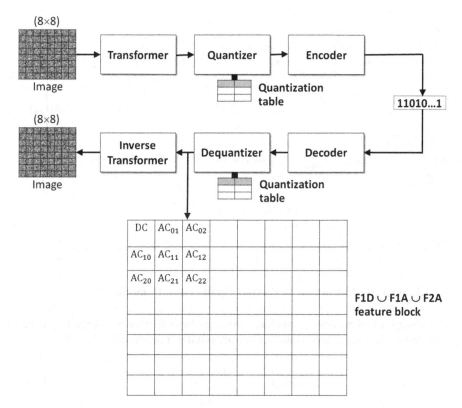

Fig. 3.4 The JPEG compression standard, and feature extraction from the low-frequency DCT coefficients

retrieval to focus on algorithms that are compatible with the new standards [83–85]. Figure 3.5 shows the JPEG2000 standard, which replaces DCT with DWT for image compression. Based on this coding scheme, the feature extraction can be done before the inverse DWT. Image descriptors can be extracted from the header of bitstream packets [86], or based on the analysis of texture and color features within the region of interests at different wavelet resolutions [79].

In the wavelet-baseline coders, the difference among the wavelet coders is only in the process of encoding wavelet coefficients. In JPEG2000, the subband samples are partitioned into small blocks of samples, called codeblocks. Each codeblock is encoded independently. In SPIHT, the wavelet coefficients are coded based on the self-similarity across scales of the wavelet transform using the tree-based organization of the coefficients. Therefore, it is appropriate to extract the descriptors directly from the DWT coefficients, in order to make the feature extraction algorithms compatible with all of the coders.

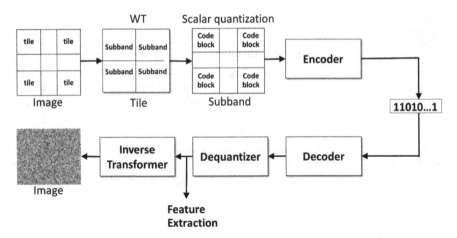

Fig. 3.5 The JPEG2000 architecture and feature extraction in the compressed domain

3.3.2.1 Feature Extraction in Wavelet Compressed Domains

The histogram of wavelet coefficients from the high frequency subbands can be modeled by the generalized Gaussian density (GGD) function [85, 87, 353],

$$p(x; \alpha, \beta) = \frac{\beta}{2\alpha \Gamma\left(\frac{1}{\beta}\right)} e^{\left(-\frac{|x|}{\alpha}\right)^{\beta}} \tag{3.18}$$

where x is the value of wavelet coefficients, α models the width of the probability density function, β is the shape parameter, and Γ is the Gamma function, i.e., $\Gamma(z) = \int_0^\infty e^{-t} t^{z-1} dt$, $z > 0$. For each subband, the parameters α and β can be estimated and utilized for image features [85]. Based on this observation, the image feature for the JPEG2000 coded image can be characterized by the variance of the DWT coefficients from the code blocks [77].

Based on Eq. (3.18), a wavelet moment method [88] can be conducted to obtain a feature related to the energy distribution of each wavelet subband. Let $W_{LL}^n(i,j)$ be the low band image at the n-th level. Also, let $W_{HH}^n(i,j)$, $W_{LH}^n(i,j)$, and $W_{HL}^n(i,j)$ be the three high band images at the n-th level in the horizontal, vertical, and diagonal, respectively. For 3-level decomposition, the wavelet moment features are computed by the first and second central moments on the absolute value of coefficients of each subband, resulting in the ten-dimensional feature vector: $f = \left[\mu_{LL}^3 \sigma_{HH}^3 \sigma_{LH}^3 \sigma_{HH}^3 \cdots \sigma_{HH}^1 \sigma_{LH}^1 \sigma_{HH}^1\right]^t$ where

$$\mu_m^n = \frac{1}{N_{mn}} \sum_{(i,j) \in W_m^n} |W_m^n(i,j)| \tag{3.19}$$

$$\sigma_m^n = \sqrt{\frac{1}{N_{mn}} \sum_{(i,j) \in W_m^n} (|W_m^n(i,j)| - \mu_m^n)^2} \qquad (3.20)$$

Also, n and m denote decomposition level and subband orientation, respectively, N_{mn} is the number of coefficients in the mn-th subband, and $W_m^n(i,j)$ is the wavelet coefficient at location (i,j) in the subband image W_m^n.

3.3.2.2 Feature Extraction from Wavelet Transform/Vector Quantization Coder

The hybrid wavelet transform/vector quantization (WT/VQ) coders have been proven to achieve high compression while maintaining good visual quality [89, 353]. Figure 3.6 shows the coder and decoder of this coding scheme. Here, a two-level wavelet decomposition scheme, with a 15-coefficient biorthogonal filter, is adopted for the analysis of images. The decomposition scheme produces three subbands at resolution level 1, and four subbands at resolution level 2. To capture the orientational characteristics provided by the wavelet-based subband decomposition, a codebook is designed for each subband. This results in a multi resolution codebook (Fig. 3.6d) that consists of sub-codebooks for each resolution level and preferential direction. Each of these sub-codebooks is generated using the Linde–Buzo–Gray (LBG) algorithm, as well as the bit allocation method (Fig. 3.6c), to minimize overall distortion. The codebook design divides a subband belonging to different images into $m \times m$ square blocks and the resulting vectors are used as the training vectors. Separate codebooks are trained for each resolution orientation subband.

For the encoding of an input image at a total bit rate of 1 b/pixel, the bit assignment is organized as follows: resolution 1 (diagonal orientation) is discarded; Resolution 1 (horizontal and vertical orientations) and resolution 2 (diagonal orientation) are coded using 256-vector codebooks resulting in a 0.5-b/pixel rate, whereas resolution 2 (horizontal and vertical orientations) is coded at a 2 b/pixel rate using 256-vector codebooks; and, finally, the lowest resolution is coded by scalar quantization at 8-b/pixel.

Figure 3.6b shows the decoding process. The feature extraction is obtained before vector dequantization. The coding labels are used to constitute a feature vector via the computation of the labels histograms. Each subband is characterized by one histogram and represents the original image at a different resolution; thus, the resulting histograms are called multiresolution histogram indexing (HMI) [90]. This method makes use of the fact that the usage of codewords in the sub-codebook reflects the content of the encoded input subband. For the two-level decomposition, five subbands containing wavelet *detail* coefficients are utilized for the construction of HMI features:

$$f_{MHI} = \left[\boldsymbol{H}^1\left(l\right), \boldsymbol{H}^2\left(l\right), \boldsymbol{H}^3\left(l\right), \boldsymbol{H}^4\left(l\right), \boldsymbol{H}^5\left(l\right) \right]^t \qquad (3.21)$$

where $\boldsymbol{H}^j\left(l\right)$ is the histogram generated from the coding label of the j-th subband, $l = 1, 2, \ldots, L$, and the sub-codebook size $L = 256$. In Fig. 3.6a, let the function $Q\left(V_i\right): \mathbb{R}^{m \times m} \rightarrow 1, \ldots, L$ be the function that quantized the value of the i-th input vector of size m-by-m to its bin. The histogram model of each subband consists then of the L values of the L bins of the histogram $\boldsymbol{H}\left(l\right) = [H\left(1\right), \ldots, H\left(l\right), \ldots, H\left(L\right)]^t$. The value of the l-th bin is calculated by:

$$H\left(l\right) = \sum_{i=1}^{N_V} \delta\left(Q\left(V_i\right) - l\right), \ l \in \{1, \ldots, L\} \qquad (3.22)$$

where δ is the Kronecker delta function, and N_V is the total number of vectors in the subband.

3.3.3 Experimental Result

The pseudo RF for adaptive image retrieval outlined in Fig. 3.3 was applied for the retrieval of compressed images. Feature space $\mathbb{F}_1$ is characterized by the compressed domain features (extracted from the DCT or WT compressed images). For relevance classification in feature space $\mathbb{F}_2$, a Gabor wavelet transform technique [91, 92] was employed. The experiments were designed to compare the performances of four methods: non-adaptive CBIR, user-controlled RF retrieval, pseudo RF retrieval, and semiautomatic retrieval. The experimental results were obtained from two image databases: DB1, the Brodatz database, which contains 1,856 texture images; and DB2, distributed by Media Graphic Inc. [93], consisting of nearly 4,700 JPEG color images covering a wide range of real-life photos, with a completely open domain. These are typical, medium-size databases that are potentially remotely accessible through Internet environments, without advanced indexing of the stored images [76].

For the DB1 test set, the visual descriptor used both WM [cf. Eqs. (3.19) and (3.20)] and MHI feature [cf. Eq. (3.21)] representations, for the characterization of the wavelet-compressed images. The WM descriptor was obtained before the invert-DWT process of the wavelet-baseline coder, whereas the MHI descriptor was obtained before VQ-decoding of the WT/VQ decoder. For the DB2 test set, the visual descriptors used are the energy histograms which were extracted directly from the compressed JPEG images after the entropy decoding process.

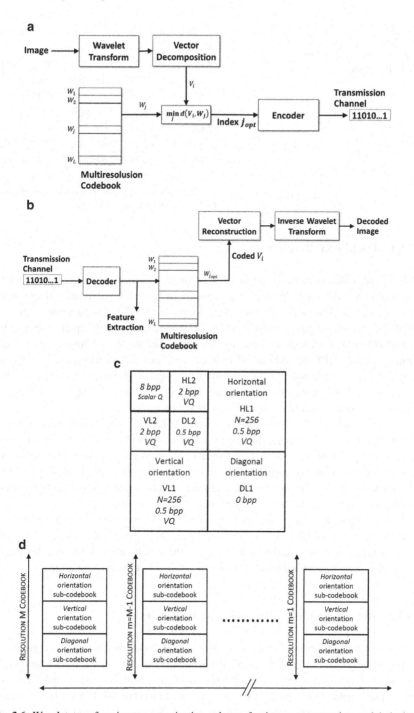

Fig. 3.6 Wavelet transform/vector quantization scheme for image compression and indexing; (**a**) coder; (**b**) decoder and MHI feature extraction; (**c**) subimages bitrate allocation for a total bit rate of 1 b/pixel and for a two-level decomposition; (**d**) multiresolution codebook

Table 3.2 Average retrieval
rate (AVR) of 116 query
images on DB1, obtained by
pseudo-RF learning

Method	Initial	Iter. 1	Iter. 2	Iter. 3	Iter. 4
Retrieval based on WM descriptor					
ARBFN	58.78	69.02	72.85	76.24	77.21
Single-RBF	58.78	66.32	68.80	70.04	71.87
QAM	53.88	57.11	59.00	60.45	60.78
Retrieval based on NHI descriptor					
ARBFN	63.42	71.66	75.22	75.86	76.51
Sigle-RBF	63.42	70.31	72.74	73.11	73.06
QAM	60.35	67.89	71.07	72.63	72.79

The initial AVR results were obtained by
Euclidean metric for ARBFN and single-RBF, and
by Cosine measure for QAM

3.3.3.1 Pseudo-RF Result

Table 3.2 provides numerical results illustrating the performance of the pseudo-RF
method on DB1 database. In all cases, relevance judgment was based on the ground
truth. Three adaptive retrieval methods: adaptive radial basis function network
(ARBFN), the single-radial basis function (RBF) method, and the query adaptation
method (QAM) were tested (these methods are discussed in Chap. 2). For each
learning method, the top 20 ranked images were utilized as training data. These
samples were input to the SOTM algorithm for pseudo labeling. The output of the
unsupervised network was in turn used as the supervisor for RF learning to update
learning parameters and to obtain a new set of retrievals.

The use of pseudo-RF learning for automatic retrieval resulted in a significant
improvement in retrieval performance over that of the non-adaptive technique. For
the automatic ARBFN, 18.4 % improvement in average precision was achieved
through four iterations of pseudo-RF, whereas the automatic single-RBF provided
a 13 % improvement. These retrievals used the WM descriptor. The results for each
learning method, with the MHI descriptor, show the same trend.

Figure 3.7 provides an example of a retrieval session performed by the automatic
ARBFN learning method, using the WM descriptor. Figure 3.7a shows retrieval
results without learning, and Fig. 3.7b shows the results after automatic learning.
The improvement provided by the automatic retrieval method is apparent.

3.3.3.2 Retrieval Results of Semiautomatic Retrieval

In order to verify the performance of the unsupervised learning of the pseudo-
RF retrieval system, its performance was compared with that of the traditional RF
method. The retrieval system was allowed to interact with the user to perform the
retrieval task, and the results obtained are provided in Table 3.3. It was observed that
user interaction gave better performance: 3.34–6.79 % improvement was seen after
one iteration, and 3.66–4.74 % after four iterations. However, it should be taken into

Fig. 3.7 (**a**) Initial retrieval
result for DB1 database;
(**b**) retrieval result after
application of automatic
ARBFN

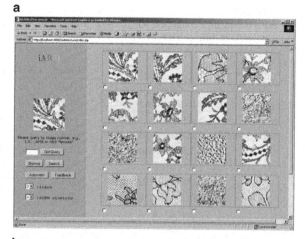

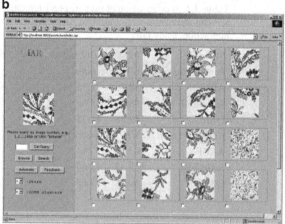

account that the users had to provide feedback on each of the images returned by a
query in order to obtain these results.

As found in the studies from Chap. 2, retrieval performance can be progressively improved by repeated relevance feedback from the user. The semiautomatic
approach reported here greatly reduced the number of iterations required for user
interaction. This significantly improved the overall efficiency of the system. In
the semiautomatic learning method, the retrieval system first performed automatic
retrieval for each query to adaptively improve its performance. After four iterations,
the retrieval system was then assisted by the users. Table 3.4 provides a summary
of the retrieval results, based on one round of user-controlled RF. It was observed
that the semiautomatic RF method was superior to the automatic method and the
user interaction method. The best performance was given by the semiautomatic
ARBFN at 83.41 % using WM descriptor, and 81.14 % using MHI descriptor.

Table 3.3 A comparison of average precision rate (AVR) (%) between pseudo-RF method and user-controlled RF method, using DB1, and MHI descriptor, where Δ denotes AVR differences between the two methods

Method		Initial	Iter. 1	Iter. 4	Number of user RF (iteration)
ARBFN	a: Pseudo-RF	63.42	71.66	76.51	–
	b: User-controlled RF	63.42	77.64	80.17	4
	$\Delta = a - b$	–	+5.98	+3.66	
Single-RBF	a: Pseudo-RF	63.42	70.31	73.06	–
	b: User-controlled RF	63.42	73.65	77.43	4
	$\Delta = a - b$	–	+3.34	+4.37	
QAM	a: Pseudo-RF	60.35	67.89	72.79	–
	b: User-controlled RF	60.35	74.68	77.53	4
	$\Delta = a - b$	–	+6.79	+4.74	

Table 3.4 A comparison of average precision rate (AVR) (%) between semiautomatic and user-controlled RF methods, after one round of user interaction, using DB1

Method	Initial	User-controlled RF	Semiautomatic RF
Retrieval based on WM descriptor			
ARBFN	58.78	77.53	83.41
Sigle-RBF	58.78	75.59	78.34
QAM	53.88	61.75	63.25
Retrieval based on MHI descriptor			
ARBFN	63.42	77.64	81.14
Sigle-RBF	63.42	73.65	77.03
QAM	60.35	74.68	76.39

Figure 3.8a–c shows the results for each method when convergence is reached. The improvement resulting from the adoption of the semiautomatic approach is indicated by a correspondingly small amount of user feedback for convergence. In particular, the semiautomatic methods can reach or surpass the best performance of user controlled RF within only one to two interactions of user feedback.

3.3.3.3 Result of Retrieval in DCT Compressed Domains

The ARBFN method utilizing pseudo-RF learning was applied for retrieval of images in DB2, JPEG photograph database [93]. The energy histograms of the lower frequency DCT coefficients [76] were used to characterize each image in the database. This constituted the feature space $\mathbb{F}_1$ for retrieval. The four coefficients bounded within the upper left corner of the DCT block are used to obtain the energy histograms. Separate energy histograms are constructed for the DC and AC coefficients of each of the color channels, and 30 bins are used for each histogram.

Fig. 3.8 A comparison of retrieval performance at convergence, between the semiautomatic and user-controlled RF methods, where the learning methods used are: (**a**) ARBFN; (**b**) single-RBF; and (**c**) QAM. The semiautomatic method can attain convergence within one to two iterations of user feedback. These results are based on the MHI feature

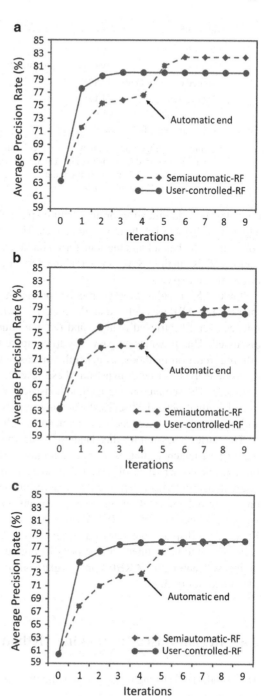

Table 3.5 Retrieval results for DB2, averaged over 30 query images

Method	Avg. relative precision (%)	Avg. number of user RF for convergence (Iter.)
Non-adaptive method	49.82	–
Pseudo-RF	79.17	–
User-controlled RF	95.66	2.63
Semi-automatic RF	98.08	1.33

Column 2: average relative precision (%); column 3: number of user feedbacks (iterations) required for convergence. The results were performed by ARBFN in both automatic and semi-automatic modes

For relevance classification on the feature space $\mathbb{F}_2$, the GWT [91, 92] was again adopted to characterize the retrieved images. The GWT was applied to the dominant colors in each channel and the transform coefficients were used to construct feature vectors. This method gives better characterization of texture information from different color spaces.

Table 3.5 provides average relative precision (ARP) figures for thirty query images. The ARP was defined as $Pr/\max(Pr)$, where Pr is the number of relevant images over 12 retrieved images, and the maximum was taken across all methods discussed. This provides an easy way to compare the relative performance among different retrieval methods. In general, conclusions similar to those for the texture database (DB1) can be drawn from these results, with regard to the retrieval performance. The semiautomatic method consistently displayed superior performance over the other methods discussed, showing improvement from 49.8 to 98.1 %, and with the number of user feedbacks reduced by half to reach convergence.

The retrieval session for this database is shown in Fig. 3.9a, b. Figure 3.9a shows the 12 best-matched images without learning, with the query image displayed in the top-left corner. It is observed that some retrieved images are similar to the query image in terms of texture features. Seven similar images are relevant. Based on this initial information, the self-organizing system dynamically readjusts the weight parameters of the ARBFN model to capture the notion of image similarity. Figure 3.9b displays the retrieval results, which are considerably improved after using the automatic interactive approach. Figure 3.9c shows the retrieval results of the semiautomatic ARBFN in comparison to the user-controlled interactions illustrated in Fig. 3.9d.

3.4   Region-Based Re-ranking Method

The pseudo-RF learning represents the blind relevance feedback, where the machine performs pseudo labeling. This process requires modeling image contents with sufficiently accurate features for the characterization of perceptual importance. This issue is especially pressing with automatic RF since, without providing some form of knowledge to the relevance classification process from the external

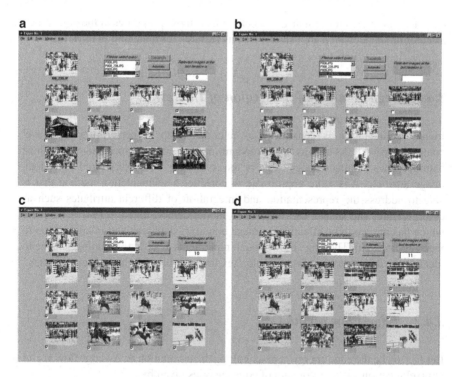

Fig. 3.9 Retrieval results for DB2, obtained by (**a**) a non-adaptive method; (**b**) automatic ARBFN; (**c**) semiautomatic ARBFN, converted by one round of user interaction; (**d**) user-controlled ARBFN, converted by two rounds of user interaction

world, the SOTM classifier cannot operate as efficiently as a user-supervised process. For example, global features of shape, color, or texture might consume an undue proportion of weights toward the judgment of image relevancy by machine vision [75]. Furthermore, these global features do not always address perceptually important regions or any salient objects depicted in an image. This is because there are more regions in an image than those which are of perceptual importance. So, higher classification accuracy may be possible with the acquisition of more precise perception information. However, the form of knowledge needed in automatic relevance feedback has to be identified before the retrieval process begins, instead of during the process as the user-controlled RF does.

In this section, an automatic adaptive image retrieval scheme is implemented with embedded knowledge of perceptual importance, the form of which is identified in advance. With a specific domain to photograph collection, the restricted goal of identifying the region of interest (ROI) is pursued. The ROI assumes that the significant objects within an image are often located at the center, as a photographer usually tries to locate significant objects at the focus of the camera's view. The Edge Flow model [94] is adopted to identify the ROI within a photograph. This ROI does not necessarily require the exact identification of a possible object in the image, but only the region selected which adequately reflects those properties of the object such as color or shape, which are usually used as features for matching in retrieval.

3.4.1 Segmentation of the Region of Interest

Image segmentation is considered as a crucial step in performing high-level computer vision tasks such as object recognition and scene interpretation [95]. Since natural scenes within an image could be too complex to be characterized by a single image attribute, it is more appropriate to consider a segmentation method that is able to address the representation and integration of different attributes such as color, texture, and shape. The Edge Flow model demonstrated in [94] is adopted, which has proven to be effective in image boundary detection and in application to video coding [96]. The Edge Flow model implements a predictive coding scheme to identify the direction of change in color, texture, and filtered phase discontinuities.

3.4.2 Edge Flow Method

Let $E(s, \theta)$ be the edge energy at pixel s along the orientation θ. An edge flow vector at pixel location s is a vector sum of edge energies given by:

$$\mathbf{F} = \sum_{\Theta(s) \leq \theta \leq \Theta(s) + \pi} E(s, \theta) \exp(j\theta) \qquad (3.23)$$

which is taken along a continuous range of flow directions that maximizes the sum of probabilities:

$$\Theta(s) = \arg\max_{\theta} \left\{ \sum_{\theta \leq \theta' \leq \theta + \pi} P(s, \theta') \right\} \qquad (3.24)$$

where $P(s, \theta)$ represents the probability of finding the image boundary if the corresponding Edge Flow flows in the direction θ. The model in Eq. (3.23) facilitates the integration of multiple attributes in each Edge Flow which is obtained from different types of image attributes. Consider,

$$E(s, \theta) = \sum_{a \in A} E_a(s, \theta) w(a) \qquad (3.25)$$

and

$$\sum_{a \in A} w(a) = 1 \tag{3.26}$$

$$P(s, \theta) = \sum_{a \in A} P_a(s, \theta) w(a) \tag{3.27}$$

where $E_a(s, \theta)$ and $P_a(s, \theta)$ represent the energy and probability of the edge flow computed from image attribute $a \in \{$intensity/color, texture, phase$\}$. $w(a)$ is the weighting coefficient associated with image attribute a.

For a given color image, the intensity of the edge flow can be computed in each of three color bands (R, G, B) and the texture edge flow can be calculated from the intensity $I = (R + G + B)/3$. Then the overall edge flow can be obtained by combining them as in Eqs. (3.25) and (3.27) with $A = \{$red, green, blue, texture$\}$. Each location s in the image is associated with the three parameters: $\{[E(s, \theta), P(s, \theta), P(s, \theta + \pi)] | 0 \leq \theta < \pi\}$. Given these parameters, Eq. (3.24) is utilized to firstly obtain the parameter $\Theta(s)$. Then, the edge flow vector $\mathbf{F}$ is identified by Eq. (3.23). The resulting $\mathbf{F}$ is a complex number with its magnitude representing the resulting edge energy and angle representing the flow direction.

The basic idea of the Edge Flow method is to identify the direction of change in the attribute discontinuities at each image location. The Edge Flow vectors propagate from pixel to pixel along the directions being predicted. Once the propagation process reaches its stable state, the image boundaries can be detected by identifying the locations which have non-zero edge flows pointing to each other. Finally, boundary connections and region merging operations are applied to create closed loop regions and to merge these into a small number of regions according to their color and texture characteristics.

3.4.3 Knowledge-Based Automatic Region of Interest

The definition of ROI is highly dependent on user needs and perception. However, specific to the current application for photographic collections, a photographer usually creates a photograph with a single focus point at the center of the picture. Based on this assumption, we can effectively attain ROI by associating it with the objects located at the center of photographs. Let $\mathscr{S} = \{\mathscr{R}_i, i = 1, \ldots, N | \mathscr{R}_i \cap \mathscr{R}_j = \varnothing, i \neq j\}$ be a set of regions generated by the Edge Flow model from one image, where $\mathscr{R}_i$ is the i-th region and N is the number of regions. Let $W_{m \times n}$ be a predefined rectangular window of size $m \times n$ pixels, whose center is located at the center of the input image. Also, let $\mathscr{W}$ be a set of label for regions that are located either partly or completely inside the $W_{m \times n}$ window, e.g., $\mathscr{W} = \{i | R_i \cap W_{m \times n} \neq \varnothing\}$. ROI is defined as a collection of regions which are members of $\mathscr{W}$:

$$\mathscr{S}' = \bigcup_{i \in \mathscr{W}} \mathscr{R}_i \tag{3.28}$$

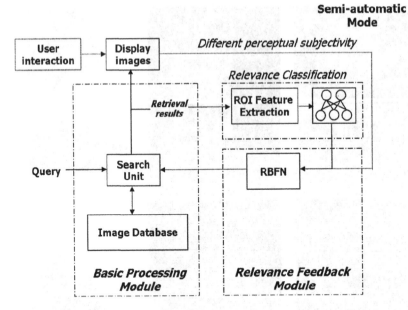

Fig. 3.11 Diagram of an automatic adaptive image retrieval system which utilizes feature sets extracted from the region-of-interest for pseudo labeling by the SOTM. The system can run in automatic as well as semiautomatic modes

followed by extracting the feature vectors in the feature space $\mathbb{F}_2$, using color histograms and Fourier descriptors.

The performance comparisons were conducted using four methods: non-adaptive method, user-controlled RF, automatic RF, and semi-automatic RF, using 20 queries from different categories. The non-adaptive method employed normalized Euclidean distance as the matching criterion. This method provided a set of retrieved images to the user-controlled RF algorithm that further enhanced the system performance by the non-linear RBF model. In comparison, in automatic RF case, the relevance identification was executed by the SOTM with two iterations of pseudo-RF. In addition, after the automatic process, the system performance was refined by a user to obtain semi-automatic RF results.

Table 3.6 presents results obtained by the four methods, measured by the average precisions of the top 16 best matches. Evidently, the automatic RF provides considerable improvement over the non-adaptive method (i.e., by more than 25 % in precision), without user interaction. The automatic result is close to 4 % lower than that of user-controlled RF method. By combining automatic learning with user interaction, it is observed that the semi-automatic RF clearly outperforms other methods discussed.

The user interaction process was also allowed to continue until convergence. It is observed that the user-controlled RF and the semi-automatic RF reached convergence at similar points within 93 %. However, in order to reach this optimum

Table 3.6 Average precision rate (%) and number of user feedback cycles, obtained by retrieving 20 queries from the Corel database, measured from the top 16 best matches

Method	Average precision (%)	Number of user RF (Iter.)
Non-adaptive method	52.81	–
Pseudo-RF	78.13	–
User-controlled RF	82.19	1
Semi-automatic RF	87.50	1

point, the user-controlled RF method used on average 2.4 cycles of user interactions, while the semi-automatic RF method used 1.6 cycles. This shows that the semi-automatic method is the most effective learning strategy in terms of both retrieval accuracy and minimization of user interaction. This also demonstrates that the application of pseudo-RF in combination with perceptually significant features extracted from the ROIs clearly enhanced the overall system performance.

3.5 Video Re-ranking

Incorporating the pseudo-RF method for improving retrieval accuracy is important. While RF for video retrieval has been implemented [98, 99], where the audio-visual information is utilized for characterizing spatio-temporal information within the video sequence, the application of RF to video files is, however, a time consuming process, since users have to play each retrieved video file, which is usually large, in order to provide relevance feedback. In practice, this is a more difficult interaction with sample video files for retrieval on Internet databases. In this section, the RF is considered an important method and is implemented in automatic fashion. The retrieval system utilizes the *template frequency model* (TFM) to characterize both spatial and temporal information. This representation allows RF to effectively analyze the dynamic content of the video. The TFM is conducted with the same principle as the bag-of-word model. It is suitably integrated with a cosine network [100] for implementing pseudo RF, to further allow improvement of retrieval accuracy, while minimizing user interactions.

3.5.1 Template Frequency Model Implementing Bag-of-Words Model

The template frequency model [101] views a video datum as a set of visual templates, in the same spirit as bag-of-words modeling. Let $\mathcal{V}$ be a video interval that contains a finite set of frames $f_1, f_2, \ldots, f_M$. Also, let $\mathbf{x}_m \in \mathbb{R}^P$ denote a feature vector (i.e., color histogram feature) extracted from the m-th frame.

Thus, the video interval $\mathcal{V}$ can be described by a set of descriptors $\mathcal{D}_{\mathcal{V}} = \{(\mathbf{x}_1, f_1), \cdots, (\mathbf{x}_m, f_m), \cdots, (\mathbf{x}_M, f_M)\}$. The indexing of each video frame is obtained by a vector quantization process. Specifically, let $\mathcal{C} = \{(\mathbf{g}_r, l_r) | \mathbf{g}_r \in \mathbb{R}^P, \; l_r \in \{1, 2, \ldots, R\}, \; r = 1, 2, \ldots, R\}$ be a set of templates (or codewords) $\mathbf{g}_r$, where l_r is the label of the r-th template. This set is previously generated and optimized by a competitive learning algorithm [331] (illustrated in Table 3.7). The vector $\mathbf{x}_m$ is mapped by $\mathbb{R}^P \rightarrow \mathcal{C}$ on the Voronoi space, i.e., quantizing the input vector by:

$$Q(\mathbf{x}_m) = \{l_{r^*}^{\mathbf{x}_m}, l_{r^*, 1}^{\mathbf{x}_m}, \ldots, l_{r^*, (\eta-1)}^{\mathbf{x}_m}\} \tag{3.30}$$

where Q is the vector quantization function, $l_{r^*}^{\mathbf{x}_m}$ is the label of the closest template, i.e.,

$$r^* = \arg\min_r (\|\mathbf{x}_m - \mathbf{g}_r\|) \tag{3.31}$$

and $l_{r^*, 1}^{\mathbf{x}_m}$ and $l_{r^*, (\eta-1)}^{\mathbf{x}_m}$ are the labels for the first and the last neighbors of the wining template $\mathbf{g}_{r^*}$, respectively.

Equation (3.30) obtains a multiple label indexing that is designed to describe correlation information between the winning template and its neighbors. Figure 3.12 shows the example of this indexing process. Here we are interested not only in the best-match template, but also the second (and up to η-th) best match. Once a cell is selected, the $\eta - 1$ neighbors which have not yet been visited in the scan are then also included in the output label set. This allows for interpretation of the correlation information between the selected cell and its neighbors. Since a video sequence usually has a very strong frame-to-frame correlation [102] due to the nature of time-sequence data, embedding correlation information through Eq. (3.30) offers a better description for video contents, and thus a means for more accurate discriminant analysis. For example, two consecutive frames which are visually similar may not be mapped into the same cell; rather, they may be mapped onto two cells in a neighborhood area, so that mapping through multiple labels using Eq. (3.30) maps two frames from the same class in the visual space into the same neighborhood area in feature space.

The visual content of the video frame f_m is therefore characterized by the membership of the label set, $\{l_{r^*}^{\mathbf{x}_m}, l_{r^*, 1}^{\mathbf{x}_m}, \ldots, l_{r^*, (\eta-1)}^{\mathbf{x}_m}\}$. The result of mapping all frames, $\{l_{r^*}^{\mathbf{x}_m}, l_{r^*, 1}^{\mathbf{x}_m}, \ldots, l_{r^*, (\eta-1)}^{\mathbf{x}_m}\}$, $\forall m \in \{1, \ldots, M\}$ from the mapping of the entire video interval V_j are concatenated into a vector $\mathbf{v}_j = \{w_{j1}, \ldots, w_{jr}, \ldots, w_{jR}\}$. The weight parameters are calculated by the $TF \times IDF$ weight scheme [323]:

$$w_{jr} = \frac{F_{jr}}{\max_r F_{jr}} \times \log \frac{N}{n_r} \tag{3.32}$$

where the weight parameter F_{jr} stands for a raw frequency of template $\mathbf{g}_r$ in the video interval $\mathcal{V}_j$, i.e.,

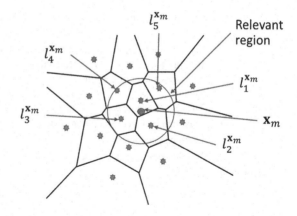

Fig. 3.12 Representation of encoding $\mathbf{x}_m$ with the set of labels $\{l_1^{\mathbf{x}_m}, l_2^{\mathbf{x}_m}, \ldots, l_5^{\mathbf{x}_m}\}$

$$F_{jr} = \sum_{m=1}^{M} \sum_{i=1}^{\eta} I\left(l_i^{\mathbf{x}_m} = l_r\right) \tag{3.33}$$

The function I is equal to 1 if the argument is true, and 0 otherwise. In addition, the maximum in Eq. (3.32) is computed over all templates mentioned in the content of the video $\mathcal{V}_j$; N denotes the total number of videos in the system; and n_r denotes the number of videos in which the index template $\mathbf{g}_r$ appears.

The weight w_{jr} balances two effects for clustering purposes: intra-clustering characterization and inter-clustering characterization. First, the intra-clustering similarity provides one measure of how well that template describes the video contents in the desired class, and it is quantified by measuring the raw frequency of a template $\mathbf{g}_r$ inside a video $\mathcal{V}_j$. Second, the inter-clustering dissimilarity is quantified by measuring the inverse of the frequency of a template $\mathbf{g}_r$ among the videos in the collection, thereby specifying that the templates which appear in many videos are not very useful for the discriminant analysis.

3.5.2 Adaptive Cosine Network

3.5.2.1 Network Architecture

The TFM video indexing characterizes the j-th video by using numerical weight parameters, w_{jr}, $r = 1, \ldots, R$, each of which characterizes a degree of importance of the templates presented in the video. In this section, an adaptive cosine network demonstrated in [100, 101] is adopted to re-organize the weight parameters on a per query basis. Using these weight parameters, video clusters, which maximize the similarity within a cluster while also maximizing the separation from other clusters, can be formed based on content identifiers, to initialize the ranking for answering a query. This ranking is now adopted to re-organize the degree of importance of the templates through the following process. First, the process identifies *effective*

Table 3.7 Summary of competitive learning algorithm for template generation for video database indexing

Input:	Set of feature vectors extracted from video frames in a given database: $\mathbf{H} = [\mathbf{h}_1, \mathbf{h}_2, \ldots, \mathbf{h}_H]^t = [h_{ji}]$, where $\mathbf{h}_j = [h_{j1}, h_{j2}, \ldots, h_{jP}]^t \in \mathbb{R}^P$ is the color histogram vector of the j-th video frame, and H is the number of training samples.
Output:	The set of weight vectors $= \{\mathbf{g}_r | r = 1, \ldots, R\}$, $\mathbf{g}_r \in \mathbb{R}^P, R \ll H$
Initialization:	Maximum number of iterations $= t_f$
	Learning parameter $= \eta_0$
	Weight vectors, $\mathbf{g}_1, \mathbf{g}_2, \ldots, \mathbf{g}_R$
Computation:	$$h_{ji} \longleftarrow \frac{(h_{ji} - \mu_i)}{\sigma_i} \quad \text{(normalized all patterns)}$$ where μ_i and σ_i are the mean value and the standard deviation of the i-th column vector in $\mathbf{H}$, respectively.
Repeat	Randomly select a pattern $\mathbf{h}$, at iteration t $$r \longleftarrow \arg\min_{r'} \|\mathbf{h} - \mathbf{g}_{r'}\| \quad \text{(classify } \mathbf{h}\text{)}$$ $$\mathbf{g}_r \longleftarrow \mathbf{g}_r + \eta(\mathbf{h} - \mathbf{g}_r) \quad \text{(weight update)}$$ $$\eta \longleftarrow \eta_0\left(1 - \frac{t}{t_f}\right) \quad \text{(parameter update)}$$
Until:	$t = t_f$
Return:	$\mathbf{g}_1, \mathbf{g}_2, \ldots, \mathbf{g}_R$

templates that are the common templates among videos in a retrieved set. Then, those templates considered to be the most significant for reweighting the existing templates of the initially submitted query are weighted, to improve the ranking performance. In other words, we allow the templates that are not presented by the initially submitted query (i.e., $w_{qr} = 0$, $r \in [1, \ldots, R]$), but are common among the top-ranked videos (i.e., the potentially relevant videos), to *expand*. This results in reorganization of the degree of importance of the query's templates for better measurement of video similarity.

The re-ranking process is performed by an adaptive cosine network [100, 101], with the network architecture presented in Fig. 3.13. The network is composed of three layers: one for the query templates, one for the video templates, and the third for the videos themselves. Each node has a connection weight communicated to its neighbors via the connection links. The query template nodes initiate the inference process by sending signals to the video template nodes. The video template nodes then themselves generate signals to the video nodes. Upon receiving this stimulus, the video nodes, in turn, generate new signals directed back to the video template nodes. This process might repeat itself several times, through the second and the

Fig. 3.13 An architecture of
the adaptive cosine network
implementing the pseudo-RF
method for video retrieval

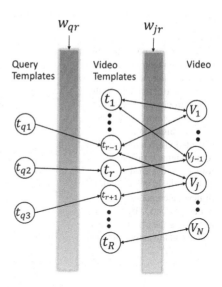

third layers, which allows the network to find templates that appear to be relevant
on the basis of the initial ranking, and use those templates to refine the ranking
process.

Figure 3.14 graphically describes the spreading activation process. Figure 3.14a
shows two query templates sending signals to the video template nodes $\{a,b\}$. The
video nodes: $\{c,d,e\}$ are activated (the application of thresholding is omitted to
simplify illustration). Figure 3.14b shows the signals propagating backward to the
video template layers. At this time, f, g and h are the newly activated nodes. After
re-calculating the node activations, the video template nodes send signals forward to
the video nodes as shown in Fig. 3.14c. This results in a new ranking, which includes
a new video node, i. We see that the network then utilizes video template node f,
present in the initial ranking, to find a higher number of relevant video nodes.

3.5.2.2 Network Adaptation and Learning

Let $\mathbf{v}_q = \{w_{qr} | \; r \in [1,\ldots,R]\}$ denote the set of the query's weight components,
obtained by converting the video query $\mathscr{V}_q$ into a set of templates, and weighting
vectors. Let $mesg_{r^{(q)} \to r^{(t)}}$ denote the message sent along the connection $\{r^{(q)}, r^{(t)}\}$
from the r-th query node to the r-th video template node. Also, let $mesg_{r^{(t)} \to j^{(v)}}$
denote the message sent along the connection $\{r^{(t)}, j^{(v)}\}$ from the r-th video
template node to the j-th video node, $j \in [1,N]$. Note that $mesg_{r^{(q)} \to r^{(t)}}$ is a
one-to-one correspondence, while $mesg_{r^{(t)} \to j^{(v)}}$ is a one-to-many correspondence.

Fig. 3.14 Signal
propagation: (**a**) signals from
the two query nodes are sent
to the video template nodes,
and three video nodes
$\{c,d,e\}$ are activated; (**b**) the
signal propagates back from
the third layer to the second
layer, resulting in more
activated video temple nodes;
(**c**) the signal propagates
forward to the third layer.
This results in the activation
of new video nodes (i.e.,
nodes $\{c,d,e,i\}$) by
expanding the original query
nodes and the activated video
nodes in (**b**)

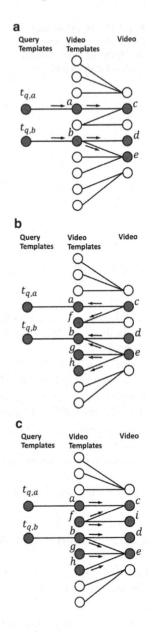

First, each query template node is assigned a fixed activation level equal to $a_r^{(q)} = 1, r \in [1,R]$. Then, its signal to the video template node is attenuated by normalized query template weights $\bar{w}_{qr}$, as follows:

$$mesg_{r^{(q)} \to r^{(t)}} = a_r^{(q)} \times \bar{w}_{qr} \tag{3.34}$$

$$\bar{w}_{qr} = \begin{cases} \dfrac{w_{qr}}{\sqrt{\sum_{r=1}^{R} w_{qr}^2}} & \text{if } \vec{\mathbf{g}}_r \in \mathcal{V}_q \\ 0 & \text{otherwise} \end{cases} \tag{3.35}$$

When a signal reaches the video template nodes, only the video template nodes connected to the query template nodes will be activated. These nodes might send new signals out, directed towards the video nodes, which are again attenuated by normalized video template weights $\bar{w}_{jr}$ derived from the weights w_{jr}, as follows:

$$mesg_{r^{(t)} \to j^{(v)}} = mesg_{r^{(q)} \to r^{(t)}} \times \bar{w}_{jr} \tag{3.36}$$

$$\bar{w}_{jr} = \begin{cases} \dfrac{w_{jr}}{\sqrt{\sum_{r=1}^{R} w_{jr}^2}} & \text{if } \vec{\mathbf{g}}_r \in \mathcal{V}_j \\ 0 & \text{otherwise} \end{cases} \tag{3.37}$$

Once the signals reach a video node, the activation level of this video node (associated with the video $\mathcal{V}_j$) is given by the sum of the signals (the standard cosine measure),

$$a_j^{(v)} = \sum_{r=1}^{R} mesg_{r^{(t)} \to j^{(v)}} \tag{3.38}$$

$$= \sum_{r=1}^{R} \bar{w}_{qr} \bar{w}_{jr} \tag{3.39}$$

$$= \frac{\sum_{r=1}^{R} w_{qr} w_{jr}}{\sqrt{\sum_{r=1}^{R} w_{qr}^2} \sqrt{\sum_{r=1}^{R} w_{jr}^2}} \tag{3.40}$$

This finishes the first round of signal propagation. The network output (i.e., $a_j^{(v)}, j = 1, \ldots, N$) is a desired ranking of the videos for retrieval. The process, however, does not stop here. The network continues the ever-spreading activation process after the first round of propagation. This time, however, a minimum activation threshold is defined such that the video nodes below this threshold send no signals out. Thus, the activation level at the r-th video template node is obtained by summing up the inputs from the activating video nodes as follows:

$$a_r^{(t)} = \sum_{j \in Pos} a_j^{(v)} \bar{w}_{jr} \tag{3.41}$$

where $a_j^{(v)}$ denotes the activation levels of the j-th video node and Pos is the set of j's such that $a_j^{(v)} \geq \xi$, where ξ is a threshold value. The activation process is allowed to continue flowing forwards and backwards between the video template nodes and the video nodes, inducing an order for the videos, based on the corresponding node activations at each stage.

A new activation level computed in Eq. (3.41) can be viewed as a modified weight of the query template, where only videos with significant activation levels are considered to be good candidates for modifying the query template activations. This considers only positive feedback. However, anti-reinforcement learning can be adopted to improve the speed of convergence [103, 323], whereby both original query components and a strategy of negative feedback can help to improve effectiveness. Thus, as an alternative to Eq. (3.41), the following formula is derived for the activation of the r-th video template node:

$$a_r^{(t)} = \frac{l_r}{\left(\sum_{r=1}^{R} l_r^2\right)^{\frac{1}{2}}} \tag{3.42}$$

$$l_r = w_{qr} + \alpha \sum_{j \in Pos} a_j^{(v)} \bar{w}_{jr} + \beta \sum_{j \in Neg} a_j^{(v)} \bar{w}_{jr} \tag{3.43}$$

where $a_j^{(v)}$ is the activation level of the j-th video, Pos is the set of j's such that $a_j^{(v)} > \xi$, and Neg is the set of j's such that $a_j^{(v)} < -\xi$, where ξ is a threshold value. In addition, α and β are the suitable positive and negative constant values.

Table 3.8 provides a summary of the pseudo-RF learning algorithm implemented by the adaptive cosine network. The input query weights $w_{qr}, r = 1, \ldots, R$ are utilized to activate video template nodes. These are then modified by the activation levels of the video nodes in the positive and negative feedback sets. The final network output is the video ranking result for video retrieval.

3.5.3 Experimental Result

This section describes an application of TFM video indexing and adaptive cosine network for video retrieval. The performance of the TFM method is compared with the key-fame-based video indexing (KFVI) algorithm [104], which has become a popular benchmark for shot-based video retrieval. Table 3.9 provides a summary of the video data, obtained from the Informedia Digital Video Library Project [105]. This is a collection of CNN broadcast news, which includes full news stories, news headlines, and commercial clips. This video has 844 video shots (see Fig. 3.15), segmented by the color histogram based shot boundary detection algorithm [106]. A 48-bin histogram computed on HSV color space is used for both shot segmentation and for the indexing algorithms. The KFVI uses a histogram vector generated from a middle frame of the video shot as a representative video shot. The resulting feature database was scaled according to Gaussian normalization. In the TFM method, a total of $R = 5,000$ templates were generated. Each video shot

Table 3.8 Summary of competitive learning algorithm for template generation for video database indexing

Input:	Query vector $= \mathbf{v}_q = \{w_{qr} \mid r \in [1,\dots,R]\}$
	Maximum number of iterations, I_{max}
Output:	The final retrieval set, containing k-relevant samples $= S_k(\mathbf{v}_q)$
Initialization:	Threshold value ξ
	Learning parameters, α and β
	Activation level of the query node,
	$$a_r^q = \begin{cases} 1, & \text{if } w_{qr} \neq 0 \\ 0, & \text{Otherwise} \end{cases}$$
Computation:	Calculate $a_r^{(t)} \equiv mesg_{r(q) \rightarrow r(t)} = a_r^{(q)} \times \bar{w}_{qr}$, for $r = 1, 2, \dots, R$,
	Calculate $mesg_{r(t) \rightarrow j(v)} = a_r^{(t)} \times \bar{w}_{jr}$, for $j = 1, 2, \dots, N$,
Repeat	1. Calculate activation level of the video nodes, for $j = 1, 2, \dots, N$,
	$$a_j^{(v)} = \sum_{r=1}^{R} mesg_{r(t) \rightarrow j(v)} = \sum_{r=1}^{R} a_r^{(t)} \times \bar{w}_{jr}$$
	2. Obtain a positive set, Pos, and a negative set, Neg,
	$$Pos = \left\{ ja_j^{(v)} \geq \xi \right\}, \quad Neg = \left\{ ja_j^{(v)} < -\xi \right\}$$
	3. Calculate the activation level of the video template node,
	$$a_r^{(t)} \longleftarrow \frac{l_r}{\left(\sum_{r=1}^{R} l_r^2 \right)^{\frac{1}{2}}}$$
	where $l_r = w_{qr} + \alpha \sum_{j \in Pos} a_j^{(v)} \bar{w}_{jr} + \beta \sum_{j \in Neg} a_j^{(v)} \bar{w}_{jr}$
Until:	Iteration $= I_{max}$
Return:	Top-k retrieval set, $S_k(\mathbf{v}_q) = \left\{ \mathbf{v} \mid a^{(v)} \geq a_k^{(v)} \right\}$
	where $S_k(\mathbf{v}_q)$ is the set of top-k vectors most similar to the query vector and $a_k^{(v)}$ is the activation level of the k-th nearest neighbor of $\mathbf{v}_q$.

was described by its associated weight vector. This was generated by the template models, using neighborhood $\eta = 5$ [cf. Eq. (3.30)].

A total of 25 queries were made and the judgments on the relevance of each video to each query shot were evaluated. In general, the relevance judgment of videos is difficult because two video clips may be related in terms of the story context, and not just visual similarity. This fact was taken into account in this experiment, so a criterion employed here is a very subjective judgment of relevance: only retrieved video shots from the *same* stories were judged to be relevant. For example, four video shots shown in Fig. 3.16a were judged to be relevant because they were parts of the same stories. Similarly, the four video shots shown in Fig. 3.16b are relevant to each other.

Fig. 3.15 Some representative key-frames extracted from a subset of 844 video shots in the test video database obtained from CNN broadcast news

Figure 3.17 shows precision results as a function of top matches, averaged over all 25 queries. It can be observed that TFM performed substantially better than KFVI for every setting of the number of top matches (the average precision was higher by more than 18 %). It is also observed that TFM is very effective in capturing spatio-temporal information from video, as seen in Fig. 3.18 which depicts retrieval results from the top sixteen best matches. It was observed that TFM allows similarity matching based on video contents, whereas the KFVI emphasis is on the content of the key-frame. There was a dominant brown color on the key-frame, degrading the performance of KFVI on this query.

Next the adaptive cosine network is applied to improve retrieval accuracy. The structure of the information in the video database can be represented by a network with 5,844 nodes and 14,800 connections. The results of three tests are shown: letting the activation spread for one, three, and twenty iterations. The parameters were set at $\xi = 0.1$, and $\alpha = 0.95$ and $\beta = -0.05$. Figure 3.19 shows the improvement of the average precision in retrieving 25 queries.

The following observations were made from the results. Firstly, the adaptive cosine network was very effective in improving retrieval performance—the average

Fig. 3.16 Two samples of subjective judgment for video relevance; (**a**) four relevant video shorts from the same news stories are judged to be relevant; (**b**) four relevant video shots from the same commercial movie are judged to be relevant. *Note*: Each video shot is shown by the corresponding key frames

Table 3.9 Description of video sequences in the database: CNN broadcast news and other video types, distributed by the Informedia Digital Library project [105]

Type of video	Number of sequences	Number of cuts	Number of frames	Length (min:s)
Commercial	20	844	98,733	54:52
Movie clip	2			
Headline and story news	46			

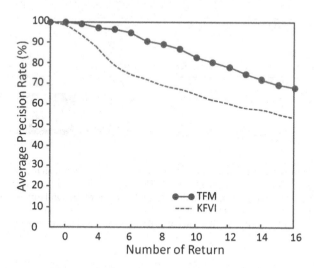

Fig. 3.17 Average precision rate (%) at different numbers of returns, obtained by retrieval of 25 queries of video shots. The TFM performance is higher than KFVI by 18 % in average precision

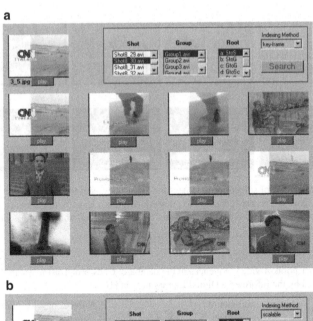

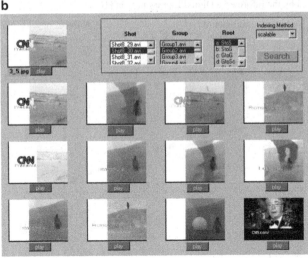

Fig. 3.18 A comparison of the retrieval performance, showing 16 top matches of video shorts; (**a**) obtained by KFVI and (**b**) obtained by TFM. The query is shown in the top-left corner, and the retrieval videos are ranked according to the descending order of the similarity scores, from left to right and top to bottom. From the result, TFM allows similarity matching based on the video contents, whereas KFVI emphasizes the content of the key-frames, resulting in the similar color of the key frames

precision increased by more than 11 %, and is particularly significant in the top 10 to 16 retrievals. Secondly, the network is stabilized very quickly. Thirdly, allowing many iterations degraded the performance slightly. Finally and most significantly, the results were achieved by simply allowing activation flow, with no user input.

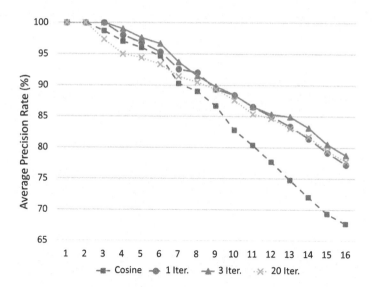

Fig. 3.19 Average Precision Rate, APR (%) obtained by the adaptive cosine network through pseudo-RF, using 25 video shots for queries. For the pseudo-RF result, the signal propagation was allowed to flow forward and backward for up to 20 iterations, and only the result after 1, 3, and 20 iterations are shown, for comparison with the non-adaptive method that used the cosine metric as the similarity matching function

It was observed that the values for ξ, α and β affected the results and confirmed the reports of other studies [103, 107, 323] with regard to the value for α. However, the identification of the proper values for these parameters was completed conveniently as they were usually found in certain ranges. It was also observed that without applying the threshold level ξ, only modest improvement is initially obtained, and all the nodes became increasingly activated. This led to a longer processing time and to a random ordering of the videos.

3.6 Summary

Automation is critical for enhancing learning efficiency and/or improving retrieval performance. The automation is done through a pseudo-relevance feedback that iteratively re-ranks database entities, in both fully-automatic and semi-automatic modes. This chapter presents various techniques for pseudo-relevance feedback, including dynamic self-organization methods and the adaptive cosine network. Both compressed and uncompressed image databases, as well as video applications are covered.

Chapter 4
Interactive Mobile Visual Search and Recommendation at Internet Scale

Abstract Mobile-based visual search and recognition has been an emerging topic for both research and engineering communities. Among various methods, visual search has its merit in providing an alternative solution, where text/voice searches are not applicable. Combining the Bag-of-word (BoW) model with advanced retrieval algorithms, a mobile-based visual search and social activity recommendation system is presented at internet scale. The merit of the BoW model in large-scale image retrieval is integrated with the flexible user interface provided by the mobile platform. Instead of text or voice input, the system takes visual images captured from the built-in camera and attempts to understand users' intents through interactions. Subsequently, such intents are recognized through a retrieval mechanism using the BoW model. Finally, visual results are mapped onto contextually relevant information and entities (i.e. local business) for social task suggestions. Hence, the system offers users the ability to search information and make decisions on-the-go.

4.1 Introduction

Mobile devices are becoming ubiquitous. People use them as personal concierge to search information and make decisions. Therefore, understanding user intent and subsequently provide meaningful and personalized suggestions is important. While existing efforts have predominantly focused on understanding the intent expressed by a textual or a voice query, this chapter presents a new and alternative perspective which understands user intent *visually*, i.e., via visual signal captured by the built-in camera. This kind of intent is named as "visual intent" as it can be naturally expressed through a visual form.

The bag-of-words (BoW) model and its application in content-based retrieval has shown promising results in desktop-based visual searches at large-scale. In this chapter, a mobile visual search algorithm is presented, by combining the BoW model's merit with user interaction through a mobile platform. An innovative context-aware search-tree is described based on the BoW paradigm, which includes both user specified region of interest (ROI) and surrounding pictorial context. There is a mutual benefit by combining the visual search using the BoW model with mobile devices.

© Springer International Publishing Switzerland 2014

P. Muneesawang et al., *Multimedia Database Retrieval: Technology and Applications*,
Multimedia Systems and Applications, DOI 10.1007/978-3-319-11782-9_4

From a retrieval point of view, although the BoW model has shown promising results in desktop-based visual searches for large-scale consortia, it also suffers a semantic gap. The BoW model is limited by its homogenous process in treating all regions without distinction. Features are extracted homogeneously, and local features are treated without emphasis. Therefore, information provided by a query image without priority can mislead the computer vision algorithm for recognition. Hence, to have a better retrieval result, there is a need to orderly utilize local visual information. Multi-touch screen and its user interaction on mobile-devices offer such a platform for users to select their ROIs as prioritized information, with surrounding context as secondary information.

From a mobile application perspective, visual search via image query provides a powerful complementary carrier besides conventional textual and vocal queries. Compared to conventional text or voice queries for information retrieval on-the-go, there are many cases where visual queries can be more naturally and conveniently expressed via mobile device camera sensors (such as an unknown object or text, an artwork, a shape or texture, and so on) [135]. In addition, mobile visual search has a promising future due to the vital roles mobile devices play in our life, from their original function of telephony, to prevalent information-sharing terminals, to hubs that accommodate tens of thousands of applications. While on the go, people are using their phones as a personal concierge discovering what is around and deciding what to do. Therefore, the mobile phone is becoming a recommendation terminal customized for individuals—capable of recommending contextually relevant entities (local businesses such as a nearby restaurant or hotel) and simplifying the accomplishment of recommended tasks. As a result, it is important to understand user intent through its multi-modal nature and the rich context available on the phone.

Motivated by the above observations, this chapter presents an interactive search-based visual recognition and contextual recommendation using the BoW model, targeting internet scale large image collection. Smart-phone hardware such as camera and touch screen, are taken advantage of in order to facilitate expressions of user's ROI from the pictures taken. Then, the visual query along with such a ROI specification go through an innovative contextual visual retrieval model to achieve a meaningful connection to database images and their associated rich text information. Once the visual recognition is accomplished, associated textual information of retrieved images are further analyzed to provide meaningful recommendations.

An actual system codename *TapTell* is implemented based on the algorithms and methodologies described in Sect. 4.2. A natural user interaction is adopted to achieve the *Tap* action, in which three gestures are investigated (i.e., circle, line, and tap). It is concluded that the circle (also called "O" gesture) is the most natural interaction for users, which integrates user preference to select the targeted object. The BoW model and a novel context-embedded vocabulary tree approach is adopted. The algorithm incorporates both ROI visual query and the context from surrounding pixels of the "O" region to search similar images from a large-scale image dataset. Through this user interaction (i.e., "O" gesture) and the BoW model with our innovative algorithm, standard visual recognition can be improved. The *Tell* action is accomplished by recommending relevant entities based on recognition results and associated metadata.

The novelty of the chapter lies in the following aspects:

- BoW model and context-aware visual search algorithm is designed with a novel context-embedded vocabulary tree (CVT). The algorithm is able to achieve better visual recognition performance by embedding the context information around the "O" region into a standard visual vocabulary tree.
- Based on the context-aware visual recognition, a real system *TapTell* is implemented to understand users' visual intents. The goal is to provide a contextual entity suggestion for activity completion that provides meaningful and contextually relevant recommendations. Advanced touch screen technology provided at the mobile platform is utilized to introduce human experts in loop for a better visual search. Three different kinds of gestures for specifying object (and text) of interest are investigated by a user study. It is concluded that "O" provides the most natural and effective way to interactively formulate user's visual intent and thus reduce ambiguity. After obtaining the recognition results, a location-aware recommendation is provided to suggest relevant entities for social task completion.

In the following, an interactive mobile visual search using the BoW model and the CVT algorithm is first presented. A viable application, *TapTell*, is introduced in detail to show how to accomplish meaningful contextually relevant recommendations through mobile recognition. Experimental results are provided to demonstrate the effectiveness of the CVT method.

4.2 BoW-Based Mobile Visual Search Using Various Context Information

This section presents the mobile visual search with context-aware image retrieval using the BoW model. Section 4.2.1 briefly reviewed the BoW model and its potential in large-scale content-based image classification, retrieval and visual search. Section 4.2.2 introduces the literature and industrial developments of mobile visual search. Section 4.2.3 describes the framework of context-aware mobile visual search. Section 4.2.4 presents the algorithm of the visual recognition by search using the BoW model with image context. Section 4.2.5 discusses a filtering process adopting sensory GPS context.

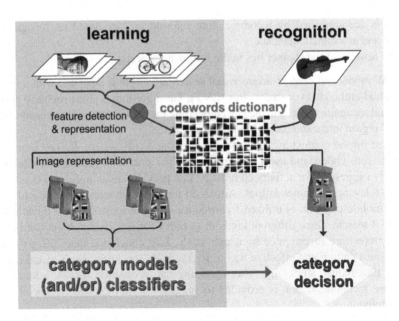

Fig. 4.1 Illustration of bag-of-words framework in computer vision

4.2.1   The Bag-of-Word (BoW) Model

Figure 4.1 shows a framework of the BoW model and its usage in computer vision. In general, there are two parts: learning and recognition. In learning, visual features are extracted from database images or video frames to generate a dictionary of codewords, which is also called a codebook in the literature. Individual images are used to project their features to the codebook to obtain a BoW representation for themselves. They are then categorized by classifiers to get ready for recognition. In recognition, a query or testing image also goes through the BoW model by mapping to the dictionary of codewords. Then, the BoW representation is categorized based on which class the query image belongs to.

To tackle the multimedia processing challenges associated with recent boom of large-scale data, the BoW model is among the most popular choices in the research community. Because of their homogenous procedures in describing images or video frames using representative local features, BoW-based methods enable researchers to conduct large-scale image analysis effectively. Large-scale image classification and retrieval have been carefully studied in recent years to catch up with the ever growing image and video datasets. Image classification and retrieval are highly interrelated research problems. Both of them are based on analyzing distinguished features of the query image, and are in attempts to bring out similar images from the database. Classification focuses on the intra-class commonalities so that the query image can find its suitable class and belonging. Retrieval, on the other hand, focuses on finding the most closely related individual images in the database and returning them as search results. In summary, classification solutions focus on feature ensembles, for instance, the histogram representation of each image. Retrieval solutions focus on both feature ensemble and individual local descriptor matches.

Csurka et al. proposed a BoW model-based algorithm for visual image classification from seven different classes, including faces, buildings, trees, cars, phones, bikes and books [115]. SIFT feature is used as the local descriptor, and Naïve Bayes, with non-linear supervised support vector machines (SVM), are used as classifiers. Deng et al. proposed a database called "ImageNet", which associates images with large-scale ontology supported by the WordNet structure [116, 117]. Currently, about nine million images are indexed and this number is still growing. Among benchmark measurements and comparisons, a spatial pyramid-based histogram of SIFT local codewords with SVMs classifiers provides the best performance. Zhou et al. proposed a method by incorporating vector coding to achieve scalable image classification [142]. They adopted vector quantization coding on local SIFT descriptors to map the features to form a high-dimensional sparse vector. Spatial information of local regions in each image is taken into account and called spatial pooling. Finally, linear SVMs are used to classify the image representations obtained from the spatial pooling.

Although non-linear SVMs classifiers perform well, they suffer from data scalability due to computational complexity. Perronnin et al. proposed several methods to improve non-linear SVMs, including square-rooting BoW vectors, kernel-PCA based embedding for additive kernels, and non-additive kernels for embedding [128,129]. In particular, an algorithm using Fisher Kernels was proposed to build gradient vectors from features, so that linear SVMs could replace those non-linear ones as less computational classifiers [127]. Hence, the scalability issue was alleviated.

Sivic and Zisserman proposed a video scene retrieval system called Video Google [264]. The goal is to retrieve similar objects and scenes and localize their occurrences in a video. MSER feature detection and SIFT feature description are used to extract local descriptors. Visual vocabulary is built by K-means clustering. A *term frequency–inverse document frequency* (tf–idf) text retrieval algorithm is used to match each visualword.

Nistér and Stewénius proposed an efficient and scalable visual vocabulary tree, so that building a large-scale retrieval system using the BoW model is possible [126]. The method adopted hierarchical K-means clustering to boost the codebook generation and retrieval process. The idea is that a query visualword does not necessarily need to go through the full comparison with the codebook. Rather, a subset of the codebook (a branch of the hierarchical K-means clustering) is sufficient. This method allows the codebook to scale up from a few thousands, to hundreds of thousands, to millions in size without much computational penalty. Although there is no automatic mechanism to determine the proper codebook size, in general, a larger vocabulary pool size described by the codebook leads to a better description of the query image with less quantization error [258].

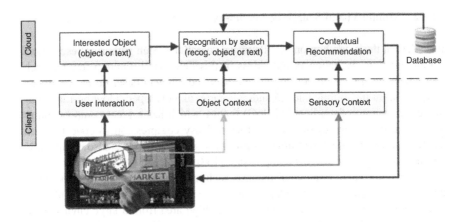

Fig. 4.2 Framework of mobile visual search and activity completion model using image contextual model, including (1) "O"-based user interaction, (2) image context model for visual search, and (3) contextual entity recommendation for social activities

images are further analyzed to provide meaningful textual-based social activity and task recommendation.

Figure 4.2 shows the framework of our visual recognition and activity recommendation model. In general, it can be divided into the client-end and cloud-end. On the client-end, a user's visual search intent is specified by the "O" gesture on a captured image. On the cloud-end, with user selected object and the image context around this object, a recognition-by-search mechanism is applied to identify user's visual intent. A novel context-embedded vocabulary tree is designed to incorporate the "O" context (the surrounding pixels of the "O" region) in a standard visual search process. Finally, the specified visual search results are mapped to associate metadata by leveraging sensory context (e.g., GPS-location), which are used to recommend related entities to the user.

The "O" gesture utilizes multi-touch screen of the smart-phone. Users do not need any training and can naturally engage with the mobile interface immediately. After the trace (the blue thin line in Fig. 4.2) has been drawn on the image, sampling points along the trace-line are collected as $\{\mathbf{D}|(x_j, y_j) \in \mathbf{D}\}_{j=1}^{N}$, which contains N pixel-wise positions (x_j, y_j). Principal component analysis (PCA) is applied to find two principal components (which form the elliptical ring depicted by thick orange line in Fig. 4.2). The purpose of this part is to formulate a boundary of the selected region from an arbitrary "O" gesture trace. Mean μ and covariances Σ are calculated, based on $\mathbf{D}$ and non-correlated assumption along the two principal components:

$$\mu = [\mu_x, \mu_y] \qquad \Sigma = \begin{vmatrix} \sigma_x^2 & 0 \\ 0 & \sigma_y^2 \end{vmatrix}. \qquad (4.1)$$

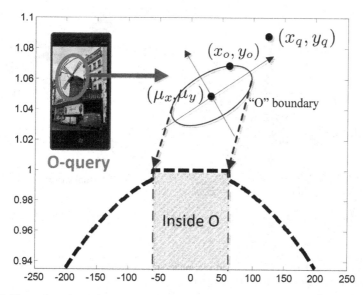

Fig. 4.3 Illustration of user indicated "O" query, and the computation of principal components of the query. (μ_x, μ_y) is the center of "O" query, (x_o, y_o) is a pixel on the "O" boundary, and (x_q, y_q) is a query pixel

Figure 4.3 shows the computation of principal components from the "O" query. Once the principal components are identified, image contextual model for mobile visual search is used to identify the object of interest indicated by the user.

The following two sections will introduce the algorithms used in the context-aware visual search. Section 4.2.4 presents the context within the query image itself using the BoW model. Section 4.2.5 discusses the context of searched images, by considering their tagged GPS information and relationship to the user's current location.

4.2.4 Context-Aware Visual Search Using the BoW Model

The visual intent recognition method is based on a retrieval scheme using the BoW model with the vocabulary tree proposed by Nister et al. [126]. This method provides a fast and scalable search mechanism and is suitable for large-scale and expansible databases because of its hierarchical tree-structured indexing. Such a method is adopted in the mobile domain, because the "O" gesture fits naturally to provide a focused object selection for better recognition. Different from using the entire image as visual query in [126], we have user-indicated ROI from the "O" gesture (called "O-query"). We design a novel context-aware visual search method in which a CVT is built to take the surrounding pixels around the O-query into consideration. The CVT algorithm focuses on first building a visualwords codebook

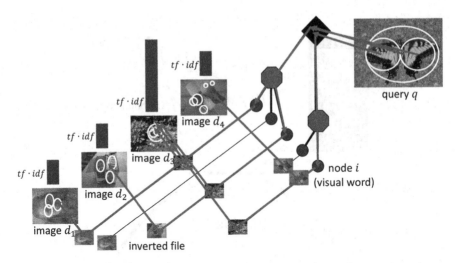

Fig. 4.4 Image search scheme with visual vocabulary tree. Note that the *white circle* in the image corresponds to a local descriptor (not an O-query)

for the BoW model to map each local feature, and subsequently, constructing a BoW representation. By establishing a hierarchical K-means clustering for the codebook, this algorithm manages to shorten the codebook generation process. Therefore, it is scalable and efficient for processing large-scale data. Specifically, the CVT algorithm is able to reduce the following ambiguities:

- Sometimes, issuing O-query only in image-based search engines may lead to too many similar results. The surrounding pixels provide a useful context to differentiate those results.
- Sometimes, the O-query may not have (near) duplicates or exist in the image database. Issuing only O-query may not lead to any search results. The surrounding pixels then can help in providing a context to search for the images with similar backgrounds.
- Hierarchically built K-means clustering for codebook generation makes the retrieval process efficient, wherein each queried local feature only goes through one particular branch at the highest level and its sub-branches instead of going through the entire codebook.

The CVT-based visual search method encodes different weights of term frequencies inside and outside the O-query. For off-line image indexing, SIFT local descriptors are extracted as a first step. Since our target database is large-scale, an efficient hierarchical K-means is used to cluster local descriptors and build the CVT. Then, the large-scale images are indexed using the built CVT and the inverted file mechanism, which is to be introduced in the following.

In on-line image searches, given a query image, we can interpret the descriptor vectors of the image in a similar way to the indexing procedure, and accumulate scores for the images in the database with a so-called *term frequency–inverse document frequency* (tf–idf) scheme [126]. This tf–idf method is an effective entropy weighting for indexing a scalable database. Figure 4.4 shows the computation of image similarity based on the tf–idf scheme. In the vocabulary tree, each leaf node corresponds to a visualword i, associated with an inverted file (with the list of images containing this visualword i). Note that we only need to consider images d in the database with the same visualwords as the query image q. This significantly reduces the amount of images to be compared with respect to q. The similarity between an image d and the query q is given by

$$s(q,d) = \| \mathbf{q} - \mathbf{d} \|_2^2$$

$$= \left(\sum_{i|d_i=0} |q_i|^2 + \sum_{i|q_i=0} |d_i|^2 + \sum_{i|q_i\neq0,d_i\neq0} |q_i - d_i|^2 \right) \quad (4.2)$$

where $\mathbf{q}$ and $\mathbf{d}$ denote the tf–idf feature vectors of the query q and image d in the database, which are consisted of individual elements q_i and d_i (i denotes the i-th visualword in the vocabulary tree), respectively. q_i and d_i are the tf–idf value for the i-th visualword in the query and the image, respectively. Mathematical interpretations are given by

$$q_i = tf_{i_q} \cdot idf_i, \quad (4.3)$$

$$d_i = tf_{i_d} \cdot idf_i. \quad (4.4)$$

In the above equation, the *inverted document frequency* idf_i is formulated as $ln(N/N_i)$, where N is the total number of images in the database, and N_i is number of images with the visualword i (i.e., the images whose descriptors are classified into the leaf node i).

The *term frequency* representations tf_{i_q} and tf_{i_d} are computed as the accumulated counts of the visualword i in the query q and the database image d, respectively. One simple means for the *term frequency* computation is to use the O-query as the initial query without considering the pixels surrounding the "O". This process is equivalent to using "binary" weights of the *term frequency* tf_{i_q}: the weight is 1 inside "O", and 0 outside "O". A more descriptive and accurate computation is to incorporate the context information (i.e., the surrounding pixels around the O-query) in the vocabulary tree. We design a new representation of the *term frequency* $tf_{i_q}^o$ for the O-query. A "soft" weighting scheme is adopted to modulate the *term frequency* by incorporating the image context outside the O-query, which was neglected in the simple binary scheme. When quantizing descriptors in the CVT, the $tf_{i_q}^o$ of the O-query for a particular query visualword i_q is formulated as:

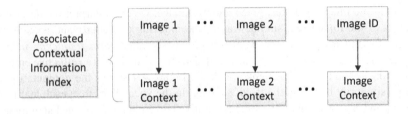

Fig. 4.5 Sensory context information index associated with each image

$$tf_{i_q}^o = \begin{cases} tf_{i_q}, & \text{if } i_q \in O \\ tf_{i_q} \cdot \min\left\{1, \frac{\Re(x_q, y_q)}{\Re(x_o, y_o)}\right\}, & \text{if } i_q \notin O \end{cases} \qquad (4.5)$$

where $\Re(x_o, y_o)$ and $\Re(x_q, y_q)$ denote the Gaussian distances of the pixel (x_o, y_o) and (x_q, y_q) with respect to the center of O-query (μ_x, μ_y). Figure 4.3 shows the definition of these pixels in the query image q. The Gaussian distance $\Re(x, y)$ for an arbitrary pixel (x, y) is given by

$$\Re(x, y) = A \cdot \exp\left\{-\frac{1}{2}\left[\frac{(x - \mu_x)^2}{\alpha \sigma_x^2} + \frac{(y - \mu_y)^2}{\beta \sigma_y^2}\right]\right\} \qquad (4.6)$$

The "soft" weighting scheme shown in Eq. (4.5), is a piece-wise, bivariate-based multivariate distribution outside the O-query, and a constant 1 inside the O-query. The position (x_o, y_o) is the boundary of the O-query contour where the weight 1 ends. In the case that a visualword i_q is outside the O-query, the modulating term is $\min\left\{1, \frac{\Re(x_q, y_q)}{\Re(x_o, y_o)}\right\}$, such that the soft weighting is guaranteed to be less than 1. The term $\frac{\Re(x_q, y_q)}{\Re(x_o, y_o)}$ is the ratio of which the query point (x_q, y_q) should be weighted with respect to its closest boundary position (x_o, y_o). Mean values μ_x and μ_y are calculated from "O" gesture sample data, while α and β are tunable parameters to control the standard deviation for the bivariate normal distribution. Figure 4.3 also illustrates this "soft" weighting schemes in the CVT when a projection view along one principal axis is sliced and presented. Parameter A is the amplitude value controlling the highest possible weighting scale. Parameters α and β reflect the importance of the horizontal and vertical axis (or directions) when employing the PCA technique. Empirically, we set α with higher value than β to indicate that the horizontal axis is usually more important than the vertical one. This is because most pictures are taken by the phone camera horizontally. As illustrated in Fig. 4.4

In the next section, a location-context-based filter process is executed, for re-ranking visual search results based on user's current location (derived from the GPS-enabled images taken by the phone camera).

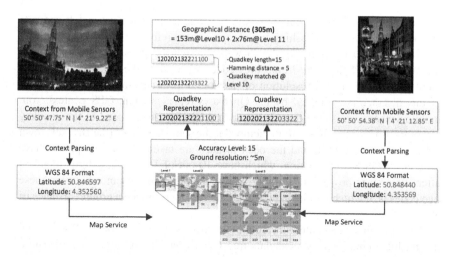

Fig. 4.6 Quadkeys quantization and hashing from GPS, and images ground distance estimation using Microsoft Bing Map service

4.2.5 GPS Context-Based Filtering

Context information collected by mobile sensors plays an important role to help to identify users' visual intents. As Fig. 4.5 illustrates, similar with the inverted file index method, each piece of image context information is indexed with the image itself during the off-line database construction.

In our system, GPS information from sensors is utilized and associated with each image taken by the phone camera. A filter-based process is used to remove the non-correlated images after the initial visual search. This is because GPS as an important context filter can be used to efficiently explore users' true intents by precisely knowing their locations. This process is formulated as:

$$S_L(q,d) = s(q,d) \cdot \phi(\mathbf{q}, \mathbf{d})$$

$$where \quad \phi(\mathbf{q}, \mathbf{d}) = \begin{cases} 1, & \text{if } dist_{quadkey}(\mathbf{q},\mathbf{d}) \in Q \\ 0, & \text{if } dist_{quadkey}(\mathbf{q},\mathbf{d}) \notin Q \end{cases} \quad (4.7)$$

The visual similarity term $s(q,d)$ is modulated by a location-based filter $\phi(\mathbf{q}, \mathbf{d})$. This filter is based on the GPS effective region Q, which describes the geographical distance between the query and the database images. We defined $dist_{quadkey}(\mathbf{q},\mathbf{d})$ as the quadkey distance between the query $\mathbf{q}$ and the database image $\mathbf{d}$.

The quadkey method is adopted from the Bing Maps Tile System.[1] It converts the GPS coordinates to a hashing-based representation for fast search and retrieval. We present an example in Fig. 4.6 to walk through the steps of conversion from the WGS-84 GPS to a quadruple tiles code. We encode the GPS to a 23 digits number with the ground resolution of possible 0.02 m accuracy. The formulation of this distance is computed by the Quadkeys representation. GPS context from mobile sensor is collected first. The standard WGS-84 is encoded to the quadkey representation. In the illustration, pictures of the same landmark (the Brussels town hall) with both the front and the back façades are taken. These two photos have different WGS-84 information, which have 10 out of 15 quadkey digits identical after Bing Maps projection. In other words, the hamming distance between these two codes is 5, which is calculated using tables to approximate a ground distance of about 305 m.

This section uses a context-aware mobile visual search based on the BoW model and the hierarchical visual vocabulary tree. Contextual GPS information is also used in filtering the visual search result. In the next section, an implementation named *TapTell* is presented based on the CVT algorithm introduced. *TapTell* is able to achieve social activity recommendations through mobile visual searches.

4.3 Mobile Visual Search System for Social Activities Using Query Image Contextual Model

TapTell is a system that utilizes visual query input through an advanced multi-touch mobile platform and rich context to enable interactive visual search and contextual recommendation. Different from other mobile visual searches, *TapTell* explores users individual intent and their motivation in providing a visual query with specified ROI. By understanding such intent, associated social activities can be recommended to users. Existing work has predominantly focused on understanding the intent expressed by text (or the text recognized from a piece of voice). For example, previous research attempts to estimate user's search intent by detecting meaningful entities from a textual query [131, 140]. However, typing takes time and can be cumbersome on the phone, and thus in some cases, not convenient in expressing user intent. An alternative is to leverage speech recognition techniques to support voice as an input. For example, popular mobile search engines enable a voice-to-search mode.[2,3] Siri is one of the most popular applications that further structure a piece of speech to a set of entities.[4] However, text as an expression of

---

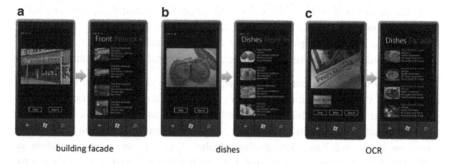

Fig. 4.7 Snapshots of *TapTell* with three different scenarios. A user can take a photo, specify the object or text of his/her interest via different gestures (e.g., tap, circle, or line), and then get the search and recommendation results through *TapTell*

user intent has two major limitations. First, it relies on a good recognition engine and works well only in a relatively quiet environment. Second, there are many cases where user intent can be naturally and conveniently expressed through the visual form rather than text or speech (such as an unknown object or text, an artwork, a shape or texture, and so on) [135]. As an alternative, we believe that image is a powerful complementary carrier to express user intents on the phone.

Since *intent* is generally defined as "a concept considered as the product of attention directed to an object or knowledge" [108], *mobile visual intent* is defined as follows:

Definition 4.1 (Mobile Visual Intent). Mobile visual intent is defined as the intent that can be naturally expressed through any visual information captured by a mobile device and any user interaction with it. This intent represents user's curiosity of certain object and willingness to discover either what it is or what associated tasks could be practiced in a visual form.

The following shows scenarios of mobile visual intent and how expressed intent may be predicted and connected to social tasks for recommendation. The goal is not only to list related visual results, but also to provide rich context to present useful multimedia information for social task recommendation.

- You pass by an unknown landmark that draws your attention. You can take a picture of it. By using visual intent analysis, the related information of this landmark is presented to you.
- You see an interesting restaurant across the street. Before you step into the restaurant, you take a picture of it and indicate your interest using your gesture. By applying visual intent analysis, the information about this restaurant or its neighborhood points-of-interest matching your preference are recommended.
- You are checking a menu inside a restaurant, but you do not speak the language or know the cuisine. You can take a photo of the menu using your phone and indicate your intended dish or text in the photo. Your visual intent on either the photo

or the description of the dish will be analyzed. For example, optical character recognition (OCR) can help you automatically recognize the indicated text, while a visual search can help you identify the dish (which may not be recognized without indication) and recommend nearby restaurants serving a similar dish.

Figure 4.7 shows three corresponding scenarios. The visual intent model consists of two parts: visual recognition by search and social task recommendation. The first problem is to recognize what is captured (e.g., a food image), while the second is to recommend related entities (such as nearby restaurants serving the same food) based on the search-based recognition results. This activity recommendation is a difficult task in general, since visual recognition in the first step still remains challenging. However, the advanced functionalities, such as natural multi-touch interaction and a set of available rich context on the mobile device, bring us opportunities to accomplish this task. For example, although one image usually contains multiple objects, a user can indicate an object or some text of interest through a natural gesture, so that visual recognition can be reduced to search a similar single object. Moreover, the contextual information, such as geo-location, can be used for location-based recommendations.

Since the *visual intent* is an original term, this chapter retrospects the evolution of intent in general and walk the readers through the formation of the *intent* from text, voice, and visual inputs, with both desktop-based and mobile domain-based searches and recognition.

For desktop user intent mining, an early study on web search taxonomy is introduced by Broder [110]. In this work, the most searched items belong to an "informational" category, in which it sought for related information to answer certain questions in a user's mind. A later work from Rose and Levinson further categorized the informational class to five sub-categories, where the *locate* of a product or service occupies a large percentage [133]. On the other hand, compared to general web searches, intents derived from mobile information have strong on-the-go characteristics. Church and Smyth conducted a diary study of user behavior of mobile-based text search and summarized a quite different categorization from its general web search counterpart [113]. Besides the informational category at 58.3%, a new geographical category which is highly location dependent takes a share of 31.1% of total search traffic. From a topic perspective, *local services* and *travel & commuting* are the most popular ones out of 17 total topics, with 24.2% and 20.2% entries respectively. It can be concluded that the on-the-go characteristics play an important role for intent discovery and understanding on mobile devices [143].

4.3.1   System Architecture

Figure 4.8 shows the architecture of *TapTell*. It extends Fig. 4.2 by including user intent. This illustration can assist readers from an implementation perspective to understand the importance in linking individual intents to final recommendations.

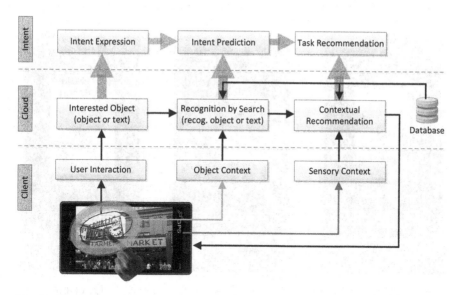

Fig. 4.8 The framework of *TapTell*, based on previously introduced visual recognition algorithm in Fig. 4.2, incorporates with the visual intents notation

Intent expression recognizes the object specified by the user–mobile interaction. Intent prediction formulates intent expression and incorporates image context. Finally, a task recommendation is achieved by taking both the predicted intent, as well as, the sensory context.

In the following, Sect. 4.3.2 presents a conducted survey and explains why the "O" gesture is chosen as the best solution among several gesture candidates. With the "O" gesture and selected ROI, visual recognition by search is achieved using the algorithm introduced in the previous section. Consequently, Sect. 4.3.3 describes the recommendation, using text metadata associated with visual recognition to achieve a better re-ranking.

4.3.2 User Interaction for Specifying Visual Intent

It has been studied and suggested that visual interface will improve mobile search experiences [114]. In this section, a user study is conducted to identify the most natural and efficient gesture for specifying the visual intent on mobile devices. By taking advantages of multi-touch interaction on smart-phones, three gestures for specifying visual intents on captured photos are defined as follows:

- **Tap.** A user can "tap" on the pre-determined image segments, in which a captured image is automatically segmented on-the-fly. Then, the tapped segments

Fig. 4.9 Different gestures for specifying user intent in *TapTell*: (**a**) "tap"—selection of image segments, (**b**) "line"—rectangular box, and (**c**) "O"—circle or lasso

indicated by user's gesture will be connected as the region-of-interest (ROI). The ROI will be further used as the visual query, as shown in Fig. 4.9a.

- **Line.** A user can draw straight "lines" to form a rectangular bounding box. The region in the box will be used as the visual query, as shown in Fig. 4.9b.
- **O (*circle*).** A user can naturally outline an object of irregular shape. The "O" gesture can be also called the *circle* or *lasso*. Note that an "O" is not limited to a circle, but any arbitrary shape, as shown in Fig. 4.9c.

A user study is performed following the principles of focus group in the field of human–computer interaction [118]. In this study, ten participants were invited. After being introduced to the basic functions of *TapTell* and getting familiar with the system, they were asked to perform several tasks using different gestures in 30 min. From this study, it is found that seven out of ten subjects thought that "O" is more natural than the other two gestures, and eight subjects were satisfied with the "O" interaction. Their comments on "tapping" and "line" are: (1) tapping is sometimes too sensitive and image segmentation is not always satisfying, and (2) the "line" is not convenient for selecting an arbitrary object.

Equipped with the "O" gesture and the user interaction platform, mobile search and recognition can be achieved effectively using the context-embedded visual approach. The next step of *TapTell* is to recommend social activities based on associated metadata and text-based search.

4.3.3   Social Activity Recommendations

Recently, Jain and Sinha proposed to re-examine the fundamental issue between content and context and why researchers should utilize both of them to bridge the semantic gap [123]. From the perspective of visual content analysis, Hua and Tian surveyed the importance of visual features to help text-based searches [122]. Although the aforementioned two studies focused on context and visual contents, respectively, they both advocate on a multi-modality structure to achieve various tasks. On the other hand, Guy et al. suggest that while machine learning and human computer interactions play key roles in recommendations, personalization and context-awareness are also crucial in establishing an efficient recommendation system [121]. Authors agree with their arguments that it is necessary to connect data and users. It is also believe that smart-phones provide perfect platforms for such data-users connection, from human computer interaction, to visual search, and finally, to the recommendation.

In the *TapTell* system, after the visual intent expression and identification, rich metadata is utilized as a better feature to search. Powerful context is used to re-rank metadata-based search result for the final task completion. To be specific, the metadata associated with the top image search result is adopted as a textual query. Then, social activity recommendations are obtained based on the text retrieval results. The Okapi BM25 ranking function is used to compute a ranking score based on text similarity [132]. Keywords $Q_t = \{q_{t_1}, q_{t_2}, \ldots, q_{t_n}\}$ are extracted by projecting the text query to a quantized text dictionary. Subsequently, relevance score of query Q_t and database image descriptions D_t are computed. Detailed score computation techniques can be referred to in [132]. In the last step, search results are ranked

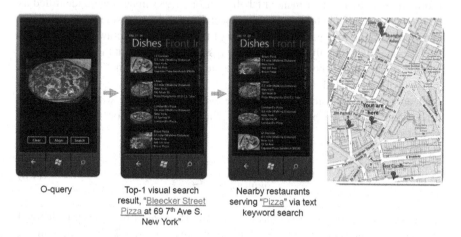

O-query   Top-1 visual search   Nearby restaurants
                 result, "Bleecker Street   serving "Pizza" via text
                 Pizza at 69 7th Ave S.   keyword search
                 New York"

Fig. 4.10 Result of recommendation list, which is visualized in a map to help users to picture the distances between the query and the results

based on the GPS distance of the user's current location. Figure 4.10 demonstrates a sample result of the recommendation list and location-based re-ranking.

4.4   Experimental Result

Experiments on evaluating the context-embedded visual recognition, social activity recommendations through the *TapTell* system, performance and complex analysis, and OCR performance, as well as subject evaluation, are presented in the following.

4.4.1   Data, Settings, and Evaluation Metrics

The client-end application is developed on a Windows Phone 7 HD7 model with 1 GHz processor, 512 MB ROM, GPS sensor and 5 megapixel color camera. In the cloud, a total of one million visualwords is built from 100 million sampled local descriptors (SIFT in this experiment). A hierarchal tree structure consisting of six levels of branches is used, where each superior branch has ten sub-branches or nodes. In constructing the vocabulary tree, each visualword takes up to 168 bytes storage, where 128 bytes are for the clustering vector (same size as SIFT), and 4 bytes for ten subordinate children nodes connection. In total, 170 megabytes of storage is used for the vocabulary tree in cache.

The dataset consists of two parts. One is from Flickr, which includes a total of two million images, with 41,614 landmarks equipped with reliable GPS contextual information. With a further manual labeling effort, 5,981 images were identified as the groundtruth such that the landmark object façade or the outside appearance can be traced from the image. The second part of the database is a crawled commercial local services data, mainly focusing on the restaurant domain. In this part, a total of 332,922 images associated with 16,819 restaurant entities from 12 US cities were crawled with associated metadata.

Mean average precision (MAP) for the evaluation is used , where MAP is the mean value of average precisions (APs). The average precision (AP) formula is presented as

$$AP@n = \frac{1}{min(n,P)} \sum_{k=1}^{min(n,S)} \frac{P_k}{k} \times I_k \qquad (4.8)$$

The number of top ranks is represented as n. The size of the dataset is denoted as S, and P is the total number of positive samples. At index k, P_k is the number of positive results in the top n returns, and I_k is described as the result of the k_{th} position.

Another performance metric is Normalized Discounted Cumulative Gain (*NDCG*). Given a query q, the *NDCG* at the depth d in the ranked list is defined by:

$$NDCG@d = Z_d \sum_{j=1}^{d} \frac{2^{r^j} - 1}{\log(1 + j)} \qquad (4.9)$$

where r^j is the rating of the j-th pair, Z_d is a normalization constant and is chosen so that the *NDCG@d* of a perfect ranking is 1.

4.4.2 Objective Evaluations

4.4.2.1 Evaluation of Location-Based Recognition

In Fig. 4.11, the CVT-based CBIR method with and without location-based GPS filter is evaluated in both MAP and NDCG measurements for different database sizes. In this case, original image query is used without any visual intent regulation. The performance suffers a degradation with the increment of database size. For the location-based recognition method, images with related geographical regions have been firstly isolated from irrelevant images, and then, recognition by search algorithm is implemented solely on the filtered dataset. Performance is maintained and demonstrates that the system is applicable for dealing with large-scale databases. For the location-based filter $\phi(\mathbf{q})$, the GPS effective region Q utilizes the Quadkey level 5, which is equivalent to the resolution of 4,891 m in ground. Since landmarks groundtruth includes various object types: from statuaries and buildings, to city skylines and famous mountains, the aforementioned contextual filter will guarantee the inclusion of enough potential image candidates. In summary, such an analysis and investigation demonstrate the usage of location-based filter as an important tool in mobile visual search and recognition.

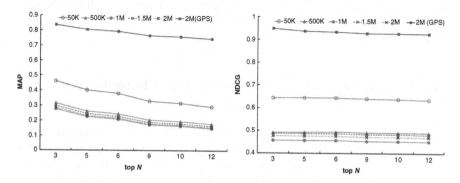

Fig. 4.11 Top N returns for both MAP and NDCG evaluations with GPS context, on the whole image itself as query

4.4.2.2   Evaluation of Context-Embedded Visual Recognition

Image contextual information and its effectiveness in recognition by search technique are investigated, using the soft weighting scheme. For the bivariate-based function $\Re(x, y)$, The amplitude A is fixed to 1 and tuned two parameters α and β to modulate the standard deviation. Two sets of experimentation were conducted with and without GPS context shown in Figs. 4.12 and 4.13, respectively. In general, using the soft weighting scheme improves search performance compared to the binary weighting method. Specifically, in Fig. 4.12, $\alpha = 50$ and $\beta = 10$ provide the best performance for both MAP and NDCG measurements. The results of this parameter choice using MAP and NDCG measures outperform the binary weight method by 12 % and 15 %, respectively.

Similarly, after incorporating the GPS context, the soft weighting method again outperformed the binary one, but in a much higher precision range. This does not surprise us since geolocation is an important feature for differentiating objects and their recognition, and eventually associated visual intent. Different from its counterpart in the non-GPS scenario, Figure 4.13 demonstrates that parameter $\alpha = 5$ and $\beta = 1$ outperforms other parameter choices, as well as the baseline binary weighting scheme. The margin difference from the soft weighting and the binary case has dropped to 2 % and less than 1 % for MAP and NDCG, respectively. This result demonstrates the importance of the GPS context.

It can be observed that parameter α is higher than parameter β for the best performance in both Figs. 4.12 and 4.13. The reason is due to the fact that most images are taken horizontally. Therefore, information is appreciated more and weighted higher by α horizontally than its counterpart β vertically. Similar patterns can also be observed in the following evaluations.

The significance of this image contextual information with soft weighting scheme allows robust user behavior and is seamlessly glued with the "O" gesture, which is spontaneous and natural. The shortcoming of the "O" is that it inevitably suffers from lack of accuracy due to device limitations in outlining the boundary, compared to other gestures, such as segmentation or line-based rectangular shape. However, soft weighting alleviates this deficiency of correctness in object selection and provides a robust method to accommodate behavioral errors when drawing the outlines of the ROI.

4.4.2.3   Evaluation and Comparison with Contextual Image Retrieval Model (CIRM)

State-of-the-art contextual image retrieval model (CIRM) [139] was implemented. Its performance is compared to our context-embedded visual recognition. The CIRM has demonstrated a promising result in desktop-based CBIR by applying a rectangular bounding box in highlighting the emphasized region, which can be achieved using mouse control at a desktop platform. The weighting scheme in CIRM model is to use two logistic functions joined at the directional (either X or Y) center of the bounding box. Then, the term frequency tf_q is formulated as:

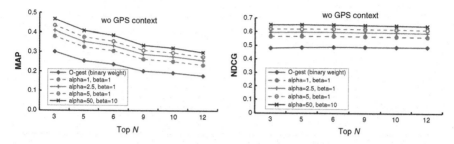

Fig. 4.12 Image contextual-based recognition by various parameter α and β, without GPS information

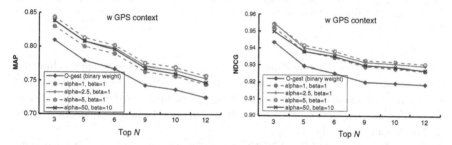

Fig. 4.13 Image contextual-based recognition by various parameter α and β, with GPS information

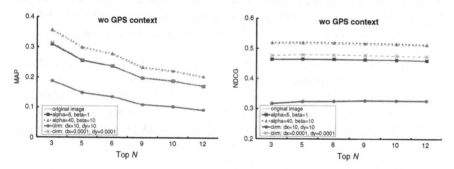

Fig. 4.14 Comparison of image contextual-based recognition by various parameter α and β, with the conventional CBIR (original), as well as the CIRM algorithm with parameter dX and dY, without GPS information

$$tf_q \propto min(\frac{1}{1+exp(\delta_X(x_l-x_i))}, \frac{1}{1+exp(\delta_X(x_i-x_r))})$$

$$* min(\frac{1}{1+exp(\delta_Y(y_t-y_i))}, \frac{1}{1+exp(\delta_Y(y_i-y_b))}) \tag{4.10}$$

where x_l, x_i, x_r represent x pixel values of the left boundary, detected feature point, and the right boundary along the x-axis direction, respectively. Similarly, y_t, y_i, y_b are the y pixel values of the top boundary, detected feature point, and the bottom boundary along the y-axis, respectively. The geometric relations $x_l < x_i < x_r$ and

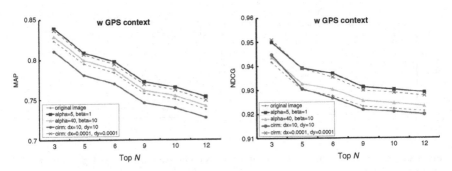

Fig. 4.15 Comparison of image contextual-based recognition by various parameter α and β, with the conventional CBIR (original), as well as the CIRM algorithm with parameter dX and dY, with GPS information

$y_t < y_i < y_b$ hold for this bounding box, such that the tf_q should be approaching the value 0, the further x_i from the bounding box; while ideally close to value 1 when the feature point is inside the bounding box. δ_X and δ_Y are two tunable parameters for finding the best performance of the bounding box. Detailed explanation of the algorithm can be found in [139].

Figure 4.14 shows MAP and NDCG measurements, by comparing the Gaussian-based contextual method with the CIRM model, as well as the CBIR method using the original image. It appears that the proposed method with parameters $\alpha = 40$ and $\beta = 10$ outperformed both CIRM in its best result with parameter $dX = 0.0001$ and $dy = 0.0001$, and the CBIR result of the original image without using contextual model.

Figure 4.15 depicts a similar comparison using the GPS context re-ranking. Again, the proposed method outperformed the CIRM method and the CBIR algorithms. However, the best performance of the CIRM model at $dX = 0.0001$ and $dY = 0.0001$ is close to the performance of the proposed contextual model at $\alpha = 5$ and $\beta = 1$. This result can be explained, such that, by adopting the GPS filtering, the margin of various methods is reduced.

4.4.2.4　Evaluation of Mobile Recommendations

For the recommendations, our method is to use the visual photo taken by users as the starting point, and to provide recommendation lists based on text searches associated with the recognized object. First, the object is identified and matched to the database. Then, the matched metadata is used as a text query to do a text-based search. The final result is then re-ranked by the relevant GPS distance from the query's image location to the ranked list image locations.

The evaluation was conducted exclusively on a vertical domain of food cuisines. A total of 306 photos were randomly picked and manually labeled and categorized them into 30 featured themes of food dishes, such as beef, soup, burger, etc. A 300

Table 4.2 MAP evaluation of the visual-based and description-based performance

MAP	@0	@1	@2	@3	@4
Visual-based	96.08	53.06	37.61	29.60	24.59
Description-based	n/a	75.65	72.66	70.78	65.93

word text dictionary was built by extracting the most frequently used words in the image description.

In order to produce a real restaurant scenario, Dishes in a menu style with both texts and images were printed out. We took pictures of the dishes as the visual query and attempted to find the duplicated/near-duplicated images from the dataset. It is assumed that the best match of the visual recognition result would be user intent. Such intent was carried by the associated metadata, which were quantized using the prepared 300-word dictionary. The quantized words were searched with a ranked list based on the text similarity. The final step was to re-rank the result list using GPS distance.

Table 4.2 presents the MAP result with the initial visual query and newly formatted text description query after visual recognition. The table demonstrates that the performance of the text description-based search is much better than the visual-based search. This result is reasonable in the sense that text is a better description than visual content once the ROI is identified and linked with precise textual metadata. However, the merit of the visual input is its role in filling the niche when an individual does not have the language tools to express him/herself articulately. It is demonstrated that during the initial visual search (@0), the visual-search result is at a high precision rate of 96.08 %. Such accuracy provides a solid foundation to utilize associated metadata as a description-based query during the second stage search. In summary, once the visual query is mined accurately, the role of the search query is then shifted from visual content to text metadata for a better result.

4.4.2.5 Time Complexity Analysis

TapTell's efficiency performance of the individual component is evaluated. A detailed analysis is illustrated in Fig. 4.16. The total time spent on the server end takes about 1.6 s, including initialization, text-based search, visual-based search, and OCR-based recognition (the system also supports OCR if the ROI corresponds to a text region). Among the visual search, local descriptor SIFT extraction takes the most time, almost 1 s. The communication time between the server and the client takes about 1.2 s, which is the wireless transmission in our experimental set-up.

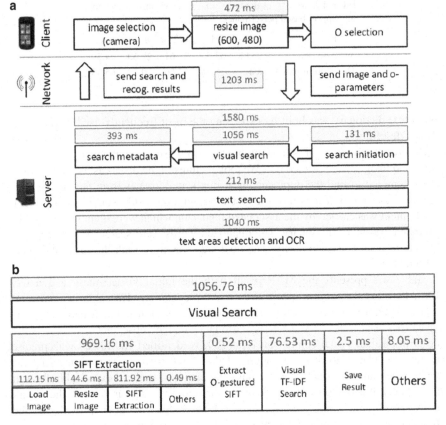

Fig. 4.16 The time analysis of the *TapTell* system as well as the visual search, based on the restaurants dataset. (**a**) Total time spent of the *TapTell* system. (**b**) Visual search time spent

4.4.2.6   Improved OCR from "O" and Visual Examples

Besides the visual content, Optical Character Recognition (OCR) is another important means to help mobile users to understand their visual intents correctly. It plays a vital role in translating from the visual feature to the text feature. However, most of the OCR techniques are sensitive to the orientation of visual input. If characters are skewed in a certain degree, current OCR techniques cannot successfully recognize the correct characters. However, such a difficulty can be alleviated by using a transform invariant low-rank textures (TILT) algorithm to align the severely tilted characters properly [141].

It is found that one of the byproducts from the "O" gesture is that it can achieve better OCR performance, if the estimation results of two principal components are utilized by the PCA in Sect. 4.3.2. Once the original text region is selected by the "O" gesture, those characters are first aligned by performing rotation alignment

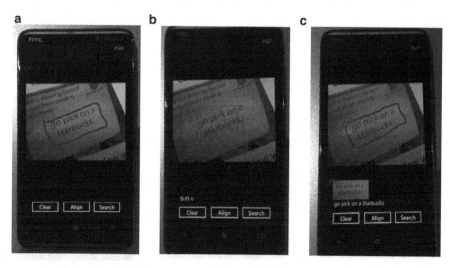

Fig. 4.17 Standard OCR failed to recognize multiple lines of skewed characters, but is successful after using the "O + TILT alignment" procedure. (**a**) original image with O. (**b**) OCR fails without O. (**c**) OCR with "O + alignment"

based on the PCA result, and then, further aligned by the TILT algorithm before the OCR process. Figure 4.17 illustrates a successful OCR detection.

Two visual examples are demonstrated in Fig. 4.18 with the visual queries associated location metadata of (a) Bleecker Street Pizza, located at 69 7th Ave S. New York. (b) Beef Marrow and Marmalade, located at 97 Sullivan St. New York.

4.4.3 Subjective Evaluation

It is conducted a subjective evaluation on user experience with the *TapTell* system. A total of 13 people participated the survey, nine male and four female. Eight out of the total participants had heard of the term content-based image retrieval, and six of them had heard of a natural user interface. During the survey, they were asked about the usefulness of and satisfaction with the system based on their experience using the prototype. The survey scale is ranked from 1 to 5 for usefulness and satisfaction, where 1 is the least and 5 is the most. Table 4.3 summarizes the survey result.

- Question 1 and 2 are about the usefulness of the "O" gesture compared to segmentation and line-based gestures, and the satisfaction of the "O" interface.
- Question 3 and 4 are about visual search satisfaction on duplication/near-duplication results, as well as semantic similar results. The rate is higher for the former, which is a fair reflection of the algorithm we took. This is because we use salient-based SIFT points, which are more suitable for duplication/near-duplication detection than object recognition.

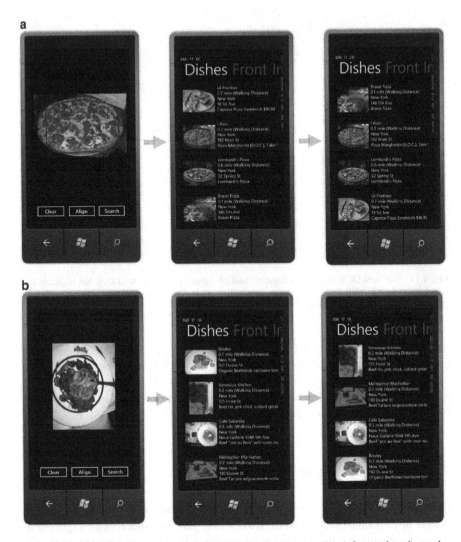

Fig. 4.18 Visual examples based on the recommendation system. The left snapshot shows the visual query. The middle snapshot is the result using metadata-based text search. The right snapshot is the re-ranking based on user's current position and location-based distance. (**a**) Bleecker Street Pizza. (**b**) Beef Marrow and Marmalade

- Question 5 and 6 are the usefulness study on the Optical Character Recognition (OCR) technique and adopted transformation invariant low-rank textures (TILT) for improving the OCR. More people are in favor of the TILT algorithm enhanced OCR method than the OCR itself [141]. (Technical details are presented in Sect. 4.4.2.6.)
- Question 7 is about the performance of text-based searches. Most people are satisfied with this feature.

Table 4.3 A summary of the subjective survey

Q#	Valid result	Criteria	1	2	3	4	5	Avg.
1	10	Useful	0	1	2	1	6	4.2
2	10	Satisfied	0	1	1	3	5	4.2
3	10	Satisfied	0	1	1	4	4	4.1
4	10	Satisfied	0	2	2	2	4	3.8
5	9	Useful	0	1	1	3	4	4.11
6	10	Useful	0	1	3	2	4	3.9
7	10	Useful	0	1	1	4	4	4.1
8	10	Useful	0	1	1	4	4	4.1
9	10	Useful	0	1	2	3	4	4.0

A scale of 1–5 is used, with 5 indicating the most useful/satisfied level, 1 indicates the least useful/satisfied level, and 3 is the neutral

- Question 8 and 9 are about the overall usefulness in terms of a recommendation system and *TapTell* as an application for mobile devices. Most people gave positive response to the usefulness of this system for both recommendations, as well as the application in general.
- The last question asks a price (in USD) they would be willing to pay at the mobile market to obtain this application. Eight out of ten people prefer a price less than $4.99, where two are not willing to pay anything. The remaining two participants are willing to pay a price above $10.

On average, questionnaire participants were satisfied with the *TapTell* system. Most responses were either 4 or 5 s on the 5-point scale. They also provided insightful comments such as

Quote 1 "Maybe can cooperate with the fashion industry."
Quote 2 "This is quick and natural. Better than pre-segmented based method. The segment results are always confusing."

4.5 Summary

A contextual-based mobile visual search utilizing the BoW model is used in this Chapter. A viable application, *TapTell*, is implemented to achieve mobile recognition and recommendations. Meaningful social tasks and activities are suggested to users with the assistance of multimedia tools and rich contextual information in the surroundings. Different gestures have been investigated from tapping the segments, to drawing the lines of rectangle, to making an "O"-circle via the multi-touch screen. It is demonstrated that the "O" behavior is the most natural and agreeable user–mobile interaction. Along with the BoW model, a context-embedded vocabulary tree for soft weighting is adopted by using both "O" object and its surrounding image context to achieve mobile visual intents mining. Various weighting schemes were evaluated with and without GPS conditions, and verified that image context outside the "O" region plays a constructive role in improving the recognition. State-of-the-art algorithms were used as comparison benchmark, and it has been demonstrated that the proposed method outperformed both the conventional CBIR using original image query and the CIRM algorithm. Moreover, a recommendation system is built upon an initial visual query input, where neither the text nor the voice has the strength in describing the visual intent. Once the context metadata is associated with the intent, more reliable contextual text and GPS features are taken advantage of in searching and re-ranking. Ultimately, interesting and related social activities are recommended to the users.

Chapter 5
Mobile Landmark Recognition

Abstract In recent years, landmark image recognition has been a developing application for computers. In order to improve the recognition rate for mobile landmark recognition systems, this chapter presents a re-ranking method. The query feature vector is modified, identifying important features and non-important features. These are performed on the ranked feature vectors according to feature selection criteria using an unsupervised wrapper approach. Positive and negative weighting schemes are applied for the modification of the query to recognize the target landmark image. The experimental results show that the re-ranking method can improve the recognition rate, as compared to previously proposed methods that utilize saliency weighting and scalable vocabulary tree encoding.

5.1 Introduction

The comparison of photos captured on mobile devices to a landmark photo database at the remote server is the main issue in mobile landmark search applications. The mobile user captures a landmark image and then uploads the image data (or a compact descriptor [144]) to the server. In an instant, related information of the captured image is returned to the user, i.e., name, geographic location, photograph viewpoints, tourism recommendations, or other value added information. This image matching tool has emerged in applications of mobile phones for not only landmark recognition, but also mobile shopping, mobile location recognition, online photographing recommendation, and content-based advertising. This chapter will focus on mobile landmark recognition, addressing this issue using the re-ranking method and saliency information, on top of the benchmark of the state-of-the art method in landmark recognition and retrieval.

In the mobile visual search scenario, instead of sending an entire photo, sending a compact descriptor computed on the mobile device allows for low bit rate search. Some compact descriptors are a low dimensional representation of the scale-invariant feature transform (SIFT) descriptor, such as [145–148]. These research efforts in compact visual descriptors provide the following benefits. Firstly, the compact descriptor reduces resource consumption (i.e., less battery and memory use), since sending large amounts of data via wireless consumes relatively large mobile resources as compared to sending a compact signature. Secondly, the internet

© Springer International Publishing Switzerland 2014
P. Muneesawang et al., *Multimedia Database Retrieval: Technology and Applications*,
Multimedia Systems and Applications, DOI 10.1007/978-3-319-11782-9_5

search system requires significant bandwidth, since at the server end, receiving multiple query photos is much more challenging than receiving texts, within the standard uplink bandwidth in a search engine.

A scalable near duplicate visual search system is typically developed based on a Scalable Vocabulary Tree (SVT) [149]. For the large size database, SVT reduces the computational cost as well as increases the performance in mobile landmark recognition. Visual vocabulary models quantize the descriptors with K-means clustering [150], vocabulary tree [149], and approximate K-means [151]. The BoW model with inverted indexing structure is usually developed for image descriptors based on SVT [149, 152–154]. However, a more compact descriptor can be obtained by the Bag-of-features histogram, which encodes the position differences of non-zero bins [155]. The inverted index structure of VST can also be further compressed with arithmetic coding to reduce the memory and storage cost to maintain a scalable visual search system.

While the aforementioned methods have been the main methods used for the construction of SVT and the associated compact descriptor, this chapter presents a method for improving the performance of SVT-based landmark recognition. As in the previous works in [156–160], the goal is to study the discriminative information of various image patches to evaluate the patch's importance. This information constitutes a weighting scheme for construction of SVT and BoW histogram features. In the conventional SVT and BoW, the local descriptors are assigned equal importance and hence feature selection for visual word generation is underutilized. However, the local descriptors for foreground landmarks should be given more importance, while the local descriptors in the background are outlines for recognition. The background information, such as sky and grass, are usually common to many different landmark categories. As such, their importance should be reduced when generating the BoW histogram [160].

In this chapter, the saliency map demonstrated in [161, 346] is adopted for construction of the saliency weighting scheme. Figure 5.1 shows the recognition process incorporating saliency maps and re-ranking. The saliency weighting is applied at various stages of the recognition process. Section 5.2 presents the generation of the saliency map. This map is applied in the construction of local descriptors in Sect. 5.3, and the construction of the SVT codebook, BoW and similarity function in Sect. 5.4. In Sect. 5.5, a new re-ranking procedure is applied to select the important BoW features for improving the recognition accuracy. Section 5.6 provides experimental results on landmark recognition from two landmark databases.

5.2   Saliency Map Generation

The goal toward the generation of a saliency map is to ultimately highlight a handful of 'significant' locations when the image is 'informative' according to the human perception. The graph-based visual saliency (GBVS) method demonstrated in [161] is applied to accomplish this. There are three stages for modeling visual saliency:

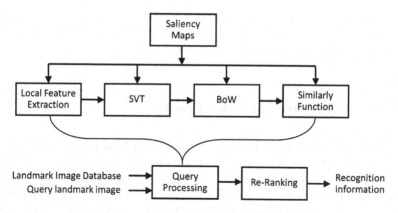

Fig. 5.1 Landmark recognition process, incorporating saliency weighting scheme and re-ranking

s1, s2, and s3. The s1 is the extraction stage, where feature vectors are extracted over the image plane. This results in a feature map $M : [n]^2 \to \mathbb{R}$, where n is the image space. The s2 is the activation stage, which forms an activation map $A : [n]^2 \to R$, such that locations $(i, j) \in [n]^2$ where the image is salient will correspond to high values of activation A. The last stage s3 will normalize the activation map.

The GBVS method is applied to the last two stages, for a given feature map M. Specifically, the dissimilarity of $M(i, j)$ and $M(p, q)$ is computed by:

$$d((i,j)||(p,q)) = \left| \log \frac{M(i,j)}{M(p,q)} \right| \tag{5.1}$$

Firstly, the fully-connected directional graph G_A is obtained by connecting every node of the lattice M, labelled with two indices $(i, j) \in [n]^2$, with all other $n - 1$ nodes. The directed edge node (i, j) to node (p, q) will be assigned a weight:

$$w((i,j),(p,q)) = d((i,j)||(p,q)) \cdot \exp\left(-\frac{(i-p)^2 + (j-q)^2}{2\sigma^2}\right) \tag{5.2}$$

where σ is a free parameter. Secondly, the graph G_A is converted to a Markov chain, and the equilibrium distribution of this chain results in an activation measure, i.e., the activation map A. Thirdly, the map is normalized to generate the final saliency map S of the image.

In the current work, at the final stage, the Sigmoid function is applied to conduct a mapping function from the activation map to saliency map [346],

$$S(i,j) = a + (1-a)\frac{1 - \exp(-b \cdot A(i,j))}{1 + \exp(-b \cdot A(i,j))} \tag{5.3}$$

where $S(i,j)$ is the saliency map at location (i,j), $a = 0.1$ and $b = 2$ are used to adjust the relative compactness of the saliency values. Equation (5.3) results in the concentration of the activation into a few key locations.

5.3 Saliency-Aware Local Descriptor

The SIFT descriptor aims at detecting and describing local visual features in two steps. In the first step, the key points are localized, while in the second step, local descriptors are built for each key point. A given image is decomposed into a set of key points $\mathbf{X} = \{x_1,\dots,x_n\}$ with their corresponding SIFT descriptors $\mathcal{S} = \{s_1,\dots,s_n\}$. In the process of obtaining the descriptors, the gradient vector for each pixel in the key point's neighborhood is computed and the histogram of gradient directions is built. Thus, the descriptor can be represented as a set of gradient histograms, and can be denoted by $s(m,n,o)$, where m,n and o are respectively the indexes of the spatial bins and orientation channels.

A 16×16 neighborhood is partitioned into 16 sub-regions of 4×4 pixels each. For each pixel within a sub-region, the pixel's gradient vector is added to a histogram of gradient direction by quantizing each orientation to one of eight directions. Each entry of a bin is further weighted by $1 - d$, where d is the geometric distance from the sample to the bin center. This reduces boundary effects as samples move between positions and orientations.

In order to incorporate the saliency information into the descriptor, when calculating the histogram, each entry of a bin is weighted by the saliency weights:

$$s(m,n,o) = \frac{\sum_{d_B(i,j)<1} M_o(i,j)(1-d(i,j))S(i,j)}{\sum_{d_B(i,j)<1} S(i,j)} \qquad (5.4)$$

where $M_o(i,j)$ represents the gradient magnitude at the location (i,j) in the o-th orientation plane, $d_B(i,j)$ is the distance between the sample at (i,j) and the center of the bin $B(m,n)$, $1 \le m,n \le 4$, and $1 \le o \le 8$.

Let R denote a region of size 16×16 pixels, chosen for obtaining the descriptor s. The saliency value associated with the descriptor is obtained by weighting the saliency map $S(i,j)$ discussed in Eq. (5.3) by a Gaussian of scale σ as follows:

$$w = \sum_{(i,j)\in C} S(i,j)\exp\left(-\frac{(i-R_x)^2 + (j-R_y)^2}{2\sigma^2}\right) \qquad (5.5)$$

where (R_x, R_y) is the center of the region R.

5.4 Saliency-Aware Scalable Vocabulary Tree

SVT is well exploited by the studies in [149, 152, 154, 155]. SVT uses unsupervised hierarchical clustering to quantize a local descriptor into discrete codewords. For a landmark image I_q with J local descriptors $\mathcal{S}_q = \{s_1^q, \ldots, s_J^q\}$, each descriptor s_i^q is traversed through the SVT hierarchy to find the nearest codeword, which quantizes $\mathcal{S}_q$ into a Bag-of-Word histogram $\mathbf{h}_q = [h_1^q, \ldots, h_M^q]^t$, where M is the number of codewords.

In the construction of SVT, the quantization process is applied to the local SIFT descriptors, where every sample receives equal importance for the calculation of cluster centers [149]. The unsupervised clustering can be improved when the sample has different weights, by considering the saliency values associated with each SIFT descriptor during the computation of cluster centers [346].

5.4.1 Weighted Hierarchical Clustering

The saliency-aware SVT can be generated by the construction of weighted hierarchical K-means. Let the training dataset be denoted by $\mathcal{S} = \{s_1, \ldots, s_N\}$, which is associated with the weights $\mathbf{w} = \{w_1, \ldots, w_N\}$. Each w_i is obtained by Eq. (5.5). The objective of the hierarchical K-means is to obtain the vocabulary tree $\mathcal{T}$ consisting of $C = B^L$ codewords, $\mathbf{v}_{l,h} \in \mathcal{T}$, where $l \in \{0, 1, \ldots, L\}$ indicates its level, and $h \in \{1, 2, \ldots, B^{L-l}\}$ is its index at a particular level, B is the branch factor, and L is the depth.

In the initial stage, the locations of the centroids, $\{\mathbf{v}_{l,h}\}_{l=1}^{L}, h \in \{1, 2, \ldots, B^{L-l}\}$ are obtained by a hierarchical clustering [149] without saliency weights. Then the following iterative algorithm is obtained to modify the centroids.

- *Step I.* the current level $l = L$.
- *Step II.* The algorithm involves an iterative updating scheme, with each iteration comprising of two substeps as follows:

  - *Winner Identification*: For every pattern $s_i, s_i \in \mathcal{S}$, its distances from each of the B^{L-l} centroids are computed. The cluster with the closest centroid will be identified as the winning. Let C_h be the winning cluster. That is, $s_i \in C_h$ if

$$h = \arg\min_{h=1,\ldots,B^{L-l}} w_i \left\| s_i - \mathbf{v}_{l,h} \right\| \qquad (5.6)$$

  In this case, s_i will be added to the winning cluster C_h, as its newest member.

– *Centroid update*: When a new vector $\mathbf{s}_i$ is added to a cluster, C_h, the old centroid of that cluster (denoted by $\mathbf{v}_{l,h}(old)$) will be updated as follows:

$$\mathbf{v}_{l,h}(old) \rightarrow \mathbf{v}_{l,h} = \frac{\sum_{s_i \in C_h} w_i \mathbf{s}_i}{(N_h) \sum_{s_i \in C_h} w_i} \tag{5.7}$$

where N_h is the total number of vectors in the cluster C_h.

These two substeps are repeated until there is no decrease of the following weighted cost function,

$$E_{SSD}(\mathscr{S}, \mathscr{V}) = \sum_{\mathbf{v}_{l,h} \in \mathscr{V}} \sum_{\mathbf{s}_i \in C_h} w_i \left\| \mathbf{s}_i - \mathbf{v}_{l,h} \right\|^2 \tag{5.8}$$

where E_{SSD} is the sum-of-squared-distance criterion, and $\mathscr{V} = \{\mathbf{v}_{l-1,(h-1)B+k}\}$, $k \in \{1, 2, \ldots, B\}$

• *Step III*. The current level is assigned with a new value, $l \leftarrow l - 1$, and Step II is repeated until $l = 0$.

5.4.2 Saliency-Aware Bag-of-Word Representation

For a query landmark image, I_q, its local descriptors can be described by $\mathscr{S}_q = \{\mathbf{s}_1^q, \ldots, \mathbf{s}_J^q\}$. These descriptors can be used for image matching, involving pairwise comparison between the descriptors [144],

$$D_d(I_x, I_q) = \sum_{j=1}^{J} \left(\left\| \mathbf{s}_{i'}^x, \mathbf{s}_j^q \right\|, \ s.t. \quad i' = \arg\min_i \left\| \mathbf{s}_i^x, \mathbf{s}_j^q \right\| \right) \tag{5.9}$$

where I_x is an input image in the database being compared, and has the descriptors $\mathscr{S}_x = \{\mathbf{s}_1^x, \ldots, \mathbf{s}_J^x\}$. For the database of size N, an optimized ranking using $\mathscr{S}_q$ is the one that minimizes the following ranking loss:

$$\mathscr{L} = \sum_{x=1}^{N} R(x) D_d(I_x, I_q) \tag{5.10}$$

$$R(x) = \exp(-rank(x)) \tag{5.11}$$

where $R(x)$ is the ranking position weight of I_x with respect to I_q. Apparently, minimizing the loss $\mathscr{L}$ with respect to D_d in Eq. (5.10), does not scale well due to the linear complexity to the image volume N. In comparison, the transformation of $\mathscr{S}_x$ to the BoW representation $\mathbf{h}_x = [h_1^q, \ldots, h_M^q]^t$, can address the scalability [149]. The matching of I_x and I_q can be obtained by comparing the BoW component h_i for the given query I_q:

$$D_d(I_x, I_q) \approx \sum_{i=1}^{M} \|h_i^x, h_i^q\| \tag{5.12}$$

$$h_i^x = |s_j^x|Q(s_j^x) = v_i| \tag{5.13}$$

$$h_i^q = |s_j^q|Q(s_j^q) = v_i| \tag{5.14}$$

where $Q(s_j) = v_i$ denotes the quantization of descriptor s_j into the codeword v_i, and h_i^x denotes the number of local descriptors of image I_x that fall into v_i. Therefore, the ranking loss $\mathcal{L}$ can be approximated by:

$$\mathcal{L} \approx \sum_{x=1}^{N} \left(R(x) \sum_{i=1}^{M} \|h_i^x, h_i^q\| \right) \tag{5.15}$$

The BoW component in Eq. (5.13) [or Eq. (5.14)] estimates the distribution of codewords in an image by assuming each descriptor to be equally important. However, the foreground object in an image is usually more important than the cluttered background, and thus they should be assigned different weights. Therefore, saliency weighting is used in the calculation of the BoW components, as follows:

$$h_i = |s_j|Q(s_j) = v_i| \tag{5.16}$$

$$= \frac{1}{\sum_{j=1}^{N_d} w_j} \sum_{j=1}^{N_d} w_j I(i = \arg\min_v(\|v - s_j\|))_{v \in \mathscr{T}} \tag{5.17}$$

where $w = \{w_1, \ldots, w_j, \ldots, w_{N_d}\}$ is the saliency weight of a landmark image, $I(\cdot)$ is the indicator function, and N_d is the number of local descriptors in the image.

The component h_i corresponds to the Term Frequency (TF) of v_i [162]. Thus, the Inverted Term Frequency (ITF) can also be obtained to make a complete weighting scheme [149]. As a result, the similarity between the query image I_q and the image I_x in the database can be obtained by:

$$D_d(I_x, I_q) = 1 - \left\| \frac{h_q \cdot f}{\|h_q \cdot f\|} - \frac{h_x \cdot f}{\|h_x \cdot f\|} \right\| \tag{5.18}$$

where $h_q = [h_1^q, \ldots, h_M^q]^t$ and $h_x = [h_1^x, \ldots, h_M^x]^t$ are the weighted BoW vectors of the query image I_q and the image I_x, respectively. f is the ITF vector [149], calculated as:

$$f = \left[\log\left(\frac{N}{N_{v_1}}\right), \ldots, \log\left(\frac{N}{N_{v_i}}\right), \ldots, \log\left(\frac{N}{N_{v_M}}\right) \right]^t \tag{5.19}$$

where N denotes the total number of images in the database, N_{v_i} denotes the number of images containing v_i, and $\log\left(\frac{N}{N_{v_i}}\right)$ is the inverted term frequency of v_i in the entire dataset.

5.5 Re-ranking Approach to Landmark Recognition

This section presents a re-ranking method for improving the performance of the recognition system employing SVT and BoW. The re-ranking method selects a suitable weighting scheme by applying an unsupervised wrapper feature selection to a training set associated with a particular query. The method is described in the following sections.

5.5.1 Building a Training Set via Ranking

Given a known database containing N landmark photos $[I_1, I_2, \ldots, I_N]$, the first step in the learning process is to obtain a subset of photos $[A_1, A_2, \ldots, A_R]$ to build a training set for a given query I_q. Here $R \ll N$, and all landmark images in the database are available with the class labels (or the information on the landmarks). Based on the distance function $D_d(I_x, I_q)$, this step outputs the following ranking list:

$$Query(I_q) = [A_1, A_2, \ldots, A_R] \tag{5.20}$$

where A_i is the i-th returning entry of the query. $[A_1, A_2, \ldots, A_R]$ are R top ranked images based on the original BoW histogram given the query.

We aim to maximally improve the ranking order by modifying the BoW of the query instead of using that of the original query.

5.5.2 Unsupervised Wrapper Feature Selection Method

As a specific subset of features is specially effective for the accurate prediction of certain query classes, the original BoW features can be modified by this subset. The unsupervised wrapper method [163] is utilized for feature selection. This process is shown in Fig. 5.2. The ranked BoW vectors can be first divided into subgroups by the unsupervised clustering. The single linkage (SL) [164] is selected to accomplish this purpose. Once each of the subgroups are artificially assigned a class label, then the wrapper method is applied.

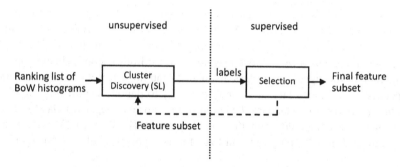

Fig. 5.2 The procedure for the unsupervised wrapper approach, where a ranking list of BoW vectors is fed into a clustering algorithm whose results are used to perform feature selection. The unsupervised cluster discovery procedure is performed by the single-linkage (SL) method, generating "class labels" for each cluster. These cluster labels are used by the feature selection method

Let $\mathbf{h}(r)$ denote the BoW vector corresponding to the r-the training image in Eq. (5.20), with h_j denoting the j-th element of any vector $\mathbf{h}$. For the ranking result in Eq. (5.20), there are a total of R training samples, each of which is denoted by an M-dimensional vectors:

$$\mathbf{h}(r) = \begin{bmatrix} h_1(r) \\ h_2(r) \\ \vdots \\ h_M(r) \end{bmatrix}, r = 1,\ldots,R \tag{5.21}$$

Then, a data matrix can be explicitly expressed as follows:

$$\mathbf{H} = [\mathbf{h}(1),\mathbf{h}(2),\cdots,\mathbf{h}(R)] \tag{5.22}$$

$$= \begin{bmatrix} h_1(1) & h_1(2) & \ldots & h_1(R) \\ h_2(1) & h_2(2) & \ldots & h_2(R) \\ \vdots & \vdots & \ddots & \vdots \\ h_M(1) & h_M(2) & \ldots & h_M(R) \end{bmatrix} \tag{5.23}$$

Let the dimension-reduced representation of $\mathbf{h}(t)$ be denoted as an m-dimensional vector:

$$\mathbf{y}(r) = [y_1(r),y_2(r),\ldots,y_m(r)]^t, \ r = 1,\ldots,R \tag{5.24}$$

where $m \leq M$. The feature selection algorithm chooses m most useful features from the original M features. Each of the new representations $y_i(r), i = 1,\ldots,m$ will be simply one of the original features.

In order to obtain $y_i(r)$, the class labels of the training data are used to define the scores of individual features. Such scores can effectively reflect the feature's capability in discriminating positive and negative classes. A feature's score can be effectively represented by its SNR (Signal-to-Noise Ratio) score, which is defined as the ratio of the signal (inter-class distinction) and noise (intra-class) perturbation respectively. We adopt $\{\mu^+, \mu^-\}$ and $\{\sigma^+, \sigma^-\}$ to denote respectively the class-conditional means and standard deviation of the (positive/negative) classes. These parameters are computed from the row vectors of $\mathbf{H}$ in Eq. (5.23). The Fisher Discriminant Ratio (FDR) [165] is utilized for the calculation of the SNR score:

$$FDR(j) = \frac{\left(\mu_j^+ - \mu_j^-\right)^2}{\left(\sigma_j^+\right)^2 + \left(\sigma_j^-\right)^2} \tag{5.25}$$

where μ_j^+, μ_j^-, σ_j^+, and σ_j^- represent the class-conditional means and standard deviations of the j-th feature, respectively.

In this case, the magnitude of scores for all features, i.e., $\{|FDR(j)|\}_{j=1}^M$ can be used to measure the relevancy of their corresponding features. More exactly, the features $\{h_j\}_{j=1}^M$ can be ranked accordingly to their scores $\{|FDR(j)|\}_{j=1}^M$, and a fraction of the lowest-ranked features will be eliminated. The selected feature set is denoted as:

$$\{y_1, \ldots, y_i, y_{i+1} \ldots, y_m\}, |FDR(i)| > |FDR(i+1)| \tag{5.26}$$

This feature set is further divided into two subsets:

$$\left\{ \underbrace{y_1, y_2, \ldots, y_{T_1}}_{Y'} \underbrace{y_{T_1+1}, y_{T_1+2}, \ldots, y_m}_{Y''} \right\} \tag{5.27}$$

where T_1 is the threshold value, and the subset Y' contains the features having SNR scores greater than those of the subset Y''.

The feature selection process can be summarized by its flowchart shown in Fig. 5.3. In the final step, the selected features in Y' and Y'' are used as a weighting factor for the original BoW features of the query, $\mathbf{h}_q = \left[h_1^q, \ldots, h_M^q\right]^t$. According to the indexes of features in Y', and Y'', the j-th element of the query is modified by:

$$h_j^q = \begin{cases} h_j^q + \varepsilon_1 y_j, & y_j \in Y' \\ h_j^q - \varepsilon_2 y_j, & y_j \in Y'' \\ h_j^q & \text{otherwise} \end{cases} \tag{5.28}$$

where ε_1, and ε_2 are the positive constants. Note that, all other features of the query $h_j^q, j \in \{1,\dots,M\}$ remain unchanged if these features are not members of the feature subsets Y' and Y''.

The query modification obtained by Eq. (5.28) is analogous to the pseudo-relevance feedback method discussed in Chap. 3. The relevant features are added to the original query, while the features with a lower degree of relevancy are subtracted from the query. In this way, the structure of the modified query will be more similar to the relevant samples, so that the cosine similarity function will be high and the distance in Eq. (5.18) will be low. This results in a reduction of the loss,

$$\mathcal{L}' < \mathcal{L} \tag{5.29}$$

$$\mathcal{L} = \sum_{x=1}^{N} R(x) D_d (I_x, I_q) \tag{5.30}$$

$$\mathcal{L}' = \sum_{x=1}^{N} R(x) D_d (I_x, I'_q) \tag{5.31}$$

where I'_q denotes the query image which has the BoW features modified according to Eq. (5.28).

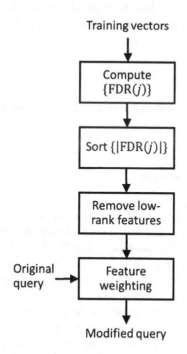

Fig. 5.3 Flowchart for feature selection and query modification

5.5.3   Recognition Function

In a landmark recognition system (e.g., [346]), the image database contains images $I_1, I_2, \ldots, I_N$, each of which belong to one of the c-classes, $\{C_1, C_2, \ldots, C_c\}$. Thus, these available class labels can be assigned to a new landmark image queried by a user. For this recognition task, the system obtains the matching image using $D_d(I_x, I_q)$, $\forall x = 1, 2, \ldots, N$ and the best matching image is selected. Its class label is then assigned to the given query I_q.

In the current work, the class assignment to the query is performed differently, by using the ranking list. The top-R retrieved images are firstly obtained, i.e., $Query(I'_q) = \{A_1, A_2, \ldots, A_R | D_d(A_i, I'_q) \le D_d(A_R, I'_q)\}$. The class labels of these images are also retrieved. Since the modified query A'_q is expected to be more effective than the original query, the retrieved image set will contain more relevant images, i.e., higher probability of relevant images in the top-R retrieved images. The probability can be measured by:

$$P(C_c | \{A_1, A_2, \ldots, A_R\}) = \frac{|C_c|_R}{R} \tag{5.32}$$

where $|C_c|_R$ is the number of occurrences of the c-th class label, C_c of the retrieved images in the top-R best matches. With this definition, the class label assigned to the query is obtained by the class labels that occur the most frequently in the top matches, i.e.,

$$c^* = \arg\max_c P(C_c | \{A_1, A_2, \ldots, A_R\}) \tag{5.33}$$

The query image will be assigned to the class c^* of the landmark images in the dataset.

5.6   Experimental Result

In the experiment, two datasets of landmark images were constructed. The first database is the Singapore landmark dataset containing 50 categories with 4,060 images in total. The second database is the World landmark dataset containing 72 categories with 8,847 images in total. Each category is associated with the landmark, and includes multiple images of each landmark. These images were originally collected from the internet. Sample images from the Singapore and World landmark databases are shown in Fig. 5.4. Images were divided into two subsets: training and testing for demonstrating the recognition performance of the system. Figure 5.5 shows samples of training and testing images from the Art Science Museum category in the Singapore landmark database. These images were taken at different viewpoints, and their apparentness are varied according to the camera viewpoints.

Table 5.1 Average recognition accuracy (%). Performance comparison for the Singapore Landmark Dataset

No.	Train:test	Method I SA + SVT + Re-ranking	Method II SA + SVT	Difference
1	90:10	81.87	78.93	2.94
2	80:20	72.67	70.68	1.99
3	70:30	65.43	63.94	1.49
4	60:40	59.67	59.11	0.56
5	50:50	56.8	55	1.8

Table 5.2 Average recognition accuracy (%). Performance comparison for the World Landmark Dataset

No.	Train:test	Method I SA + SVT + Re-ranking	Method II SA + SVT	Difference
1	90:10	77.25	76.01	1.24
2	80:20	67.89	66.36	1.53
3	70:30	60.58	59.41	1.17
4	60:40	56.82	55.67	1.15
5	50:50	52.24	50.83	1.41

The experimental results were analyzed in two parts. The first part presented the performance of the re-ranking method with the procedural parameter adjustment. In the second part, the recognition accuracy of the re-ranking method was measured at different ratios of training images and testing images, and compared to the previously proposed method discussed [346].

The procedural parameters for the re-ranking approach are: R [the number of top retrievals for training in Eq. (5.20)], and the weight parameters $\varepsilon_1, \varepsilon_2$ in Eq. (5.28). The system was tested at $(\varepsilon_1, \varepsilon_2) = \{(0.2, 0.8), (0.5, 0.5), (0.8, 0.2)\}$. For each setting, the value of R was varied from $R = 3, \ldots, 20$. It was observed that the recognition accuracy for the Singapore landmark database at 90:10 ratio of training and testing was at 81.6% at $R = 4$ and $(\varepsilon_1, \varepsilon_2) = (0.5, 0.5)$. Next, R was fixed at 4 and the values of weights $(\varepsilon_1, \varepsilon_2)$ were varied from 0.1 to 0.9. The best result was obtained at 81.9% at $\varepsilon_1 \geq 0.6$ and $\varepsilon_2 \leq 0.3$. According to Eq. (5.28), this result indicates that the new query should be modified by adding the most important features and subtracting the less important features. The parameter ε_1 should be greater than ε_2.

In the second part of the experiment, both of the datasets were used. The dataset in each category was divided into two groups; training group and testing group, in the ratios of 90:10, 80:20, 70:30, 60:40 and 50:50. This experiment compared the two methods, which were the re-ranking method implementing SA, SVT, and re-ranking, and the SA and SVT methods demonstrated in [346]. The experimental result is shown in Tables 5.1 and 5.2.

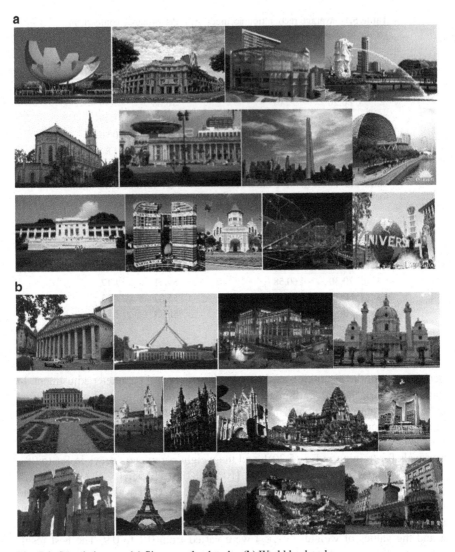

Fig. 5.4 Sample images. (**a**) Singapore landmarks. (**b**) World landmarks

Table 5.1 shows the comparison of the percentage accuracy of recognition for the Singapore landmark database, obtained by the SA + SVT + Re-ranking method and SA + SVT method. The highest recognition rate was 81.87 % at the training and testing ratio of 90:10. It is observed that the SA + SVT + Re-ranking method has a greater percentage accuracy than the SA + SVT method, regardless of the ratios of training and testing discussed. At 90:10 ratio, the best performance of both methods can be attained.

a

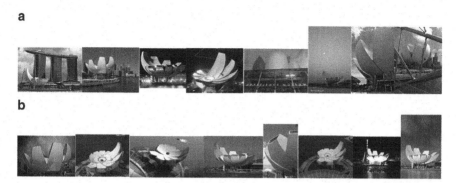

b

Fig. 5.5 Samples images used for (**a**) training and (**b**) testing in the Art Science Museum category

Table 5.2 shows the comparison of the percentage accuracy for the World landmark database. The highest score was 77.25 % at the 90:10 ratio, obtained by the SA + SVT + Re-ranking method. The results observed for the Singapore landmark database can also be observed for the World landmark database with regard to the performance of the methods being compared. The system which implemented the re-ranking method outperformed the baseline recognition system which implemented the SA and SVT methods.

5.7 Summary

The chapter extends the conventional Bag-of-Words (BoW) method for image content indexing to a discriminating BoW method for landmark recognition. Both scalable vocabulary tree (SVT) and BoW representation can be applied with the nonlinear discrimination power, by taking into account saliency weighting in image recognition. The discriminating BoW model is obtained by the feature selection and re-ranking processes, based on an unsupervised wrapper approach. This feature selection method has a great effect on learning efficiency and/or prediction performance.

Chapter 6
Image Retrieval from a Forensic Cartridge Case Database

Abstract This chapter presents a content-based image retrieval method for firearm identification. The reference and the corresponding cartridge base case images are aligned according to the phase-correlation criterion on the transform domain. The informative segments of the breech face marks are identified by a cross-covariance coefficient in a window located locally in the image space. Measurements of edge density for these segments are made to compute effective correlation areas for image matching. This image matching system can attain significant improvement in image-correlation results, compared with traditional image-matching methods for firearm identification. The system will enable forensic science to compile a large-scale image database to perform a correlation of cartridge case bases, in order to identify firearms that involve pairwise alignments and comparisons.

6.1 Introduction

The comparison of ballistic images taken from ballistic evidence found at a crime scene against reference images is the main issue in forensic science for firearm identification. The development of accurate analytical tools and systems is highly desirable. This chapter presents a method to address this issue based on two techniques: automatic registration of images containing breech face marks, and content-based matching of cartridge base case images.

Recently, there has been much research interest in techniques dealing with image processing and the statistical methods used to ascertain ballistic specimens [166]. By employing such techniques, a ballistic information system (BIS) can provide the automated association of ballistic samples—correlation lists against a given query specimen. In view of the difficulty in obtaining a complete match, this system can only provide a statistically viable match or an investigative lead that allows a forensic examiner to microscopically examine the evidence, to then arrive at an identification that can be used to apprehend and convict a criminal.

An effective correlator is therefore the most important module in the BIS. It interprets the contents of ballistic images in a collection, and ranks these images according to the degree of relevance to the user query. This chapter presents a

© Springer International Publishing Switzerland 2014
P. Muneesawang et al., *Multimedia Database Retrieval: Technology and Applications*,
Multimedia Systems and Applications, DOI 10.1007/978-3-319-11782-9_6

method for improving the accuracy of the correlator, which is based on the selection of effective correlation areas (ECAs), preventing bad areas from being used for correlation purposes. Bad areas are areas of the ballistic image that do not contain useful, reproduced toolmarks. Generally, these areas are consciously ignored by a firearm examiner during his visual checking. But including data located in bad areas in the correlation results in a lower correlation score, and can seriously compromise the performance of an automated system.

Given that the cross-correlation function is important for the ballistic image comparison as demonstrated by Chu et al. [167], Vorburger et al. [168, 169] and Weller et al. [170], in the current work, a method is presented for improving the discriminating power of the correlator using automatic image registration and the characterization of the ECA. The proposal for the adoption of automatic registration takes into account the translation of images in all three axes, as well as a scaling change for the proper alignment of the compared images. Unlike the works of Vorburger et al. [168, 169], in which the image correlation is obtained right after registration, the current work extracts the ECA before obtaining the similarity score. This increases the score value of the potential match, as well as the discriminating capability of the system, increasing the accuracy of firearm identification.

6.1.1   Firearm Identification Procedure

Traditionally, investigators identify the ballistic specimen from a crime scene with a reference specimen, by mapping the marks with visual images from two cameras. Images of the cartridge case of the firearm are captured using a personal computer and frame-grabber in conjunction with 40× microscopes fitted with two color charge-coupled device (CCD) cameras (Fig. 6.1). A ring light source is adopted, which can provide uniform lighting conditions. In order to match both specimens, a number of features within the identifying marks are chosen for their apparent uniqueness. A decision is made as to whether the same firearm made the marks under examination at the crime scene and in reference specimens. The critical step here is the selection of the mark or set of marks for examination and comparison. Figure 6.2 shows some examples of matching marks obtained by the system.

In comparison, Fig. 6.3 shows the automatic system for matching cartridge base case images. Images of the reference specimens are stored in the database, and each of them is compared to the image of the ballistic specimen from the crime scene. The identification process consists of the following three steps: *L2-norm energy normalization, image registration,* and *ECAs-based image matching.*

The quality of the captured image of a cartridge specimen can be affected by noise and lighting conditions. Poor lighting conditions and wrong setting of the lens aperture during image acquisition can result in a low-contrast image. Thus contrast-enhancement transformation is used when the image is obtained by the system.

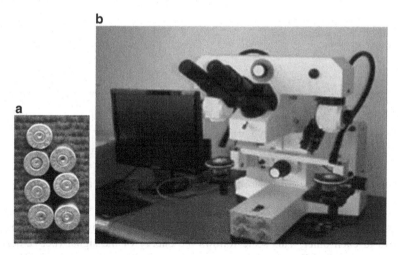

Fig. 6.1 Cartridge base cases and 40× microscopes fitted with two color charge-coupled device (CCD) cameras

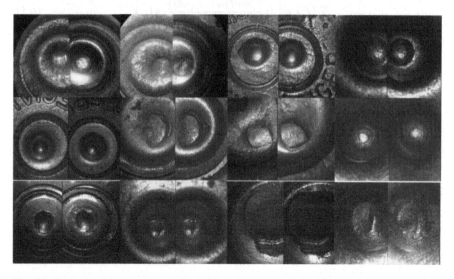

Fig. 6.2 Example of images captured by the imaging system, organized as image pairs showing similar marks from the same firearm

The contrast-enhancement transformation is applied to the image by the L2-norm energy normalization. This utilizes a *relative gray scale* to enhance the two images being compared according to their energy. The enhancement method is different from the traditional enhancement methods, which usually transform image intensity into some standard scales. Let $\{f[i,k]\}$ and $\{g[i,k]\}$ be, respectively, the reference image and the corresponding cartridge case images being compared, where i,k

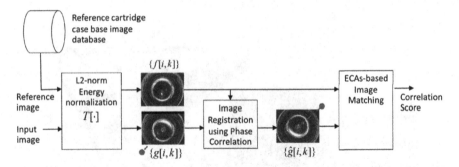

Fig. 6.3 Flow diagram describing automatic matching of cartridge base case images

represent the pixel indices. The two images are enhanced by the contrast scale relative to each other. This scale follows the energy of the signal (i.e. *l2*-norm), which is shown as follows:

$$\mathscr{T}\left[f\left[i,k\right]\right] = \frac{round\left(a \times f\left[i,k\right]\right)}{\|f\left[i,k\right]\|}, \forall \left(i,k\right) \tag{6.1}$$

$$\mathscr{T}\left[g\left[i,k\right]\right] = \frac{round\left(a \times g\left[i,k\right]\right)}{\|g\left[i,k\right]\|}, \forall \left(i,k\right) \tag{6.2}$$

where $\mathscr{T}$ is the transformation function, a is the average of the *l2*-norm of $\{f\left[i,k\right]\}$ and $\{g\left[i,k\right]\}$. Based on Eqs. (6.1) and (6.2), the energies of the two images are adjusted to the same base line, using the averaging of the *l2*-norm.

In the second step, image registration is used in the geometric transformation of the image $\{g\left[i,k\right]\}$. The image is adjusted according to translation, rotation, and scaling. The registration uses the image $\{f\left[i,k\right]\}$ as the reference image and adjusts the image $\{g\left[i,k\right]\}$. We denote $\{\hat{g}\left[i,k\right]\}$ as the geometric transformation of $\{g\left[i,k\right]\}$. As a result, as shown in Fig. 6.3, the image $\{\hat{g}\left[i,k\right]\}$ is adjusted according to the reference image $\{f\left[i,k\right]\}$, with the same translation, rotation, and scaling.

In the third step, the two images are matched by a correlator. The correlator utilizes the cross-correlation coefficient of the two images, which is defined as [171]:

$$C\left(f,\hat{g}\right) = \frac{\sum_{i=1}^{M}\sum_{k=1}^{N}\left(f\left[i,k\right] - \mu_f\right)\left(\hat{g}\left[i,k\right] - \mu_{\hat{g}}\right)}{\sigma_f \times \sigma_{\hat{g}} \times M \times N} \tag{6.3}$$

The C value in Eq. (6.3) is the normalized cross-correlation coefficient of the two images: $\{f\left[i,k\right]\}$ and $\{\hat{g}\left[i,k\right]\}$ of size $M \times N$. In addition, both σ_f and $\sigma_{\hat{g}}$ values are the standard deviations of the two images. Moreover, both μ_f and $\mu_{\hat{g}}$ values are the mean of the two images. It follows from Eq. (6.3) that $|C| \leq 1$. If $|C| = 1$ then both $\{f\left[i,k\right]\}$ and $\{\hat{g}\left[i,k\right]\}$ images agree with each other; however, if $|C| = 0$ then both $\{f\left[i,k\right]\}$ and $\{\hat{g}\left[i,k\right]\}$ images disagree with each other.

The similarity function in Eq. (6.3) has been demonstrated by the related works [168–170]. In comparison, the method introduced in the current work extracts ECAs before computing the similarity. This increases the discriminating power of the correlator in identifying the firearm. The method for extraction of ECAs is explained in Sect. 6.3.

6.2   Image Registration Using Phase-Correlation Method

Image registration is the process of determining the correspondence between two or more images in a point-by-point manner. These images may be taken of a scene at different times, by different sensors, or from different viewpoints. The parameters that make up the registration transformation consist of translation in x and y, rotation angle around z, and scaling. These can be computed directly, or determined by finding an optimum of some functions defined on the parameter space. In the domain of image analysis for ballistic identification, Chu et al. [167] calculated these parameters by optimizing a specified similarity metric using the Newton–Raphson method. Chu et al.'s work [167] is an attempt to register pairs of topography measurements of standard cartridge cases. The image registration is applied to align the master standard cartridge case and its replicas before the similarity between them is calculated.

In the current work, the phase correlation technique demonstrated by Reddy and Chatterji [172] is adopted to obtain parameters for image registration. Unlike the registration method in Chu et al. [167] that uses image pixel values directly, the current work proposes the adoption of the algorithm that uses the frequency domain. The Fourier domain approach is used to match images that are translated, rotated, and scaled with respect to one another. The algorithm searches for the optimal match according to information in the frequency domain. The mathematical algorithms for translation, rotation, and scaling are described in the following sections.

6.2.1   Parameter Estimation for Translation

Let $\{f[i,k]\}$ denote the reference image, $0 \leq i \leq M-1$, and $0 \leq k \leq N-1$, for an image with M row pixels and N column pixels. Let $\{g[i,k]\}$ be the reference image with shifted position by a pixels in row direction and b pixels in column direction, that is:

$$g[i,k] = f[i-a,k-b] \tag{6.4}$$

According to Gonzalez and Woods [173], we can find the Fourier transform of image $\{g[i,k]\}$ using:

$$G[m,n] = \frac{1}{MN} \sum_{i=0}^{M-1} \sum_{k=0}^{N-1} g[i,k] e^{-j2\pi\left(m\frac{i}{M}+n\frac{k}{N}\right)} \tag{6.5}$$

Substituting $g[i,k] = f[i-a,k-b]$ in (6.5) yields:

$$G[m,n] = \frac{1}{MN} \sum_{i=0}^{M-1} \sum_{k=0}^{N-1} f[i-a,k-b] e^{-j2\pi\left(m\frac{i}{M}+n\frac{k}{N}\right)} \tag{6.6}$$

$$= \frac{1}{MN} \sum_{u=-a}^{M-1-a} \sum_{v=-b}^{N-1-b} f[u,v] e^{-j2\pi\left(m\frac{u+a}{M}+n\frac{v+b}{N}\right)} \tag{6.7}$$

$$= e^{-j2\pi\left(m\frac{a}{M}+n\frac{b}{N}\right)} F[m,n] \tag{6.8}$$

The relation between the first line and the second line is obtained by substituting index i and k with $i = u+a$ and $k = v+b$, and $F[m,n]$ is the Fourier transform of image $\{f[i,k]\}$. Taking the complex conjugate $F^*[m,n]$ to multiply the relation in Eq. (6.8) produces:

$$G[m,n] F^*[m,n] = e^{-j2\pi\left(m\frac{a}{M}+n\frac{b}{N}\right)} F[m,n] F^*[m,n] \tag{6.9}$$

$$= e^{-j2\pi\left(m\frac{a}{M}+n\frac{b}{N}\right)} |F[m,n]|^2 \tag{6.10}$$

$$= e^{-j2\pi\left(m\frac{a}{M}+n\frac{b}{N}\right)} |G[m,n]|\, |F[m,n]| \tag{6.11}$$

The relation from the second line to the third line is obtained by substitution of $|F[m,n]|$ with $|F[m,n]| = |G[m,n]|$. Equation (6.11) can be written in the form of a cross-power spectrum as:

$$\frac{G[m,n] F^*[m,n]}{|G[m,n]|\, |F[m,n]|} = e^{-j2\pi\left(m\frac{a}{M}+n\frac{b}{N}\right)} \tag{6.12}$$

According to Gonzalez and Woods [173], we can obtain the inverse Fourier transform of the cross-power spectrum using:

$$\sum_{m=0}^{M-1} \sum_{n=0}^{N-1} e^{j2\pi\left(m\frac{i-a}{M}+n\frac{k-b}{N}\right)} = \begin{cases} MN, & i=a,\ k=b \\ 0, & i \neq a,\ k \neq b \end{cases} \tag{6.13}$$

$$= MN \cdot \delta[i-a,k-b] \tag{6.14}$$

where $\delta[i-a,k-b]$ is equal to zero at index $i \neq a$ and $k \neq b$, whereas $\delta[i-a,k-b]$ is equal to one at index $i = a$ and $k = b$. At this position, we can find the parameters for image translation between the two images in the row direction by a pixels and in the column direction by b pixels.

6.2.2   Parameter Estimation for Rotation

Let $\{g[i,k]\}$ be the reference image $\{f[i,k]\}$ that rotates by θ_0 and translates by a pixels in the row direction and b pixels in the column direction. The relation of the gray scale corresponding image can be written as:

$$\{g[i,k]\} = f[i\cos\theta_0 + k\sin\theta_0 - a, \ -i\sin\theta_0 + k\cos\theta_0 - b] \tag{6.15}$$

where index $0 \le i \le M-1$ and $0 \le k \le N-1$ for an image of size M row-pixels and N column-pixels. Following the property of Fourier transformation [173], we can obtain the Fourier transformation of $\{g[i,k]\}$ that is related to the Fourier transform of $\{f[i,k]\}$ by:

$$G[m,n] = e^{-j2\pi\left(m\frac{a}{M}+n\frac{b}{N}\right)} \times F\left[m\cos\theta_0 + \frac{nM}{N}\sin\theta_0, -\frac{mN}{M}\sin\theta_0 + n\cos\theta_0\right] \tag{6.16}$$

with the corresponding magnitude of $G[m,n]$ which is equal to:

$$\left|F\left[m\cos\theta_0 + \frac{nM}{N}\sin\theta_0, -\frac{mN}{M}\sin\theta_0 + n\cos\theta_0\right]\right| \tag{6.17}$$

When $M = N$, we have the following relationship:

$$|G[m,n]| = |F[m\cos\theta_0 + n\sin\theta_0, -m\sin\theta_0 + n\cos\theta_0]| \tag{6.18}$$

Let $|G[m,n]| = M_G[m,n]$ and $|F[m,n]| = M_F[m,n]$, and then the relationship shown in Eq. (6.18) can be rewritten as:

$$M_G[m,n] = M_F[m\cos\theta_0 + n\sin\theta_0, -m\sin\theta_0 + n\cos\theta_0] \tag{6.19}$$

From the relationship in Eq. (6.19), the translation parameters disappear, leaving only rotation parameters. The estimation of the parameters for rotation starts with changing the magnitude of the Fourier transform from rectangular coordinates $[m,n]$ to polar coordinates $[r,\theta]$ by substituting index $m = r\cos\theta$ and index $n = r\sin\theta$ into Eq. (6.5). The Fourier transform in polar coordinates can be obtained by:

$$G[r,\theta] = \frac{1}{MN}\sum_{i=0}^{M-1}\sum_{k=0}^{N-1} g[i,k] e^{-j2\pi\left(r\cos\theta\frac{i}{M}+r\sin\theta\frac{k}{N}\right)} \tag{6.20}$$

Similarly, the Fourier transform in polar coordinates of $f[i\cos\theta_0 + k\sin\theta_0 - a, \ -i\sin\theta_0 + k\cos\theta_0 - b]$ can be obtained by:

$$\frac{1}{MN}\sum_u\sum_v f[u,v] e^{-j2\pi\left((m\cos\theta_0 + n\frac{M}{N}\sin\theta_0)\frac{u}{M}+(-m\frac{N}{M}\sin\theta_0 + n\cos\theta_0)\frac{v}{N}\right)} \tag{6.21}$$

Next, substituting $m = r\cos\theta$ and $n = r\sin\theta$ into Eq. (6.21) produces the Fourier transform in polar coordinates:

$$\sum_u\sum_v \frac{f[u,v]}{MN} e^{-j2\pi\left(r\cos(\theta-\theta_0)\frac{u}{M}+r\sin(\theta-\theta_0)\frac{v}{N}\right)} = F[r,\theta-\theta_0] \tag{6.22}$$

From the relations in Eqs. (6.17)–(6.22), we can write the relationship between the magnitudes of the Fourier transform of the two images in polar coordinates as:

$$M_G[r, \theta] = M_F[r, \theta - \theta_0] \tag{6.23}$$

From the relationship between the magnitudes in Eq. (6.23), it can be viewed as a function having an independent variable in rectangular coordinates with $r \cong i$ and $\theta \cong k$, the same as for Eq. (6.4). Thus, we can obtain the cross-power spectrum as in Eq. (6.12) and the inverse Fourier transform of the cross-power spectrum as in Eq. (6.14). This yields the result in the form of a delta function, that is,

$$N^2 \delta[r, \theta - \theta_0] \tag{6.24}$$

It can be observed that the maximum peak value of this function is attained at $\theta = \theta_0$, which is the parameter for the rotation of the images.

6.2.3   Parameter Estimation for Scaling

If $\{g[i,k]\}$ is scale replica of $\{f[i,k]\}$ with scale factor α, we can write the relation $\{g[i,k]\} = \{f[\alpha i, \alpha k]\}$. According to the Fourier scale property, the discrete-time Fourier transform of $\{g[i,k]\}$ and $\{f[i,k]\}$ are related by:

$$G[m,n] = F\left[\frac{m}{\alpha}, \frac{n}{\alpha}\right] \tag{6.25}$$

By converting the axes to logarithmic scale, scaling can be reduced to a translation movement,

$$G[\log m, \log n] = F[\log m - \log \alpha, \log n - \log \alpha] \tag{6.26}$$

That is,

$$G[m', n'] = F[m' - \alpha', n' - \alpha'] \tag{6.27}$$

where $m' = \log m$, $n' = \log n$, and $\alpha' = \log \alpha$.

According to Eqs. (6.23) and (6.25), if $\{g[i,k]\}$ is translated, rotated, and scaled to replicate $\{f[i,k]\}$, their Fourier magnitude spectra in polar representation are related by:

$$M_G[r, \theta] = M_F\left[\frac{r}{\alpha}, \theta - \theta_0\right] \tag{6.28}$$

In log-polar coordinates [174], the logarithm of the radius axis is taken by: $(r', \theta) = (\log r, \theta)$. Thus the relationship in Eq. (6.28) can be viewed in the logarithmic scale as:

$$M_G\left[r', \theta\right] = M_F\left[r' - \alpha', \theta - \theta_0\right] \tag{6.29}$$

From the relationship of their magnitude spectra, Eq. (6.29) can be viewed as the function with independent variables in Cartesian space with $r' \cong i$ and $\theta \cong k$, same as for Eq. (6.4). Thus, the phase correlation technique can be applied using Eq. (6.12) followed by the inverse Fourier transform Eq. (6.14). This results in the delta function,

$$N^2 \delta\left[r' - \alpha', \theta - \theta_0\right] \tag{6.30}$$

where $r' = \log r$, and $\alpha' = \log \alpha$. It is observed that the maximum value of this function is attained when $\theta = \theta_0$ and $r' = \alpha'$.

6.2.4   Registration Accuracy

In order to measure the efficiency of the algorithm for automatic alignment of the cartridge base case images using the phase-correlation technique, the following mean square error was employed:

$$\rho_m = \frac{\sum_{i=1}^{M}\sum_{k=1}^{N}(g\,[i,k] - \hat{g}\,[i,k])^2}{\sum_{i=1}^{M}\sum_{k=1}^{N}(g\,[i,k])^2} \times 100\,\% \tag{6.31}$$

where $g\,[i,k]$ and $\hat{g}\,[i,k]$ are respectively the grayscales of the target image and the reference image after they were geometrically transformed with registration parameters (i.e. translation, rotation, and scaling). In addition, the error of the estimated parameters between the reference image and the target image was measured by ρ_p,

$$\rho_p = \frac{\sum_{j=1}^{K}(q\,[j] - \hat{q}\,[j])^2}{\sum_{j=1}^{K}(q\,[j])^2} \times 100\,\% \tag{6.32}$$

where $q\,[j]$ are the parameters used for geometric transformation between the reference image and the target image; $\hat{q}\,[j]$ are the parameters used for geometric transformation estimated using the phase-correlation technique; and K is the total number of parameters used for the experiment.

In the experiment, the test was conducted for three cases of translation, rotation, and scaling. The first case estimated the parameters for translation. In Fig. 6.4, a reference image of size 480×640 was translated from 0 to 40 pixels, increasing

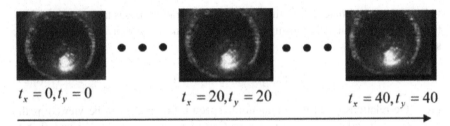

$t_x = 0, t_y = 0$ $t_x = 20, t_y = 20$ $t_x = 40, t_y = 40$

Translation by t_x, t_y

Fig. 6.4 Image samples generated by translation of the reference image of size 480×640 from 0 to 40 pixels increasing along the vertical and horizontal axis with the step size of 5 pixels

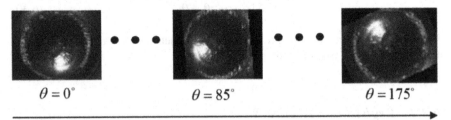

$\theta = 0°$ $\theta = 85°$ $\theta = 175°$

Rotation by θ

Fig. 6.5 Image samples generated by rotation of the reference image of size 480×640 from 0 to 175° with a step size of 5°

along the vertical and horizontal axis with a step size of 5 pixels, producing a total of 80 samples. In the second case, we estimated that the rotation parameters of the image changed from 0 to 175° with a step size of 5°, producing a total of 36 samples, as shown in Fig. 6.5. Finally, the third case estimated that the parameters for scaling ranged from 0.1 to 2.0.

The experimental results from the first case for 80 translated images showed that the error rate from the registration of images caused by translation was 0 % for all samples (i.e. $\rho_m = 0\%$). This is shown by the graph in Fig. 6.6. In addition, when compared with the graph of the translation parameters between the real value and the estimated value in the horizontal plane (t_x) and in the vertical plane (t_y), the graphs are straight lines passing through the origin with a slope of one. This shows that the error of the estimated translation parameters was zero, $\rho_p = 0\%$ for all samples in both horizontal and vertical directions.

When testing the algorithm with the pair of images obtained by rotation of the image with size 480×640 pixels for all 36 pairs from 0 to 175°, it was found that the error of image registration caused by rotation was less than 4.73 % for all samples (i.e. $\rho_m \leq 4.73\%$). This is shown by the graph in Fig. 6.7a. Moreover, a comparison between the real θ_0 parameter and the estimated $\hat{\theta}_0$ parameter for the rotation in Fig. 6.7b shows that the graph is a straight line. Table 6.1 summarizes the

Table 6.1 Comparison of rotation parameters for image registration for real values of rotation parameter (θ_0) versus the estimated values ($\hat{\theta}_0$) obtained by phase correlation

θ_0	$\hat{\theta}_0$	ρ_m	θ_0	$\hat{\theta}_0$	ρ_m
0	0	0.00	90	90.5	2.49
5	5.0	0.02	95	95.5	2.62
10	10.1	0.06	100	100.6	2.75
15	15.1	0.12	105	105.6	2.90
20	20.1	0.20	110	110.6	2.99
25	25.1	0.30	115	115.6	3.07
30	30.2	0.41	120	120.7	3.18
35	35.2	0.54	125	125.7	3.30
40	40.2	0.67	130	130.7	3.44
45	45.3	0.80	135	135.8	3.66
50	50.3	0.97	140	140.8	3.77
55	55.3	1.14	145	145.8	3.90
60	60.3	1.33	150	150.8	4.04
65	65.4	1.54	155	155.9	4.17
70	70.4	1.74	160	160.9	4.30
75	75.4	1.96	165	165.9	4.43
80	80.4	2.15	170	170.9	4.57
85	85.5	2.33	175	176.0	4.73

The table also shows the mean square error of image registration (ρ_m)

comparison of rotation parameters between the real value and the estimatedvalue for all samples, which shows that the error rate for parameter estimation was $\rho_p = 0.37\%$.

Table 6.2 shows the experimental result for registration with scaling parameters. The proposed algorithm estimates all 20 scale factors at the error of $\rho_p = 0.01\%$. This causes the mean square error for image registration to be $\rho_m \leq 5.3\%$ for all samples.

According to the above results for all three cases, it can be observed that the estimated parameters for translation for the registration of the 480×640 image were the perfect result. However, the estimation of the rotation and scaling parameters produced error rates of less than 4.73 % and 5.3 %, respectively. The factor that influenced the rotation error arose because the dimension of the two images was not rectangular, as assumed by the estimation process described by Eqs. (6.24) and (6.30).

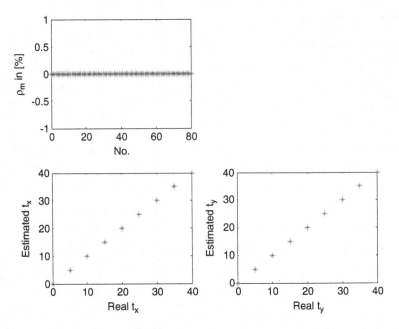

Fig. 6.6 Registration error by translation: (*top panel*) mean square error of image registration from translation of 80 couple images from 0 to 40 pixels; (*bottom panel*) comparing the real and estimated values of translation parameters

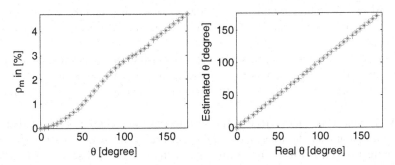

Fig. 6.7 Registration error by rotation: (*left*) mean square error of image registration from rotation of 36 couple images from 0 to 175°, (*right*) comparing between the real and estimated values of rotation parameters

6.3   ECA-Based Image-Matching Method

One of the critical parts of a matching operation is the creation of ECAs from the acquired images. This is particularly true for practice cartridge-case images, which contain a lot of random masks that are not relevant to the matching operation. These random masks are consciously ignored by a human examiner during his/her

Table 6.2 Comparison of scaling parameters for image registration between real values of scale parameter (α) and the estimated values ($\hat{\alpha}$) obtained by phase correlation

α	$\hat{\alpha}$	ρ_m
0.100	0.100	5.3
0.200	0.199	2.5
0.300	0.301	1.8
0.400	0.399	1.2
0.500	0.500	0.9
0.600	0.603	1.1
0.700	0.700	0.5
0.800	0.798	0.5
0.900	0.902	0.6
1.0000	1.0000	0.0
1.100	1.088	2.6
1.200	1.184	3.1
1.300	1.288	1.6
1.400	1.388	1.4
1.500	1.483	2.2
1.600	1.583	1.8
1.700	1.691	0.9
1.800	1.788	1.0
1.900	1.874	2.2
2.000	1.983	1.1

The table also shows the mean square errors of image registration (ρ_m)

visual checking. Specifically, a selected matching area is determined based on its capability of characterizing the impression marks on the reference image, which is highly correlated with the corresponding area on the target image at a suitable alignment position. In addition, the selected area is conveyed as a mark instead of a background or other normal area, because the mark is usually described by a certain magnitude of gray-level discontinuity as constituting a significant edge feature.

The adoption of the current ECA method is motivated by the observation of this human approach to visual checking with regard to the notion of the selected matching area. To incorporate this criterion into the image matching process, it is natural to adopt the ECA-extraction method where each selected-matching area is designated by its corresponding high value of the similarity score using a cross-covariance coefficient (CCC). This process ignores non-relevant areas where the CCC value is below a predefined threshold value. Edge-density measurement is also used to ensure that the selected area contains the features. In view of this, both the CCC value and the edge density are utilized to select an ECA located locally on the pair consisting of the reference image and the target image.

Let $f[i,k]$ be the reference image, and $\hat{g}[i,k]$ be the target image after registration to the reference image. In a matching process, the cross-correlation function (CCF) is usually applied to measure the similarity between the reference image $f[i,k]$

and the target image $\hat{g}[i,k]$ [cf. Eq. (6.3)]. In the current work, however, ECAs are extracted from the two images before the CCF values are calculated. Both images are spatially normalized so that the pixel values outside the ECAs are taken to be zero. This normalization process results in the output images, $f'[i,k]$ and $\hat{g}'[i,k]$, which are then used to obtain the CCF value for similarity measurement. This is explained in Sects. 6.3.1 and 6.3.2.

6.3.1   Local Normalization with Cross-Covariance Function

The CCC is referred to as a bias-independent measure for two-dimensional discrete data [175]. For extraction of ECAs, the CCC is first used for characterization of the similarity of the individual parts of the image in order to eliminate the local irrelevant region, thus defining the locally-normalized image data. Specifically, each coefficient CCC_s for $s = 1,\ldots,S$ is associated with a subset $\mathscr{R}_s \subset \mathscr{X}$, where $\mathscr{X}$ denotes the set of points in a $N_y \times N_x$ image lattice:

$$\mathscr{X} = \left\{(i,k) : 1 \leq i \leq N_y, 1 \leq k \leq N_x\right\} \tag{6.33}$$

and where the regions $\mathscr{R}_s$ forms a partition of $\mathscr{X}$

$$\mathscr{R}_{s_1} \cap \mathscr{R}_{s_2} = \varnothing, s_1 \neq s_2 \tag{6.34}$$

$$\bigcup_{s=1}^{S} \mathscr{R}_s = \mathscr{X} \tag{6.35}$$

Here, image lattice $\mathscr{X}$ is partitioned into non-overlapping square blocks of size $n \times n$.

The selection strategy is to first classify each region $\mathscr{R}_s$ for $s \in \{1,\ldots,S\}$ as relevant or non-relevant, and then derive the normalized image data. The preliminary classification was performed by adopting the following local CCC_s measure [176] for each region:

$$CCC_s\left(f_s, \hat{g}_s\right) = 1 - \sqrt{\frac{\sum_{k=1}^{n^2} \left(q_1[k] - q_2[k]\right)^2}{\sum_{k=1}^{n^2} \left(q_1[k]\right)^2}} \tag{6.36}$$

where $\{f_s[i,k]\}$ denotes the grayscale value of the reference image within the region $\mathscr{R}_s$, that is, $\{f_s[i,k]\} = \{f[i,k] : (i,k) \in \mathscr{R}_s\}$, and $\{\hat{g}_s[i,k]\}$ denotes the grayscale value of the target image within the region $\mathscr{R}_s$, that is, $\{\hat{g}_s[i,k]\} = \{\hat{g}[i,k] : (i,k) \in \mathscr{R}_s\}$. The $\{q_1[k]\}$ sequence in Eq. (6.36) is a feature sequence whose elements in descending order are obtained from the auto-covariance matrix of the reference image $\{f_s[i,k]\}$; that is, $C_{ff}[i,k]$ defined as [171]:

$$C_{ff}[i,k] = \frac{\sum_{x=1}^{n}\sum_{y=1}^{n}\left(f_s[x,y]-\mu_{f_s}\right)\left(f_s[x-i,y-k]-\mu_{f_s}\right)}{\sigma_{f_s}^2 \times n \times n} \tag{6.37}$$

where μ_{f_s} and $\sigma_{f_s}^2$ are the mean and the variance of the reference image $\{f_s[i,k]\}$, respectively. Furthermore, the $\{q_2[k]\}$ sequence in Eq. (6.36) is a feature sequence whose elements in descending order are obtained from the cross-covariance matrix between two images: $\{f_s[i,k]\}$ and $\{\hat{g}_s[i,k]\}$; that is, $C_{f\hat{g}}[i,k]$ defined as [171]:

$$C_{f\hat{g}}[i,k] = \frac{\sum_{x=1}^{n}\sum_{y=1}^{n}\left(f_s[x,y]-\mu_{f_s}\right)\left(\hat{g}_s[x-i,y-k]-\mu_{\hat{g}_s}\right)}{\sigma_{f_s} \times \sigma_{\hat{g}_s} \times n \times n} \tag{6.38}$$

where $\mu_{\hat{g}_s}$ and $\sigma_{\hat{g}_s}$ are the mean and the standard deviation of the reference image $\{\hat{g}_s[i,k]\}$, respectively. It may be observed that if the cross-covariance coefficient CCC_s approaches unity, both images absolutely agree with each other.

The current region, $\mathcal{R}_s$ is then classified as either relevant or non-relevant according to the value of $CCC_s(f_s,\hat{g}_s)$ relative to a threshold value of ξ_{COV}. This results in:

$$\mathcal{I} = \{s : CCC_s \geq \xi_{COV}\} \tag{6.39}$$

where $\mathcal{I}$ is the set of selected indices and $s \in \{1,\ldots,S\}$. By Eq. (6.39), we can define all the relevant image regions as:

$$\mathcal{R}' = \bigcup_{s\in\mathcal{I}} \mathcal{R}_s \tag{6.40}$$

and the resulting output image lattice containing those relevant points can be obtained from:

$$\mathcal{X}' = \{(i,k) : (i,k) \in \mathcal{R}'\} \tag{6.41}$$

Finally, the normalized versions of the reference image and the target image are obtained by:

$$\{f'[i,k]\} = \{f[i,k] : (i,k) \in \mathcal{X}'\} \tag{6.42}$$

$$\{\hat{g}'[i,k]\} = \{\hat{g}'[i,k] : (i,k) \in \mathcal{X}'\} \tag{6.43}$$

In the normalized images, pixels located outside the relevant region, that is, at position $(i,k) \notin \mathcal{X}'$, are set to zero.

6.3.2   Edge-Density Measurement

In the previous section, the ECAs are characterized by the degree of similarity (the CCC_s value) between the reference and the target images within a predefined region, $\mathscr{R}_s$. The resulting ECAs may not be representative of the impression marks, since images containing no marks can contribute to the high value of CCC_s if the two images are highly correlated. In other words, in the first stage, we only locate the highly-correlated area on the two images. Here, the second stage requires the specification of a measurement which describes the notion of a significant mark area. Edge-density measurement as demonstrated in Chu et al. [177] was applied to accomplish this task. The adoption of the current measurement technique was motivated by the previous research results showing that a striation mark produced on the bullet surface image constitutes a significant edge feature. This criterion is incorporated into the ECA-detection process by using edge density measurement and applying it to the predefined region, $\mathscr{R}_s$.

The edge detection is used to localize the edge in the region $\mathscr{R}_s$ of the reference image $\{f_s[i,k]\}$. The Canny edge detector [178] is used to perform edge detection. Instead of using a global threshold value specified by the user, the Canny edge detector adopts the so-called hysteresis thresholding operation, in which a significant edge is defined as a sequence of pixels with the edge magnitude of at least one of its members exceeding an upper threshold value, and with the magnitudes of the other pixels exceeding a lower threshold value. The pixel points judged to be edges are evaluated as "1", while other pixel points judged to be non-edge are evaluated as "0". The edge density (ED) [177] is utilized to describe the ratio of the number of edge pixel points to the total pixel points of the $n \times n$ reference image $\{f_s[i,k]\}$,

$$ED_s = \frac{number\ of\ pixels\ at\ the\ edges}{n^2} \tag{6.44}$$

The ED_s value quantifies that the region $\mathscr{R}_s$ contains all detected features on reference image $\{f_s[i,k]\}$. This includes useful features associated with the impressions. The ED_s value is used together with the CCC_s value to classify the current region $\mathscr{R}_s$ as either a relevant or non-relevant area according to a threshold value of ξ_{EDG}. Thus, the Eq. (6.39) can be rewritten as:

$$\mathscr{I} = \{s : (CCC_s \geq \xi_{COV}) \wedge (ED_s \geq \xi_{EDG})\} \tag{6.45}$$

where "$\wedge$" is the logical AND operation. The remaining process of the extraction of the ECA then follows Eqs. (6.40)–(6.43). With this definition, any region $\mathscr{R}_s$ is regarded as an ECA if the associated sub-images of the reference and the target images are highly correlated and the sub-image of the reference contains a sufficient edge feature relative to a predefined threshold value.

Table 6.3 Averaged cross-correlation scores for the ten pairs of cartridge cases fired from ten shotguns

Cartridge cases being correlated	CCF of the original	CCF after registration	
		Without ECA	With ECA
Code 101 vs. Code 102	0.7972	0.7784	0.9276
Code 201 vs. Code 202	0.4029	0.1632	0.8158
Code 301 vs. Code 302	0.4307	0.2920	0.8540
Code 401 vs. Code 402	0.1567	0.0036	0.8776
Code 501 vs. Code 502	0.3584	0.3025	0.8611
Code 601 vs. Code 602	0.4158	0.5749	0.8724
Code 701 vs. Code 702	0.5140	0.4985	0.8116
Code 801 vs. Code 802	0.0996	0.0139	0.7434
Code 901 vs. Code 902	0.2913	0.0348	0.8123
Code 1001 vs. Code 1002	0.3026	0.3559	0.8874
Average	*0.3769*	*0.3017*	*0.8463*

6.4 Experimental Result

In the experiment, the system performance was measured when the system was utilizing the registration algorithm, cross-covariance function, and edge mask for characterization of the ECA. All test fires were taken from twenty test fires (2 cartridges × 10 firearms) that were imaged by 40× microscopy at a resolution of 480×640 pixels. Each unit had its image measured in the region of the firing-pin impression and breech-face impression. The ten firearms used in this study are the same type of shotgun, the same brand of 'Remington', and the same model of 812 with four different serial numbers: C109219, C88922, C123355 and C86487. The images were indexed according to their classes: images named Code 101 and Code 102 are from class 1, whereas Code 201 and 202 are from class 2, and so on. A program has been developed, which automates the methods discussed previously, and produces cross-correlation scores for each pair of cartridge cases. Table 6.3 shows a list of averaged CCF values for all ten pairs of cartridge cases fired from ten different shotguns. The matching methods that were compared are Method 1: CCF of original images, as presented in Geradts et al. [179]; Method 2: CCF of the original images after registration, as presented in Vorburger et al. [168]; and Method 3: CCF of the pairs with ECA extraction presented in the current work. Note that the normalization process discussed in Eqs. (6.1) and (6.2) was applied for all three methods. The CCF value-matching pair is close to one for a perfect match.

For all ten lists, the average CCF obtained by the ECA method had a value of 0.85, where a value of 1.0 would be a perfect score. This matching rate is about 47 % higher than that obtained with a widely-used system in which the images are directly correlated without the selection of effective correlation areas and registration [179], and about 55 % higher than that of Method 2. This quantity can be used to indicate the reliability of identifying cartridge cases fired from the same firearm using a correlator. It can be observed from Table 6.3 that CCF values obtained by the pairs of the originals after registration were the lowest. This result indicates that the image registration did not help to achieve a better matching result, but only achieved greater alignment between the image pairs.

The discriminating power of the ECA image-matching method was then examined. Ten images of cartridge cases were selected as queries, each from different classes. Ranking lists were then developed for each query according to CCF scores from correlations with the other nineteen cartridge cases in the data set. For each of these ten ranking lists, the other cartridge case fired from the same identical firearm should have the highest correlation scores and should occupy the top position in the list. The recall rate was used for measuring the retrieval accuracy of the system. In an ideal situation of two cartridge cases being fired through the same firearm, if one of them is retrieved in the top best matches, the recall value should be unity.

Figure 6.8 shows the experimental result—the recall rates averaged by all ten queries obtained by the ECA matching-method are compared with those of the other two methods. It can be observed that the ECA method provides high retrieval performance with significant improvement in the recall rate at all settings of the top n best matches. The average recall rate was 22.6 % and 17.9 % higher than those obtained with Methods 1 and 2, respectively. This improvement was calculated using $\sum_{n=1}^{19} \frac{(R(n)_{ECA} - R(n)_1)}{19} \times 100\%$, where $R(n)_{ECA}$ and $R(n)_1$ are the averaged recall rates obtained by the ECA method and Method 1, respectively. The magnitude was observed to be $0.1 \leq (R(n)_{ECA} - R(n)_1) \leq 0.6, \forall n = 1, \ldots, 19$. It can also be

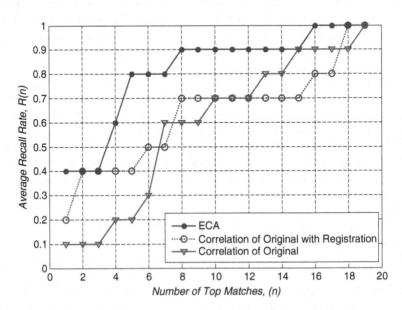

Fig. 6.8 Recall range, $R(n)$, as a function of the number of top matches, averaged over all ten queries

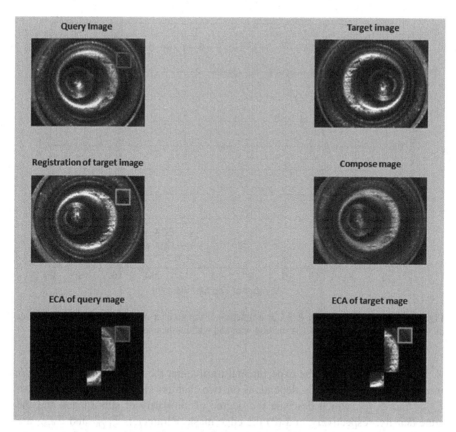

Fig. 6.9 Examples of screen shots captured from the proposed system, obtaining the correlation between the query image and the target image. The parameters estimated by the registration algorithm are: $\theta_0 = 180°, \alpha = 1, t_x = 0, t_y = 0$. The ECAs of both images are clearly extracted. This results in a CCF score of 0.85

observed that the system correctly retrieved eight out of ten classes from the top five best matches (e.g. $R(5) = 0.8$) by using the ECA method. In comparison, Method 1 required the top sixteen best matches (e.g., $n = 16$) to attain this level of performance. This high performance of the ECA method is very important for a retrieval system with a high volume of databases.

Figure 6.9 shows examples of screen shots captured from the system to obtain the correlation between the query image and the target image. Both were in the same class. The target image was aligned with the query using the image registration algorithm. The estimated parameters were: rotation $(\theta_0) = 180°$, scaling $(\alpha) = 1$, and translation $(t_x, t_y) = (0, 0)$. The ECAs of both images were extracted, which covered the area where edge density and the cross-covariance function were greater than the predefined threshold values. It can be observed from the result that ECAs are clearly extracted from both images. This results in a CCF score of 0.85, which is much higher than that of Method 1, at 0.36.

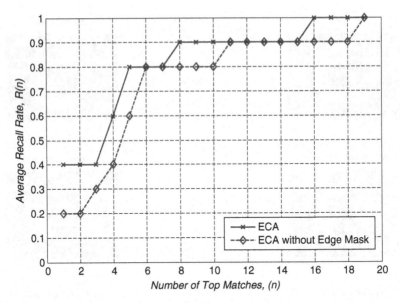

Fig. 6.10 Average Recall rate, $R(n)$, as a function of the number of top matches, averaged over all ten queries, comparing the ECA method with and without the application of an edge mask

It was observed from the experimental results that the performance of the ECA image-matching method is dependent on two factors: (1) the two parameters of ξ_{COV} and ξ_{EDG}, which describe the degree of similarity of sub-images and the edge density, respectively, and (2) the edge mask. Parameters ξ_{COV} and ξ_{EDG} are experimentally chosen, and the values of $\xi_{COV} = 0.7$ and $\xi_{EDG} = 7\%$ provide the best results. These were used throughout for all the experiments reported in Table 6.3 and Fig. 6.8. For the second factor, Figure 6.10 shows the comparison of an averaged recall rate between the ECA methods with and without the application of the edge mask. It can be seen from the figure that the averaged recall rate drops by 7.9 % when the ECA method is used with no application of the edge mask.

6.5   Summary

An image matching process which emphasizes on saliency information could have significant potential for digital forensic applications. The chapter demonstrates that saliency information in the form of the effective correlation areas on the image-data pair can improve accuracy for cartridge case image matching. In view of the fact that segmenting an effective correlation area will inevitably throw away some information in the image, it is imperative to determine the best matching positions. This work shows that these positions can be determined by cross-covariance coefficients and edge density. It is also shown that as far as localization accuracy is concerned, alignment of images is required for further processing of pairwise comparisons. The experimental results confirm that the current system may be successfully applied for the matching of cartridge cases to obtain accurate firearm identification.

Chapter 7
Indexing, Object Segmentation, and Event Detection in News and Sports Videos

Abstract A video parsing algorithm in the compressed domain is first introduced in this chapter. The algorithm is based on the conventional solution, where energy histograms of DC coefficients are used to calculate the distance between consecutive I/P frames, and the DC coefficients of the P-frames are obtained by frame conversion. The detection results are enhanced by using the ratio between two sliding windows to amplify the transitional regions. Secondly, in order to index news video at various levels, a template-frequency model is utilized to characterize the spatio-temporal information of news stories. The system employing this indexing structure is highly applicable for news-on-demand applications. Thirdly, a method for video object segmentation using Graph Cut and histogram of oriented gradients is presented. This method enhances the segmentation of objects that do not segment well, due to either poor luminance distribution, weak edges, or backgrounds with similar color and movement. Fourthly, the chapter presents an automatic and robust method to detect human faces from video sequences that combines feature extraction and face detection based on local normalization, Gabor wavelet transform, and AdaBoost algorithm. Finally, an application system is presented for the classification of American Football videos according to events of interest. The system consists of two stages. The first stage is responsible for play event localization and the latter stage is responsible for feature mapping and classification. The first stage employs MPEG-7 motion activity descriptors to detect the starting point of a play event, whereas the second stage uses MPEG-7 motion and audio descriptors along with Mel Frequency Cepstrum Coefficient features to classify the events using Fisher's LDA.

7.1 Introduction

News and sports video database applications require video-on-demand technology to allow users to select and watch video content on demand. Towards the goal of a database system which can implement on-demand technology, the system requires tools for automatically tagging video content to support end-user interactions such as search, filtering, mining, content-based routing, personalization, and summarization. Such tools will enable the system to decompose video images into semantic primitives that the user can employ to define "interesting" or "significant" events, which are then utilized to build up a semantic description of video data that will facilitate both tracking and searching for more instances of any given event. For example, in the domain of news videos, an anchor shot can be detected as a significant event by using a face detection technique. Given this anchor shot, we then can use existing knowledge representation techniques to build up a news headline for querying news story units. Similarly, semantic descriptions of sport videos can be described by play events, such as pass and run in American football, which are considered as the highlights for a game.

In order to realize the goal of building automatic tagging video data, this chapter presents the methods for video parsing, indexing and content characterization of news units (short, group, and story), video object segmentation, face detection in news video, and event detection in sports video. These methods can be applied for *content characterization*, which is the prerequisite for the construction of semantic description.

Section 7.2 presents a video parsing method to segment video sequences into video shots, which then allows subsequent operations such as feature extraction and shot characterization. The section will look into an algorithm to detect shot transitions (sharp and dissolved transitions) from the compressed domain, using the energy histograms of DC coefficients. The segmentation result is enhanced by using the ratio between two sliding windows to attenuate the low-pass filtered frame distance and to amplify the transitional regions. This provides the advantage of achieving high detection rates with low computational complexity. In the subsequent content analysis, the resulting shots can be combined to the higher levels, such as group of shorts, and video story.

Since news events happen daily, a person cannot afford to view all news on all channels in discriminately. To alleviate the problem, we need to develop a news video database that digitally stores full news story units, and provides interactive retrieval interface by letting new headlines function as quires. In this way, it is necessary to organize video content in terms of small, single-story units, instead of shots which do not usually convey any coherent semantics to users. The users are seeking the video contents in terms of events or stories but not in terms of changes in visual appearance as in shots. Section 7.3 will look into the content characterization of videos at the group and story unit levels, and demonstrate the retrieval of full news stories by using news headlines functioning as quires.

Section 7.4 presents video segmentation methods based on the object of interest. This method generates a segment form an input video sequence, which is more descriptive than the full portion of the video, since the objects are automatically detected and tracked from the input video according to the user preference. The method incorporates *shape prior* to implement Graph Cut for video object segmentation. This shape prior enhances the segmenting of objects with weak edges, poor luminance distribution, and backgrounds with similar color and movement.

Section 7.5 presents a method to detect human faces from video sequences, which incorporates the local histogram with optimal adaptive correlation. This alleviates a common problem in conventional face detection methods, i.e., inconsistent performance due to the sensitivity to lamination variations such as local shadowing, noise, and occlusion.

Section 7.6 presents a method for detecting events, and its application for the classification of American Football videos. The starting point of play events is detected by the MPEG-7 motion activity descriptors and the mean of the motion vector magnitudes. Then, the descriptors from multi modalities, including MPEG-7 motion, audio descriptors, and Mel Frequency Cepstrum Coefficients descriptors, are utilized to classify video shots into events, such as pass plays, run plays, field goal/extra point plays and kickoff/punt plays.

7.2   Video Parsing in Compressed Domain

Video parsing is the segmentation of video sequences into video shots, which then allows subsequent operations such as feature extraction, shot characterization, and key frame selection. Therefore, it is crucial that video parsing can correctly detect the shot transitions present, or else the quality of shot representation can be affected.

Since the original video data are large in size, they are compressed to preserve storage space. The computational cost of decompression is extremely high for most compression algorithms, and hence efficiency can be improved by performing operations on video data in the compressed domain. MPEG is one of the widely adopted compression standards [183], and many content-based video operations in the compressed domain have been developed [180]. In particular, research has shown that the DC coefficients can be used to detect shot transitions in MPDG [184]. Previous work using Motion-JPEG indicated that AC coefficients could be used to detect scene changes [185]. This section presents a new method called Twin-Window Amplification Method (TWAM) [181, 182] for detecting scene changes. This algorithm greatly enhanced the performance of the conventional method used in [184], and is comparable to the more complex methods in [186].

7.2.1   Conventional Method

Scene change detection is the process of dividing a video stream into shots based on the content of the video, where a shot is a sequence of continuous frames representing a continuous action in time and in space. In general, there are two types of transitions: sharp transitions and gradual transitions. A sharp transition is an abrupt transition between two shots that exists only between two frames, whereas a gradual transition requires several frames to complete the changeover. The most frequently encountered type of gradual transition is the dissolve transition, and it involves the fading-out of the leading shot and the fading-in of the trailing shot.

Traditionally, energy histograms of DC coefficients are chosen to represent the content of each frame. Since adjacent frames tend to be similar in content, only Intra (I)- and Predictive (P)-frames are examined. The first step is to obtain the DC coefficients in the compressed frames. As DC coefficients in the P-frames are not readily available, frame conversion [187] or approximation methods [188] need to be performed in order to extract the DC coefficients. In this work, the frame conversion method [187] is selected as it introduces less error terms.

An energy histogram of a DCT coefficient is obtained by counting the number of times an energy level appears in the DCT coefficient blocks of a DCT encoded frame. For each of the luminance and chrominance components, one histogram is created independently. The City block distance function is used to calculate frame distance for component i, and it is defined as:

$$D_i(n) = \frac{1}{T_i} \sum_{t=1}^{M} |h_{n-1}(t) - h_n(t)| \tag{7.1}$$

where $h_{n-1}(t)$ and $h_n(t)$ are the energy histograms of frames $n-1$ and n respectively. M is the number of histogram bins. The histograms are usually zero padded and aligned such that bins in the same position represent the same energy range. T_i is the number of DC coefficients of component i in the frame, and it is used to normalize the component frame distance D_i. Thus, the value D_i has an upper bound of 2, which occurs when the energy ranges of $h_{n-1}(t)$ and $h_n(t)$ do not overlap at all prior to zero padding. The component frame distances are then combined to form the overall frame distance $D(n)$ by averaging the three components:

$$D(n) = \frac{1}{3} \sum_{i \in \{Y, Cb, Cr\}} D_i(n) \tag{7.2}$$

The presence of a sharp transition is indicated by a sharp impulse in the frame distance function, and it can be detected with ease by thresholding. Alternatively, $D(n)$ is differentiated before thresholding is applied, and this reduces the difficulty in threshold selection. In the case of a gradual transition, its presence is indicated by a small peak with a width larger than 1. A sliding window is usually used to accumulate frame distances caused by gradual transitions. However, since these transitions can vary greatly in length, it is difficult to set the size of the window. Even with an optimal window size, it is still possible miss a gradual transition due to a small value of the accumulated frame distance.

7.2.2   Twin Window Amplification Method

The twin window amplification method (TWAM) was initially designed to enhance gradual transitions. Before explaining this technique, we first need to discuss the noise signals present in the frame distance function. During the MPEG compression of a video stream, quantization error and truncation error are introduced. These errors are lossy and thus cannot be removed from the decompressed data. In order to reduce the noise signals, we decided to apply a FIR low-pass filter (LPF) to the frame distance function. Low-pass filtering is implemented by using a sliding window of length L, and the average of the frame distance values in the sliding window is used to replace the current frame distance. The low-pass filtering function is as follows:

$$F(D(n), L) = \frac{1}{L} \sum_{j=0}^{L-1} D(n-j) \qquad (7.3)$$

Although the quantized value should be rounded to the nearest integer during quantization, it is common practice to round it down to increase the compression ratio. MPEG has two default quantization matrices for intra-frames and non-intra frames, and it also supports user defined quantization matrices. Depending on the quantization matrix used and the bin size of the energy histogram, the de-quantized DC coefficients of a data block can be shifted to a different energy range, leading to noise in the frame distance function. By using a sliding window, this noise signal is reduced and becomes less significant.

Floating point calculation is performed during MPEG compression and the process of obtaining DC coefficients from P-frames. This truncation error accumulates until the next I-frame is encountered, and thus it resembles a triangular signal. This noise signal tends to peak when the current frame is an I-frame, and it is the least significant when the previous frame is an I-frame. For a pure triangular signal with a period of T, it can be reduced to a DC signal by using a sliding window of length T. Since there is usually one I-frame in a group of pictures (GOP), we set the length of the filter L to be equal to the total number of I- and P-frames in a GOP. By using a LPF, the noise signal caused by truncation error is attenuated.

MPEG achieves a high compression ratio by taking advantage of temporal redundancy. In a GOP, I- and P-frames are used as references in motion compensation. Therefore, it is reasonable to assume that the contents of I- and P-frames in the same GOP are similar, except when there is a scene change present. For a MPEG video with a frame rate of 29.97 fps and GOPs of length 15, the duration of a GOP is only 0.5 s. In this case, the contents of adjacent GOPs are highly correlated, and the average frame distances of the two GOP are similar in magnitude. That is, the ratio between the two average frame distances has a value close to 1. Since the presence of a transition is indicated by an increase in frame distance, this ratio would have a value larger than 1 when there is a transition in the current GOP. As transitions could involve more than one GOP, it is more appropriate to consider the ratio between two sliding windows instead of two actual GOPs. This leads to the TWAM:

$$D_{TWAM}(n) = A(D(n), L_1) * F(D(n), L_2) \qquad (7.4)$$

$$= \left(\sum_{j=0}^{L_1-1} D(n-j) \middle/ \sum_{j=L_1}^{2L_1-1} D(n-j) \right) * \frac{1}{L_2} \sum_{j=0}^{L_2-1} D(n-j) \qquad (7.5)$$

where L_1 is the number of I- and P-frames in a GOP, L_2 is the size of the sliding window used in LPF, and A is the ratio between the average frame distances of two sliding windows. $D_{TWAM}(n)$ reduces the noise in the frame distance $D(n)$ by low-pass filtering, and scales the filtered signal by the ratio between the two sliding windows. By setting L_2 to the number of I- and P-frames in a GOP as discussed previously, $D_{TWAM}(n)$ can be simplified and written in a recursive format:

$$D_{TWAM}(n) = A(D(n),L) * F(D(n),L) \tag{7.6}$$

$$= \frac{p^2(n,L)}{L*q(n,L)} \tag{7.7}$$

where

$$p(n,L) = p(n-1,L) + D(n) - D(n-L) \tag{7.8}$$

$$q(n,L) = q(n-1,L) + D(n-L) - D(n-2L) \tag{7.9}$$

This can be implemented with a circular buffer of length $2L$, which involves only two additions, two subtractions, two multiplications and one division once the current frame distance $D(n)$ is obtained. Conventional methods such as thresholding can be applied to locate the scene changes in $D_{TWAM}(n)$.

7.2.3   Demonstration

Two MPEG-1 video files obtained from [189] are selected to demonstrate the effect of TWAM. Although the files are MPEG-1 encoded, the algorithm can be adjusted to accommodate MPEG-2, Motion-JPEG, and H.263 video data. Figures 7.1a and 7.2a show the unprocessed frame distance plots, and Figs. 7.1b and 7.2b show the TWAM version of video files V_1 and V_2 respectively. V_1 has 14 sharp and dissolve transitions, and the transitional regions are marked by the plot with an offset of 1.8 in the vertical direction. Figure 7.1b shows a peak near frame 0, which is caused by the initialization of the circular buffer and is ignored during thresholding. Transitions 1, 6, 8, 13, and 14 are dissolve transitions, and it can be seen in Fig. 7.1b that TWAM leads to an increase in frame distance for all of them. In particular, the peak of transition 6 is increased from 0.23 to 0.42. This transition involves two shots that are similar in content, and the transition could not be detected by the conventional method. The magnitudes of five sharp transitions are reduced after TWAM, but they remain as local maxima and can still be detected. Although some of the non-transitional regions are amplified by TWAM, it is possible to detect all 14 transitions with no false alarms using a threshold value between 0.3 and 0.42.

V_2 has ten sharp and dissolve transitions, with transitions 3, 4, 6, 7, 8, 10 being dissolve transitions. Similarly, V_2 has the same problem with the circular buffer and the peak near frame 0 is ignored. Again, all six dissolve transitions are amplified by TWAM as shown in Fig. 7.2b. The most important enhancement is during transition 3, where the frame distance is increased from 0.22 to 0.84, thus making detection possible. In the case of sharp transitions, all four of them are amplified by TWAM. By using TWAM with a threshold value between 0.3 and 0.7, it is possible to detect all ten transitions with one false detection near frame 1600. This false alarm is caused by a large object moving across the frame, which is similar to a gradual transition called wipe. As TWAM cannot distinguish wipes from motions of large objects, the frame distance is amplified in both cases. This is a problem for video shots that involve large objects moving across the frame frequently and usually results in false alarms.

7.3 News Video Retrieval

In the video parsing, the videos are segmented into camera shots. Consequently, a high-level technique is required to group individual shots into a more descriptive segment of the video sequence and to characterize video content and further extracting intelligent annotation from the segment. While the techniques for news video story parsing [190] and segmenting story units [191] have been developed successfully, this section presents the method for content characterization and indexing videos into group and story units. The template-frequency modeling (TFM) method discussed in Chap. 3 is applied for video indexing and retrieval for a news video database. In a news-on-demand application, a "news story" has been chosen as the appropriate unit of segmentation. Entire segmented news stories are the video document units indexed and returned by the retrieval system in response to a query. These news stories are the units of video presented in the result list and played back when selected by the user.

7.3.1 Characterization of News Video Units

A video database is a collection of raw video streams. A video stream F is a finite set of frames $f_1, f_2, \ldots, f_n$ that are ordered with respect to the index time n. If $f_s, f_e \in F$ and $s < e$, then a video interval $I[f_s, f_e]$ over F is the set of frames $\{f_k \in F | s \le k \le e\}$. f_s and f_e of $I[f_s, f_e]$ are the starting frame and the ending frame, and they are denoted by $start(I)$ and $end(I)$, respectively. A video interval $I[f_s, f_e]$ is simply denoted by I, and $I(F)$ denotes the set of all intervals over F.

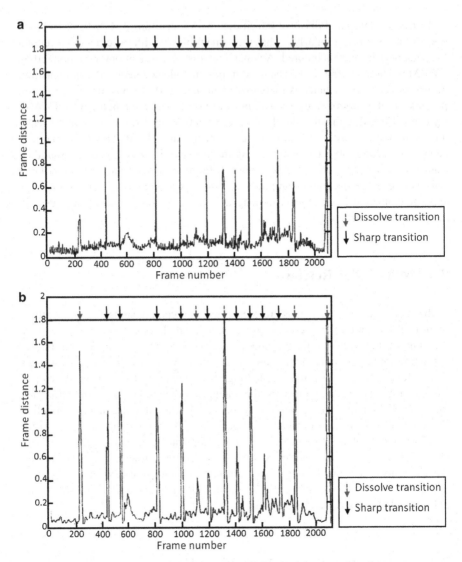

Fig. 7.1 (a) The unprocessed frame distance of V_1; (b) the TWAM enhanced frame distance of V_1

A news video F can be organized into three levels: shot, group, and story levels. So, $I_{Shot}(F)$, $I_{Group}(F)$ and $I_{Story}(F)$ denote a set of all intervals over F for shot, group and story levels, respectively. A video group, then, is the stream of continuous shots having some contextual meaning. A video interval at the group level is defined by:

$$I_{Group} = \{I_{i,Shot} | i = 1, 2, \ldots, S1\}, I_{i,Shot} \in I_{Shot}(F) \qquad (7.10)$$

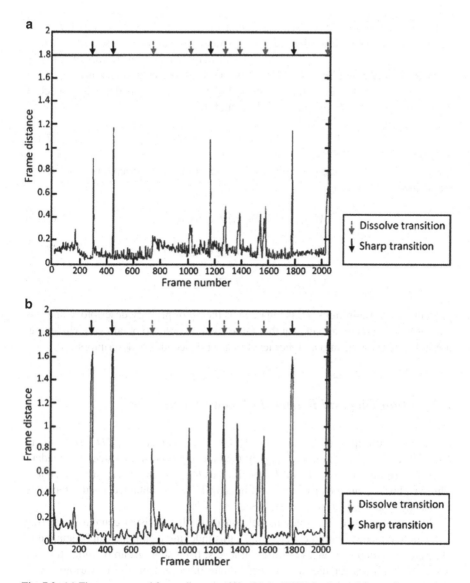

Fig. 7.2 (a) The unprocessed frame distance of V_2; (b) the TWAM enhanced frame distance of V_2

Similarly, the story interval is defined by:

$$I_{Story} = \{I_{i,Shot} | i = 1, 2, \ldots, S2\}, I_{i,Shot} \in I_{Shot}(F) \tag{7.11}$$

As story is the highest or most complex level, it usually contains a larger number of shots (i.e., $S1 < S2$).

Let $\mathbf{x}_i \in \mathbb{R}^P$ represent a visual descriptor of frame f_i. A video interval $I[f_s, f_e]$ at any level is characterized by a set of video descriptors represented by $D_I = \{(\mathbf{x}_s, f_s), (\mathbf{x}_{s+1}, f_{s+1}), \ldots, (\mathbf{x}_e, f_e)\}$. denotes a set of primary descriptors of I. It will be used for obtaining a secondary descriptor used for the video indexing.

Intuitively, a video descriptor database VD for a video F is defined as a set of video descriptors for F and has the following form:

$$VD = \{(D_{I_1}, I_1), (D_{I_2}, I_2), \ldots, (D_{I_J}, I_J)\} \tag{7.12}$$

Based on Eq. (7.12), video descriptor databases at the shot, group, and story levels are defined as follows:

$$VD_{Shot} = \{(D_{I_i}, I_i) | I_i \in I_{Shot}(F)\} \tag{7.13}$$

$$VD_{Group} = \{(D_{I_i}, I_i) | I_i \in I_{Group}(F)\} \tag{7.14}$$

$$VD_{Story} = \{(D_{I_i}, I_i) | I_i \in I_{Story}(F)\} \tag{7.15}$$

In the above definitions, D_I is regarded as the set of primary descriptors, and it is only used to characterize video at the frame level. In order to obtain video indexing, it will be reorganized into a higher level as a set of secondary descriptors.

7.3.2   Indexing and Retrieval of News Video

For a video descriptor database $VD = \{(D_{I_1}, I_1), \ldots, (D_{I_j}, I_j), \ldots, (D_{I_J}, I_J)\}$, where $D_I = \{(\mathbf{x}_s, f_s), (\mathbf{x}_{s+1}, f_{s+1}), \ldots, (\mathbf{x}_e, f_e)\}$, the indexing process produces a secondary video descriptor for each interval I_j, specified as $\tilde{D}_{I_j} \equiv \mathbf{v}_j = [w_{j1}, \ldots, w_{jr}, \ldots, w_{jR}]^t$. The weights w_{jr} are positive and non-binary. They are obtained by the template frequency model (TFM) discussed in Sect. 3.5, Chap. 3.

Since the template-frequency model considers all the visual contents occurring in a video sequence (with the weight w_{jr}), this indexing technique can be applied to characterize video sequences at different levels, from shot, group of shots, to story levels. This allows for the system to facilitate the user's access to various levels as depicted in Fig. 7.3: (a) shot-to-shot, (b) shot-to-group, (c) group-to-group, (d) group-to-story, and (e) shot-to-story.

This architecture is able to accommodate retrieval from the lower to higher levels, e.g., retrieval of a video group or story by using a query from the shot or group levels. A user is generally seeking information across the different levels defined in the segmented videos. To satisfy this demand, it is expected that at a higher level, the video story should contain most of the visual contents occurring at the lower one. For instance, to retrieve a full news story, a small shot that contains the anchor of the news story can be utilized as a query.

Let I_{Group} be the video interval at the group level, which contains a total of $S1$ video shots, $I_{Group} = \{I_{1,Shot}, \ldots I_{i,Shot}, \ldots, I_{S1,Shot}\}$. Then, the video descriptor for I_{Group} is given by:

$$\tilde{D}_{I_{Group}} \equiv \mathbf{v}_{Group} = [w_{1,Group}, \ldots, w_{r,Group}, \ldots, w_{R,Group}]^t \qquad (7.16)$$

where

$$w_{r,Group} = \sum_{i=1}^{S1} w_{ir,Shot} \qquad (7.17)$$

$w_{ir,Shot}$ is the r-th weight component of the i-th video shot $I_{i,Shot}$. Equations (7.16) and (7.17) are also applied to obtain a set of descriptors for a video interval at the story level, $\tilde{D}_{I_{Story}}$. A summary of the video description databases for each level is as follows:

$$VD_{Shot} = \{(\tilde{D}_{I_{i,Shot}}, I_i) | I_i \in I_{Shot}(F)\} \qquad (7.18)$$

$$VD_{Group} = \{(\tilde{D}_{I_{i,Group}}, I_i) | I_i \in I_{Group}(F)\} \qquad (7.19)$$

$$VD_{Story} = \{(\tilde{D}_{I_{i,Story}}, I_i) | I_i \in I_{Story}(F)\} \qquad (7.20)$$

In the querying process, a query can be chosen from VD_{Shot} or VD_{Group}, according to the links in Fig. 7.3. In these conditions, a query interval should have two properties: first, it should be short enough to not contain many lengthy scenes. Second, it should be long enough such that the context does not break down. This means that an interval from a story database may not be a suitable interval query.

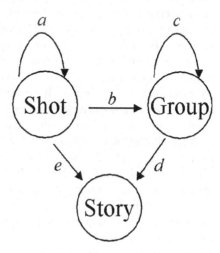

Fig. 7.3 Multiple-level access to video database, (*a*) shot-to-shot, (*b*) shot-to-group, (*c*) group to-group, (*d*) group-to-story, (*e*) shot-to-story

7.3.3   Demonstration

The CNN news video database discussed in Table 3.9 was used for the evaluation of video characterization and retrieval methods discussed in Sect. 3.5.3. The experiment was to demonstrate that the TFM can be adapted for retrieval beyond the shot level. There were 844 video shorts in this database. According to the time line in the original un-segmented video, shots are jointed into the meaningful groups and stories. Although there is an automatic technique available for detecting the news story [190, 191], this has been done manually to ensure the quality of the segmented videos used for this experiment. Three feature databases were created to describe the videos in the three levels. The lengths of the video clips were between 0.5 and 43.5 s for the group level, and 5.7–180.3 s for the story level.

In order to retrieve the video groups, six sets of video intervals were obtained for querying, $\{(I_{1,Shot}, I_{1,Group})_{q1}, \ldots, (I_{6,Shot}, I_{6,Group})_{q6}\}$, each of which was obtained from different stories. In the same set, the shot interval $I_{i,Shot}$ was one part of the group interval $I_{i,Group}$. This allows a comparison of the performance between query-by-video-shot and query-by-video-group. It is noted that the lengths of the queries are as follows: $\{(1s, 1.9s)_{q1}, (2.1s, 3.3s)_{q2}, (2.4s, 12.3s)_{q3}, (15.3s, 39.3s)_{q4}, \quad (2.8s, 4.5s)_{q5}, (1.3s, 3.5s)_{q6}\}$.

Figure 7.4a, b shows the precision versus recall figures for all six sets of the test queries, resulting from the retrieval of the video groups. Figure 7.4c shows a comparison between two querying methods: shot-to-group (STG) and group-to-group (GTG). Evidently, the TFM exhibits a good accuracy for video group retrieval. We have an average precision of 90 % at 50 % recall, and more than 60 % at 100 % recall. It can be observed that querying by GTG provides higher precision at lower recall levels, while the STG is superior at higher recall levels. This is because video intervals at the group level usually contain more information and are longer than at shot levels. On the other hand, a video shot usually contains less information, but can pinpoint the relevance for ranking a video at higher recall levels.

Figure 7.5 shows a group retrieval session, where a query clip contained two shots in a total length of 1.8 s. For convenience, each of the retrieved clips is represented by a set of frames. It can be seen that the top five retrieved video clips are all relevant and are actually from the same story. A precise ranking of the relative similarity (to the query) among these retrievals may also be observed.

A possible application for retrieval of the video story is to utilize a news headline to retrieve the full news story. This enables one user to go directly to the full story from the headline of interest. Five news stories that are introduced with at least two headlines (summarized in Table 7.1) are examined. Then five shots and five video groups from the news headline are utilized for querying. Figure 7.6 shows the system performance in retrieving the news stories by employing the shots and groups from news headlines as queries. It is observed that all relevant video segments related to the same story were retrieved with close to 50 % precision (at 100 % recall). This means that, on average, all relevant video intervals can be

Fig. 7.4 Precision and recall rates of retrieval of the video groups, using six query sets, employing the two querying methods: (**a**) Shot-to-Group (STG) and (**b**) Group-to-Group (GTG). The average precision of (**a**) and (**b**) are shown in (**c**)

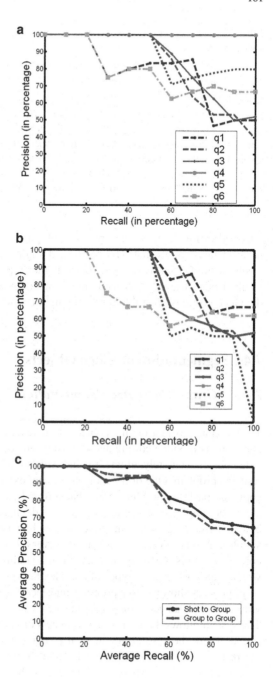

Table 7.1 Story retrieval results, obtained by two querying methods: shot-to-story (STS) and group-to-story (GTS)

Query	Story	Retrieval result (recall, precision)	
		Shot-to-story	Group-to-story
Query 1	S7, S22, S31	(0.33, 1), (0.67, 0.50), (1, 0.50)	(0.33, 1), (0.67, 0.50), (1, 0.50)
Query 2	S5, S8, S14, S28, S29	(0.20, 1), (0.40, 0.67), (0.60, 0.50), (0.80, 0.11), (1, 0.10)	(0.20, 1), (0.40, 0.50), (0.60, 0.50), (0.80, 0.50), (1, 0.23)
Query 3	S1, S26, S46	(0.33, 1), (0.67, 1), (1, 0.75)	(0.33, 1), (0.67, 1), (1, 1)
Query 4	S36, S37, S50, S55	(0.25, 1), (0.50, 1), (0.75, 1), (1, 0.50)	(0.25, 1), (0.5, 1), (0.75, 0.38), (1, 0.31)
Query 5	S7, S36, S39	(0.33, 1), (0.67, 0.40), (1, 0.50)	(0.33, 1), (0.67, 0.52), (1, 0.43)

retrieved within the first ten retrievals. In Figure 7.7, a comparison of STS and GTS performances shows that STS performed slightly better than GTS at lower recall levels, while GTS was much better at higher recall levels. This is opposite to the results from retrieving video groups. In this case, a great deal of information from the video group is favorable for retrieving the video story.

7.4 Segmentation of Video Objects

7.4.1 Graph Cut Video Segmentation

The automatic extraction of an object of interest in a video has immediate important applications in video editing and indexing. The development of ways to segment a video object accurately, efficiently and with minimal user interaction is an ongoing research problem. One of the most prominent examples of the use of a video object copy and paste is the blue screen background used by many television studios to allow for simple color keying. This takes advantage of the fact that colors such as blue and green are rare in an indoor setting like a news anchorman. This process is simple and can be done in real-time; however it is limited by the use of a background color. It requires the setup of a screen in a studio setting, and does not generalize well to outdoors or other types of complex backgrounds.

Figure 7.8 shows a user program interface for segmentation of objects in news videos. A user can get a rough estimate of a video object by just marking one frame. The system allows the user to mark objects of interest in blue, and the background in red. Then, the system automatically segments all following frames and shows the result of an anchor object segmented. Similarly, Fig. 7.9 shows the result of object segmentation, where the user marks the sailboat in Frame 2. The system automatically tracks and cut the same object past Frame 30, even if the object moves and changes its shape. In general, tracking and segmentation continues until a scene changes or when there is severe occlusion.

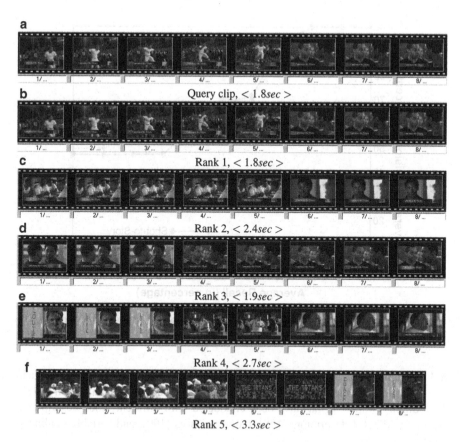

Fig. 7.5 Top five retrievals (**b**)–(**f**) answering to a query clip that contains two video shots (**a**), using the group-to-group querying method. Note that the first ranked video is the query itself. All of the retrieved clips are originally from the same story

This section introduces a novel way to implement Graph Cut for video object segmentation with shape information. Graph Cut is a very efficient algorithm for image segmentation, whereas Histogram of Oriented Gradients (HOG) is useful in detecting humans. The HOG feature is combined to incorporate a shape prior into the Graph Cut algorithm as a new way to enhance video object segmentation accuracy.

Graph Cut methods were applied for image and video segmentation. For image segmentation [192], a 2-D graph is constructed from the image color information, with each pixel representing a node in the graph. The nodes are connected by arcs or edges that represent the energy cost for *cutting* that edge. This is the pairwise energy, commonly assigned a cost relative to the intensity difference between adjacent pairs of pixels. For video object segmentation, the structure of Graph Cut is conducted as

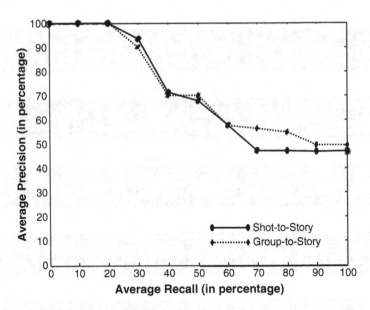

Fig. 7.6 Precision and recall rates of retrieval of the video stories, employing the two querying methods: Shot-to-Story (STS) and Group-to-Story (GTS)

a 3-D graph [193–195], and has been implemented with different topologies, such as a hierarchical graph topology [196] and a pyramidal hierarchical graph [197]. In addition, Graph Cut has also been conducted with different video descriptors, including MPEG4 descriptors [198], motion vectors [199], and variable nonlinear shape priors [200].

In order to improve performance, there are different techniques to improve Graph Cut for video; one is to reduce the number of nodes and pixels directly, via clustering of pixels or regions. Another technique is to firstly use a scalable or hierarchical method for computing a simplified solution, and then iterate over to obtain more accurate results. Tradeoffs in processing time and memory become the key issue for long videos with a high resolution or objects with complicated object borders.

This section addresses the problem of segmentation of objects with weak edges. Since the Graph Cut algorithm depends on the pair wise luminance of pixels, it is dependent only on intensity distribution, and it does not take into account any shape information of the object that should be segmented. To address this problem, an accurate method, HOG, is introduced as a way to incorporate shape information.

The HOG was demonstrated for detecting humans in images [201]. HOG is locally normalized histograms of image gradient orientations in a dense grid. It uses the idea that the appearance and shape of local objects can often be characterized rather well by the distribution of local intensity gradients or edge directions.

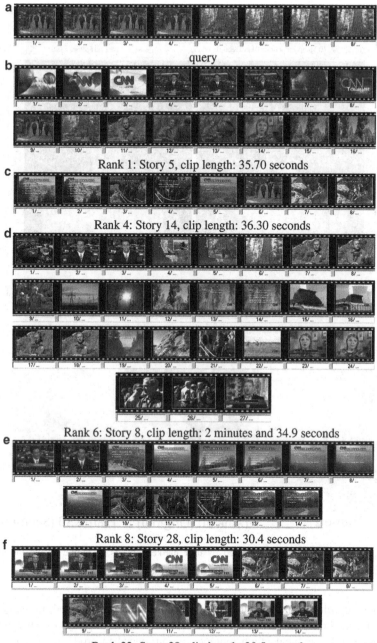

Fig. 7.7 Story retrieval using group-to-story querying method; (**a**) query clip containing two video shots (3.7 s). There are a total of five relevant stories in the database, showing President G.W. Bush visiting a national park: (**b**) the first segment (35.7 s) is ranked at no. 1; (**c**) the second segment (36.3 s) is ranked at no. 4; (**d**) the third segment (34.9 s) is ranked at no. 6; (**e**) the fourth segment (30.4 s) is ranked no. 8; (**f**) the fifth segment (20.5 s) is ranked at no. 22

Fig. 7.8 User interface for the video object segmentation program

Fig. 7.9 Object segmentation, obtained by user marked objects in Frame 2, and the system automatically tracks and segments the objects until Frame 30

Thus, in order to further enhance the current Graph Cut method, in the current work, the method is combined with HOG. A combination of pre-processing of pixel regions and hierarchical graph topology is introduced to produce efficient video object segmentation.

7.4.2 Object Segmentation

Graph Cut solves for the cut that minimizes the energy of an object/background pixel assignment A:

$$E(A) = \lambda \sum_{p \in P} R_p(A_p) + \sum_{\substack{(p,q) \in N \\ A_p \neq A_q}} B_{(p,q)} \tag{7.21}$$

where P represents all image pixels, N all unordered neighborhood pixel pairs, A is a binary vector whose components A_p specify assignments to pixel p in P, and λ specifies the relative importance of the first and the second terms. R_p is the prior probability, represented by how likely the pixel is to be of object or background label A in the set of pixels P. $B_{(p,q)}$ is the pairwise edge energy represented by the probability that there exists an edge between the pair of pixels (p,q) in the set of neighborhood pixels N.

To calculate R_p, the pixel values are compared with the color histogram to calculate how similar the pixel is to the user seeded region. To calculate $B_{(p,q)}$, the pairwise pixel luminance difference $I_p - I_q$ is mapped to an exponential function representing how likely is there to be an edge between the pair, shown in Eq. (7.22).

$$B_{(p,q)} \propto \exp\left[-\frac{(I_p - I_q)^2}{2\sigma^2}\right] \cdot \frac{1}{\|p,q\|} \tag{7.22}$$

In the calculation of pairwise luminance difference, a pixel can be connected to 4 or 8 of its immediate neighbors. The number of connections is set to reduce processing complexity, and it is possible to connect a pixel not only to its adjacent pixels, but also nearby pixels or pixels which are frames away.

Graph Cut can easily be extended for videos using a 3-D graph structure. The temporal information added allows it to track a segmented object effectively. Most implementations of Graph Cut require the user to seed the image by indicating the desired region versus the background (in our implementation, blue and red strokes, respectively). The unique strength of Graph Cut is that when given the connected graph topology, it can propagate the information across the sequence of images.

One of the main problems in using the Graph Cut algorithm in 3-D for video segmentation is in the growing complexity of the number of nodes and edges. Given a graph $G(N_n, N_e)$, where N_n is the number of nodes and N_e is the number of edges, which are both proportional to the number of pixels, the relationships of $N_e \cong 4N_n$ and $N_e \cong 6N_n$ hold for a 4-connected and 8-connected neighbor graph, respectively (Fig. 7.10). In 3-D, connecting immediately to the neighboring temporal frames will increase to $N_e \cong 6N_n$ and $N_e \cong 26N_n$ for 4 or 8-connected neighbors. With a $720 \times 480 \times 100$ pixel video, there will be 34×10^6 nodes and 207×10^6 edges. Given that the Graph Cut algorithm's polynomial run time depends on N_n and N_e, using Graph Cut in 3-D is still quite infeasible at the pixel level. Unfortunately, the technique does not scale well with resolution, especially for videos.

Fig. 7.10 3-D lattice
topology

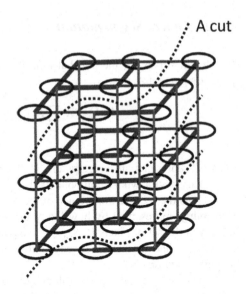

A cut

7.4.3 Histogram of Oriented Gradients

In the calculation of pairwise luminance difference, a pixel can be connected to 4 or 8 of its immediate neighbors. The number of connections is set to reduce processing complexity, and it is possible to connect a pixel not only to its adjacent pixels, but also to nearby pixels or pixels which are frames away.

To calculate the HOG feature on a detection window, two basic steps are taken: (1) divide the window into small spatial regions, (2) calculate the histogram of gradient directions over the pixels in that cell. For the task of human detection, HOG is tiled over the detection window in variable scales and the combined feature vector is used for human detection using a trained classifier.

HOG can not only be used for detecting humans, but any type of objects, as it is a robust scale-invariant feature. In the current work, each detection window is divided into cells of size 8×8 pixels, with each cell containing a 9-bin HOG and each group of 2×2 cells is integrated into a block. Each block is thus a 36-D feature vector.

Equations (7.23) and (7.24) explained below are used to incorporate shape prior information from the calculated HOG features. $R_p(O)$ now contains an extra weighted term $\ln P(O_p)$ representing how likely there is an object O_p there. is calculated using a specific trained HOG model.

$$R_p(O) = \begin{cases} K, & p \in O \\ 0 & p \in B \\ \mu P(O_p) & p \notin O \cup B \end{cases} \qquad (7.23)$$

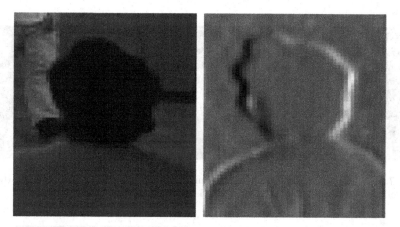

Fig. 7.11 A training sample and its gradient for the construction of the HOG model for the characterization of shape information of a human's head and shoulder

$$R_p(B) = \begin{cases} 0, & p \in O \\ K & p \in B \\ P(O_p) & p \notin O \cup B \end{cases} \tag{7.24}$$

where O and B denote the subsets of pixels a priori known to be a part of "object" and "background", correspondingly. The subsets $O \subset P$ and $B \subset P$ are such that $O \cap B = \emptyset$. In addition,

$$K = 1 + \max_{p \in P} \sum_{q:\{p,q\} \in N} B_{(p,q)} \tag{7.25}$$

In the experiment, a HOG model is trained by a collection of human head and shoulders as shown in Fig. 7.11. With the prior of a shape of a head, when the same algorithm is run on Akiyo shown in Fig. 7.12, it improves the segmentation results because of the preference for the overall shape of a human. In Fig. 7.12b, the Akiyo sequence shows positive response to the HOG filter near the center of the frame, increasing the likelihood that there is an object of interest there.

The additional results from video object segmentations are shown in Figs. 7.13, 7.14, 7.15 and 7.16. The user marked the objects at Frame no. 1, and the system performed segmentation through the following frames. The results at Frame no. 10 are shown in the figures. It was observed that the system's performance was satisfy and after final user marking, perfect segmented results could be attained. In the bus sequence (Fig. 7.13), the algorithm was robust enough to track the bus object thru the lamppost at the left side of the video. As the bus passed thru the lamppost, it was occluded and split into two separate objects. The algorithm still can segment the bus, but the frontal white edge of the bus is lost. A simple marking of the bus in Fig. 7.13a allows the bus to be segmented correctly. Other segmented objects in the images are

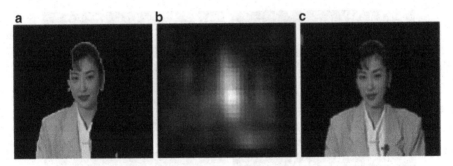

Fig. 7.12 Segmentation of Akiyo sequence, obtained with and without the application of the HOG model. (**a**) Segmentation without HOG. (**b**) HOG model. (**c**) Segmentation with HOG

Fig. 7.13 Segmentation of Bus sequence, (**a**) Frame no. 1 with the user mark, (**b**) the segmentation result at Frame no. 10

from the similarity prior probability calculation, as they match the marked bus more than the marked background, which is mostly green. Using a weighted value of λ in Eq. (7.21) can resolve the problem.

The foreman sequence (Fig. 7.14) was segmented effectively for the face. However, the hat and the background are very similar with the contour of the hat, and the hat was not detected by using the user marking. As shown in Fig. 7.14b, the segmentation of the hat can be fixed and enhanced with a shape prior information, in addition to the pairwise luminance difference $B_{(p,q)}$.

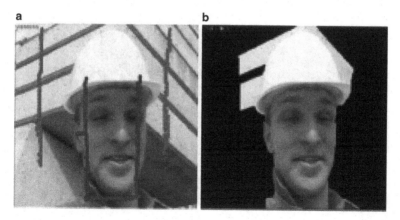

Fig. 7.14 Segmentation of Foreman sequence, (**a**) Frame no. 1 with the user mark, (**b**) the segmentation result at Frame no. 10

Fig. 7.15 Segmentation of MPEG sequence, (**a**) Frame no. 1 with the user mark, (**b**) the segmentation result at Frame no. 10

7.5   Segmentation of Face Object Under Illumination Variations

The video segmentation for face objects is more complex than other pattern detection problems. This is not only because the faces are non-rigid and have a high degree of variability in location, color and pose [202, 203], but also due to the illumination variations. The illumination component of the video frame varies a great deal, often more than the reflection component. Occlusion and lighting distortion can change the overall appearance of face objects. A non-uniform illumination will change the values of gray level distribution of a human face, and the edge of face will be blurred. Such change will cause the large intra-class

Fig. 7.16 Segmentation of Tennis sequence, (**a**) Frame no. 1 with the user mark, (**b**) the segmentation result at Frame no. 10

variations of the face distribution to be highly nonlinear and complex. The detection rate usually drops quickly under this condition.

In this section, a robust and effective method is presented for detecting faces in video sequences. The key step and the main contribution of this work is the incorporation of a normalization technique based on normalized local histograms with an optimal adaptive correlation (OAC) technique. This alleviates the common problem of illumination.

Face detection techniques have been studied extensively, which include feature based methods using geometric information, such as skin color, geometric shapes, motion information, and machine-learning based approaches, such as neural networks, Gaussian mixtures, Support Vector Machines and statistical modeling [204–206]. In automatic face detection algorithms, at the initial step, a pyramid of downscaled copies of the given input image is produced. Then, a sliding window scans each of the downscaled images and finally a classifier is applied on all possible window locations to decide whether the region contains a face object or not.

Practically, the number of windows or equivalently the number of times the classification will be processed is typically tens of thousands depending on the image size and demagnification factor. AdaBoost algorithm [207] employs this method in a fast way and has been widely investigated in video face detection systems. The key point is that fast, but less discriminating classifiers can reliably reject most of the windows containing non-face objects while passing the windows containing the maybe-face objects to a second level classifier, which is slower than the previous one but has higher discriminating power. This procedure iteratively continues and can provide high detection performance with much less computational expense.

Since illumination is one of the most important factors that determine success or failure in face detection, many approaches have been proposed to handle the illumination problem. Most algorithms for face detection presume that the illumination variation is uniform or lighting must be controlled. Georghiades et al. [208] demonstrated that face images with the same pose, under different illumination conditions form a convex cone. Ramamoorthi [209] and Basri and Jacobs [210] independently used the spherical harmonic representation to explain the low dimensionality of face images under different illumination conditions.

However, most previous face recognition and detection systems imposed strict restrictions on the input data and worked with the assumption that the location of the face within a frame is known. Although their works obtained good detection results, these systems face two main limitations: the requirement for calibrated multicameras and the restriction of usage for certain specific applications.

7.5.1   Automatic Face Detection using Optimal Adaptive Correlation Method with Local Normalization

The key step of the current work is the incorporation of local normalization with OAC technique to conventional classifiers for automatic face detection on video sequences. Each frame of the input video sequence is first extracted and regularized by local normalization. Face candidate regions are then roughly located by OAC. The Gabor wavelets filters are applied for local feature extraction after preprocessing. In the final step, the face region is detected through a cascade classifier consisting of detectors with AdaBoost algorithm.

7.5.1.1   Local Normalization

Due to the fact that variant light conditions definitely cause low detection rates and can be eliminated by illumination normalization, normalization techniques should be well considered in an automatic face detection system so that the system resistance can be evaluated for the most common classes of natural illumination variations. Most methods exploited were typically characterized by relatively low spatial frequencies. We use local normalization in this important step in order to keep all the useful information in illumination invariant form to facilitate accurate and robust feature extraction and detection. The local normalization composes of the illumination compensation and the candidate selection processes.

7.5.1.2   Illumination Compensation

The illumination normalization process consists of several stages, including gamma intensity correction (GIC), difference of Gaussian (DoG), local histogram matching (LHM) and local normal distribution (LND). GIC corrects the overall brightness variation of the input image $g(x,y)$, where (x,y) is the pixel location. This procedure compensates the pixel values of an image, under unknown lighting conditions, by exponentiation to best match a canonically illuminated image $g_{O(x,y)}$, under normal lighting conditions. The GIC corrected image $g'(x,y)$ is computed by transforming the input image pixel by pixel over its position (x,y) with an optimal Gamma coefficient γ^*,

$$g'(x,y) = G(g(x,y),\gamma^*) \qquad (7.26)$$

$$= e \cdot g(x,y)^{1/\gamma^*} \qquad (7.27)$$

where e is a gray stretch parameter, and γ^* is computed as:

$$\gamma^* = \arg\min \sum_{x,y} [G(g(x,y),\gamma) - g_O(x,y)]^2 \qquad (7.28)$$

γ^* is approximated by the golden section search with parabolic interpolation [357]. GIC can enhance the local dynamic range of the face in dark or shadowed regions, compress values of pixels in bright regions, and compensate for the global brightness changes of an image.

Intensity gradients such as shading effects are removed through a DoG filter, a popular method to obtain the resulting bandpass behavior for images. The selected values of smaller or inner Gaussians are typically quite narrow so the detailed spatial information in high frequency is kept, while the outer ones might have more contents for the low frequency range.

The main motivation of the application of LHM after GIC and DoG is to take into account histogram distribution over local windows and integrate it to global histogram distribution. To get the LHM transfer function, the histogram distribution of the input image and its local window are calculated first. The levels of the input image from previous processing are equalized by

$$s_k = T(r_k) = \sum_{j=0}^{k} \frac{n_j}{n}, k = 0,1,\dots,L-1 \qquad (7.29)$$

where s_k is the transformation of the pixel value r_k in the original image, n is the total number of pixels, n_j is the number of pixels with gray level r_j, and L is the number of discrete gray levels. The histogram distribution function $G(z)$ from the local window is obtained by:

$$G(z_j) = \sum_{j=0}^{z} p_z(z_j) \approx \sum_{i=0}^{k} \frac{n_i}{n} = s_k \qquad (7.30)$$

where $p_z(z)$ represents the specified desirable probability density function for the output image in a local window, and follows the transform $G(z) = T(r)$. The inverse transformation function, $z = G^{-1}(s)$ is then applied to the levels obtained in Eq. (7.29). The new, processed version of the original image consists of gray levels characterized by the specified density $p_z(z)$ which is normalized using Eq. (7.31),

$$z = G^{-1}(s) \tag{7.31}$$

$$= G^{-1}[T(r)] \tag{7.32}$$

Finally, LND is applied on the result image by assuming the gray values are drawn form a normal distribution. The output image $h(x,y)$ is normalized using Eq. (7.33),

$$h(x,y) = \frac{G^{-1}(s) - \mu_i}{\sigma_i} \tag{7.33}$$

where μ_i and σ_i are the mean and standard deviation of $G^{-1}[T(r)]$ over the whole image.

This illumination compensation procedure can account for the effects of illumination variations, local shadowing and highlights for faces in the original image, therefore, the procedure preserves the essential elements of visual appearances for detection.

7.5.1.3 Candidate Selection

After illumination compensation, a modified OAC method [211] is applied to the normalized image $h(x,y)$ to locate face candidates. Compared with common automatic face detection algorithms, this method does not need to use a pyramid of downscaled copies of the input image and thus speeds up the processing. The normalized image has similar power spectra and can be efficiently implemented in the spatial domain in a running window that approximately meets the requirements of the OAC process. This algorithm is adaptive to the input normalized image, and is designed to complete the segmentation in a single iteration in Hilbert space $\mathbf{H}$, through the kennel function $\mathbf{H}$ transform. The transform of the normalized image is a correlation image with normalized values ranging from zero to one. The OAC detector examines this image and segments it according to the range of correlation values. The image is then split into two segments after the correlation examination that corresponds to face candidates and background regions, which can be used conveniently by the later fine classifier with Gabor and AdaBoost algorithm.

Assume we have a normalized image $h(x,y)$ with multiple faces part $h_f(x,y)$ and complex background part $h_b(x,y)$, i.e.,

$$h(x,y) = h_f(x,y) + h_b(x,y) \tag{7.34}$$

The face part h_f and background part h_b can be modulated as uncorrelated independent signals, so we have

$$h(x,y) = \sum_{k=1}^{l} \xi^k \otimes \bar{h}_f(x,y) + h_b(x,y) \tag{7.35}$$

where the face part h_f is now composed by the averaged face template $\bar{h}_f$, the eigenface though gain mapping matrix ξ, and l is the number of faces. The OAC transform for the entire image is

$$H(X,Y) = H_f^T(X,Y) \Big/ |H_b(X,Y)|^2 \qquad (7.36)$$

where H_f and H_b are the nonlinear mapping response in Hilbert space $\mathbf{H}$ of h_f and h_b, respectively, T denotes the complex conjugate operation, and X,Y are the two-dimensional transform domain indices. The labeled graph (LG) generated by this transform is the adaptive ratio of target (face) signal peak height to the standard deviation of the clutter (non-face) background of the image. From the fact that the background power spectrum $|H_b(X,Y)|^2$ is unknown, we instead estimate it from the spectrum of the entire image $H(X,Y)$. So we can calculate the adaptive priori for a given image. The OAC detector is defined as

$$D(X,Y) = M^T \otimes |H(X,Y)|^2 \qquad (7.37)$$

where M is a 5×5 matrix.

We then use kernel canonical correlation analysis (KCCA) [212] to get the nonlinear correlation between $D(X,Y)$ and $H(X,Y)$. A pair of directions ω_D and ω_H are obtained, such that the correlation between the two projections ω_D^T and ω_H^T is maximized.

For a given normalized image, we can estimate the face candidates in the segmented image by arguing the OAC value of $D(X,Y)$ and $H(X,Y)$,

$$C^* = \arg\max\left(\frac{a_i}{b_i}\right) \qquad (7.38)$$

where a_i and b_i are respectively the projections of the variables $\Phi(D)$ and H on the projection vector $\omega^i_{\Phi(D)}$ and ω^i_H, and $\{\omega^i_{\Phi(D)}, \omega^i_H\}^t_{i=1}$ is the t pair directions of OAC.

$$a_i = (\omega^i_{\Phi(D)})^T \Phi(D) \qquad (7.39)$$

$$b_i = (\omega^i_H)^T H \qquad (7.40)$$

where $\Phi(D)$ is the diagonal of $D(X,Y)$ in the Hilbert space $\mathbf{H}$. The segmentation image mask $m(x,y)$ for the original image $g(x,y)$ is then generated from the correlation image $h(x,y)$ as

$$m(x,y) = \begin{cases} 0 & Th_{h(x,y)} < C^* \\ 1 & Th_{h(x,y)} \geq C^* \end{cases} \qquad (7.41)$$

where $Th_{h(x,y)}$ is the threshold parameter for pixels corresponding to the face candidates.

7.5.1.4 Recognition Stage

The face detection stage consists of two main components: Gabor wavelets feature extractions and AdaBoost detection algorithms. Gabor wavelets demonstrate two desirable characteristics, spatial locality and orientation selectivity, which has shown its effectiveness in automatic face detection and recognition. Boost algorithm is adopted to reduce the redundancies of the high dimensional feature space and computational cost.

The AdaBoost algorithm [358] was demonstrated to have a very low false positive rate for face detection and can detect faces in real time. It can be trained for different levels of computational complexity, speed and detection rates which are suitable for specific applications. The performances of Real AdaBoost, Gentle AdaBoost and Modest AdaBoost for face detection are compared in the current work based on video sequences. Real AdaBoost is the generalization of a basic AdaBoost algorithm and is treated as a fundamental boosting algorithm. Gentle AdaBoost is a more robust and stable version of Real AdaBoost. It is shown that Gentle AdaBoost performs slightly better than Real AdaBoost on regular data, and considerably better on noisy data. It is also much more resistant to outliers. Modest AdaBoost is a regularized tradeoff of AdaBoost, mostly aimed at better generalization capability and resistance for certain specific sets of training data.

7.5.2 Experimental Result

The performance of the methods for human face detection and segmentation were evaluated on two video datasets with different illumination conditions. The first test video dataset was recorded under conditions of good brightness. The dataset includes eight subjects (2 Italian, 2 Chinese, 2 Pakistani, 1 Persian, and 1 Canadian) and comprises 520 video clips in total. The second dataset (647 clips in total) consists of commercial films and includes videos available on the Web under complex illumination conditions. Videos in the second dataset also contain single or multiple faces occurring at different sizes, in different poses, and at various positions with respect to each other.

The videos with good lighting conditions were collected for the purpose of human emotion recognition. Each human subject showed the six fundamental human emotional states: happiness, sadness, anger, disgust, fear and surprise. The variations among the emotional states make the face detection task more challenging, since the training images were essentially photographed in the neutral state.

For the training of the face detector, face images and non-face images are collected from the extended Yale Database and CMU Database, which are the publicly available face detection databases with large illumination variations. The detector is trained to detect a face centered in a standard window with a size of 54×48, and all training images are so resized to 54×48 pixels.

For the local normalization method, the nonlinear histogram equalization was applied by taking into account histogram distribution over the local window and combining it with the global histogram distribution. Examples of the filtered results of the original images are shown in Fig. 7.17. By the local normalization, it can be observed from Fig. 7.17 that the histograms of all input images are widely spread to cover the entire gray scale. The distribution of pixels is not too far from uniform. As a result, dark images, the histogram components of which are concentrated at the low end of the gray scales, bright images, the histogram components of which are biased toward the high end, and low contrast images, the histogram components of which are narrow and centered toward the middle of the gray scale, are significantly enhanced to give an appearance of high contrast. By applying local normalization, an image with varying lighting conditions shows a great deal of gray level detail and has a high dynamic range. So the system resistance to natural illumination variation is improved.

Gabor wavelet filters with four scales and eight orientations were applied for feature extraction. For the purpose of training the detector, a total of 15,599 subjects (8,754 positives and 6,845 negatives) were used. The detector was trained through cascade AdaBoost classifiers. Real AdaBoost, Gentle AdaBoost and Modest AdaBoost were compared for error checking with 200 boosting iterations. Gentle AdaBoost returned a better face detection rate, and was selected as the detection algorithm.

For testing, the face detection methods were applied to the two databases, containing various practical aspects in face detection, such as changes in illumination, poses, size and various faces. Figure 7.18 shows the overall performance of the methods using ROC curves. The detection results were obtained by setting the window size of the local normalization to 5×5. The detection method labeled as GW utilized Gabor wavelets features only, and the method labeled as GW + LN used combined features of GW and local normalization. These methods were applied to video data at different illumination conditions. The experimental results demonstrated that the face detection accuracy is considerably improved by about 10–15 % by incorporating local normalization in the critical regions of detection rate vs. false positives. At the same time, false detection rates dropped by approximately 15 %.

Figures 7.19 and 7.20 show the face detection results from video sequences under good illumination conditions and bad illumination conditions. It can be observed that all faces were detected under varying illumination conditions. The size of the bounding box was determined using the scale of the detected face on the image.

Finally, the face detector was applied on the video sequences containing rotating poses, varying sizes, and multiple faces. The detection rates are given in Table 7.2. Columns 2, 3, 4, and 5 indicate video sequences with good illumination conditions,

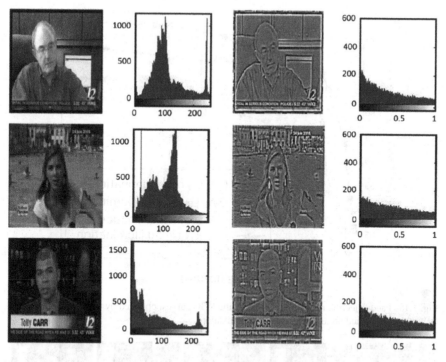

Fig. 7.17 Example images and the application of nonlinear histogram equalization: (*first column*) the original images; (*second column*) histograms of the original images; (*third column*) filtered images; (*forth column*) histograms of the filtered images

Table 7.2 Face detection results for the two testing databases

Methods	Good illumination case (348 samples)	Bad illumination case (427 samples)	Changing head poise/sizes (249 samples)	Multiple faces (143 samples)
GW	87.50	75.25	72.49	70.14
GW + LN	93.74	85.69	89.06	81.38

bad conditions, changing head poses/sizes and multiple faces, respectively. It can be observed that the application of local normalization to the face detection algorithm provides significant improvement in detection rates for all cases discussed.

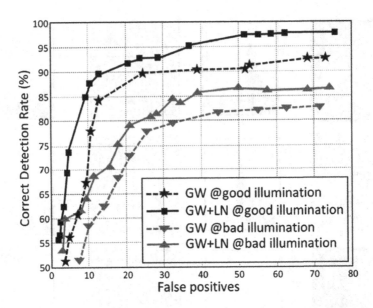

Fig. 7.18 Face detection results, explained by the ROC curves, obtained by the GW method, and GW with LN method under good and bad illumination

Fig. 7.19 Face detection result obtained by the application of the trained face detector to the video frames under good illumination

Fig. 7.20 Face detection result obtained by the application of the trained face detector to the video frames under bad illumination

7.6 Play Event NFL Video Classification Using MPEG-7 and MFCC Features

Most professional sports leagues and teams in North America have a digital channel boasting On-Demand programming and statistics. This requires time consuming post-production work to prepare the highlights of a game.

The Highlights-On-Demand for a game needs a system that can analyze the contents of the broadcast and derive the semantics from the input videos. These semantics can be made available to the users for querying in order to create a true On-Demand experience. This section addresses this issue by presenting an application system to classify American Football (NFL) video shots, using MPEG-7 motion descriptors, and enhancing the indexing capabilities of the system with MPEG-7 audio and Mel Frequency Cepstrum Coefficients (MFCC) features.

Recently, some research has been conducted on automating the process of indexing and annotating sports video streams. Nearly all the major sports have been used to test the indexing and retrieval systems. One of the major projects working on the generation of semantic sports video annotations is the ASSAVID project. As detailed in [213], this project focuses on developing a system that can categorize different types of sports and provides users with an interface to query events in a particular sport.

In [214], audio, textual and visual information are used to classify NFL video into events like touchdowns and field goals. In [215], different types of formations within NFL games were classified using the natural language commentary from the game, the geometrical information about the play and the domain knowledge. In [216], closed caption text and audio visual information were utilized to classify plays into three categories namely: scrimmage, FG/XP and K/P.

The aforementioned works rely on domain knowledge to classify different high level concepts within American football. On the other hand, the video classification system in the current work classifies recurring events of the game without using any domain knowledge. These recurring events are the most basic components of the game. By classifying these basic components first we can look for higher concepts contained within each of the basic events and thus generate a hierarchical graph of concepts which varies from low level to high level. The standard descriptors of MEPG-7 are utilized as the basic feature set. In [217], the author shares proposed applications for generating summary highlights in the sports domain using MPEG-7 motion descriptors, but MPEG-7 audio and motion descriptors have not been used to index recurring events in the American football domain.

7.6.1   Localization of Play Events

Sports have a very well defined structure. They have a set of rules that must be followed in order for the game to be played properly. Many sports such as golf, baseball, bowling and American football have a requirement that the team or players must be in a distinctive position before each play begins. In golf, the player positions himself by the ball in order to hit it in a certain direction. Likewise in American football, the two teams first line up face to face before the ball is snapped to begin the play. The common theme among all these sports is that before the play starts, the level of motion activity in the video is lower compared to when the play has started. This distinction in the motion activity is utilized in the proposed algorithm to segment play events from non-play events. Figure 7.21 shows the magnitude of motion vectors in different types of NFL plays.

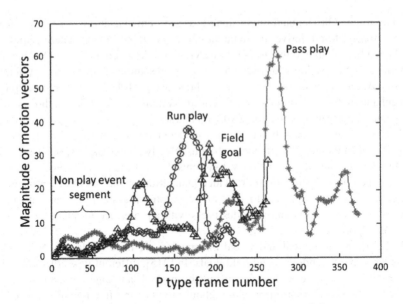

Fig. 7.21 Comparison of motion vector magnitudes for different types of play

7.6.1.1 Play Event Detection Algorithm

The primary objective of the algorithm is to detect the key frame that can be used as the starting point of the play event in the shot. The end point of the play event does not have to be extracted, as in most American football video shots containing play events, the shot usually terminates at the end of the play. In order to extract the intensity of the motion descriptor, MPEG-1 video motion vectors are used. Only the motion vectors from the P frames are analyzed in order to speed up the processing time. In MPEG-7, the motion activity descriptor represents the standard deviation of the motion vector magnitudes within a frame. This is given by the following equation.

$$\sigma_{mv} = \sqrt{\frac{\sum_1^N (MAG_{mv} - \mu_{mv})^2}{N}} \tag{7.42}$$

where MAG_{mv} is the magnitude of the motion vector with coordinates (x, y), and is calculated by $MAG_{mv} = \sqrt{x^2 + y^2}$. μ_{mv} is the mean of the motion vector and is defined as:

$$\mu_{mv} = \frac{\sum_1^N MAG_{mv}}{N} \tag{7.43}$$

where N is the number of macro-blocks that have a motion vector coded in the MPEG-1 stream. The number N varies from frame to frame, as not all the macro-blocks are coded with a motion vector. The two features μ_{mv} and σ_{mv} are used collaboratively in the algorithm to detect the starting point of the play event. In practice, in order to detect the starting point, a set of video shots can be selected from each category, and used to estimate the thresholds for the mean and standard deviation of the motion vectors.

Figure 7.22 shows the flow chart of the algorithm to estimate the frame which represents the starting point of the play event. The following steps detail the algorithm:

Step 1: Find a P frame with a mean value of 4 or higher.

Step 2: Determine the gradient of the mean values within a window (three or four adjacent frames).

Step 3: If the gradients are all positive, mark the frame as a possible starting point, else go back to Step 1.

Step 4: If the intensity of the motion descriptor has a value of 2 or higher, return the frame number as the starting point.

Step 5: Otherwise, determine the gradient of the standard deviation values within a window (three or four adjacent frames).

Step 6: If the gradients are all positive, return the frame number as the starting point, else go back to Step 1.

7.6.1.2   Evaluation of Play Event Detection Algorithm

The play event detection algorithm was tested on the American football video shot database which consists of 200 video shots taken from 4 different games and 4 different networks. In order to measure the performance of the algorithm, we have to establish some ground truths about the starting point of the play event within each video shot. This was accomplished by having an observer manually index the frame number which best represented the start point of the play event.

Comparison of results was done by getting the delta between the ground truth frame number and the frame number estimated by the algorithm. The results still needed to be evaluated in terms of what this delta meant in actual time domain. That is, we need to determine if the algorithm is estimating a starting point too early or if it is estimating the starting point after a certain amount of delay.

Since MPEG-1 video has a frame rate of 30 frames/s, building a histogram with a bin size of 30 frames would give a general idea of how far apart the estimated frame numbers are from the ground truth in actual time domain. Figure 7.23 shows a histogram of the number of shots within each time unit. Negative time units represent early detection and positive time units represent a delayed detection.

From Fig. 7.23, we can see that the algorithm detects the starting points of the play with 83 % accuracy. That is, 166 of the 200 video shots in the database had the starting points detected within ± 1 s of the original starting point. The accuracy of the algorithm can be increased to 86.5 % by increasing the window size from three

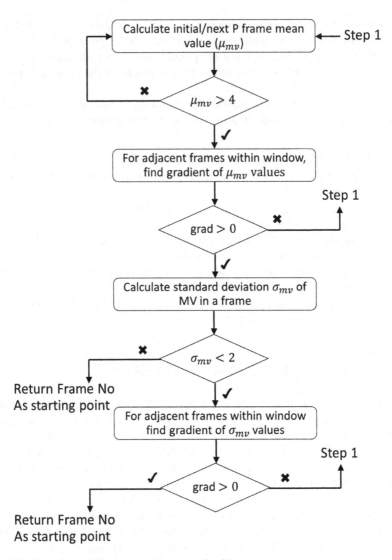

Fig. 7.22 Flow chart of the play event detection algorithm

to four frames. But this change in window size has its side effects. By increasing the window size, we are looking for motion activity being sustained for a longer period of time, which means we will get more shots with delayed detection.

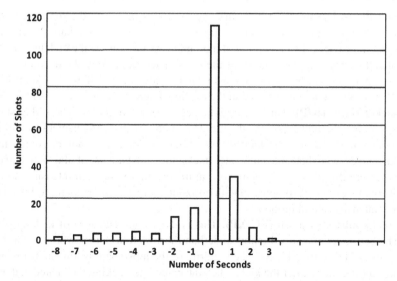

Fig. 7.23 A histogram of the number of shots within each time unit. Negative time units represent early detection and positive time units represent a delayed detection

7.6.2   Classification of American Football Events

In the domain of American football, visual or motion features play a significantly dominant role in discriminating between different types of plays as evident from Fig. 7.21. Therefore first we evaluate the efficacy of using motion descriptors for an American football video indexing system and then we evaluate the changes in system performance by adding audio descriptors and MFCC features.

7.6.2.1   Motion Feature Mapping

The motivation behind using the motion descriptors was due to the fact that in American football, the global motion between different types of plays provides a variety of clues. In order to understand fully the difference in motion between the plays, first we require a detailed explanation of the general motion involved in the plays:

1. **Pass Plays**: During a pass play, first the motion is lateral in order to track the movements of a quarterback who is going to throw the ball. Then it is followed by rapid zoom out and followed by a lateral movement to follow the throw. At the end of the play the motion is tracking the player to whom the ball was thrown. Therefore, the movements for a pass play involve first low intensity lateral movement followed by high intensity zoom out and lateral movement and then in the end low intensity lateral movement.

2. **Run Plays**: During a run play, first the motion is lateral as the runner gets the ball. Then the camera zooms in, to track the movements of the ball carrier. This zoom in provides the perception of high intensity motion. At the end, the camera laterally tracks the movements of the ball carrier. Therefore, the movements of a run play involve firstly low intensity lateral movement, followed by short high intensity lateral movement and in the cud low intensity lateral movement.

3. **Kickoff/Punt (K/P)**: This is the first category of kicking play. The kicker starts by kicking the ball high into the air. This motion causes the camera to rapidly zoom out to capture the kicked ball. After the kick, the camera zooms into the player who has the ball, and tracks the movements of the ball carrier. Therefore this play has movements that involve firstly the high intensity motion of zooming out and zooming in with horizontal direction movement, followed by low intensity lateral motions.

4. **Field goal/Extra point (FG/XP)**: This is the second category of kicking play. The ball is long snapped (short underhand throw) to a holder who sets the ball up to be kicked by a kicker. The majority of the movement is low intensity with most of it coming after the kick, when the camera is tracking the kicked ball as it sails towards the goal post. Therefore the majority of motion in this category is vertical and low intensity.

The global motion of camera, the intensity of motion and the direction of motion provide valuable discriminating information regarding the different types of plays. In the current work, the motion based feature set is developed by utilizing the intensity of the motion descriptor and dominant direction descriptor in MPEG-7. The motivation behind using a combination of the two descriptors comes from analyzing the different plays as defined above.

The magnitude of motion vectors was calculated by extracting the encoded motion vector given by coordinates (x, y) from the macro blocks within P frames of the MPEG-1 video stream. The magnitude and the direction of the motion vector are given by the following equations:

$$MAG_{mv} = \sqrt{x^2 + y^2} \tag{7.44}$$

$$\Theta_{mv} = \arctan\left(\frac{y}{x}\right) \tag{7.45}$$

According to the MPEG-7 description [218], the standard deviation of the magnitude of the motion vectors can be used to derive the intensity of the motion descriptor. The descriptor takes on the value of 1–5, with a low value meaning a low intensity of motion. Experiments done by using five levels showed that most of the motion descriptors were quantized into two or three levels. Thus to provide better motion activity resolution, the descriptor was quantized into 12 levels. Similarly, according to the MEPG-7 description, the dominant direction descriptor is calculated by quantizing the angles of the motion vectors into 8 levels. In this work, the same eight quantization levels were used to define the dominant direction descriptor.

Fig. 7.24 Motion feature map

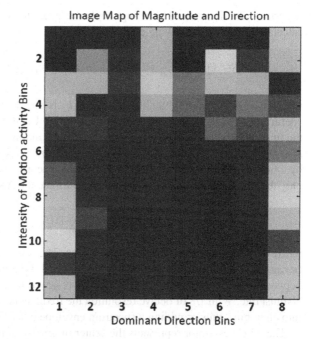

A 2D feature map is created by combining the two motion activity descriptors. The motivation behind this is to create a feature set that can model both the intensity of motion and the direction of motion, thus discriminating between high intensity motion in the upward direction versus high intensity motion in the lateral direction. As can be seen from Fig. 7.24, the feature map provides a unique representation of only 12×8 dimensions for both the intensity and direction of motion. In the feature map, blue color corresponds to low values and red color corresponds to high values.

7.6.2.2 Audio Features Mapping

The motivation behind using audio descriptors is due to the fact that most sports have a certain vocabulary associated with each event. Almost all the announcers will utilize some of the vocabulary to describe similar events. Therefore we wanted a compact representation of audio characteristics to describe the general tone and pitch of the announcer. The objective is to analyze the similarity in the spoken sounds between similar events.

Three MPEG-7 basic spectral audio features were used to achieve our objective, namely: Audio Spectrum Envelope (ASE), Audio Spectrum Centroid (ASC) and Audio Spectrum Flatness (ASF).

The ASE descriptor represents the power spectrum of an audio signal and can be calculated by taking the Fast Fourier transform (FFT) of the audio signal which is windowed using a Hamming window with an overlap of 50 % between adjacent windows. The size of the Hamming window is taken to be 10 ms. This descriptor is calculated using the following equation [220]:

$$S(l,k) = \sum_{n=0}^{N-1} s(n+lM)w(n)\exp\left(-j(\frac{2\pi}{N})nk\right) \tag{7.46}$$

where $s(n)$ is the original audio signal, $S(l,k)$ is the short time Fourier transform coefficient, N is the size of the transformed signal, k is the frequency bin index, l is the time audio frame index, $w(n)$ is the analysis window function of length lw and M is the hop size. The short time Fourier transform $S(l,k)$ needs to be normalized by a factor of N in order to preserve Parseval's Theorem and since ASE represents only the power spectrum, therefore we can estimate the ASE descriptor as follows:

$$ASE(l,k) = \frac{1}{\alpha \cdot N}|S(l,k)|^2 \tag{7.47}$$

where α is the window normalization factor. The number of frequency bins can be varied based on the octave resolution required. One bin is reserved for power between 0 and 62.5 Hz, while another one is reserved for power between 8 kHz and Nyquist rate. With 1/8 of octave resolution the frequencies in the middle are divided into eight bins, thus providing a spectrum envelope consisting of ten bins.

The ASC descriptor represents the center of gravity of the power spectrum. This is calculated by adding the energy in each frequency bin in the FFT spectrum and dividing it by the total energy in the frame, as shown below:

$$ASC(l) = \frac{\sum_{k=0}^{K-1} k \cdot |ASE(l,k)|^2}{\sum_{k=0}^{K-1} |ASE(l,k)|^2} \tag{7.48}$$

where k is the frequency bin's index. The descriptor shows which frequencies are dominant in the spectrum.

The ASF descriptor represents the overall tonal component in the power spectrum of the audio signal. It is calculated by calculating the geometric mean of the audio frame and dividing it by the arithmetic mean of the audio frame, as shown by the equation:

$$ASF(l) = \frac{\left(\prod_{k=0}^{K-1} |ASE(l,k)|^2\right)^{\frac{1}{N}}}{\frac{1}{N}\sum_{k=0}^{K-1} |ASE(l,k)|^2} \tag{7.49}$$

where k is the frequency bin's index and N is the size of the short time Fourier transform window.

All the above descriptors were quantized into 10 levels, thus providing a feature set of 30 dimensions.

7.6.2.3   MFCC Feature Mapping

Due to the fact that most of the video shots contained a lot of crowd noise, and our wish to extract the perceived rhythm and sound of the spoken content, we needed a feature that could model the human hearing and also works well under noisy conditions. MFCC has been used extensively in speech recognition systems, as it tries to emphasize the frequencies that are more perceptible to the human ear.

First the audio file is pre-processed in order to remove the silent segments. Then 13 MFCC coefficients are extracted for each segment. Each of the segments have 50 % overlap, and thus there is lot of redundancy between adjacent MFCC values. In order to reduce the dimension of the matrix, the MFCC values are passed to a feature reduction stage. The MFCC features are reduced to a 12×64 matrix.

7.6.3   *Experimental Results*

Fisher's Linear Discriminant Analysis (LDA) is employed as a classification scheme to evaluate the efficacy of the feature set. In a specific sense, LDA also commonly refers to techniques in which a transformation is done in order to maximize between-class separability and minimize within-class variability. LDA works on the feature set with no prior assumptions about the nature of the data set. It tries to compute a weight vector $\mathbf{w}$, which when multiplied by the input feature vector $\mathbf{x}$ would generate discriminant functions $g_i(\mathbf{x})$. For C class problems, we define C discriminant functions $g_1(\mathbf{x}), g_2(\mathbf{x}), \ldots, g_C(\mathbf{x})$. The feature vector $\mathbf{x}$ is assigned to a class whose discriminant function is the largest value of $\mathbf{x}$.

All the results were based on Fisher's LDA classification technique. In order to minimize the bias of the sample set, leave-one-out classification was implemented. With this method, one sample from the database sample set is removed and used as the test set. The classifier is trained with the rest of the samples. This process is repeated with each sample in the database. This process ensures that classification scheme does not contain bias due to the sample set size [219].

Feature selection was also performed using Wilk's Lambda criterion in order to optimize the feature space. The dimension of the feature space was large and some of the features did not enhance discrimination between classes. Therefore, in the feature selection phase, the features that provided redundancy and deteriorated the performance of the overall classification accuracy were taken out of the equation.

The test database consists of 200 video shots with durations varying from 5 s to about 25 s. In the database, there are 88 pass plays, 67 run plays and 45 kicking plays. A total of eight different teams were used to create the database from four

Table 7.3 Play event classification results, obtained by multiple feature types

Play category	MPEG-7 audio + MFCC	MPEG-7 motion + audio	MPEG-7 motion + MFCC	MPEG-7 motion + audio + MFCC
Pass	70.0 %	85.2 %	85.2 %	94.3 %
Run	59.7 %	91.0 %	92.5 %	89.6 %
FG/XP	75.0 %	87.5 %	87.5 %	93.8 %
K/P	69.0 %	82.8 %	82.8 %	93.1 %
Overall	*67.0 %*	*87.0 %*	*87.5 %*	*92.5 %*

Table 7.4 Play event classification results, obtained by three sets of features, based on motion combined with other modalities

Method	Pass	Run	EG/XP	K/P
MPEG-7 motion	79.5 %	92.5 %	87.5 %	65.5 %
MPEG-7 motion + audio	85.2 %	91.0 %	87.5 %	82.8 %
MPEG7 motion + audio + MFCC	94.3 %	89.6 %	93.8 %	93.1 %

different networks. This variety in the database ensured that the sample space of the current work was diverse and included all the major broadcasters.

Table 7.3, shows the indexing results of using MPEG-7 motion and audio descriptors along with MFCC features. From table, we can see the classification accuracy increased with the combining of multi-modal features. In the case of combining the MPEG-7 audio with MFCC features, we see an overall increase of 10 %, while combining the audio features with motion descriptor features shows an increase of 5 %. Combining all three features produces an overall classification result of 92.5 %.

Combining multi-modal features in a reasonable fashion can enhance the classification. But always there are trade-offs that need to be considered. Some features may reduce the accuracy of classification of a particular category but may enhance the overall performance of the system. Table 7.4 shows the variations in classification that results from adding audio features to the motion features.

7.7   Summary

The chapter covers a broad spectrum of video segmentation, indexing, retrieval, and classification techniques applicable to news and sports videos. Based on the energy histogram of DCT coefficients, a shot detection algorithm for MPEG video data in the compressed domain can be developed. The detection results can be enhanced by using the ratio between two sliding windows to attenuate the low-pass filtered frame distances. The advantage is in achieving high detection rates with low computational complexity. In a subsequent process, news videos can be segmented into shot, group-of-shots, and story levels, where the template frequency model can be applied to capture the spatio-temporal information. This facilitates video retrieval via a multiple-level database access technique, which is highly desirable for news-on-demand applications.

To enhance the robustness of video object segmentation, histograms of oriented gradients may be incorporated into the conventional Graph Cut algorithm. This leads to a new way of enhancing video segmentation accuracy, thereby incorporating a shape prior into the algorithm for segmentation of pre-trained objects such as humans.

In addition, the chapter presents an effective and robust method for detecting faces in video sequences based on a coarse-to-fine strategy. A local normalization technique is incorporated into a conventional face detector to alleviate the illumination variation problem. It is demonstrated that the method can improve the face detection rate and reduce the processing time. Compared with face detection without local normalization, the current method has the following advantages: it alleviates illumination variation problems, decreases computing time, locates faces automatically on single frames to eliminate the manual initiation step, and is able to detect a variety of faces reliably.

Finally, the indexing of NFL video using MPEG-7 descriptors is presented. The current work develops a system with two main components. The first component finds the starting points on play events within a video shot. The second component is responsible for indexing and classifying events in American football. Both the components of the system utilize MPEG-7 motion descriptors, while MPEG-7 audio and MFCC features are added to enhance the indexing capabilities of the system.

Chapter 8
Adaptive Retrieval in a P2P Cloud Datacenter

Abstract This chapter presents indexing and retrieval methods for image and video on cloud datacenters. The application is based on a peer-to-peer (P2P) network in both structured and unstructured network organizations. Firstly, a cluster-identification search system is developed on the Chord layers to organize nodes as a structured peer-to-peer network. The system derives automatic clustering for the organization of nodes in a distributed hash table for effective node searching and retrieval of multimedia objects. Secondly, pseudo-relevance feedback using the self-organizing tree map is implemented for image database retrieval on a P2P network. The query processing is carried out on an unstructured P2P network, through the discovery of a community of neighbors and by performing automatic retrieval within the nodes of the community. Thirdly, based on the unstructured P2P network, the adaptive cosine network is also implemented for video database retrieval.

8.1 Introduction

In a cloud datacenter, multimedia objects are distributed over the nodes in an overlay network. The searching of these objects requires a large number of query transactions. Retrieval of a particular multimedia object involves finding the relevant nodes owning objects potentially relevant to the query, concatenating relevant objects, and obtaining a shortlist of relevant objects in an accurate manner. In this regard, automation is highly appropriate for clustering multimedia objects and indexing nodes in a distributed hash table (DHT) for computing in a cloud network. In addition, for achieving accurate re-ranking of multimedia objects, automatic clustering offers pseudo labeling used by the relevance feedback process. This further minimizes bandwidth since the transferring of training files can be avoided.

This chapter starts with a presentation of a peer-to-peer (P2P) architecture of a distributed database system in Sect. 8.2, and a presentation of the cluster-identification search system (CSS) in Sect. 8.3. The (CSS) organizes the nodes in the network as a structured P2P network. It involves the process of partitioning multimedia objects into disjoint groups, using a self-organizing tree map (SOTM). Here, the performance of cluster discovery depends on two key factors: the number of clusters and the topology of node-vectors. The automatic clustering allows the partition of nodes on the network in the DHT and Chord layers, according to the

© Springer International Publishing Switzerland 2014

P. Muneesawang et al., *Multimedia Database Retrieval: Technology and Applications*,
Multimedia Systems and Applications, DOI 10.1007/978-3-319-11782-9_8

cluster identification. This indexing stage facilitates online search by pinpointing the relevant nodes without traversing all the participating nodes. Subsequently, improvement of retrieval can be accomplished using relevance feedback within the relevant nodes.

As an alternative to the structured P2P network, Sect. 8.4 presents an unstructured P2P network. This is realized by the discovery of a community of neighbors and performing automatic retrieval within nodes of the community. The search is done by an incremental process of P2P retrieval whereby the relevant node performs pseudo-RF and forwards the modified query to its neighbors. The system continuously increases retrieval accuracy without transferring training samples over the network during adaptive searching.

Section 8.5 presents pseudo-RF for video retrieval, by firstly discovering the neighborhood community, followed by re-ranking videos via a three-layer cosine network. The retrieval process is adaptive via intra- and inter-peer signal propagation, which can achieve high retrieval accuracy while minimizing network resources.

8.2   Distributed Database System

8.2.1   Cloud Datacenter

A cloud datacenter enhances capabilities in distributed storage and retrieval [227–230]. In order to establish high-performance datacenters for searching large volumes of multimedia data, an appropriate topology must be chosen. The datacenter architecture can be categorized into two types: centralized and distributed.

A centralized system, as offered by most commercial cloud services, maintains central nodes to handle the query requests. Upon retrieving the relevant multimedia objects according to the feature similarity measures, the universal content locator (URL) will be returned to the requesting host. The actual content will be transferred directly from the content server to the requesting host. The centralized systems keep the entire feature descriptor database in centralized servers. The real multimedia content may or may not be located on the same server. The centralized system retrieves relevant content based on the feature-descriptor database. The drawback of a centralized system is its limited scalability for handling growing volumes of retrieval requests and larger multimedia databases.

In order to provide better scalability and adaptability, decentralized systems are designed according to the Peer-to-Peer (P2P) paradigm. Each node in the P2P based datacenter acts both as a client for requesting multimedia objects and a server for re-distributing the multimedia objects. Since a peer can join and leave the network at any time, a challenge of using of such a distributed retrieval system is to address the non-guaranteed level of service of the P2P network. To localize the search, the query packet is always associated with certain Time-to-Live (TTL) levels. Database storage on distributed servers has been utilized in the industry to provide high availability (continuous service if one or more servers are unintentionally out of service) and efficiency (access from the geographically closest server). P2P network is a special case of such a network, where each node in the network behaves as a database server.

8.2.2 Application of a Multimedia Retrieval System in a P2P Datacenter

Figure 8.1 shows the application of a multimedia retrieval system in a P2P datacenter using centralized and decentralized architectures. In this system, content providers can be cloud providers or cloud customers. The providers transfer files including images, videos, and plain text into datacenters from any device, such as smart phone, tablet computer, or other lightweight device. The search starts with the cloud customer issuing a query request. The datacenter receives the query and takes charge of search processing and the query results are sent back to the customer. In the cloud datacenter, when a peer has a file to share, it makes it available to the rest of the peers. This file may be copied to some interested peers, and become available to the group. Since lists of peers may grow and shrink, the challenge is to locate files and keep track of the locations of the files.

In a centralized P2P network, as shown in Fig. 8.1a, the search directory (listing of the peers and what they offer) is centralized, but the storing and serving of files are done using the P2P paradigm. For this reason, a centralized P2P network, such as Napster [221] is referred to as a hybrid P2P network. In this type of network, a peer first registers itself with a server, and sends a list of all the files to the server. A cloud customer looking for a file goes to the server and issues a query. The server searches its directory and responds with the IP addresses of the peers that are sharing the file. The cloud customer then contacts one of the peers and downloads the file directly. The search index is constantly updated as nodes join or leave the peer. This offers greater simplicity in the maintenance of the search directory. However, using centralized networks has some drawbacks, such as the accessing of the search index generating a huge traffic load which slows down the system.

Figure 8.1b, c shows a decentralized P2P network that does not depend on a centralized directory system. In this model, peers arrange themselves into an *overlay network* as either an unstructured (Fig. 8.1b) or a structured (Fig. 8.1c) logical network. An unstructured P2P network has nodes that are linked randomly, whereas a structured P2P network has nodes that are linked according to a predefined set of rules for efficient query routing. The unstructured P2P network, such as Gnutella [222], works by broadcasting the query with non-zero Time-To-Live (TTL) to all the neighboring hosts. It may find a node with the desired file after a few levels of search in the network. However, the system causes a lot of network flooding during a query [223]. In Sects. 8.4 and 8.5, the retrieval system adopts an unstructured P2P network using a strategy of searching within the neighborhood community. This community

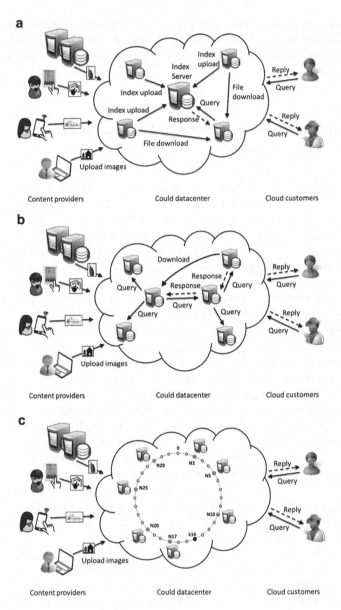

Fig. 8.1 Multimedia retrieval system applied in a P2P datacenter. (**a**) Centralized P2P network. (**b**) Unstructured P2P network. (**c**) Structured P2P network

is a list of peers that have similar image/video categories. The construction of a table of neighbors in the community allows minimum network traffic when conduct a repeat search.

A structured P2P network, as shown in Fig. 8.1c, uses a DHT to link nodes so that a query can be effectively and efficiently resolved. This will be discussed in the following section.

8.3 Adaptive Image Retrieval in a Self-organizing Chord P2P Network

8.3.1 System Architecture

In a distributed system, images are located at participating nodes across the network. It is impractical for an image query to traverse all the participating nodes due to the high communication cost. Thus, one way to make a distributed search system efficient is by performing a pre-computation, a *search index* before queries are made. While answering quires, these indices can be used to precisely locate the nodes serving the matching images without having to communicate with all the nodes.

Instead of storing the entire index in one server, a distributed indexing system distributes the index to multiple nodes in the network. Thus, the challenge is finding the right scheme to partition the index across the nodes in the network. A solution is to partition indexes by *cluster identifications* (IDs) of an image and store all index entries of a given cluster ID on a specific node. In this scheme, a user searches for images using the cluster ID of a query image, while the system utilizes the cluster ID as a *key*. To process a query, the system needs to fetch the image list for the key from the network. Once the list has arrived, the images that appear in the list are the matching images for the query.

This section presents the Cluster-identification Search System (CSS), that generates index entries with *cluster ID* as a key. Figure 8.2 shows the overview of the CSS, which proceeds in two stages, indexing and query processing. Due to its simplicity and elegant approach to routing queries, the Chord protocol [226] is selected to implement the system. The processing is conducted between the application layer and the DHT layer. In the indexing stage in Fig. 8.2a, each node has a local image database to be shared with other nodes. The image feature extractor accesses each image in the local database and then performs mapping via SOTM (discussed in Chap. 3). This results in a cluster ID of the best matched SOTM cluster. The mapping provides an index entry $< clusID$, URL$>$ for the input image, where *clusID* is the cluster ID, and the URL contains IP addresses, port numbers, and image names of the owner node. It also applies to all images in the local database, resulting in index entries corresponding to various cluster IDs. All index entries for a given cluster ID will be stored on a particular node. The node is chosen by hashing the cluster ID, using a hashing function and Chord. Specifically, the command put(key, data) is the application programing interface (API) that lets the application layer put a data item (i.e., index entry) in the nodes in the P2P network. DHash layer works by associating the keys with data items in the nodes.

A put call first uses Chord to map a node using the lookup service, and does a put in its local index storage using the cluster ID as the key.

In Fig. 8.2b, users search for image files using cluster IDs extracted from a query image, where one query image may be characterized by more than one cluster ID. A set of cluster IDs are obtained by self-organized mapping of the query feature vector. A get call uses Chord to map the Cluster ID to a node, and does a get in its local database using the cluster ID as the key. The image list (i.e., index entries) for each cluster ID is then fetched from the network and the system aggregates the results. The query node sorts the results list using a similarity measurement between the query vector and the feature vectors list, and returns the top matching images to the user. Furthermore, the adaptive retrieval method is used for relevance feedback of the initial retrieval set and improves the ranking result.

8.3.2   Indexing of Nodes and Data Items on the Distributed Hash Table

A DHT distributes data among a set of nodes to allow each peer to become responsible for a range of data items. Each peer has partial knowledge about the network, and this knowledge will allow the network to route the queries about the data items to the responsible nodes using efficient and scalable procedures. The DHT utilizes a circular ring for indexing of nodes and data items. Each data item or a peer is mapped to a point in a large address space of size 2^m, where $m = 160$, i.e., m-bit integer. A node on the network is indexed by a node identification (ID),

$$\text{node ID} = \text{hash}(\text{peer IP address}) \tag{8.1}$$

by using a mathematical hash function. A data object to be shared is also hashed to an m-bit integer,

$$\text{key} = \text{hash}(\text{Object ID}) \tag{8.2}$$

This object is related to the pair (key, data), where data is the data itself or a reference to the data object.

In the CSS, as illustrated in Fig. 8.2, when a node wants to share an image, the feature vector of the image is first extracted. Then, the SOTM is applied to map the feature vector to the cluster ID. The mapping is denoted by: $\mathbb{R}^d \to Z$, from the real-d dimensional vector to an integer. Then the cluster ID is hashed and an index message is sent to the node responsible for the ID through the DHT layer.

Let $\mathscr{C} = \{\mathbf{w}_i | \mathbf{w}_i \in \mathbb{R}^d, \ i = 1, 2, \ldots, C\}$ be the set of SOTM weight vectors $\mathbf{w}_i$ previously generated. For an input feature vector $\mathbf{f}_v \in \mathbb{R}^d$, its corresponding cluster ID is constructed by:

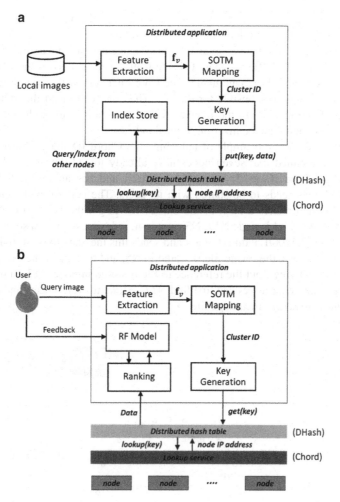

Fig. 8.2 Overview of CSS, which proceeds in two stages, (**a**) indexing and (**b**) query processing. Each peer has CSS, DHash, and Chord layers. Peers communicate with each other using asynchronous remote procedure calls

$$clusID = Q(\mathbf{f}_v) = \arg\min_i (\|\mathbf{f}_v - \mathbf{w}_i\|) \tag{8.3}$$

where $Q(\mathbf{f}_v)$ is the mapping function. To construct the key for this data object, the consistent hash function SHA1 is employed,

$$key = \text{SHA1}(clusID) \tag{8.4}$$

This distributes indexes as symmetrically as possible on the Chord ID space in order to keep the load balanced. In this way, if $\mathbf{f}_{v1}$ and $\mathbf{f}_{v2}$ are the feature vectors of two similar images, i.e., $\mathbf{f}_{v1} \cong \mathbf{f}_{v2}$, Eq. (8.3) will quantize them into the same cluster: $Q(\mathbf{f}_{v1}) = Q(\mathbf{f}_{v2})$. They will have the same hash value.

After the key of an image is obtained, the system can construct an index entry in the form of $< \text{key}, \mathbf{f}_v, \text{URL} >$, where $\mathbf{f}_v$ is the feature vector; URL is the IP address, the port address, and the image name. The Chord network will forward this index message to the node responsible for the key. The node will insert this index entry into its local storage, where the indexes with the same key are gathered into the same list to facilitate the localization of local indexes.

Figure 8.3 shows an example of indexing on a Chord ID space of size 2^5, i.e., $m = 5$. It is assumed that seven nodes have already joined the group. The node N5 is assigned the ID as $5 = \text{hash}(18.175.6.2)$, and has an image file named "Landmark" that needs to be shared with its peers. The node uses the cluster ID of the image and makes a hash of the cluster ID, to get the key $= 14$. Since the closest node to key 14 is node N17, N5 creates an index message $<\text{hash}(clusID), \mathbf{f}_v,$ http://18.175.6.2:5200/Landmark.jpg> and sends this message to be stored in node N17. In other words, the image file is stored in N5, and the key of the file is k14 (a point in the DHT ring), but the reference to file is stored in node N17. In the query processing state, other nodes can first find N17, extract the references, and then use the references to access the image file.

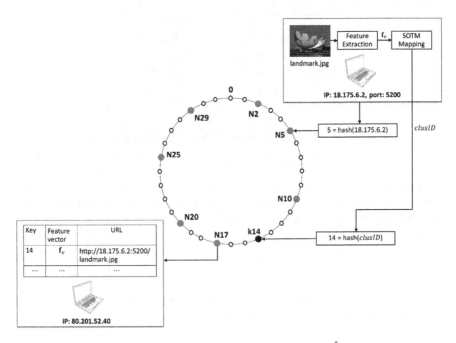

Fig. 8.3 Indexing of nodes and data items on a Chord ID space of size 2^5

8.3.3 Query Processing on the P2P Network

8.3.3.1 Query Indexing

In the query processing stage (cf. Fig. 8.2b), the query feature vector is mapped into the SOTM, similarly as in the indexing stage. However, the multiple-cluster mapping method is employed here to improve retrieval accuracy. Figure 8.4 illustrates a simplified example of dividing data samples (represented in dots) into six clusters, where the cluster centers are denoted by crossed-circles. If the query image (represented as a triangle) is located close to the boundary between multiple clusters, retrieval precision drops if the search is done for only the closest cluster. As shown in Fig. 8.4, relevant images may reside under multiple clusters (such as the samples covered by the circle surrounding the query). Therefore, if the query image is located at equal or nearly equal distance to multiple cluster centers, multiple clusters should be chosen to avoid a significant degradation in the retrieval precision.

When a node issues a query, it converts the query image to a set of cluster IDs, and then sends the query message to the nodes responsible for the cluster IDs. In order to obtain the cluster IDs for the query, a multiple-cluster mapping denoted by: $\mathbb{R}^d \to Z^k$ is employed. This is done by vector quantization of the query feature vector, $\mathbf{f}_q$:

$$Q(\mathbf{f}_q) = \{clusID_1, clusID_2, \ldots, clusID_k\} \qquad (8.5)$$

where $clusID_1$ is the closest (winning) cluster to the query, i.e.,

$$clusID_1 \equiv \arg\min_i \left(\|\mathbf{f}_q - \mathbf{w}_i\| \right) \qquad (8.6)$$

and $clusID_2$ and $clusID_k$ are respectively the cluster ID of the second and the k-th neighbor of the winning cluster.

Afterwards, the node sends the query messages in the form of $<$ key$_i$, IP address $>$, where $i = 1, 2, \ldots, k$, and key$_i$ is obtained by:

$$\text{key}_i = \text{SHA1}(clusID_i), i = 1, 2, \ldots, k \qquad (8.7)$$

Using the query routing scheme in the Chord, each query message is only forwarded to the node responsible for the keys. The number of query messages depends on the parameter k. Increasing k also expands the number of clusters that are close to the query, and thus, increase the probabilities of finding the relevant images.

Figure 8.5 shows the precision results as a function of k, the number of clusters selected for an indexing query in Eq. (8.5). The database was the Corel database [224], containing 40,000 images. Each image was characterized by color histogram, color moment, Gabor wavelet for texture, and Fourier descriptor, as discussed in Chap. 2 (Table 2.7). The application of SOTM resulted in 233 clusters (the number of clusters was automatically generated) [359]. The figure shows the average

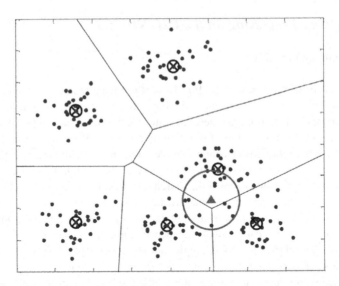

Fig. 8.4 Example illustrating cluster selection for a query

precision of searching 20 query images selected from Boeing airplanes and Bonsai classes. The result shows that the precision increased with the number of clusters, k. However, after $k = 8$, there was no improvement at all. It is also observed that, beyond $k \geq 8$, all the additional similarity matching efforts (i.e., up to approximately 90 % of all images) are wasted. Figure 8.6 shows the number of total images (i.e., search space) belonging to these clusters. It is observed that the number of images continuously increased as k increased.

8.3.3.2   Routing of Query

In order to facilitate routing queries, the Chord offers an identifier space of size 2^m. This space is used to distribute data items and nodes in a circle in a clockwise direction, as illustrated in Fig. 8.3 for $m = 5$. The identifier of a data item is referred to as k (for *key*) and the identifier of a peer is referred to as N (for *node*). The closest peer with $N \geq k$ is called the successor of k, and hosts the index entry $< k, \mathbf{f}_v, \text{URL} >$ in which k is the key (hash of *clusID* of an image), and URL is the data containing information about the peer server that has the image.

To find an image that has the same cluster as a query (a relevant image), a peer needs to know the node that is responsible for that image: the peer that stores the index entry (a reference to that image). As discussed previously, a peer that is the successor of a key in the ring is the responsible peer for the key. Let us define the function successor(k) as the node identifier of the first actual node following k around the circle clockwise. Finding the responsible node is actually finding the successor of a key. For example, in Fig. 8.3, successor(k14) = N17.

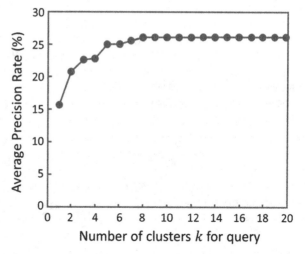

Fig. 8.5 Average precision rate, obtained for different numbers of clusters, k, for a query

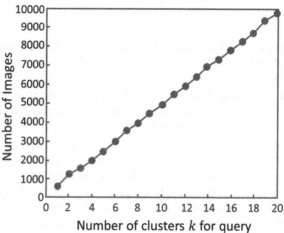

Fig. 8.6 Total number of images to be searched as a function of k

In order to find the successor of a given key, each node has a routing table called a *finger table*. The finger table has multiple columns; two of them represent the target key and the successor of the target key. The target key at row i is $N + 2^{i-1}$, where N is the current node. Figure 8.7 shows an example of nodes with the finger tables on the identifier space of size 2^5. The table size is a maximum of m rows, and the first row ($i = 1$) gives the node successor. In addition, the table also has a predecessor node ID that is used to identify the node previous to the current node.

To find the successor of a key, the system performs the *lookup* operation, as outlined in Fig. 8.8. If the node is responsible for the key, it returns its own ID; otherwise, it needs to help other nodes find the predecessor of a key. The node firstly searches its finger table to find another node that is closer to the predecessor node than itself. It then passes the duty of finding the predecessor node to the other node. The task is forwarded from node to node until the predecessor node of the

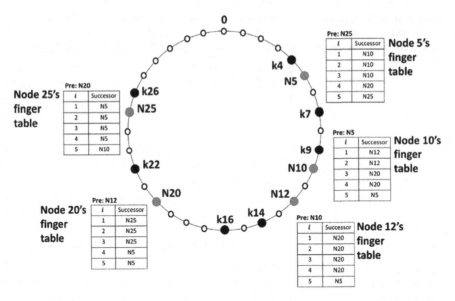

Fig. 8.7 A set of nodes and keys arranged on the 32 node identifier space, and examples of the finger tables. "Pre" is an abbreviation for "predecessor"

key is found. Let N and x be the objects in the object-oriented programing, which respectively represent the current node and the next node. The node x is closer to the predecessor node of the key than node N. The lookup operation contains three functions as shown in Fig. 8.8. At the current node, N, the "find closest predecessor" function finds the closest predecessor of the key by searching N's finger table. Searching uses the for-loop lookup table starting from the m-th row down to 1. Once the closest predecessor is found, the next node, x is set to the closest predecessor (i.e., $x = \text{finger}[i]$). The "find predecessor" function checks if the key is in between this node and its successor (i.e., key $\in (x, x.\text{finger}[1])$). If this is true, x is the predecessor of the key. Otherwise, the procedure jumps back to the first function to search for the closest predecessor again in the finger table of x (the current node). Finally, the "find successor" function will take the predecessor ID from the previous function and obtain the ID of the successor node of the key (i.e., $x.\text{finger}[1]$).

An example of the lookup procedure is as follows. Assume that the current node is N10 in Fig. 8.7, and needs to find the responsible node for k = 22. Node N10 searches its finger table, and the "find closest predecessor" function returns N12. However, N12 is not the predecessor of k22 since k22 $\notin$ (N12, N20). The system then sets N12 as the current node to find the closest predecessor of k22. This time the "find closest predecessor" function returns N20. Node N20 is in fact the predecessor of k22 since k22 $\in$ (N20, N25]. The "find predecessor" function passes this information to the "find successor" function. The system then returns the finger[1] of N20, which is N25, the successor of k22.

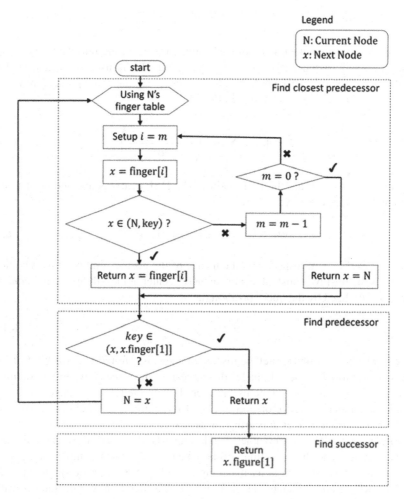

Fig. 8.8 The Lookup operation, which takes the key as an input and outputs the node ID responsible for the key

8.3.3.3   Single- and Multi-Click Relevance Feedback

For each $key_i, i \in \{1,2,\ldots,k\}$ of the query, the Chord layer returns the responsible node IDs, and thus, the query messages are only forwarded to these nodes by the DHT layer. Each of the responsible nodes checks the local index storage to find a list of index entries corresponding to the given key, and replies to the query node. After the query node receives all the results corresponding to key_i, $i = 1,2,\ldots,k$, it merges the results and performs a similarity measurement. The system computes the ranking of data items by calculating similarity scores between $\mathbf{f}_q$ and $\mathbf{f}_v$, where $v = 1,2,\ldots,V$, and V is the total number of data items. The top-T indexes are chosen, and the corresponding image files are transferred from the data owner to the query node.

The relevance feedback is employed for re-ranking of the retrieved images, by using the single-radial basis function (RBF) method (discussed in Chap. 2). The similarity between the RBF center $\mathbf{c} = [c_1, \ldots, c_i, \ldots c_P]^t$ and the input feature vector $\mathbf{f}_v = [f_{v1}, \ldots, f_{vi}, \ldots f_{vP}]^t$, is computed by:

$$S(\mathbf{c}, \mathbf{f}_v) = \sum_{i=1}^{P} \exp\left(\frac{-(c_i - f_{vi})^2}{2\sigma_i^2}\right) \tag{8.8}$$

where $\sigma_i, i = 1, \ldots, P$ are the RBF widths. The RBF center is updated prior to the computation of $S(\mathbf{c}, \mathbf{f}_v)$ by:

$$\mathbf{c}(t+1) = \bar{F}^+ + \alpha_N\left(\mathbf{c}(t) - \bar{F}^-\right) \tag{8.9}$$

where $\bar{F}^+$ and $\bar{F}^-$ are respectively the means of the positive and negative samples, and α_N is the positive constant. $\mathbf{c}(t)$ is the RBF center at the t-th feedback iteration, and it is initialized by the query position, i.e.,

$$\mathbf{c}(t=0) = \mathbf{f}_q \tag{8.10}$$

The relevance feedback method discussed above is referred to as *multi-click RF*, where all the top-T retrieved images that appear on the screen have to be examined by a user. The feedback is done by the user clicking the relevant images, followed by a feedback button. Therefore, multi-click RF requires $n+1$ clicks, where n is the number of relevant images appearing on the screen.

Single click RF, on the other hand, requests the user to select only one relevant image, and this selection will be taken as a feedback sample. The system immediately performs similarity matching using Eq. (8.8) after the single click. At the later RF iteration, images selected on an earlier iteration will be automatically selected as the relevant images. In this way, the single click RF considers only one positive sample at each iteration, while the multi-click RF requires users to examine all positive and negative images in the retrieved image set. The single-click RF can reduce the number of clicks and the user workload, as compared to multi-click RF.

Since the negative samples are not considered in the single-click RF, the process of updating the RBF center with Eq. (8.9) is reduced to:

$$\mathbf{c}(t+1) = \bar{F}^+ + \alpha_N \mathbf{c}(t) \tag{8.11}$$

Figure 8.9 illustrates the retrieval results for the Corel database as used for the experimental data in Fig. 8.5. Fifty images of flags, balloons, bonsai, fireworks, and ships (ten images of each category) are taken as the query images, to perform single-click and multi-click RF for ten iterations. Figure 8.9a compares the retrieval precision versus iteration. The plot shows increased retrieval precision is attained with higher RF iteration. As we may have anticipated, the multi-click RF performs better than single-click RF, but with a higher number of clicks (i.e., a high level of user involvement). In order to compare the performance between the two methods at the same level of number of clicks, a plot of the precision versus clicks is done, as illustrated in Fig. 8.9b. Since some queries may have different numbers of feedback, it is observed that the precision is more versatile against clicks than feedback iterations. In general, the retrieval precision versus clicks plots for both methods indicate the relationship resembles an increasing function. It is observed that single-click RF outperforms multi-click RF, for the same level of user interactions.

8.4 Social Network Image Retrieval Using Pseudo-Relevance Feedback

As an alternative to the structured P2P architecture, this section presents a method for social network image retrieval on an unstructured P2P network. The search system works by broadcasting the request message with non-zero time-to-live (TTL) to all the neighboring hosts. This is to form a social network group and perform a search within this group. Each peer in the P2P network maintains two tables of neighbors. The first type of neighbors are called the *generic neighbors* which typically represent the neighbors with the least physical hop counts. The other type of neighbors are called the *community neighbors* and they have a common interest which is shared among the community. Two stages of operations are required: *social network discovery* and *query within the social network*.

Automation in adaptive image retrieval is employed to improve retrieval accuracy, and to reduce the task of transferring actual image files over a network as required in user-controlled RF. The SOTM is employed for implementing pseudo-RF, and new techniques are utilized to improve its performance in automatic retrieval. This helps reduce the bandwidth requirement and subjective errors caused by user feedback in the scenario of distributed content-based retrieval.

8.4.1 Social Network Discovery

Figure 8.10a illustrates the process of community neighborhood discovery for the construction of a social network. A peer node originates the query request for its generic neighbors in the P2P network. Whenever a peer node receives a query request, it will (1) decrement the TTL, and forward the request to the generic neighbors when TTL > 1, and (2) perform a content search within the peer's feature descriptor database. The retrieval results of each peer are transmitted to the original query peer directly in order to improve the efficiency.

Fig. 8.9 Comparison of
retrieval performance in
terms of retrieval precision as
functions of (**a**) iterations and
(**b**) clicks

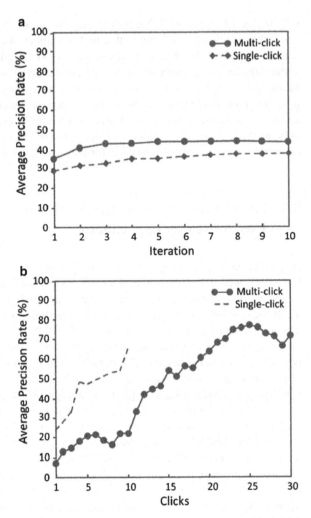

Like most P2P applications, this system applies an application layer protocol, such that the system can be realized on today's internet without modifying the underlying network infrastructure. The query packet format that traverses the P2P network is shown in Fig. 8.10c. Once the destination peer receives the query and performs a feature match, it will issue a query reply to the query requester directly. The query results are in the form of filenames and distances. The actual file transfer is not part of the protocol, and protocols like HTTP, RTP, with or without encryption, may be applied depending on the application. Transferring the actual image content is coupled with the feature descriptor transmission, to eliminate the need to re-compute the feature descriptors upon receiving a new image. The query search and query response packet format which travels through the P2P network are shown in Figs. 8.10b and d, respectively.

The query peer maintains a table of community neighbors based on past retrieval results to identify the peers which collect a similar image database.

8.4.2 Query Within the Social Network

Once the social network is identified, subsequent queries will be made to limited peers within the social network, as illustrated in Fig. 8.10b. To improve the communication efficiency, instead of forwarding the request hop-by-hop in the social network discovery stage, direct communication between the peers is utilized. The same packet format is used for query and query response within the social network.

Each peer in the social network collects more than one category of images, with at least one common category as the requesting peer to satisfy the criteria to be listed in the social network. Therefore, the same image appearing in multiple peers is likely to belong to a common category in the social network. Let $Ret(Q, P_n)$ denote the retrieval result using query image Q from peer P_n, where P_n is the n-th member of social network. Also, let $N(\cap Ret(Q, P_n))$ denote the number of occurrences of each retrieved image I. We can calculate an occurrence distance D_O for each retrieved image, with the normalized value of $N(\cap Ret(Q, P_n))$. This can be used to adjust the ranking of images, in addition to the distance D_F that is usually calculated by feature vectors. The integration of D_O and D_F is done by a weight assignment, with the weighting factor $\mathbf{w}_{p2p} = [w_F \ w_O]$. In this way, the similarity ranking for image I denoted by $Rank(I)$, is obtained as:

$$Rank(I) = \mathbf{w}_{p2p} \cdot [D_F \ D_O]^t \qquad (8.12)$$

This integration of the two distances is referred to as the occurrence weighting scheme [361].

8.4.3 Pseudo Relevance Feedback in the Distributed Database System

While pseudo RF reduces the need for user interaction in relevance feedback, integrating pseudo RF into the distributed retrieval system gives rise to new challenges for repeated requests to multiple peers, which consumes bandwidth and computational resources. To address this issue, an incremental searching mechanism is introduced to reduce the level of transactions between the peers.

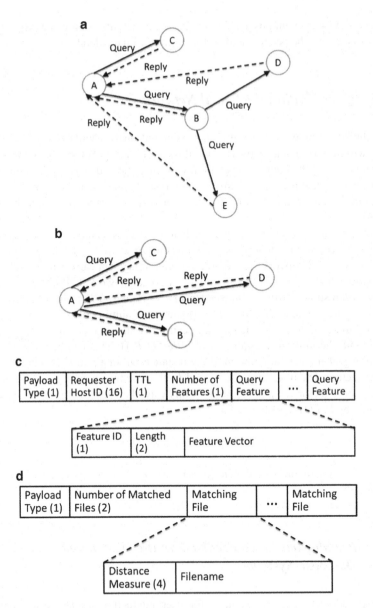

Fig. 8.10 (**a**) Neighborhood discovery, (**b**) search within community neighborhood, (**c**) packet format for query, (**d**) packet format for query reply

8.4.3.1 Incremental Search System

Figure 8.11a illustrates the implementation of pseudo-RF with an incremental search technique. Peer A originates a query request to its nearest neighbor Peer B. Peer B performs the query, and returns the top matched feature descriptors to

Peer A. Consequently, Peer A evaluates the retrieval results using pseudo-RF, and generates a new feature vector (i.e., RBF center). A new query request using the new feature vector will be sent to Peer B, as well as incrementing the audience to Peer C. The query request and automated retrieval evaluation process is repeated until a pre-defined number of peers is reached.

The pseudo-RF is implemented by the SOTM algorithm discussed in Chap. 3. SOTM is applied for the pseudo labelling of retrieved samples, and the single-RBF method is applied for relevance feedback. In the SOTM algorithm, steps 1–5 are the same as the ones discussed in Sect. 3.2.2. However, the updating of the winning node $\mathbf{w}_{j*}$ in step 3 [cf. Eq. (3.3)] is modified to:

$$\mathbf{w}_{j*}(t+1) = \mathbf{w}_{j*}(t) + \alpha(t)\beta(\mathbf{v}(t))[\mathbf{v} - \mathbf{w}_{j*}] \qquad (8.13)$$

where $\beta(\mathbf{v},t)$ is the ranking function which is inversely proportional to the ranking of the feature vector $\mathbf{v}$ at iteration t. This ranking is obtained by the similarity scores between the query feature vector and the feature vector $\mathbf{v}$. A large value of $\beta(\mathbf{v}(t))$ indicates a high relevance of the feature vector compared with the respective query feature [361]. As a result, the prototype vectors $\mathbf{w}_j$ are adjusted so that they learn more from statistically similar inputs and less from statistically irrelevant ones.

The RBF method [i.e. Eqs. (8.8)–(8.9)] is utilized for nonlinear similarity measurement by the adjustment of RBF centers and widths. Since pseudo-RF may cause some errors in the pseudo labeling of retrieved samples, the error will propagate into subsequent modification of the RBF center. To minimize the error preparation, a bias weighting γ is introduced to the original query vector corresponding to the initial RBF center $\mathbf{c}(0)$ in Eq. (8.10). The new RBF center updating function is obtained by:

$$\mathbf{c}(t+1) = (1-\gamma)\bar{\mathbf{F}}^+ + \gamma\mathbf{c}(0) + \alpha_N\left(\mathbf{c}(t) - \bar{\mathbf{F}}^-\right) \qquad (8.14)$$

This formula weights the importance of the original query and the mean of the positive samples, and will replace Eq. (8.9) for calculation of the RBF center in the RF learning.

8.4.3.2   Offline Feature Calculation

Online feature calculation requires high computational resources and results in delay in content retrieval. Redundant online feature computation can be eliminated by the following specifications:

- Each image stored in the social network is attached with its feature descriptor.
- When a peer creates a new image, the feature descriptors will be computed and attached with the image file before announcing the availability of the new image.
- Any image transmission over the social network will be coupled with the transmission of the image's feature descriptor.

8.4.3.3   Advanced Feature Calculation

For extensibility, apart from offline feature calculation, an ideal retrieval system should also allow new features to be computed on the fly. These new features, which typically address the specific feature for a query image, are best implemented with the pseudo RF such for more accuracy in the classification of image relevancy. The advanced feature descriptors for the distributed retrieval systems can be generated by the following two approaches: query node pseudo-RF and agent-based pseudo-RF.

Query Node Pseudo RF

As illustrated in Fig. 8.11a, the query node, Peer A, makes the initial request to the destination node, Peer B. The destination nodes will transfer the retrieved images to the query node. The query node will calculate the advanced feature descriptor on the fly and perform pseudo RF. A new query message will be generated and sent from the query node to the destination nodes repeatedly, until a pre-defined number of iterations is met. This new query message contains updated RBF parameters (i.e., RBF centers and widths) which are used to perform content search within the destination nodes.

The query node pseudo-RF approach requires bandwidth for multiple retrieved data transmission to the query node, and the computation for the query node to calculate advanced features.

Agent-Based Pseudo RF

A software agent technique [225] can be applied to offload the bandwidth and computation cost from the query node. As shown in Fig. 8.11b, the query node, Peer A, initiates a software agent to carry the query vector using a standard feature descriptor, and the algorithm for computing advanced features, to the destination node, Peer B. Peer B performs the retrieval with pseudo RF using the advanced features computed on-the-fly. The software agent carries the new query vector, advanced feature extraction algorithm, and the retrieved data from Peer B, to the subsequent neighbor node, Peer C. Upon reaching a pre-defined number of neighbors, the software agent will carry the retrieved data back to the query node.

Offloading computational cost from the query node to destination nodes raises security concerns, as the flexibility of remote procedure execution opens the doorway for various malicious attacks. Therefore, authenticating as well as validating the integrity of the software agent is required.

Fig. 8.11 Advanced feature calculation: (**a**) incremental P2P retrieval method; (**b**) agent-based retrieval method

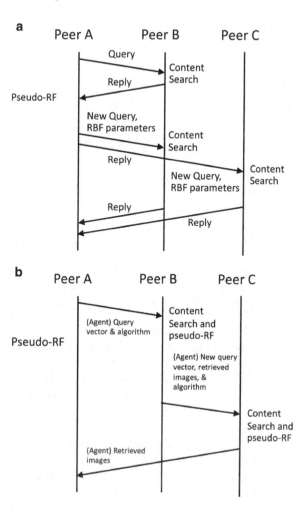

8.4.4   Experimental Result

The simulation was performed using the Corel photo image database, which consists of 40,000 images. For off-line feature calculation, the set of stand features were used, which include color histogram, color moment, wavelet moment, and Fourier descriptor (explained in Table 2.7). For specific feature calculation, the Gabor wavelet texture feature was obtained and used in the pseudo labeling process. The statistical results were computed from averaging the 100 queries in the categories of bird, canyon, dog, old-style airplane, airplane model, fighter jet, tennis, Boeing airplane, bonsai, and balloon.

In the experiment, a P2P network was constructed using an evenly distributed tree structure and each peer was connected to five other peers. The number of image

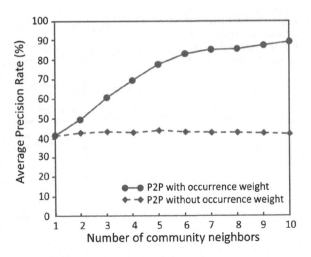

Fig. 8.12 Average precision rate, obtained by retrieval in the P2P network using a simple search with and without the application of the occurrence weight, for different numbers of community neighbors

Table 8.1 Average precision rate (%) obtained by the pseudo-RF method on the P2P network, where the bias weight γ is applied for obtaining the RBF center [cf. Eq. (8.14)], and the parameter β is applied for the SOTM [cf. Eq. (8.13)]

Bias weight	With β	Iter. 0	Iter. 1	Iter. 2	Iter. 3	Iter. 4	Iter. 5
$\gamma = 0$	✓	44.75	57.15	68.30	77.45	79.50	82.05
$\gamma = 0.2$	✓	44.75	58.15	71.35	77.90	80.85	83.25
$\gamma = 0.2$	×	44.75	57.10	68.60	76.15	79.20	82.30

categories which each peer falls under followed a normal distribution, with mean $\mu_{cat} = 10$ and standard deviation $\sigma_{cat} = 2$. The number of images per category was also normally distributed, with mean $\mu_{image} = 50$, and standard deviation $\sigma_{image} = 5$.

Firstly, the retrieval system was conducted by a simple search strategy, where image ranking was done by an occurrence weighting scheme [cf. Eq. (8.12)]. Figure 8.12 shows the statistical analysis of the size of social network with respect to retrieval precision. It was observed that the retrieval precision steadily increased against the size of the community neighborhood. Such characteristics serve as the foundation of the current P2P retrieval system.

Next, the retrieval system utilized a pseudo-RF approach, where SOTM was employed for pseudo labeling and the single RBF method was employed for similarity measurement. Since the pseudo labeling can cause an error in the classification of image relevancy, the bias weight parameter γ was used for updating the RBF center [cf. Eq. (8.14)]. Table 8.1 shows the average precision as a function of feedback iterations, when the system utilized $\gamma = 0$ and 0.2. Regardless of the setting of the bias weight, the retrieval performance significantly improved from 44.75 to 83.25 % at the fifth iteration. At each iteration, the system with $\gamma = 0.2$ provided better retrieval accuracy than that of the system with $\gamma = 0$. This system adaptively improved retrieval accuracy without user interaction. Figure 8.13 shows

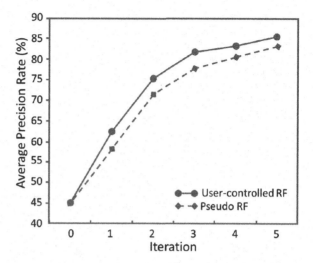

Fig. 8.13 Average precision result, obtained by the pseudo-RF method in comparison with the user-controlled-RF method, on the P2P network

the comparison of retrieval performance between the user-controlled RF and the pseudo-RF methods. It was observed that the pseudo-RF method performed very close to that of the user-controlled RF method.

The application of the ranking bias β in updating the SOTM prototypes also influenced the system performance. Since the output at each feedback stage was ranked according to the RBF function, it was observed that by adding the ranking bias β to the construction of the prototypes as in Eq. (8.13), the retrieval precision was improved. The result is also shown in Table 8.1.

The inter-dependence between each individual image database can be used to improve the retrieval precision for a centralized retrieval system, using the same algorithm applied for a distributed retrieval system. While the centralized retrieval system typically includes a higher order database, greater diversity is expected. In this simulation, the number of images per category was also normally distributed, with $\mu_{cat} = 20$, $\sigma_{cat} = 5$, $\mu_{image} = 50$, and $\sigma_{image} = 5$. Comparisons between the retrieval methods in the centralized system, the centralized system accounting for inter-dependencies between individual databases, and the P2P system, are illustrated in Fig. 8.14. Here the relevance feedback was done manually. Accounting for the overlap between relevant databases used in the distributed P2P system, as described in Sect. 8.4.2, it was observed that there was improvement in the retrieval precision for the centralized retrieval system that used the occurrence weighting scheme.

Figure 8.15 compares the experimental results between the semi-automatic RF and the user-controlled RF, applied to the P2P retrieval system. The x-axis indicates n, the number of manual RF performed. For the semi-automatic RF, the plot is coupled with $5 - n$ pseudo RF. The user-controlled RF was conducted solely from the manual RF, whereas the semi-automatic started with the pseudo RF and was followed by the manual RF. It can be observed that, while n is small, the semi-automatic RF is a better method providing a significant improvement over the user-controlled RF, where both methods use the same amount of manual RF.

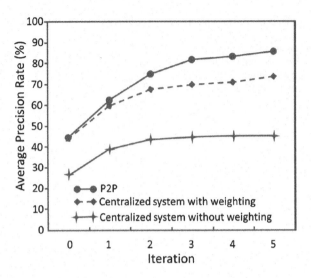

Fig. 8.14 Average precision result, obtained by the centralized system with and without the application of occurrence weighting, compared to P2P retrieval. All these methods used manual RF

An improvement of 38.5 % can be attained at $n = 0$, and 20.5 % at $n = 1$. The two plots converge to the same precision rate at $n = 5$.

Screen shots of a query for an airplane, from the centralized database, with the first and fifth iteration of manual RF, and with pseudo-RF on the distributed P2P retrieval system, are shown in Fig. 8.16a–d, respectively.

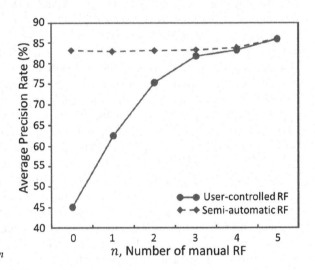

Fig. 8.15 Average precision rate, obtained by user-controlled RF and semi-automatic RF, at the same number of manual RF, n

8.5   Video Re-ranking on the Social P2P Network

The video re-ranking method, presented in Chap. 3, is suitable for the implementation of a video search engine on a P2P network since there is no requirement to conduct relevance feedback from users. In this application, a video database in a peer is indexed by the template-frequency model (TFM) and organized by the 3-layer cosine network. The video retrieval is performed by pseudo-RF through forward–backward signal propagation between peers. This process does not require bandwidth to actually transfer video files over the network during the RF learning process. The video re-ranking system is explained in the following sections.

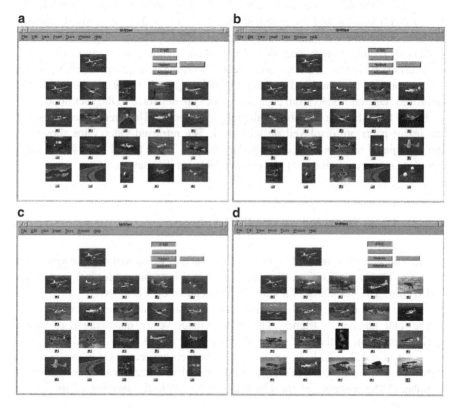

Fig. 8.16 (**a–c**) Retrieval results obtained by user-controlled RF on the centralized database; (**a**) at Iteration $= 0$, the retrieval precision was 0.55; (**b**) at Iteration $= 1$, the retrieval precision was 0.70; (**c**) at Iteration $= 5$, the retrieval precision was 0.80, and (**d**) in the retrieval result obtained with a P2P retrieval system with pseudo-RF, the retrieval precision was 0.95

8.5.1   System Architecture

The system adopts the two stage search approach discussed in Fig. 8.10a, b as a means for discovering and interacting with other peers. Each node is assumed to have a local database containing video clips, each of which is indexed with a vector. Figure 8.17 shows the connection of peers after the social network has been formed. The search is started by the user node to discover its neighbors. The user node sends a packet containing query vector $\mathbf{v}_q$ to the other nodes in the list though Java socket programing. The retrieval process is conducted according to the sequence diagram illustrated in Fig. 8.18.

In the diagram, once received, the query vector is used to search through similar video files in the peer nodes locally. Retrieval results are used to modify the query vector automatically, and the modified query, $\mathbf{v}'_{q,i}, i = 1, 2, \ldots, n$ is routed back to the user node, where n is the total number of nodes. Consequently, the user node gathers all modified query vectors and uses them to adjust the components of the previous query vector. All steps are repeated with the new query vector, $\mathbf{v}'_q$. After several rounds of forward and backward signal propagation between the nodes, the improved retrieval results from each peer nodes are delivered to the user node.

Figure 8.19 shows a snapshot of the retrieval process. The query video clips and the list of peers are displayed on left panel. The retrieved video clips shown on the right panel are represented by the key frames. The retrieval results after each iteration of query modification are also available for the users.

8.5.2   Video Indexing on the P2P Network

A video file can be segmented into video clips, each of which may contain more than one shot. The TFM technique discussed in Chap. 3 is employed for indexing of the video clips. The descriptor of a video clip is denoted by $VD = \{\mathbf{x}_1, \ldots, \mathbf{x}_i, \ldots, \mathbf{x}_N\}$, where $\mathbf{x}_i \in \mathbb{R}^P$ is the visual descriptor of the corresponding i-th frame, and N is the total number of frames. The TFM utilizes vector quantization to assign each video frame to the best matched visual template. A set of visual templates, $C = \{\mathbf{g}_j | j = 1, 2, \ldots, J\}$, is generated by competitive learning (as explained in Table 3.7), where $\mathbf{g}_j \in \mathbb{R}^P$ is the j-th visual template and J is the total number of templates. The mapping of the i-th frame is given by the labeling of its feature vector, i.e.,

$$\mathbf{x}_i \Rightarrow l^{\mathbf{x}_i}_{j^*,1}, l^{\mathbf{x}_i}_{j^*,2}, \ldots, l^{\mathbf{x}_i}_{j^*,\eta} \tag{8.15}$$

$$l^{\mathbf{x}_i}_{j^*} = \arg\min_j \left(\|\mathbf{x}_i - \mathbf{g}_j\| \right) \tag{8.16}$$

where $l^{\mathbf{x}_i}_{j^*,1}, l^{\mathbf{x}_i}_{j^*,2}$, and $l^{\mathbf{x}_i}_{j^*,\eta}$ are the labels of the η best matching templates. By mapping all $\mathbf{x}_i, i = 1, \ldots, N$, in the input video clip, the resulting labels,

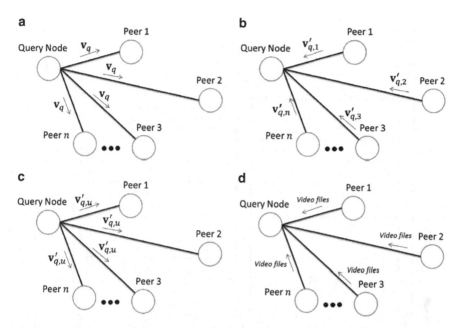

Fig. 8.17 The re-ranking procedure for modification of a query for video retrieval on a peer-to-peer network; (**a**) the user node sends query packets to its peers in the neighborhood community; (**b**) the query is modified by the peer nodes and sent back to the user node; (**c**) the user node gathers the modified queries and computes the second modified query and sends it to the peer nodes; (**d**) the final retrieval results (video files) are sent to the user node

$\left\{l^{\mathbf{x}_i}_{j^*,1}, \ldots, l^{\mathbf{x}_i}_{j^*,\eta}\right\}^N_{i=1}$, $l_j \in \{1, 2, \ldots, J\}$, can be obtained. In this way, the label l_j represents the occurrence of template $\mathbf{g}_j$ in the input video. Thus, the term-vector model [360] can be applied to the resulting set of labels. The number of times $\mathbf{g}_j$ present in the video can be viewed as the *term frequency* (TF). We can formally formulate the corresponding term-weighting vector as: $\mathbf{v} = [w_1, \ldots, w_j, \ldots, w_J]^t$ where w_j represents the multiplication of the term frequency (TF) and the inverse term frequency (ITF) of the j-th template $\mathbf{g}_j$ for the input video.

8.5.3   Re-ranking Approach to P2P Video Retrieval

Each node in the P2P network shown in Fig. 8.17 stores a collection of video clips, each of which is indexed by a weight vector. All the members of the neighborhood community are assuming the use of a single set of visual templates $C = \{\mathbf{g}_j | j = 1, 2, \ldots, J\}$. The peers may have a different number of video files. Figure 8.20 illustrates the zoom version of Peer n. Video indexing within this peer can be viewed as a network of three layers: (first) the query vector, (second)

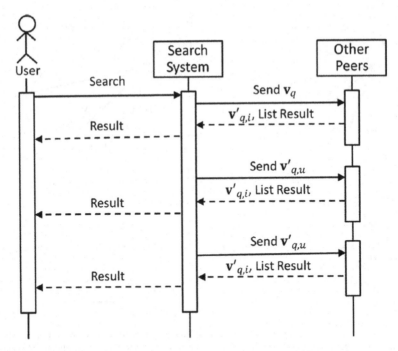

Fig. 8.18 Sequence diagram of video retrieval using pseudo-RF on a P2P network

the visual template, and (third) the video nodes. The network's signal propagation process implements a query expansion method that modifies the query components according to the initial search result. The modified query is expected to be effective, as compared to the original query. This process contains *intra-peer* signal propagation, which results in a new query which is then sent back to the query peer in the subsequent *inter-peer* signal propagation.

8.5.3.1 Intra-Peer Signal Propagation

The adaptation process is implemented by forward–backward signal propagation between the three layers. The network contains the query node (v_q) at the first layer, video template nodes (g_j, $j = 1, \ldots, J$) at the second layer, and video nodes (v_i, $i = 1, \ldots, I$) at the third layer. The connection between the second and the third layers are the weight components w_{ij}, $i \in \{1, \ldots, I\}$, $j \in \{1, \ldots, J\}$.

As shown in Fig. 8.20, at the first round of forward signal propagation, some video nodes at the third layer are activated. The activation level of the i-th video node, $a_i^{(v)}$ is calculated by taking the sum of the signals $mesg_{g_j \to v_i}$. That is:

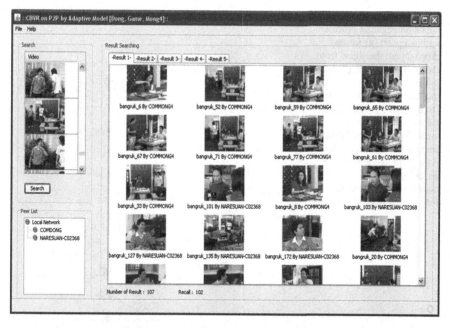

Fig. 8.19 Snapshot of retrieval process using video re-ranking on the P2P network. The *left frame* shows the query interface and the list of peers. The *right frame* shows the retrieval result which is the videos clips after five iterations

$$a_i^{(v)} = \sum_{j=1}^{J} mesg_{\mathbf{g}_j \to \mathbf{v}_i} \qquad (8.17)$$

$$= \frac{\sum_{j=1}^{J} w_{qj} w_{ij}}{\sqrt{\sum_{j=1}^{J} w_{qj}^2} \sqrt{\sum_{j=1}^{J} w_{ij}^2}} \qquad (8.18)$$

where $mesg_{\mathbf{g}_j \to \mathbf{v}_i}$ is the message sent from the j-th video template node, $\mathbf{g}_j$ to the i-th video node, $\mathbf{v}_i$.

After finishing the forward signal propagation, the activation level of all video nodes, $a_i^{(v)}$, $i = 1, \ldots, I$ are the desired ranking of the videos for retrieval. However, the signal propagation process does not stop here. The activated video nodes will send the signal backward to the templates nodes at the second layer. This time, however, a minimum activation threshold is defined such that the video nodes below this threshold send no signal out. The activation level of the j-th template node during the backward propagation is obtained by:

$$a_j^{(\mathbf{g})} = \sum_{i \in Pos} a_i^{(v)} \bar{w}_{ij} \qquad (8.19)$$

Fig. 8.20 Example of the
signal propagation process
within a peer; (**a**) forward
propagation: the signal from
the query templates g_1 and g_4
in the second layer is sent to
the third layer (video nodes);
(**b**) backward propagation:
the signal from the activated
video nodes, v_1, v_3 and v_4 is
sent back to the second layer.
As a result, the templates g_1,
g_3, and g_6 are newly
discovered and set as the
relevant template nodes

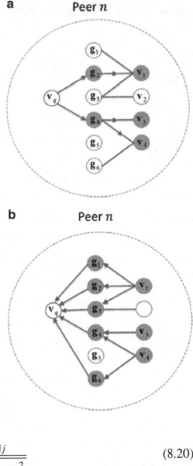

$$\bar{w}_{ij} = \frac{w_{ij}}{\sqrt{\sum_{j=1}^{J} w_{ij}^2}} \qquad (8.20)$$

where $a_i^{(v)}$ is the activation level of the i-th video node and *Pos* is the set of i's such
that $a_i^{(v)} > Tr$, where Tr is a threshold value.

8.5.3.2   Inter-Peer Signal Propagation

As shown by the example in Fig. 8.20, the forward–backward signal propagation
process will introduce new template nodes which are relevant to the query. We draw
on the observation that, with more templates in the query, it is more likely that a
video relevant to this query is indexed under at least one of the query templates. This
process automatically expands a short query with additional relevant templates. The
activation level $a_j^{(g)}$ in Eq. (8.19) can be viewed as the degree of relevance of the

corresponding template $\mathbf{g}_j$. From this, a new query $\mathbf{v}'_q = \left[w'_{q,1}, \ldots, w'_{q,j}, \ldots w'_{q,J} \right]^t$ is obtained, where $w'_{q,j}$ are calculated from the activated templates as the following:

$$w'_{q,j} = \begin{cases} \frac{\sum_{i \in Pos} w_{i,j}}{M} & \text{if } a_j^{(g)} > 0 \\ 0 & \text{otherwise} \end{cases} \tag{8.21}$$

where M is the number of video nodes in the *Pos* set. The new query template, $w'_{q,j}$ is obtained by the mean value of the j-th template of the activated video nodes.

In Fig. 8.17, the peers on the network will create the new set of query vectors, $\mathbf{v}'_{q,i}, i = 1, \ldots, n$. These new queries are sent back to the user node, and the second modified query is computed from this set of query vectors. At the user node, the modified query is obtained by concatenating the modified queries from all peers to the original query:

$$\mathbf{v}'_{q,u} = \mathbf{v}_q + \beta \sum_{i=1}^{n} \mathbf{v}'_{q,i} \tag{8.22}$$

where $\mathbf{v}'_{q,u}$ is the new query obtained at the user node and β is the positive constant. The query $\mathbf{v}'_{q,u}$ is sent to all nodes to perform the subsequent search operation.

8.5.4 Experimental Result

In the experiment, the retrieval system was firstly implemented on a local server, where all indexed video files were located in a single server. Five videos were segmented into video clips, and the video indexing process was obtained by the TFM method. In the off-line process, the color histogram on RGB color space was used for content characterization of video frames. The resulting histogram vectors were vector quantized using the procedural parameter $\eta = 5$. Each video was indexed by the $TF \times IDF$ weight vector. In the on-line process, video retrieval was obtained by the adaptive retrieval process, where the initial query was modified through signal propagation by the 3-layer cosine network. At the first iteration of forward signal propagation, Eq. (8.18) was used to obtain the activation level of video nodes. Then, for the backward signal propagation, the video nodes whose activation levels were greater than the threshold $Tr = 0.9$, were set as relevant, and used to obtain relevant templates with Eq. (8.21). In the successive iteration, the new query was obtained by Eq. (8.22) and used for retrieval.

Next, the video database was divided and distributed to nodes in the P2P network. The retrieval process was obtained by the peer-to-peer system (as explained in Fig. 8.17), through inter- and intra-peer signal propagations. Table 8.2 shows the retrieval results obtained after five iterations by the retrieval results from the single server and the peer-to-peer system. Here, the comparison was conducted

Table 8.2 Average recall
rate (%), obtained by the
video re-ranking method on
the centralized and the P2P
database systems

	Average recall rate (%)				
	1 Iter.	2 Iter.	3 Iter.	4 Iter.	5 Iter.
Centralized database	53.31	61.04	61.44	61.44	61.44
P2P database	53.31	62.02	62.99	63.87	64.35

between the non-adaptive retrieval method (1st iteration) and the adaptive retrieval method (2nd–5th iteration), and not between the centralized and distributed database systems. It can be observed that the re-ranking process by the adaptive network significantly improved retrieval performance. The recall rate at the first iteration was 53.31% and increased to 62.02% after one iteration of query modification. The system converged quickly after two to three iterations. It can be observed that the retrieval result for the peer-to-peer system was slightly better than that of the centralized database system. This is because the query modification process explained in Eq. (8.22) allowed each peer node to modify the query (i.e., $\mathbf{v}'_{q,i}, i = 1, \ldots, n$) before computing the final modification of the query at the user node. By computing $\sum_{i=1}^{n} \mathbf{v}'_{q,i}$ in Eq. (8.22), the relevant templates were weighted more than those of the centralized system, in the order of n times.

Figure 8.21 shows the average precision rate for the top 10, 20, and 30 retrievals, obtained by the re-ranking of videos on the P2P network. The precision achieved for the top ten retrievals was measured to be 80.63% (more than eight relevant videos were presented out of the top ten retrieved videos). The precision increased with the number of iterations of the query modification, and converged to about 84% precision.

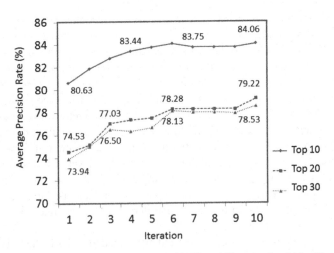

Fig. 8.21 Average precision measured for the top 10, 20, and 30 retrievals, obtained by re-ranking videos in the P2P database

a

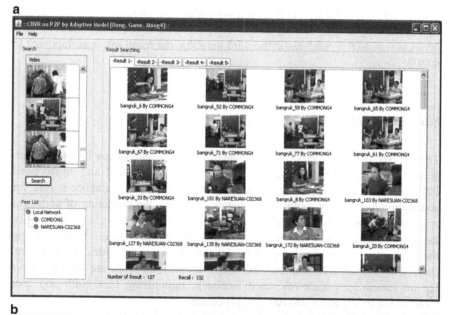

b

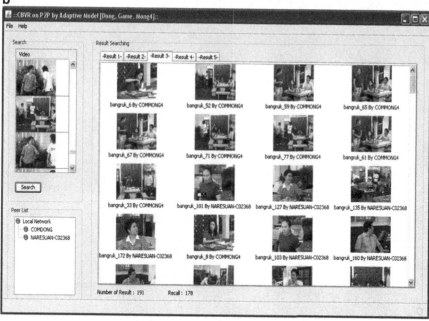

Fig. 8.22 Snapshots of video retrieval in the P2P network after (**a**) one iteration, and (**b**) three iterations of re-ranking

Figure 8.22a, b illustrates retrieval results after three iterations of query modification, showing snapshots from the P2P retrieval system. The recall rate at the first iteration was 46.6 %, whereas at the third iteration, the recall rate was improved to 80.9 %.

8.6   Summary

The chapter presents methods for organizing images and videos in a cloud datacenter. A distributed database can be managed by structured and unstructured P2P networks. In both scenarios, self-organization plays an important role for automatic clustering of multimedia objects, and thus, the clustering of nodes for effective indexing and retrieval. The self-organizing tree map is employed for the cluster-identification search system, which offers online search by pinpointing the relevant nodes without traversing all the participating nodes. Furthermore, the self-organizing tree map and the adaptive cosine network are effective tools for implementing pseudo-relevance feedback, minimizing bandwidth and user workload in image and video retrieval processes.

Chapter 9
Scalable Video Genre Classification and Event Detection

Abstract This chapter focuses on a systematic and generic approach which is experimented on scalable video genre classification and event detection. The system aims at the event detection scenario of an input video with an orderly sequential process. Initially, domain-knowledge independent local descriptors are extracted homogeneously from the input video sequence. Then the video representation is created by adopting a Bag-of-word (BoW) model. The video's genre is firstly identified by applying the k-nearest neighbor (k-NN) classifiers on the initially obtained video representation. Various dissimilarity measures are assessed and evaluated analytically. Then, at the high-level event detection, a hidden conditional random field (HCRF) structured prediction model is utilized for interesting event detection. The input of this event detection relies on middle-level view agents in characterizing each frame of video sequence into one of four view groups, namely closed-up-view, mid-view, long-view and outer-field-view. Unsupervised probabilistic latent semantic analysis (PLSA) based approach is employed at the histogram-based video representation to achieve these middle-level view groups. The framework demonstrates the efficiency and generality in processing voluminous video collection and achieves various tasks in video analysis. The affectiveness of the framework is justified by extensive experimentation. Results are compared with benchmarks and state of the art algorithms. Limited human expertise and effort is involved in both domain-knowledge independent video representation and annotation free unsupervised view labeling. As a result, such a systematic and scalable approach can be widely applied in processing massive videos generically.

9.1 Introduction

The bag-of-words (BoW) model and its application in image classification have been used in various aspects of video analysis. Because of its robustness in matching semantic objects using local descriptors, the BoW concept has been used in video object reoccurrence detection [231, 232], semantic shot detection [233, 234] and grouping [235], and object-based video retrieval [236, 237]. Some other representative works in video analysis adopted BoW models with feature tracking along the temporal course, including matching semantically similar videos built by local features using spatiotemporal volumes [238]; content-based video

© Springer International Publishing Switzerland 2014   247
P. Muneesawang et al., *Multimedia Database Retrieval: Technology and Applications*,
Multimedia Systems and Applications, DOI 10.1007/978-3-319-11782-9_9

copy detection using high-level descriptions derived from the BoW representation [239]; and, person spotting and retrieval based on their faces features in videos [240]. In the field of video event analysis, Zhou et al. applied the BoW model to Gaussian mixture models to represent news videos and utilized kernel-based supervised learning in classifying news event [241]. The BoW model was also used in video clip representation in Xu and Chang's work of video event recognition, where a multilevel temporal pyramid was adopted to integrate information from different sub-clips for pyramid match using temporal alignment [242].

Aforementioned video analysis methods using BoW models have their individual merits. However, there is a lack of systematic investigation, which is important in connecting individual aspects of the video analysis, from raw input video clip genre categorization, to middle level semantic view or shot understanding, to eventually high-level semantic event analysis. Furthermore, large-scale video data often contains many hours with a lot of insignificant information. The nature of large-scale video data is that it requires an automatic and orderly analysis to obtain efficient information extraction. In this chapter, we propose a BoW model to represent video frames and clips. We also propose an unsupervised learning approach to utilize the BoW-based video representation. We manage to tackle a series of video analysis challenges for unlabeled large-scale video consortia. As a result, a systematic analysis of video data is achieved.

In order to evaluate the effectiveness of the BoW model in the systematic video analysis, we need a valid and meaningful test ground. We believe that large-scale sports videos are ideal. First, sports video is truly a large-scale consortia. It also contributes significantly to the total collection of digital content. Second, sources of sports video collection are also various: from daily-basis public recreations to professional sports games broadcasting; from amateur digital camcorder to professional TV broadcasting, and plenteous but low-quality online streamed videos. Third, sports video analysis is closely connected with real applications, due to its huge popularity and vast commercial value.

Although analysis of sports video has drawn much attention in the research community, most of the literature focus on particular sports and tasks, utilizing domain knowledge and production rules [243–247]. Supervised learning is an important characteristic adopted by these works to fill the semantic gap. These stand-alone methods have little inter-connection and also suffer from a lack of generality and scalability to the large-scale data for two reasons. First, with various video content of different themes and cinematographic techniques, domain knowledge associated methods have difficulties in extensibility. Second, labeled data is required for supervised learning, while the majority of multimedia data available is currently unlabeled. In order to tackle these two issues, our proposed algorithm focuses on using a local domain knowledge-independent SIFT feature to represent video clips using the BoW model and utilizes an unsupervised learning paradigm to deal with unlabeled large volume data.

In this chapter, a generic and systematic framework is proposed with experimentations on a large-scale sports video dataset. Three tasks are introduced such that the output from the previous tasks are utilized as the input to the next task.

Event detection is the third and final quest with two preceding tasks, video genre categorization and semantic view type classification. By accomplishing these three tasks, event detection can be achieved with minimum domain knowledge and partially labeled data. Although we perform our methods on sports video, the generic nature makes the proposed framework valid in evaluating other video consortia.

The novelty of this framework lies in the following three aspects:

1. Domain knowledge-free local descriptors are extracted using a homogeneous process. The BoW model is used to build a histogram-based distribution to represent video clips. The BoW based video representation using local features is the natural selection for generically processing videos due to its domain knowledge-free properties.
2. An unsupervised classifier with homogeneous process is proposed. This choice of method is because that unlabeled data takes the major portion of all digital content. Thus, an automatic and systematic process can be deployed towards a large-scale dataset. Since sports videos have well defined semantic view types from their production characteristics, local features combined with the BoW model is a perfect candidate in view classification. Such a combination has also been proven successful in computer vision and object recognition. Therefore, a probabilistic latent semantic analysis (PLSA)-based method for semantic view classification is preferred due to its unsupervised nature and applicability to the BoW model.
3. A structured prediction model is adopted for taking labeled middle-level agents as input to achieve high-level semantics. This choice is because that sports videos have distinguishable temporal patterns often consisting of sequences of middle-level agents. In our work, since semantic view types have been classified in part (2), an appropriate method is to take the view results as input and achieve semantic event detection. Therefore, hidden conditional random field (HCRF) is introduced as a rational choice. The significance of the HCRF is its generalized modeling, which resides in both the relaxation of the Markov property and incorporation with hidden states of the conditional random field (CRF) modeling.

In the following, an overview of the proposed system is first presented with a flowchart, followed by video representation using the BoW model and low-level genre categorization. Then, the proposed techniques are introduced, including unsupervised learning for middle-level view classification and HCRF for high-level event detection. Experimental results are then provided to demonstrate the effectiveness of the proposed method.

9.1.1 Overview

This section provides an overview from a holistic perspective as illustrated in Fig. 9.1. The input video is analyzed systematically using a generic and sequential framework. This video is interpreted in a way such that the result from a preceding

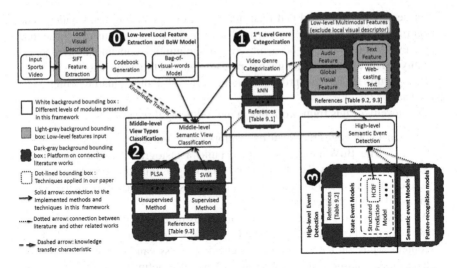

Fig. 9.1 A flowchart of the proposed generic framework with one module of generic video representation and three task modules in sequence

process is the input to the next process in a consistent and coherent fashion. There are four modules in total: module 0 is the infrastructure for low-level feature extraction and video representation using the BoW model. Module 1–3 are tasks introduced in this chapter. The highlights of this framework include the following.

1. A generic foundation using domain knowledge-free local feature was developed to represent input large-scale videos. This method fits the general framework in video analysis and provides an alternative solution to alleviate generality, scalability, and extensibility issues.
2. A thorough and systematic structure starting from genre identification is presented, which was ignored in some related work that assumed the genre type as prior knowledge.
3. A general platform is introduced to associate our method with the abundant and valuable existing literature, as well as various and innovative features input.

At module 0, the low-level local feature utilization incorporated with codebook generation and the BoW model provides an expandable groundwork for the semantic tasks of genre categorization, view classification, and high-level event detection. Most of the literature discusses domain knowledge and production rules at the feature extraction level. In our structure, a homogenous process is first introduced for extracting domain knowledge-independent local descriptors. The BoW model is used to represent an input video by mapping its local descriptors to a codebook, which is generated from an innovative bottom-up parallel structure. The histogram-based video representation is treated as the sole input (no other feature models) to both the genre categorization and the view classification modules. Such a concise representation built from the BoW model benefits users in homogenously extracting visual features and representing videos in a compact and collective form.

In the 1st module, videos are categorized by genre. Video genre nomenclature is used to describe the video type, which is defined as the highest level of granularity in video content representation. Since the video genre categorization task directly relies on low-level features, the proposed feature extraction of the target video sequence is used in categorization. In large-scale videos, a successful identification of the genre serves as the first step before attempting higher level tasks. For instance, in sports event detection, an unknown "shooting" event is the target quest, which could be from a ball game or a shooting sport. By indiscriminately treating the entire dataset, this event will be searched through all types of sports. However, since sports like figure-skating and swimming have no "shooting" at all, the effort to search this event within those non-relevant sports becomes infeasible. Instead of treating all data indifferently, a more efficient method is to identify the genre of the query video first; and then, deploy middle/high-level tasks. As the survey shows in sports video analysis, most of the related works on view classification and event detection assume the genre by default. This framework, however, provides a system that automatically identifies the genre from various types of sports data before further analysis.

In the middle-level and the 2nd module, semantic view types are classified using an unsupervised PLSA learning method to provide labels for video frames. View describes an individual video frame by abstracting its overall content. It is treated as a bridge between low-level visual features and high-level semantic understanding. In addition, unsupervised learning saves a massive amount of human effort in processing large-scale data. Moreover, the supervised methods can also be implemented upon our proposed platform. Therefore, a SVM model is executed as the baseline for comparison.

Finally in the 3rd module, a structured prediction HCRF model using labeled inputs is a natural fit for the system to detect semantic events. This choice can be justified in that a video event occupies various length along the temporal dimension. Thus, the state event model-based HCRF is suitable to deploy. Less comprehensive baseline methods, such as the hidden Markov model and the conditional random field, can also be applied on this platform.

Besides the three-level modules in the *white background bounding boxes*, this framework, illustrated in Fig. 9.1, also highlights the relationship between our system and existing literature, which are shown in the *dark-gray background bounding box*. Associated Table references are also indicated in each module. Multimodal features excluding local visual features are also introduced at various stages by the literature. The *Dotted arrows* are used to represent these associations. The *solid arrows* denote the proposed and implemented techniques in our work. The *dashed arrow* represents a knowledge transfer characteristic of the generated codebooks. In summary, codebooks generated from certain sports with abundant resources, can be transferred and utilized in classifying other sports materials with scarce resources.

9.2   Video Representation and Genre Categorization

This section covers the first part of our proposed framework, generic feature extraction with the BoW model, and systematic genre categorization. Figure 9.2 illustrates details of each process.

9.2.1   Related Work

Video genre and its categorization was one of the earliest video analysis which drew researchers' interests. The main task of this genre categorization starts from a diverse group of videos, such as sports, music, news, movies etc., and gradually moves to a more discriminating categorization such as identifying the sports genres. Various works have been highlighted as follows. However, a major and common disadvantage of these works is their heavy dependency on domain knowledge.

Fischer et al. [248] first proposed a classification method based on five different video genres. Brezeale and Cook [249] provided an extensive survey in this field. Incorporating the survey and most recent works, a concise summary is provided in Table 9.1. Color features with C4.5 decision trees were used in [250]. Camera motion features with statistical classifiers were chosen to classify six sports genre in [251]. A principal component analysis (PCA) modified audio-visual feature was used to train a Gaussian mixture model (GMM) classifier in [245]. Semantic shots (views) were used to help in genre categorization in [252]. Motion and color, as well as audio features, were applied in [253]. Color features with a hierarchical support vector machine (SVM) were used in [254]. High-level MPEG-7 features were extracted and applied in multi-modality classifiers in [255]. The best classification result at the moment has an accuracy of 95 % using a dataset of eight different genres [256]. These methods used various domain knowledge with supervised classifiers to achieve the automatic genre categorizations.

As defined in [257], domain knowledge-based features can be divided into two categories, cinematic-based features and object-based features. The cinematic feature involves middle to high level semantics from common video composition or production rules such as shots/views or events, while object-based features are described by their special properties, such as color, shape, and texture, as well as spatial–temporal-based object motions. As Table 9.1 shows, all reviewed works are domain knowledge-dependent, either object-based or cinematic-based. A lack of diversity, that is, the number of different genres in the database, restricts these methods from generality.

Table 9.1 Summary of previous video genre categorization methods

References	No. of genres	Data size Hours	Domain knowledge Object based	Domain knowledge Cinematic based	Genre categorization method	Accuracy (%)
2000 [250]	4	8	Yes	Yes	C4.5 decision tree	83
2003 [251]	6	33.75	Yes	Yes	Statistics based	n/a
2003 [245]	5	5	Yes	No	PCA & GMM	86.5
2004 [252]	4	n/a	Yes	Yes	Decision tree and HMM	91.6
2006 [253]	3	16	No	Yes	Pseudo-2D-HMM	n/a
2006 [254]	6	33.33	No	Yes	Hierarchical SVM	94
2008 [255]	5	5	Yes	Yes	Multimodel	88.5
2008 [256]	8	100	Yes	Yes	Parallel neural networks	95

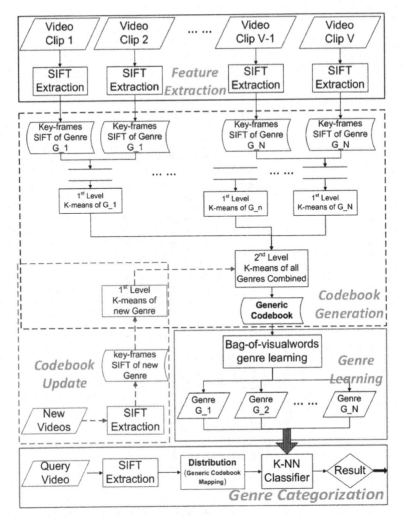

Fig. 9.2 Feature extraction and genre categorization framework using data parallelism and bottom-up structure for codebook generation

9.2.2 Bottom-Up Codebook Generation

Local invariant features are chosen for homogenous feature extraction due to their domain knowledge-free properties. The scale, rotation, and illumination invariant properties make these descriptors good candidates in preserving the similarities for semantic objects and events matching and detection. Global features, on the other hand, rely on domain knowledge and have difficulties in robust concept and event detection, especially in the presence of noise and occlusion [258]. Scale-invariant feature transform (SIFT), developed by Lowe [259], is selected as feature descriptors in this work. The SIFT method extracts key-points of an image and describes these points using local neighborhood regional information. Since no prior and domain knowledge is required, SIFT is an ideal option in the large-scale automatic and homogenous process. By processing image sequences sampled from video clips, each frame is represented by a magnitude of hundreds of SIFT descriptors. After homogenous local descriptor extraction, the BoW model is applied, whose effectiveness relies on a robust codebook design. In order to achieve this resiliency, we propose a two-level bottom-up K-means clustering for codebook generation. The advantages of the bottom-up structure are efficiency, scalability, and robustness.

The BoW model is adopted by first synthesizing a representing codebook using codewords which are exemplars of combining sampled SIFT local descriptors. Consequently, a video clip is characterized by mapping its SIFT feature points to a generated codebook; and then, a histogram distribution is obtained. Compared to the original footage, this compact representation preserves enough information for differentiation, only using a small size in storage. In addition, random noise can be suppressed by using this proposed frequency-based histogram representation.

With the large-scale dataset, efficiency and robustness of the codebook formation have been important concerns for the BoW model. Heuristically, the larger the codebook size, the better the classification results (with certain saturation limitations) [260,261]. Different codebook sizes have been explored, ranging from several hundred [262, 263] to thousands [264] to hundreds of thousands [260]. Since they all use different datasets, no conclusions have been drawn to make a standard rule. In this chapter, choices of codebook sizes are based on the empirical studies.

K-means clustering is utilized to generate a codebook by finding and appointing cluster centers as codeword values. In a large-scale domain, satisfactory performance has been reported using a top-down structure for categorization [265]. In that work, a two-layer top-down structure is used for sports genre categorization. At the first-layer, a general codebook (size 800) is generated using single K-means, in which a query video is only categorized to one of the predefined bigger groups consisting of several genres. Such a group is determined by those sports sharing similar semantics. At the second-layer after the membership of the bigger group is identified, an individual codebook (size 200) for this bigger group is used to decide the video genre. For instance, *judo* and *boxing* are combined into a bigger group named *martial arts*, where *martial arts* is used as the first-layer candidate. Subsequently, Judo and Boxing are differentiated in the second-layer categorization. Although good classification accuracy has been reported, efficiency and robustness are problems for such a method in terms of creating a general codebook using single K-means clustering. This is because most computation of K-means lies in calculating the distances between individual points to their cluster centers in each iteration. A single K-means clustering using large-scale data is heavy in computation and sometimes inaccurate due to K-means own limitations. Since more than 3 million high-dimensional SIFT points are used for building the codebook in our application, one single K-means clustering becomes inefficient.

Therefore, a two-level bottom-up structure is proposed in this work for efficient codebook generation. At the bottom layer, individual genre codebooks are generated in 1st-level K-means clustering. At the upper layer, the 1st-level codebooks are used as the input for the 2nd-level K-means to build the generic codebook. By using this bottom-up structure, we reduce the heavy computation in measuring individual point-to-cluster-center distance in the K-means algorithm. Moreover, since the 1st-level K-means are independent from each other, distributed computing methods can be applied to further reduce the computation time. The numerical analysis is referred to in Sect. 9.4.1.

Another advantage of bottom-up K-means clustering resides in the system update and scalability. In the case of new genre videos added to the dataset, a codebook update module is applied to find the new genre's individual codebook. The result, together with existing codebooks, is used to generate the new generic codebook by only re-running the 2nd-level K-means. In the case that new videos are imported for an existing genre, the corresponding 1st level K-means is applied to achieve the updated individual codebook; and then, 2nd-level K-means is re-run to update the generic codebook.

9.2.3 Low-Level Genre Categorization

In our proposed method, at the genre categorization stage, a query video is expressed as a histogram Q that also uses the generic codebook and the BoW model. Then, a k-Nearest Neighbor (k-NN) classifier is applied with a defined dissimilarity measurement between the query Q and a trained individual genre P. Consequently, the query video is identified as the genre whose distribution is closest to that of the query within measure. Technical details are presented in Sect. 9.4.1.

By identifying the genre of this query video, subsequent processes are confined to a focused group, and the scale of computation is decreased. Therefore, advanced and sophisticated techniques can be used in middle/high-level video analysis. In the next step, training data is characterized by frequency-based histogram representation. The individual genre is modularized as a distribution denoted by P using training data of its own kind.

9.3 High-Level Event Detection Using Middle-Level View as Agent

Content-based video event detection is among the most popular quest for high-level semantic analysis. Different from video abstraction and summarization, which targets any interesting events happening in a video rush, event detection is only constrained to a predefined request type (such as the third goal or the second penalty kick in a particular soccer match). In sports videos, a consumer's interest in events resides in the actual video contents, more than just the information delivered.

For instance, a user wants to watch particular goals in basketball games, or replays in soccer matches. S/he is not only interested in the information like who/how/what, but more importantly, the visual contents rendered from the sports clips. On the other hand, sports videos also have very strongly correlated temporal structures. In a way, the structure can be interpreted as a sequence of video frames which have patterns and internal connections. This pattern is ubiquitous due to the nature of sports, a competition where players learn from the standard in order to excel. Therefore, an intuitive approach is to find such patterns using certain representation; and in turn, to learn the temporal structure. Luckily, the PLSA algorithm provides such a labeled frame sequence. What we need is a clever technique to analyze portions of the video and determine what structured prediction model to use. In the following, we will first review the literature. Then, we will introduce a coarse-to-fine scheme and hidden conditional random field (HCRF) for event detection.

9.3.1 Related Work

As one of the most popular semantic tasks in video analysis, event detection has been a popular topic from the beginning of multimedia research. Despite different definitions of event detection by different researchers, commonly acknowledged properties of an "event" can be summarized as follows. An event occupies a period of time and is described using salient aspects of the video sequence input, which consists of smaller semantic units or building blocks [266]. Lavee et al. also summarized and classified event detection algorithms into three categories: (a) pattern-recognition models, (b) semantic event models, and (c) state event models. Pattern-recognition models focus on direct classification from low-level features, but lacks semantic linkage. Semantic models target high-level semantic rules and constraints with domain-knowledge. These models require a lot of human involvement in creating rules and regulations using prior information. State models utilize abstracted middle-level agents, as well as the intrinsic structure of the event itself.

By comparing these three categories of event modeling with examples in the literature, we think that the pattern-recognition model is heavily dependent on classifiers, which at the moment, are not intelligent enough to understand all semantics from low-level features. On the other hand, the semantic model considerably relies on human expertise; and thus, underestimates the accuracy and efficiency provided by classification tools. From our experience, the state model incorporates the strength of pattern recognition at low-level with classifiers at high-level so that it utilizes both feature extraction power and classification intelligence. Moreover, the state model also accommodates an automatic process and unsupervised learning, which reduces human input into the system. Therefore, state event models are suitable for analyzing large-scale datasets, from both generic and systematic point of views. A coarse-to-fine strategy fits well into such state event models, by first roughly localizing the event with context information and then precisely detecting the event using an advanced structure model.

Although we prefer the state event model for its natural fitness to the proposed systematic approach in this work, two other models are still valued for their efficiencies in analyzing sports videos and utilizations in applications. In the following, state-of-the-art algorithms are summarized and compared.

Support vector machine (SVM) is a popular pattern-recognition model algorithm [266]. Some groups use rich audiovisual features, such as face detection, scoreboard information, and, geometry of the field, to find certain semantic events. Saldier and O'Connor [267] used SVM to classify "scoring" events for four different field sports. Xu et al. [268] analyzed tennis videos by using hierarchical-SVM applied on fused audio-visual modalities. Similarly, Ye et al. [269] utilized middle-level view labels as well as shot length and camera motion descriptors. An SVM-based incremental learning scheme using updated data is proposed in detecting soccer events, along with a predefined temporal structure. A similar method combining SVM and predefined temporal structure was proposed by Li et al. [270], targeting basketball events using optical flow patterns.

Some semantic event models using rules and logic and semantic relationships are presented. Babaguchi et al. [271] used closed caption text streams with audiovisual features and the intermodal correlation between them to search a "touch down" event from 4 h of American football videos. Zhang et al. [272] also focused on superimposed caption frames and used decision trees to decide the event, such as "scoring" or "last pitch" for baseball games. Ekin et al. [257] incorporated production rules and soccer sport rules to detect certain events such as "goal", "referee", and "penalty-box".

In terms of state event models, one of the earliest works targeting structures of videos was from Nepal et al. [246], who empirically studied the temporal model in basketball videos based on manual observation, using heuristic methods and low-level audio-visual features. Duan et al. [273] also generated a temporal structure using multimodality with heuristic experience on tennis events. Another approach of learning temporal structure is from the data mining perspective, where Tien et al. [274] focused on a tennis match event detection by creating a max-subpattern tree and learning the frequent patterns from it.

Another important branch of state event models are structured prediction models such as hidden Markov models (HMMs) and their variations, Bayesian networks, as well as discriminative conditional random fields (CRFs). Zhang et al. [275] proposed an HMM-based statistical method for classifying middle-level agents generated from web-casting texts. Tong et al. [276] used Bayesian networks to classify "shoot" and "card" events in soccer videos, by applying decision tree-based intermediate-layer concept units. Mei and Hua [277] proposed an innovative mosaic-based middle-agent for key-event mining using HMMs. Wang et al. [278] proposed a CRF model on detecting semantic soccer events, and the performance turned out to be better than both SVM and HMMs. A similar algorithm was also proposed by Xu et al. [279] using CRFs for basketball and soccer event detection where a webcast text feature was obtained to achieve middle-level concepts.

An interesting event tactic analysis is proposed by Zhu et al. [247], which is beyond the conventional event and adopts the cooperative nature and tactic patterns of team sports. Extensive experiments have been conducted on soccer.

Table 9.2 provides a comparison of the aforementioned literature from a feature utilization point of view. Most of the methods utilize multimodality schemes of features input. By comparing the number of events processed, it appears that the state event model has better scalability in examining various event scenarios. It is also interesting to point out that local visual features have not been utilized in any of the methods. In addition, many of the methods, especially state event models, require middle-level semantic agents to bridge the gap between the low-level features and the high-level events. Such middle-level agents have to be labeled data. However, for the generic method presented in this work, we tackle event detection problem using the input obtained by unsupervised learning and unlabeled data.

9.3.2   Middle-Level Unsupervised View Classification

Once a video genre is identified, the next step is to achieve view classification of each of the video frames in the query sequence. We present a literature review first, followed by the proposed unsupervised method.

9.3.2.1   Related Work

We summarize related works so that readers can compare popular supervised means with proposed unsupervised PLSA. Additionally, there are only two works using unsupervised techniques based on our study. We present them for completeness of the review [280, 281].

Although there may be different nomenclatures, the fundamental purpose of the middle-level views (shots) is to involve certain production rules to aid in high-level tasks. This frame-based label concept was first introduced by Xu et al., who defined three groups of views: global, zoom-in, and close-up [243]. Ekin and Tekalp [244] used a slightly different notation which includes long-shot, middle-shot, and close-up/out-of-field. Duan et al. [282] used a finer view/shot group classification, supported by innovative semantic features. These pioneering methods, along with other works such as [283–285] focus on using decision tree classifiers to link the low-level features to view/shot types. Xu et al. [243] and Ekin et al. [244] applied color-based grass detector and field/object size to determine view types. Incorporating previously mentioned features, Tong et al. [283] added head-area detection, as well as a grey-level co-occurrence matrix(GLCM) to improve the decision tree on classification. Wang et al. [284] used field region extraction, object segmentation and edge detection for view type decision making. Duan et al. [282] first extended the research from single genre (soccer) to multiple genres (four sports) using individual genre-based decision trees. Different from previous visual feature

Table 9.2 Comparison of event detection models emphasizing feature utilization from both low-level features and middle-level semantic agents

Event detection algorithm category	Year Reference	Nature of data	Number of events	Low-level multimodal features	Visual features		Middle-level semantic agents
					Global-based	Local-based	
Patten-recognition model	2003 [268]	Tennis	5	AVM	Yes	No	Yes
	2005 [267]	Four field sports	2	AVS	Yes	No	No
	2005 [269]	Soccer	1	n/a	n/a	n/a	Yes
	2009 [270]	Basketball	5	VM	Yes	No	No
Semantic event model	2002 [271]	Football	3	VST	Yes	No	No
	2002 [272]	Baseball	2	VT	Yes	No	No
	2003 [257]	Soccer	3	VS	Yes	No	Yes
	2001 [246]	Basketball	1	AVMT	Yes	No	No
	2003 [273]	Tennis soccer	16	AVMT	Yes	No	Yes
State event model	2004 [276]	Soccer	2	VM	Yes	No	Yes
	2006 [278]	Soccer	5	AVM	Yes	No	Yes
	2007 [275]	Basketball	5	VT	Yes	No	Yes
	2008 [274]	Tennis	4	AVS	Yes	No	No
	2008 [277]	Soccer	3	VM	Yes	No	Yes
	2008 [279]	Soccer basketball	17	VTS	Yes	No	Yes
	2009 [247]	Soccer	6	VMTS	Yes	No	Yes

In the "Low-level Multimodal Features" column, various features are utilized, including audio (A), visual (V), text (T), motion feature (M), and video shot detection (S), as well as an "n/a" label in the case when no low-level feature mentioned in the related works

extraction methods, Kolekar and Palaniappan [285] took a top-down approach. They first used audio features to find exciting video clip. The motion features of the whole image volume along with the background color information are then utilized for view-type classification. Benmokhtar et al. [286] took an approach on feature level fusion using dynamic PCA with information coding neural-network (NN). At the classification level, another NN is used to fuse multi-modality inputs. However, these supervised methods are limited by the labeled data; and thus, constrained from being expanded to larger scales.

Some other researchers pursued unsupervised methods for view classification. Wang et al. [280] proposed an information-theoretic co-clustering method, in which mutual information was maximized by treating shot classes and features as two random variables. As a consequence, color histogram and perceived motion energy features are used with a test set of four sports video genres. Zhong et al.'s method was inspired from spectral theory conventionally used to solve segmentation problem in graph theory [281]. They proposed a spectral-division algorithm to find the proper video shot clustering, which were tested in three sports videos using the HSV space color feature. Although good performances have been obtained in these methods, the extensibility and flexibility towards diverse genres and large-scale datasets are very limited. This limitation is again due to the domain knowledge dependency of the extracted features.

Table 9.3 compares the aforementioned methodologies from angles of feature utilization and classification techniques. Color and texture are two major global features used by most works. Duan et al.'s work is the only one that proposed middle level features developed from low-level global features. The rest of the work either adopted additional popular global feature schemes, such as audio feature or Gabor feature, as well as some production rule-based features, or did not utilize any. While various global features are used, none of the local features have been applied. Moreover, most of the supervised methods (except Duan et al.'s work) focus on a single (soccer) sport, while unsupervised techniques use various types of sports.

9.3.2.2   Unsupervised View Classification

This section introduces the middle-level view classification, where the previously built BoW model is also used as feature representation. Since this work targets large-scale videos, an unsupervised solution is more viable and applicable. Therefore, we chose to use unsupervised probabilistic latent semantic analysis (PLSA)-based models. PLSA has demonstrated promising results in analyzing co-occurrence data of words and documents in text retrieval [287]. From a matrix factorization point of view, PLSA belongs to a subgroup called non-negative matrix factorization, where the factorized matrices are non-negative [288]. Because the codebook paradigm with codewords is adopted in mapping visual features to a probability-based histogram which has to be non-negative, PLSA becomes a more suitable selection compared to other factorization techniques, such as singular value decomposition or principle component analysis.

Table 9.3 Comparison of view classification techniques in literature, emphasizing on features utilization and classification methods

Year	Nature	Global features			Local-feature	
Reference	of data	Color based	Texture based	Others (yes/innov)	based	View classification method
2001 [243]	Soccer	Yes	No	No	No	Thresholding (S)
2002 [244]	Soccer	Yes	No	Yes	No	Morphological operations (S)
2003 [282]	Four sports	Yes	Yes	Innov	No	Decision tree (S)
2004 [283]	Soccer	Yes	Yes	Yes	No	Decision tree (S)
2007 [280]	Four sports	Yes	Yes	Yes	No	Spectral clustering (UnS)
2008 [286]	Soccer	Yes	Yes	Yes	No	Neural-network (S)
2008 [281]	Three sports	Yes	No	No	No	Spectral-division algorithm (UnS)
2009 [285]	Soccer	Yes	No	Yes	No	Decision tree (S)

In the "Global Features" column with "Others (yes/innov)" category: "yes" means other than color and texture global features are used while not innovative, while "Innov" means newly designed features are used. For the "View Classification Method" column, S indicates an supervised method, while UnS indicates the unsupervised method

PLSA relies on the likelihood function of multinomial sampling and aims to reach an explicit maximization of the predictive power of the model. Incorporating the PLSA plate notation in Fig. 9.3 with the view classification application, the observed state w is defined as codewords with a predefined codebook of size M. An individual video frame is denoted by d with a total number of training frames N. Latent state z is the view type and parameter K is the total number of view classes, and in this work, K equals four. The likelihood function is given in Eq. (9.1). The probabilistic distribution is defined as $p(w_i|d_j)$, where w_i is an individual codeword, and d_j is a training frame. Such distribution can be represented by a sum-of-product of two distributions, $p(w_i|z_k)$ and $p(z_k|d_j)$. The former is interpreted as an impact on codewords by a view type, while the latter is the probability of a particular view type given a training frame. The number of codeword w_i appearing in a frame d_j is denoted as $n(w_i, d_j)$. The argument of maximum posterior (MAP) estimate z^* is optimized by using an expectation maximization (EM) as shown in Eq. (9.2).

$$L = \prod_{i=1}^{M}\prod_{j=1}^{N} p(w_i|d_j)^{n(w_i,d_j)}$$

$$= \prod_{i=1}^{M}\prod_{j=1}^{N}\left(\sum_{k=1}^{K} p(w_i|z_k)p(z_k|d_j)\right)^{n(w_i,d_j)} \tag{9.1}$$

$$z^* = \arg\max_{z} p(z|d) \tag{9.2}$$

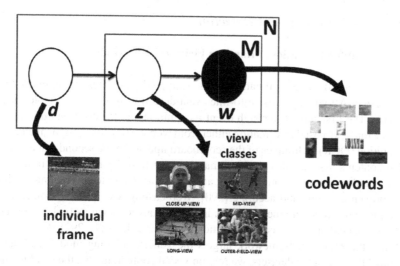

Fig. 9.3 Illustration of the PLSA model in plate notation and its connection with view type classification

Since SVMs have demonstrated great performance in the field of classification, it is adopted in our view classification task for comparison purposes. In general, supervised models tend to yield better results but require predefined knowledge. A typical radial basis function (RBF) is used as the non-linear kernel in SVM [289] and shown in Eq. (9.3). In this equation, x_i and x_j represent the codewords, and γ is the kernel parameter of the RBF.

$$K(x_i, x_j) = \exp\left(-\gamma \|x_i - x_j\|^2\right), \quad \gamma > 0. \tag{9.3}$$

Four view types are defined, namely close-up-view, mid-view, long-view and outer-field-view. This definition is also popular among other work in this field [243, 244, 273]. For the PLSA-based model, the number of view types is required, while labeling effort is not needed for individual frames. On the contrary, SVM-based models demand both semantic predefined view types as well as all frames labeled with groundtruth, which could be unaffordable when the video is large in size.

As a result of the view classification task, the query video sequence is labeled with view types. In the next section, models which take labeled video sequence as input for detecting interesting events are introduced.

9.3.3 High-Level Event Detection

9.3.3.1 Hidden Conditional Random Field (HCRF) Model

Before learning the temporal patterns, a starting and entry point of an event needs to be seized. A two-stage coarse-to-fine event detection strategy is suitable for this scenario. The first stage is a rough event recognition and localization utilizing rich and accurate text-based information either from web-casting text or optical character recognition (OCR) techniques of the scoreboard update. In the second stage, precise video contents associated with the semantic event have been detected in terms of event boundary detection and accuracy analysis. The coarse-to-fine techniques have been proven effective and accurate [290]. Web-casting text for coarse-stage event detection and video alignment was studied and analyzed such as replaying scenes and various goal and shot scenes detection in soccer video [291, 292].

Since the proposed framework targets the generic learning model that can be extended to large-scale datasets, we rely on visual content, that is, the local features extracted and middle-level views classified from such features. To demonstrate the effectiveness of the proposed model, we focus on a particular basketball score event detection. We adopted the previously developed scoreboard update detection method for a coarse-stage process in order to obtain the time-stamp [290]. The fine-stage process focuses on robust and accurate visual content detection from the score event. The video sequence is analyzed by distinguishing the actual score event from false alarm events, such as timeouts or intermission, which are also concurrent with scoreboard information. We propose a HCRF-based structured prediction model utilizing previously classified views, thereby completing the generic approach. For example, the HCRF model can be used to detect the score event in basketball for exciting events and highlights. Such an HCRF technique belongs to the state event model defined in related works. Therefore, HCRF takes the labeled sequences as input in a natural and seamless fashion. On the other hand, HCRF is a comprehensive model which can be degraded to hidden Markov models (HMM) or conditional random fields (CRF) with certain constraints. The merits of HCRF compared with the other two models are its resilience and robustness with a combination of both the hidden states and the Markov property relaxation. Technical details are examined in the following.

There are several advantages of using HCRF in large-scale datasets, rather than HMM, or CRF models. First, HCRF relaxes the Markov property, which assumes that the future state only depends on the current state. In our generic framework, video frames are uniformly decimated and sampled, regardless of the temporal pace of the video itself. In some cases, several consecutive frames have the same labeling, while in other cases, different labels are assigned. Markov property-based models such as HMM are appropriate for the former scenarios, but not suitable for the latter ones, since the future state in HMM only cares about the current state label, but not previous states. On the other hand, HCRF is flexible and takes surrounding states from both before and after the current state. Thus, HCRF is more robust for dealing with large-scale homogeneous processes and uniform sampling with no prior knowledge. For instance, if a key frame immediately preceding the current state is missed due to uniform sampling, such information loss could be compensated by including and summing up distant informational frames (both previous and future) from uniform sampling without misclassifying the event.

Second, HCRF has merit in its hidden states structure, which helps to relax the requirement of explicit observed states. This relaxation property is also an advantage in dealing with large-scale uniformly sampled video frames. It is because of this configuration, CRF model outputs individual result labels (such as event or not event) per state and requires separate CRFs to present each possible event [279]. In HCRF, only one final result is presented in terms of multi-class events occurring probabilities. From the point of view of robustness, a CRF model can be easily ruined by semantically unrelated frames due to automatic uniform sampling. A multi-class HCRF, on the other hand, can correct the error introduced by such unrelated frames using probability-based outputs [293].

Moreover, HCRF is also appealing for allowing the use of not explicitly labeled training data with partial structure [293]. From the literature, HCRF has been successfully used in gesture recognition [293, 294] and phone classification [295].

Figure 9.4a illustrates an HCRF structure in which label $y \in Y$ of event type is predicted from an input $\mathbf{X}$. This input consists of a sequence of vectors $\mathbf{X} = \mathbf{x}_1, \mathbf{x}_2, \ldots, \mathbf{x}_m, \ldots, \mathbf{x}_M$, with each $\mathbf{x}_m$ representing a local state observation along the HCRF structure. In order to predict y from a given input $\mathbf{X}$, a conditional probabilistic model defined in [293] and in Eq. (9.4) is adopted. In the equation, model parameter θ is used to describe the local potential function ψ, which is expanded in Eq. (9.6). A sequence of latent variables $\mathbf{h} = h_1, h_2, \ldots, h_m, \ldots, h_M$ are also introduced in Eq. (9.4), which are not observable from the structure of Fig. 9.4a. Each h_m member of $\mathbf{h}$ corresponds to a state of s_m. The denominator $Z(\mathbf{X}; \theta)$ is the normalization factor, which is expanded in Eq. (9.5).

$$P(y|\mathbf{X}, \theta) = \sum_{\mathbf{h}} P(y, \mathbf{h}|\mathbf{X}, \theta) = \frac{\sum_{\mathbf{h}} e^{\psi(y, \mathbf{h}, \mathbf{X}; \theta)}}{Z(\mathbf{X}; \theta)} \tag{9.4}$$

$$Z(\mathbf{X}; \theta) = \sum_{y', \mathbf{h}} e^{\psi(y', \mathbf{h}, \mathbf{X}; \theta)} \tag{9.5}$$

$$\psi(y, \mathbf{h}, \mathbf{X}; \theta) = \sum_{t} \sum_{k} \theta_k^1 f_k^1(y, h_t, \mathbf{X}) + \sum_{t} \sum_{k} \theta_k^2 f_k^2(y, h_{t-1}, h_t, \mathbf{X}) \tag{9.6}$$

In the event detection application, each $\mathbf{x}_m$ from $\mathbf{X}$ is a vector descriptor called local observation. In the notation, the $\mathbf{x}_m$ value at a time t is defined as $\mathbf{x}_m(t) = [p_{ws_1}(t), p_{ws_2}(t), p_{ws_3}(t), p_{ws_4}(t), p_{wc}(t)]$, with each entry of $\mathbf{x}_m(t)$ calculated from an average result of a sliding window centering at time t, as Fig. 9.5 shows. The first four entries of $\mathbf{x}_m(t)$ are the probabilities of four possible view types, where $p_{ws_{j=1,2,3,4}}(t)$ associates with close-up-view, mid-view, long-view, and outer-field-view by $j = 1, 2, 3, 4$ respectively. The fifth $p_{wc}(t)$ value is an associated directional

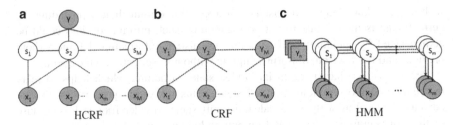

Fig. 9.4 Structured prediction models: **(a)** hidden conditional random field (HCRF); **(b)** conditional random field (CRF); **(c)** hidden Markov model (HMM)

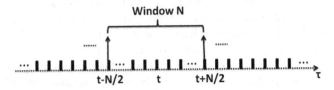

Fig. 9.5 HCRF input shown in Eq. (9.7), by sliding window average result on view types of decoded image sequence

motion descriptor, introduced by Tan et al. [296]. The formula to calculate the average values at time-stamp t are given in Eq. (9.7), where individual frame-based probabilities are $p_{s_{j=1,2,3,4}}$ and p_c.

$$p_{ws_j}(t) = \frac{1}{N} \sum_{\tau=t-N/2}^{t+N/2} p_{s_j}(\tau) \quad with \ j = 1,2,3,4$$

$$p_{wc}(t) = \frac{1}{N} \sum_{\tau=t-N/2}^{t+N/2} p_c(\tau) \tag{9.7}$$

A label and training sequence pair is defined as $(y_i, \mathbf{X}_i)$ with the index number $i = 1, 2, \ldots, n$. For each pair, $y_i \in Y$ and $\mathbf{X}_i = \mathbf{x}_{i,1}, \mathbf{x}_{i,2}, \mathbf{x}_{i,m}, \ldots, \mathbf{x}_{i,M}$ are the event label and observed states as Fig. 9.4a depicts. For instance, $\mathbf{x}_{i,m}$ is interpreted as the mth sampled time state of the ith training sequence, where $\mathbf{x}_{i,m}(t) = [p_{i,ws_1}(t), p_{i,ws_2}(t), \ p_{i,ws_3}(t), p_{i,ws_4}(t), p_{i,wc}(t)]$.

During HCRF training, parameters θ_k^1 and θ_k^2 need to be learned. As Eq. (9.6) shows, θ_k^1 and θ_k^2 are coefficients for the state feature function f_k^1, which contains a single hidden state, and the transition feature function f_k^2, which involves two adjacent hidden states, respectively. In order to find the optimal parameters, a log-likelihood objective function is used, as shown in Eq. (9.8), with a shrinkage prior (the second term in the equation) in order to avoid the excessive parameter growth. A limited-memory version of the Broyden–Fletcher–Goldfarb–Shanno (L-BFGS) quasi-Newton gradient ascent method [297] is applied to find the optimal $\theta^* =$

argmax£(θ). The L-BFGS algorithm is chosen due to this method's efficiency and performance from both theory [298] and application [279].

During the optimization process, the conditional probability in Eq. (9.8) is substituted by the explicit form in Eq. (9.4) to get Eq. (9.9). Then, partial derivatives of a training sample $£_i(\theta)$ with respect to θ_k^1 and θ_k^2 are derived in Eqs. (9.10) and (9.11), respectively.

$$£(\theta) = \sum_i \log p(y_i|\mathbf{X}_i, \theta) - \frac{1}{2\delta^2}\|\theta\|^2 \tag{9.8}$$

$$£(\theta) = \sum_i \log\left(\frac{1}{Z(\mathbf{X}_i;\theta)}\sum_\mathbf{h} e^{\psi(y_i,\mathbf{h},\mathbf{X}_i;\theta)}\right) - \frac{1}{2\delta^2}\|\theta\|^2 \tag{9.9}$$

$$\frac{\partial £_i(\theta)}{\partial \theta_k^1} = \sum_t P(h_t|y_i,\mathbf{X}_i)f_k^1(y_i,h_t,\mathbf{X}_i)$$
$$- \sum_{t,y'} P(h_t,y'|\mathbf{X}_i)f_k^1(y',h_t,\mathbf{X}_i) \tag{9.10}$$

$$\frac{\partial £_i(\theta)}{\partial \theta_k^2} = \sum_t P(h_{t-1},h_t|y_i,\mathbf{X}_i)f_k^2(y_i,h_{t-1},h_t,\mathbf{X}_i)$$
$$- \sum_{t,y'} P(h_{t-1},h_t,y'|\mathbf{X}_i)f_k^2(y',h_{t-1},h_t,\mathbf{X}_i) \tag{9.11}$$

9.3.3.2 Comparison with Conditional Random Field (CRF) and Hidden Markov Model (HMM)

For comparison purposes, we also utilized conventional CRF models as depicted in Fig. 9.4b. By following definitions in [299], the conditional probability function is shown in Eq. (9.12), with the normalization factor in Eq. (9.13). The potential function is defined in Eq. (9.14), where $v_j(Y_{t-1}, Y_t, \mathbf{x})$ is a transition feature function between state positions t and $t-1$ within the observation sequence; while $s_k(Y_t, \mathbf{x})$ is a state feature function at state position t. Parameters λ_j and μ_k are estimated for transition and state feature functions, respectively.

$$P(\mathbf{Y}|\mathbf{x}) = \frac{1}{Z(\mathbf{x})} \cdot exp\left(\sum_{t=1} F(\mathbf{Y},x,t)\right) \tag{9.12}$$

$$Z(\mathbf{x}) = \sum_{Y'} exp\left(\sum_{t=1} F(Y',\mathbf{x},t)\right) \tag{9.13}$$

$$F(Y,\mathbf{x},t) = \sum_j \lambda_j v_j(Y_{t-1}, Y_t, \mathbf{x}) + \sum_k \mu_k s_k(Y_t, \mathbf{x}) \tag{9.14}$$

The HMM algorithm is also provided in Eq. (9.15) and depicted in Fig. 9.4c.

$$P(Y|X) = P(X,Y)/P(X)$$
$$= \prod_t P(X_t|Y_t) \cdot P(Y_t|Y_{t-1}) \tag{9.15}$$

The aforementioned three structured prediction models use different decision-making schemes for the final event detection. For the HMM, the query sequence is tested. The highest likelihood of the HMM provides the final decision in event detection. On the other hand, in the CRF model, since each state variable $Y(t)$ requires a label, as Fig. 9.4b shows, a majority-rule voting scheme in which the most event labels along the Y sequence decide the event result. For the HCRF model depicted in Fig. 9.4a, a multi-class training process recognizing all classes at the same time is adopted. Therefore, a detected event with the highest probability is considered the final result for the query sequence.

9.4 Experimental Result

In the following section, experimental results are presented to justify the properties of the proposed generic framework, specifically using a relatively large-scale video collection that includes 23 genres with a total of 145 h gathered by the authors and his co-workers, named the 23-sports dataset. To our best knowledge, this dataset is the most diverse in video genres, collected from both the internet and television. All the video clips have the same length of 167 s with a total of 500 uniformly sampled frames at a sampling rate of three frames per second. This dataset is composed with 3,122 clips. In training, 1,198 clips are used, in which a subset of 46 clips (2 clips per sport) are used in codebook generation with a total of 3,112,341 SIFT points. In testing, the other 1,924 clips are selected.

Various codebook sizes were studied at first. Then, the proposed system was evaluated in three experiments, with a particular event detection as its ultimate measurement: (1) genre categorization using the proposed bottom-up codebook generation is analyzed; (2) view classification results are assessed and compared using both supervised and unsupervised classifiers; (3) finally, the coarse-to-fine event detection is examined by investigating the basketball score event. The validity on the score event detection can be extended to other event scenarios with labeled video sequences. The detailed argument can be found in Sect. 9.4.3.

To investigate the codebook size effectiveness, a subset of the 23-sports dataset of 14 sports was used. The clip numbers of these sports range from 70 to 106, averaging 87, while each individual clip is a uniform 167 s in length. Two experiments were conducted on the codebook size selection for genre categorization and view classification, respectively. For genre categorization, the average accuracy performance of all sports as a function of different codebook sizes is shown in Fig. 9.6a. The plot reaches a plateau after codebook size 800, and starts to drop

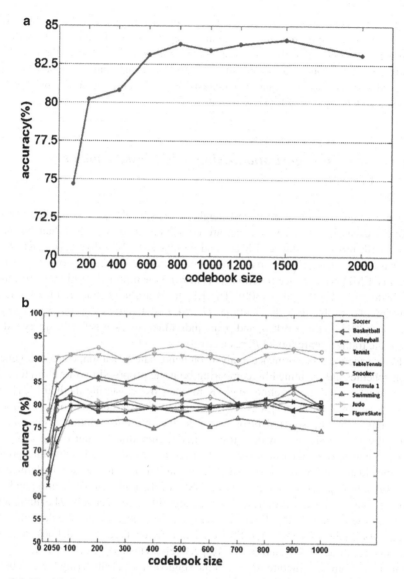

Fig. 9.6 Empirical studies on codebook size selection. (**a**) Average sports accuracy performance for genre categorization. (**b**) Individual sport accuracy performance for view classification

at codebook size 1,500. For view classification, the accuracies of individual sport as a function of different codebook sizes are shown in Fig. 9.6b. Although various accuracy levels are observed for each sport, the individual performance follows a similar plateau trend. Based on these empirical studies, it is concluded that the performances are proportional to codebook sizes, with stable results at codeword ranges of 800–1,500 and 800–1,000 for genre categorization and view classification, respectively. This study is also consistent with existing research [258, 260, 261]. In the following experimentation for genre categorization with a total of 23 sports types, it is predicted that the codebook size should be bigger than in the tested 14 sports case. Therefore, a codebook size of 1,600 is chosen, and a codebook size of 800 is also applied as a comparative analysis. For view classifications involving 14 sports, a codebook size of 800 is selected.

9.4.1 Genre Categorization Using K-Nearest Neighbor Classifier

In genre categorization, a K-nearest neighbor (k-NN) classifier is applied. Three different dissimilarity measurements are compared, including Euclidian distance (ED), earth mover's distance (EMD), and Kullback–Leibler divergence (KL-div). ED is used for measuring the spatial distance in Euclidian space in between two histograms. EMD is a distance function for achieving the minimal cost in transforming one histogram into the other [300]. The KL-div is a non-symmetric measurement between two probability distributions Q and P defined as $D_{KL}(Q||P) = \Sigma_i q_i \cdot \ln(q_i/p_i)$ [301]. In this work, q_i and p_i are individual codewords for the query video Q and the trained genre model P, respectively.

Before accuracy performance analysis on genre categorization, codebook generation schemes are examined by comparing both the proposed two-level bottom-up (BU) structure and the baseline single K-means (SK) clustering method [301]. As pointed out by Jain et al. [302], K-means clustering is considered a partitional algorithm using the squared error to reach the optimum solution. The sum of squared errors (SSE) is a widely used criterion function for clustering analysis, which quantitatively measures the total difference between all individual points to their clustering centers [301]. An SSE deviation percentage δ_{dev} is defined in Eq. (9.16). Let ξ_{BU} and ξ_{SK} represent the SSEs of the bottom-up clustering and the single K-means clustering at the end of each algorithm, respectively. The numerator is the absolute value of the difference between ξ_{BU} and ξ_{SK}, and the denominator is ξ_{SK}. As Table 9.4 shows, the SSE deviation percentages at codebook sizes of 800 and 1,600 are 1.4 % and 3.7 %, respectively. Thus, we can conclude that in using the bottom-up structure instead of the single K-means clustering for codebook generation, the deviation of SSE is trivial.

$$\delta_{dev} = \frac{|\xi_{BU} - \xi_{SK}|}{\xi_{SK}} \cdot 100\% \tag{9.16}$$

Codebook computation effort of the bottom-up structure is also compared with single K-means clustering in Table 9.4. Both bottom-up and single K-means clustering are employed on a single Quad CPU at 2.40 GHz with 4.0G RAM machine, in which the bottom-up is only simulated as parallel computing in a serial sequence. To generate a codebook with size 800, the single K-means clustering uses

Table 9.4 SSE deviation percentage δ_{dev} and computation time in codebook generation using bottom-up (BU) and single K-means (SK) structures

Codebook size	$cb_{BU} = 800$	$cb_{SK} = 800$	$cb_{BU} = 1{,}600$	$cb_{SK} = 1{,}600$
Computation	4 h	350 h	9 h	648 h
δ_{dev}	1.4 %		3.7 %	

350 h, while the bottom-up clustering only takes 4 h. When the codebook size is doubled to 1,600, the computation for single K-means and bottom-up clustering are 648 and 9 h, respectively. With a truly distributed processing environment using multiple computers, bottom-up processing time will be further reduced. This comparison of computational complexity demonstrates that our generic framework using robust bottom-up clustering for codebook generation can replace the single K-means in dealing with large-scale and diverse datasets.

For the accuracy performance using k-NN and various dissimilarities, Table 9.5 shows the average genre categorization results for 23 different sports. The proposed bottom-up codebook generation manifests a better and more robust performance than single K-means codebook generation in both EMD and KL-div measurements. By comparing the row-wise's dissimilarities, the bottom-up structure is more consistent with codebook sizes of 800 and 1,600. On the contrary, the single K-means codebook generation is unstable for both histogram and mLDA-based distributions. For instance, the performance at a codebook size of 800 using EMD has about a 7 % increment from ED dissimilarity (75.33 % vs. 68.31 %), while the counterpart at a codebook size of 1,600 using EMD has dropped 1.1 % from ED dissimilarity (64.28 % vs. 65.39 %). One reason is that the single K-means clustering on over three million input SIFT points hardly reaches the optimal value. As a summary, KL-div performs the best among three dissimilarity measures. Using the bottom-up structure, results of the codebook size 1,600 outperform the cases with size 800 in all measurements with consistency. Oppositely, single K-means clustering results are not consistent.

Another merit of the bottom-up structure is its preservation of individual genre characteristics from the 1st-level K-means. On the contrary, single K-means codebook generation covers all the data; thus, a weakly distinguishable genre is easily overruled by a strong one. This reasoning explains why with the increase of codebook size from 800 to 1,600, the bottom-up process has about a 4 % improvement for KL-div, while the single K-means process has only a 2 % increment for KL-div.

The individual sport genre classification result is illustrated in Fig. 9.7. On average, a codebook size of 1,600 gives an average of 3.6 % higher than the codebook size of 800, which corresponds with the empirical studies from other research groups [258, 261].

To evaluate the generic and extensive properties of our proposed method, experimental results on the 23-sports dataset are compared with results in Li et al.'s work [265], where a top-down process was adopted using single K-means as its

Table 9.5 Average categorization results (%) of 23-sports data with codebook size 800 and 1,600

Measurement	ED	EMD	KL-div
$cb_{BU} = 800$	61.54	75.80	78.59
$cb_{SK} = 800$	68.31	75.33	73.49
$cb_{BU} = 1,600$	65.68	78.94	82.16
$cb_{SK} = 1,600$	65.39	64.28	75.75

BU: codebook generated using bottom-up structure. SK: codebook generated using single K-means structure

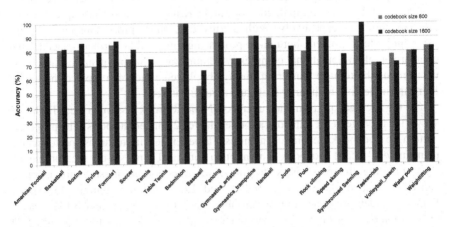

Fig. 9.7 Genre categorization for the 23-sports dataset with codebook sizes of 800 and 1,600

top layer general codebook. The best performance in two-layer and single-layer structures are 83.83 % and 81.2 %, respectively [265]. In their work, speeded up robust features (SURF)-based method is adopted. Similar to SIFT, SURF is also a scale and rotation-invariant interesting point feature extraction algorithm, which focuses on the computational efficiency [303]. Although SURF and SIFT adopt different key points detection techniques, these two descriptors are comparable in characterizing local features of sampled frames from a video sequence. Therefore, such a comparison is valid in genre categorization performances, regardless of the feature extraction difference. Considering the increment of data in scale about 27 % (145 h vs. 114.2 h), and in variety about 64 % (23 genres vs. 14 genres), using the bottom-up structure with a codebook size of 1,600 and KL-div measurement, our experimentation provides comparable results of 82.16 %, with a degradation of 1.67 %.

Although the performance is maintained on average, we also observed that the individual performance has been fluctuating. This fluctuation is mainly due to the nature of the adopted k-NN classifier, where distance-based measurement can be overruled by a strong representation in a large and sparse dataset. We acknowledge that k-NN may not be the most robust algorithm towards the very large-scale dataset. However, the k-NN is an efficient method in batch processing. It can be used as

Table 9.6 Genre categorization accuracy between various video clips with uniform sampling-based and key-frame/shot-based methods

Three minutes clip		Ten seconds clip	
Uniform sampling	Key-frame/shot	Uniform sampling	Key-frame/shot
83.83 %	79.41 %	71.90 %	63.10 %

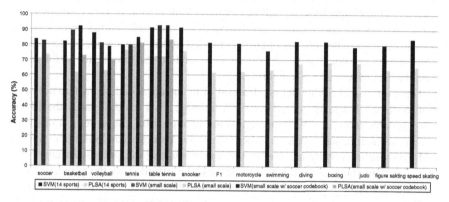

Fig. 9.8 View type classification using supervised SVM and unsupervised PLSA. First two columns are with codebook size 800 for 14 sports

a coarse and preliminary execution to quickly prune off the large portion of the irrelevant data.

From a different perspective, generic properties of the proposed method are assessed using various video clip lengths and frame sampling methods. As detailed in Table 9.6, better performance is acquired using longer lengths of video clips, while a generic and automatic uniform sampling method outperforms the key-frame sampling. It is because the proposed method is based on local key-point descriptors. Therefore, a longer video clip with denser sampling frames provides more key-points and consequently builds a better distribution than a shorter clip with less sampled key-frames/shots. Such experimentation demonstrates the merit of our proposed generic method towards a truly large-scale dataset.

9.4.2 Middle-Level View Classification Using Supervised SVM and Unsupervised PLSA

Experiments in this section focus on middle-level view classification by utilizing extracted low-level histogram-based representations. A subset of 14 sports of all 23 sports was used as test data. Figure 9.8 compares both supervised SVM and unsupervised PLSA results as the 1st and 2nd columns, respectively. On average, supervised SVM has a classification accuracy of 82.86 %, and unsupervised PLSA has an average of 68.13%, in which the SVM technique outperforms the PLSA algorithm by 14.73%.

It needs to be pointed out that this evaluation is based on predetermined semantic view types, which are in favor of the SVM algorithm. It is because such a semantic definition has become considerably involved in SVM training, while barely being used in PLSA training. In the SVM method, labeled training data associated with each predefined view type are indispensable for building the classifier. On the other hand, the PLSA model training merely requires a specified number of view types, which is similar to the number of clusters needed for training a K-means clustering. Thus, it is anticipated that the supervised SVM method will have better performance than the unsupervised PLSA algorithm.

However, the PLSA model is advanced in its unsupervised characteristics such that the labeled data is not necessary in training. This feature makes the PLSA more suitable than the SVM and significant in supporting the generic framework dealing with large-scale datasets, where automatic processes and minimum human and expertise interventions are essential. For evaluating our proposed framework, a trade-off in the classification accuracy can be afforded, if the ultimate event detection results are comparable using either the PLSA or the SVM view results.

In order to analyze the generic and scalable properties, a subset with small-scale five-sports dataset is applied, including {soccer, basketball, volleyball, table tennis, tennis}. The SVM and PLSA view classification performance of this small-scale dataset is presented in the 3rd/4th columns of Fig. 9.8, respectively. The baseline on the small-scale data, the 14-sports, has a 0.27 % performance drop in SVM and an improvement of 1.76 % in PLSA. With similar results, compared with the five-sport small-scale data, the 14-sport view dataset has a lot more data in both variety and volume.

Based on the preceding analytical results, the extrapolated performance from this current relatively large-scale dataset to a truly large-scale dataset should be maintained, especially for the PLSA method. The reasoning is twofold: first, large-scale data is normally sparse; PLSA, as a generative model, has a characteristics in probabilistically mapping data from a high-dimensional space to a low-dimensional space. Hence, more information brought by the new data can help in finding significant representatives in the lower dimensional space. Second, since the number of view classes are fixed at four types, more variety and volume will not affect the performance much.

Additionally, a knowledge transfer property is investigated by using the same five-sport dataset. It can be seen that an individual sport from insufficient resources {basketball, volleyball, table tennis, tennis} can be assisted by borrowing the codebook from an abundant sport resource {soccer}. As Fig. 9.8 depicts, these limited-source four sports in the 5th/6th columns, the codebook transfer mechanism has improved about 2.07 % and 5.05 % for the SVM and PLSA on average, respectively. The margin of improvement using the PLSA is bigger than its counterpart in SVM. This result can be explained by the nature of two different techniques. PLSA is a probabilistic-based dimensional reduction technique. Therefore, more data will provide a more thorough characterization of the low-dimensional model.

On the contrary, SVM is a technique mapping from a low dimensional space to a higher dimensional space. More information brought by the codebook may be overwhelmed by the SVM process and may not necessarily provide a better classification in the higher-dimensional space. Therefore, such a knowledge transfer property could help the unsupervised PLSA in further improving its performance for sports with scarce resources.

9.4.3 Event Detection Using Coarse-to-Fine Scheme

In previous experiments, the proposed framework provides an application to identify video genres by directly utilizing domain knowledge-free SIFT descriptors and a BoW model. After the genre is determined, individual frames of the query video sequence are labeled by the middle-level semantic views via either supervised or unsupervised classifiers. In this experiment, the task on basketball score event detection is investigated by employing this labeled video sequence. A two-staged coarse-to-fine scheme is adopted that first detects scoreboard information change, introduced by Miao et al. [290]. By adopting this technique, an entry point of an interesting event is located. However, this coarse detection only provides a static frame-based rough estimation as an entry point. Since scoreboard information not only appears in score events, but also in time-out events or intermission events, individual frame-based detection without temporal structured information cannot provide robust and satisfactory results. Therefore, a fine-tuning process in finalizing detection is adopted to ensure that the query video truly conveys the score event as its semantic theme. The proposed HCRF model is deployed as the fine-tuning process after the first-stage coarse detection. Experimental results using this HCRF model are compared with CRF and HMM baselines.

Two video groups consisting of four matches are utilized, which are defined as (a) Dataset A: using two NBA games for training and using another two Olympic Games for testing; (b) Database B: using one NBA game for training and using another NBA game for testing. Frame-based views from the PLSA model and the SVM model are applied to Dataset A and B. Therefore, four combinations of view labels and datasets are defined as $PLSA + A$, $PLSA + B$, $SVM + A$, and $SVM + B$. Each video clip used in both training and testing is automatically decimated and consists of 500 uniformly sampled frames. We use a window size $N = 20$, which is introduced in Fig. 9.9 and Eq. (9.7) from Sect. 9.3.3, with a window N sliding every ten frames. The final number of the states sequence for HCRF is thus calculated as $49 = 500/(20 - 10) - 1$.

Fig. 9.9 HCRF input shown in Eq. (9.7), by sliding window average result on view types of decoded image sequence

Fig. 9.10 Current state influenced by surrounding observed states

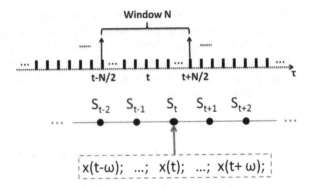

Table 9.7 Precision and recall results of basketball score events detection at the first (coarse) stage

Correctly detected score	Detected score	Correct total score	Precision	Recall
True positive	Correct result	Obtained result	%	%
231	251	268	92.03	86.19

The number of approximated events detected after the first stage is given in Table 9.7. The precision and recall of the coarse-stage basketball score detection are 92.03 % and 86.19 % respectively. In the second stage, the proposed HCRF-based model and state-of-the-art HMM and CRF models are evaluated and compared. The advantage of HCRF over HMM is its relaxation on the Markov property that the current state S_t can be inferred from both current observations, as well as surrounding observations, as illustrated in Fig. 9.10. In the experiment, the circumferential range number is selected at $\omega = 0, 1, 2$. As shown in Table 9.8, the HCRF has better performance than the CRF for the same ω values, while both models outperform the HMM baseline. When using different ω values for both CRF and HCRF, $\omega = 1$ provides better results than $\omega = 0$, in which neighboring information assists in better decision-making. However, when $\omega = 2$ is used for HCRF, the performance has been dropped for all cases compared with $\omega = 1$. This performance degradation can be viewed as an overfitting issue, in which adding more surrounding information limits the structured prediction ability. A similar overfitting problem is also observed in gesture recognition research using HCRF [293]. In summary, the proposed HCRF-based model with parameter $\omega = 1$ outperforms both CRF and HMM models. The best results are obtained at 93.08 % and 92.31 % by taking SVM- and PLSA-based input labels, respectively.

On the other hand, by comparing the proposed PLSA with SVM benchmark, performance discrepancy of the event detection has been shortened, despite the input view classification (as shown in Fig. 9.8) has PLSA (70.14 %) outperformed by SVM (82.00 %) with 11.86 %. For Dataset A, the average difference shows that SVM outperforms PLSA by 3.65 %, while in Dataset B, such a difference is only 0.47 %. This tolerable difference demonstrates the robustness and resilience

Table 9.8 Performance comparison on score event detection in basketball

	Accuracy			
	Dataset A (NBA/Olympics)		Dataset B (NBA/NBA)	
	SVM + A (%)	PLSA + A (%)	SVM+B (%)	PLSA + B (%)
HMM $\omega = 0$	78.28	75.29	87.50	85.94
CRF $\omega = 0$	78.16	74.57	87.43	86.52
CRF $\omega = 1$	79.52	76.82	88.52	87.89
HCRF $\omega = 0$	80.93	75.53	90.00	90.77
HCRF $\omega = 1$	83.26	80.24	93.08	92.31
HCRF $\omega = 2$	82.09	77.88	91.46	91.77

Dataset A: NBA matches as training, Olympic matches as testing. Dataset B: NBA matches for both training and testing

of structured prediction models in accommodating poorly labeled video sequences from PLSA, yet achieving comparable performance with those labeled sequences from SVM. Therefore, the event detection presented in this work achieves similar results by both unsupervised and supervised learning. However, due to PLSA's reduced human involvement, the unsupervised classifier is preferred in large-scale video analysis.

Experimental result discrepancies using Dataset A and Dataset B are also compared. Although both datasets belong to basketball, Dataset B (with NBA matches for both training and testing) outperformed Dataset A (with NBA matches for training and Olympics matches for testing) by 10.9% on average. It suggests that albeit Datasets A and B are of the same genre and event detection task, a significant difference exists. Such a difference can be explained by assuming that NBA and international basketball (FIBA) are two different styles of the same genre. In terms of computer vision and structured prediction, NBA and FIBA have related but different temporal patterns even in the same semantic event. Thus, by training/testing in the same style, it is expected to have a better detection rate than training/testing using different styles. This is also an example of the semantic gap–that semantic event recognition with discrepant conditions is still not perfect.

Although there is only one event detection example discussed, it is believed that the method can be extended and generalized to a bigger pool of event scenarios. The reason is fourfold: First, the experiment data of the basketball score event are multi-source and non-simplex. Videos are collected from both internet and TV recordings, and there are different production rules of NBA and Olympics basketball. Second, the video representation module using local features and the BoW model is domain knowledge-free and with no production rules involved. Such a generic approach has been proven to be effective in genre categorization of 23 sports, view classification of 14 sports, and the basketball score event. Third, the event detection algorithm utilizing HCRFs, as well as baseline HMMs and CRFs are structured prediction models and belong to the category of state event model. By comparing the number of events analyzed using different event models from Table 9.2, the state event model, a recently popular approach in literature, is capable in handling more events than the other two model types (i.e. pattern-recognition model and semantic event model). In addition, among the state event models, most methods utilize middle-level semantic agents. In our work, the adopted four-category view type definition is one of the most popular classification schemes in literature. Last and most important, the input of our event detection model is a sequence of labeled views which is the result of a domain knowledge-free method (either PLSA or SVM), using generic video representation. With better accuracy achieved by the proposed HCRF-based model than baselines HMM- and CRF-based models, the performance should be maintained with other labeled sequences which could form various event scenarios. Moreover, utilizing sequences labeled by the middle-level agents as input, is also popular among peers' work with state event models [275, 276, 278, 279].

9.5 Summary

This chapter focuses on scalable video genre classification and event detection with the help of middle-level view agent. We introduce the BoW model, with its incorporation of unsupervised learning algorithms, in analyzing large-scale video dataset generically and systematically. Three video tasks are investigated in a coherent and sequential order. After processing all data indifferently at the feature extraction stage using domain knowledge-free local SIFT descriptors, video sequences are represented by utilizing compact and concise BoW model. Then, a systematic scheme is employed for interesting event detection, by taking the video sequence as query. In this framework, after its genres identified using a k-NN classifier, the query video is evaluated by a semantic view assignment as the second stage using the PLSA model. Both genre identification and view classification tasks utilize the initially processed video representation as input, and unsupervised algorithms as classifiers. Finally in the third task, the interesting event is detected by feeding the view labels into an HCRF-structured prediction model.

Overall, this framework demonstrates the efficiency and generality in processing voluminous data from a large-scale video collection and achieves various tasks in video analysis. The effectiveness of the framework is justified by extensive experimentation and results are compared with benchmarks and state-of-the-art algorithms. As a conclusion, with little human expertise and effort involvement in both domain knowledge-independent video representation and annotation-free unsupervised view labeling, the proposed generic and systematic method using the BoW model is promising in processing videos, and has the potential for even larger and more diverse datasets.

Chapter 10
Audio-Visual Fusion for Film Database Retrieval and Classification

Abstract This chapter presents the techniques for the characterization and fusion of audio and visual content in videos, and demonstrates their applications in movie database retrieval. In the audio domain, a study is conducted on the peaky nature of the distribution of wavelet coefficients of an audio signal, which cannot be effectively modeled by a single distribution. Thus, a new modeling method based on a Laplacian mixture model is studied for analyzing audio content and extracting audio features. The dimension of the indexed features is low, which is important for the retrieval efficiency of the system in terms of response time. Together with the audio feature, the visual feature is extracted by template frequency modeling. Both features are referred to as perceptual features. Then, a learning algorithm for audiovisual fusion is presented. Specifically, the two features are fused at the late fusion stage and input into a support vector machine to learn semantic concepts from a given video database. Based on the experimental results, the current system implementing the support vector machine-based fusion technique achieves high classification accuracy when applied to a large volume database containing Hollywood movies.

10.1 Introduction

Content-based video retrieval methods are highly applicable to movie on demand and movie production applications. These methods can be implemented by a recommender system for content-based filtering to assist users in finding relevant entities according to their individual preferences. A central design issue of recommender services is in addressing how to suggest relevant, yet unknown entities. The system based on video indexing using text descriptors usually provides great generic and broad categories. In comparison, a *perception-based descriptor* implemented by a content-based recommender system provides a more focused scope of relevant entities. Such descriptors aggregate several different types of modality to compute relevancy. The variety of the integrated modality allows us to consider different relevant criteria, helping users to explore new entities. To that

© Springer International Publishing Switzerland 2014
P. Muneesawang et al., *Multimedia Database Retrieval: Technology and Applications*,
Multimedia Systems and Applications, DOI 10.1007/978-3-319-11782-9_10

end, this chapter presents the application of perception-based features extracted from different modalities and fused through a machine learning process in order to retrieve and classify relevant movie clips.

Video content analysis tasks, such as the detection of complex events, are intrinsically multimodal problems, since both the audio and visual channels provide important clues. Recognition of video entities such as events in the visual domain alone is challenging enough since a video contains large variations in lighting, viewpoint, camera motion, etc. However, video also contains audio information which provide an extra useful clue for content analysis. The video content captured is multimodal, and the task of video content analysis requires a *fusion model* to capture both consistent and inconsistent audio-visual patterns for video indexing and retrieval.

In Sect. 10.2, we begin with the method for audio content analysis and indexing. The modeling scheme based on the Laplacian mixture model (LMM) is presented and demonstrated for indexing and retrieval of videos using audio content. The LMM is utilized to capture the peaky distribution of wavelet coefficients. The LMM's parameters provide a low-dimension feature vector for video indexing, as well as an efficient audio feature that is helpful for finding clues to the video events.

Section 10.3 presents the application of the template-frequency modeling (TFM) method for visual content characterization of movie clips, and experimentally explores its efficiency and robustness. The TFM performance is also compared to the single/multi frame-based video indexing, which performs frame clustering for video indexing. A movie search engine is developed which addresses the difficulty in video retrieval with automatic and semi-automatic relevance feedback.

While the previous sections explain the extraction methods for perception-based features, Sect. 10.4 presents a learning algorithm for audio-visual fusion and demonstrates its application for video classification in a movie database. The perception-based features are extracted from different modalities and fused through a machine learning process. In order to capture the spatial–temporal information, TFM is applied to extract visual features, and LMM is utilized to extract audio features. These features are fused at a late fusion stage and input to a support vector machine (SVM) to construct a decision function for the classification of videos according to a given concept. The experimental results show that the system implementing this fusion method successfully attained high classification accuracy when applied to a large database containing various types of Hollywood movies.

10.2   Audio Content Characterization

The users of the video data are often interested in certain action sequences that are easier to identify in the audio domain. Audio is effective in linking visually different but semantically related video clips. In this section, a statistical approach is adopted to analyze the audio data and extracts audio features for video indexing. Wavelet transformation is applied to the audio signal and the LMM is utilized for characterization of audio content.

Wavelet transform is a powerful tool for analyzing signal content. It is applied for audio signals in the current work. Wavelet coefficients are sparsely distributed due to their energy packing property. Therefore, the distribution of the wavelet coefficients is non-Gaussian and peaky. This type of peaky distribution can be modeled using a mixture of Gaussians. In theory, any arbitrary-shaped distribution can be modeled using mixture of Gaussians, if there are an infinite number of components in the mixture. Modeling the wavelet coefficients is a typical example in which a large number of components in the Gaussian mixture may be required to catch the peaky distribution. This is however practically infeasible. Studies on the nature of wavelet coefficient distributions in high-frequency subbands have shown that the distributions have a Laplacian-like density [325]. Taking into account the peaky nature, a LMM may provide a better alternative for modeling the distributions of wavelet coefficients.

10.2.1 Finite Mixture Model

The wavelet transforms are sparse due to them compression property. There are a few wavelet coefficients that have large values and carry most of the information, while most of the other coefficients have small values. This energy-packing property of the wavelet coefficients results in a peaky distribution [328]. This type of peaky distribution is heavy-tailed and difficult to model with a single distribution. Mixture modeling techniques provide an excellent and flexible alternative for this kind of complex distribution. Finite mixture models are widely used in statistical modeling of data. It is a very powerful tool for probabilistic modeling of the data produced by a set of alternative sources. Finite mixtures represent a formal approach to unsupervised classification in statistical pattern recognition. The usefulness of this modeling approach is not limited to clustering. They are also able to represent probability density functions (pdf) of arbitrary complexity [327].

Let $\mathbf{x} = [x_1, \ldots, x_d]^t$ be a particular observation of a random variable. We assume that the data has been generated by a finite mixture of components. The pdf of this random variable is then defined as [326]:

$$p(\mathbf{x}|\Theta) = \sum_{m=1}^{M} \alpha_m p_m(\mathbf{x}|\theta_m) \tag{10.1}$$

where $\alpha_1, \ldots, \alpha_M$ are the mixing probabilities, θ_m is the parameter set representing the m-th component, $\Theta = \{\theta_1, \ldots, \theta_M, \alpha_1, \ldots, \alpha_M\}$, and M is the number of components. Therefore the complete set of model parameters Θ is to be calculated to specify the mixture. In addition, since $\alpha_1, \ldots, \alpha_M$ are probabilities,

$$\alpha_m \geq 0, \sum_{m=1}^{M} \alpha_m = 1 \tag{10.2}$$

The mixtures can be built with different types of components. However, it is usually assumed that the components of the mixture have the same functional form, such as Gaussian or Laplacian. In the following, the LMM is utilized and the parameters defining the mixture model is estimated by the expectation–maximization (EM) algorithm.

10.2.2   Laplacian Mixture Model and Parameter Estimation

The univariate Laplacian distribution is defined as:

$$p(x) = \frac{1}{2b} \exp\left(-\frac{|x - \mu|}{b}\right) \tag{10.3}$$

where x is an instance of the random variable, μ is the location parameter, and b represents the width of the distribution. A Laplacian distribution with $\mu = 0$ and $b = 1$ is shown in Fig. 10.1. Previous studies have shown that the density of the wavelet coefficients is symmetrically centered at zero [325]. This is due to the fact that most of the wavelet coefficients in a frequency sub-band have small magnitudes close to zero. Therefore, we assume that the underlying distribution is a mixture of M Laplacian components centered at zero. Then the probability function of the i-th data point, $p(x^{(i)}|\theta_m)$ is simply a conditional probability of generating given that the m-th model is chosen:

$$p(x^{(i)}|\theta_m) = \frac{1}{2b_m} \exp\left(-\frac{|x^{(i)}|}{b_m}\right) \tag{10.4}$$

The EM algorithm is applied for the estimation of the parameters. We assume the existence of a hidden variable $\mathbf{z} = [z_1, \ldots, z_M]^t$ whose values are not known. This M-dimensional hidden variable $\mathbf{z}^{(i)}$ is associated with each data point $\mathbf{x}^{(i)}$ and indicates which component of the mixture has generated $\mathbf{x}^{(i)}$. For example, if a data value has been generated by the m-th component of the mixture, then the m-th component of this vector $z_m^{(i)} = 1$ and all other component values will be 0. Here, i represents the index of the data point and $i = 1, \ldots, N$ because the total number of observations are taken to be N. In the presence of both $\mathbf{x}$ and $\mathbf{z}$, the complete likelihood can be written as follows:

$$L_c(\Theta, \mathbf{x}, \mathbf{z}) = \sum_{i=1}^{N} \sum_{m=1}^{M} z_m^{(i)} \ln\left(p(\mathbf{x}^{(i)}|\theta_m) + \ln \alpha_m\right) \tag{10.5}$$

The EM algorithm proceeds by alternatively applying the following two steps:

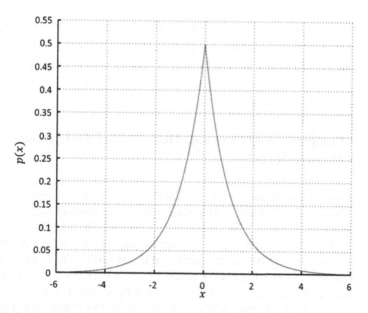

Fig. 10.1 Laplacian distribution with $\mu = 0$ and $b = 1$

- **M-Step**: There is only one parameter in Eq. (10.4) i.e., b_m. Now we have the model parameter set given by $\theta_m = [\alpha_m, b_m]$ for each mixture component. Using the maximum likelihood principle, and enforcing the condition $\sum_{m=1}^{M} \alpha_m = 1$, we get the following update equations for b_m and α_m;

$$b_m = \frac{\sum_{i=1}^{N} \left\langle z_m^{(i)} \right\rangle \left| x^{(i)} \right|}{\sum_{i=1}^{N} \left\langle z_m^{(i)} \right\rangle}, \tag{10.6}$$

$$\alpha_m = \frac{\sum_{i=1}^{N} \left\langle z_m^{(i)} \right\rangle}{N} \tag{10.7}$$

where $\langle \cdot \rangle$ is the expectation operator.

- **E-Step**: To maximize the incomplete log-likelihood $p(x^{(1)}, \ldots, x^{(N)} | \Theta)$, we take the expectation w.r.t. the posterior distribution of $\mathbf{Z}$ namely $p(\mathbf{Z} | x^{(1)}, \ldots, x^{(N)}, \Theta)$, where $\mathbf{Z} = \left\{ z^{(i)} \right\}_{i=1}^{N}$. Therefore, each of the expectations $\left\langle z_m^{(i)} \right\rangle$ that appear in the above update equations is computed as follows:

$$\left\langle z_m^{(i)} \right\rangle = \frac{p(x^{(i)} | \theta_m) \alpha_m}{\sum_{j=1}^{M} p(x^{(i)} | \theta_j) \alpha_j} \tag{10.8}$$

The parameter $[\alpha_m, b_m]$ are initialized and the value of the hidden variable $\left\langle z_m^{(i)} \right\rangle$ is calculated. The value of b_m and α_m are then updated by using the new value of $\left\langle z_m^{(i)} \right\rangle$ using Eq. (10.6) and Eq. (10.7). This is done iteratively until the algorithm converges.

10.2.3   Comparison of Gaussian Mixture Model and Laplacian Mixture Model

In order to make a comparison between GMM and LMM, a study was performed on the Brodatz image database. The images from the Brodatz image database were decomposed to three levels using the Daubechies db4 wavelet kernel. The wavelet coefficients in all the high-frequency subbands (9 for 3-level decomposition) were modeled with two components, GMM and LMM. The model accuracy was measured using the Kullback–Leibler Divergence (KL). KL is a quantity which measures the difference between two probability distributions. KL can be considered as a kind of distance between the two probability densities. But it is not a real distance measure because it is not symmetric. The likelihood of the model can be measured in terms of the KL between the observed density and the density as calculated by the model. The KL between two probability distributions of a discrete variable is defined as,

$$KL(p,q) = \sum_{x} p(x) \log \frac{p(x)}{q(x)} \tag{10.9}$$

where $p(x)$ is the estimated probability distribution from GMM or LMM, and $q(x)$ is the normalized histogram of the wavelet coefficients. There are a total of 16,704 high-frequency subbands for 3-level decomposition of 1,856 images ($1,856 \times 9$). The wavelet coefficients of high-frequency subbands at the first, second, and third levels of decomposition are quantized into 256, 128 and 64 levels respectively, to properly represent the resolutions of different decomposition levels. A normalized histogram is constructed that represents the true distribution $q(x)$ of the coefficients. The distributions using LMM and GMM models are then calculated. The KL distance is calculated between normalized histograms and the distributions obtained from the GMM and LMM models. It is observed that, out of 16,704 total cases, LMM gives a lower value of KL in 16,494 cases. In the remaining 210 cases, KL was lower in case of GMM. These results indicate that in 98.74 % of the test cases, the LMM model with two components is closer to the true distribution in terms of KL statistics. This evaluation indicates that LMM is a more appropriate model for the wavelet coefficient distribution and can model it with only two components. The fitting of the GMM and LMM models for a typical high-frequency wavelet subband of an image from the Brodatz image database is illustrated in Figs. 10.2 and 10.3.

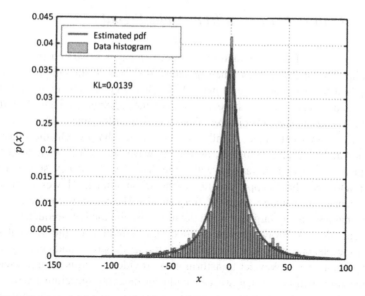

Fig. 10.2 LMM fit for a high-frequency subband

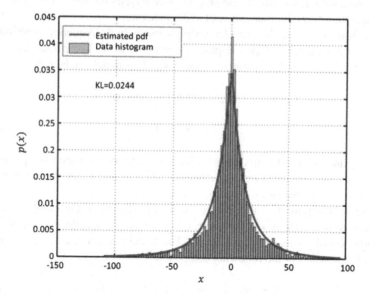

Fig. 10.3 GMM fit for a high-frequency subband

10.2.4   Feature Extraction from Audio Signal

In order to obtain feature extraction, an audio signal is separated from the input video clip. The audio signal is then re-sampled to a uniform sampling rate. It is decomposed using a one-dimensional DWT. This decomposes audio signals into two subbands at each wavelet scale; a low-frequency subband and a high-frequency subband. The audio signal is different from a gray or color image signal. In images, the values of adjacent pixels usually do not change sharply. On the other hand, the digital audio signal is a form of oscillating waveform, which includes a variety of frequency components varying with time. The low-frequency subband of the image is a low-resolution approximation of the original image. However, most audio signals consist of a wide variety of frequencies. The wavelet coefficients of the audio signal have many large values in detail levels, and the low-frequency subband coefficients do not always provide a good approximation of the original signal. The wavelet decomposition scheme matches the models of sound octave-divisions for perceptual scales. Wavelet transform also provides a multiscale representation of sound information, so that we can build an indexing structure based on this scale property. Moreover, audio signals are nonstationary signals whose frequency contents evolve with time. Wavelet transform provides both frequency and time information simultaneously. These properties of wavelet transform for sound signal decomposition form the foundation of audio indexing.

The distribution of the wavelet coefficients in high-frequency subbands are modeled by a mixture of two Laplacians centered at 0. The parameters of this mixture model are used as features for indexing. The model can be represented as:

$$p(\mathbf{w}^{(i)}) = \alpha_1 p_1(\mathbf{w}^{(i)}|b_1) + \alpha_2 p_2(\mathbf{w}^{(i)}|b_2) \tag{10.10}$$

$$\alpha_1 + \alpha_2 = 1 \tag{10.11}$$

where α_1 and α_2 are the mixing probabilities of the two components p_1 and p_2, respectively. $\mathbf{w}^{(i)}$ are the wavelet coefficients while b_1 and b_2 are the parameters of the Laplacian distributions p_1 and p_2, respectively.

Table 10.1 summarises the feature extraction algorithm that employs the EM algorithm to obtain the model parameters. In practice, the wavelet decomposition of the audio signals is taken up to L levels. The feature vector used for indexing the video clips consists of the following components:

$$\mathbf{f}_a = \left\lfloor \{m_0, \sigma_0\}, \{\alpha_{1,l}, b_{1,l}, b_{2,l}\} \right\rfloor, l = 1, 2, \dots, L-1 \tag{10.12}$$

where $\mathbf{f}_a$ denotes the feature vector describing the audio content. This composes of the mean and standard deviation of the wavelet coefficients in the low-frequency subband; model parameters calculated for each of the high-frequency subbands.

10.2.5 Performance of Video Retrieval Using Audio Indexing

The experimental results obtained in this section were conducted on a database consisting of 24 full-length and mostly recent mainstream Hollywood movies chosen to represent the more popular films, music videos, and commercials. This included the Titanic, the Patriot, the Postman, Pakistani music videos and films. All video files were segmented into 6,000 clips, each of which contained one to three shots, and was approximately 6 s long.

The feature extraction algorithm explained in Table 10.1 was applied to obtain the audio feature. A wavelet transform with nine-level decompositions was applied to the audio signal from each video clip. The coefficients in each high frequency subband were then characterized by the LMM. The resulting model parameters and the mean and standard deviation of wavelet coefficients in the low-frequency subband were used to obtain feature vectors according to Eq. (10.12). In addition, as feature components represent different physical quantities and have different dynamic ranges, the Gaussian normalization technique [329] was employed to convert the vector component to $[-1, 1]$.

A total of 25 queries were generated from different high-level query concepts that included "Fighting", "Ship Crashing", "Music Video", and "Dance Party". These concepts were chosen based on the fact that audio information was the dominant feature in these concepts. Five queries were performed for each concept, and the retrieval precision was measured from 16 best matches. Table 10.2 shows the retrieval results obtained by using the audio description for video retrieval, at 7-level and 9-level wavelet decompositions. The results are obtained by averaging the precisions within the individual query concepts, as well as within the overall queries. These results clearly indicate the power of audio descriptors in finding the video clips containing the specified concepts. The retrieval results varied depending on the characteristic of the query, and the performance was the highest in cases with dialogues. An average-retrieval precision of 84.2 % was achieved based on 9-level decomposition. This precision value was 6.4 % better than that based on 7-level decomposition. Further increasing the level of decomposition may improve the performance, but at the expense of more computational overhead.

The similarity concept is hard to define because of the subjectivity of the matter. But we can define a notion of similarity based on the concept of the clip. In the case of music videos, the clips are considered similar if they belong to the same song. Similarly, in the case of audio clips which contain a dialogue, the clips belonging to the same movie are taken as similar because they involve similar characters. The lowest performance is obtained in the case of "Ship Crashing" due to its audio similarity with the "Sound Effects" class. Both classes are overlapping in meaning in that they contain similar audio content. Performance is enhanced with the increase in the number of decomposition levels.

Table 10.1 Feature extraction for audio signal

Input	Audio signal, $s(t)$
Output	Feature vector, $\mathbf{f} = \left\lfloor \{m_0, \sigma_0\}, \{\alpha_{1,l}, b_{1,l}, b_{2,l}\} \right\rfloor, l = 1, 2, \ldots, L-1$, where m_0 and σ_0 are the mean and standard deviation of the wavelet coefficients in the low-frequency subband, $\{\alpha_{1,l}, b_{1,l}, b_{2,l}\}$ are the model parameters obtained from wavelet coefficients from the l-th high-frequency subband, and L is the decomposition level.
Computation	1. Apply DWT to $s(t)$ and obtain wavelet coefficients of the low-frequency subband $\{\mathrm{w}^{(i)}\}_{Low}$ and the high-frequency subband $\{\mathrm{w}^{(i)}\}_{High,l}, l = 1, 2, \ldots, L-1$
	2. Compute $\{m_0, \sigma_0\}$ from $\{\mathrm{w}^{(i)}\}_{Low}$

	3. Compute $\{\alpha_{1,l}, b_{1,l}, b_{2,l}\}, l = 1, 2, \ldots, L-1$
	 begin initialize $l \leftarrow 0$
	   do $l \leftarrow l+1$, $\{\mathrm{w}^{(i)}\} \leftarrow \{\mathrm{w}^{(i)}\}_{High,l}$
	     begin initialize $[b_1, b_2]$ and $[\alpha_1, \alpha_2]$, $j \leftarrow 0$ *(EM algorithm)*
	     do $j \leftarrow j+1$
	       E-step: compute the expected value of the hidden variable for each wavelet coefficient
	
	 $$\left\langle z_1^{(i)} \right\rangle = \frac{\alpha_1(j)p(\mathrm{w}^{(i)}|b_1(j))}{\alpha_1(j)p(\mathrm{w}^{(i)}|b_1(j)) + \alpha_2(j)p(\mathrm{w}^{(i)}|b_2(j))}$$
	
	 $$\left\langle z_2^{(i)} \right\rangle = \frac{\alpha_2(j)p(\mathrm{w}^{(i)}|b_2(j))}{\alpha_1(j)p(\mathrm{w}^{(i)}|b_1(j)) + \alpha_2(j)p(\mathrm{w}^{(i)}|b_2(j))}$$
	
	 M-Step: update the parameters $[b_1, b_2]$ and *a priori* probabilities $[\alpha_1, \alpha_2]$,
	
	 $$\alpha_1(j+1) = \frac{\sum_{i=1}^{N} \left\langle z_1^{(i)}(j) \right\rangle}{N}$$
	
	 $$\alpha_2(j+1) = \frac{\sum_{i=1}^{N} \left\langle z_2^{(i)}(j) \right\rangle}{N},$$
	
	 $$b_1(j+1) = \frac{\sum_{i=1}^{N} \left\langle z_1^{(i)}(j) \right\rangle \left| \mathrm{w}^{(i)} \right|}{\sum_{i=1}^{N} \left\langle z_1^{(i)}(j) \right\rangle}$$
	
	 $$b_2(j+1) = \frac{\sum_{i=1}^{N} \left\langle z_2^{(i)}(j) \right\rangle \left| \mathrm{w}^{(i)} \right|}{\sum_{i=1}^{N} \left\langle z_2^{(i)}(j) \right\rangle},$$
	
	       where N is the number of wavelet coefficients.
	       until convergence is reached
	       return $[\alpha_1, b_1, b_2]$
	     end
	   until $l = L$
	   return $\{\alpha_{1,l}, b_{1,l}, b_{2,l}\}, l = 1, 2, \ldots, L-1$
	 end

Table 10.2 Video retrieval results, obtained by LMM-based audio indexing, using 25 queries

| LMM features | Average precision (%) | | | | | | |
	Music video	Fighting	Ship crashing	Dance party	Dialogues	Sound effects	Average
Seven-level wavelet decomposition	80.0	77.5	67.2	60.0	92.2	89.6	77.74
Nine-level wavelet decomposition	83.8	83.8	65	78.8	100	93.8	84.2

10.3   Visual Content Characterization

This section demonstrates the application of the template-frequency model (TFM) for video indexing. The TFM was discussed in Chap. 3, but its performance has not been compared to other methods. In the following, a summary of TFM for video indexing is given, and a demonstration is performed by applying it to the movie database.

10.3.1   Visual Indexing Algorithm

The TFM for video indexing is summarized in the following steps:

- **Step 1**: Template generation. A competitive learning algorithm [330, 331] is applied to generate prototype vectors, $C = \{\mathbf{c}_1, \ldots, \mathbf{c}_j, \ldots, \mathbf{c}_{T_c}\}, \mathbf{c}_j \in \mathbb{R}^d$, where $\mathbf{c}_j$ is obtained by modification of input color histograms, and T_c is the total number of prototypes (templates).
- **Step 2**: Multiple label vector quantization. For a given video clip, a primary descriptor is obtained: $D = \{\mathbf{h}_1, \ldots, \mathbf{h}_i, \ldots, \mathbf{h}_{T_d}\}$, where $\mathbf{h}_i$ is the 48-bin color histogram vector of the i-th frame, and T_d is the total number of frames. Each vector $\mathbf{h}_i$ is quantized by the prototype vectors in C using multiple labels:

$$Q(\mathbf{h}_i) = \{l_1^{(\mathbf{h}_i)}, l_2^{(\mathbf{h}_i)}, \ldots, l_k^{(\mathbf{h}_i)}\}, l_j^{(\mathbf{h}_i)} \in \{1, 2, \ldots, T_c\} \qquad (10.13)$$

where $l_1^{(\mathbf{h}_i)}$ is the label of the best-match template, and $l_k^{(\mathbf{h}_i)}$ is the label of the k-th best match template.
- **Step 3**: $TF \times IDF$ weighting. The resulting $Q(\mathbf{h}_i), i = 1, \ldots, T_d$ give a set of labels corresponding to the entire video frames, which are concatenated into a single weight vector, $\mathbf{f}_v = [f_1, \ldots, f_j, \ldots, f_{T_c}]^t$. The weight parameter f_j is obtained by:

$$f_j = \frac{fr(\mathbf{c}_j)}{\max_j\{fr(\mathbf{c}_j)\}} \times \log \frac{N_v}{n(\mathbf{c}_j)} \qquad (10.14)$$

where $fr(c_j)$ stands for a raw frequency of template c_j (the number of times the template is mentioned in the input video sequence). The maximum is computed over all templates mentioned in the content of the input video; N_v denotes the total number of videos in the system and $n(c_j)$ denotes the number of videos in which the index template c_j appears.

10.3.2   Performance Comparison for Retrievals from Movie Database

An Interactive-based Analysis and Retrieval of Multimedia (iARM) system is a web-based search engine [324], and has been implemented using TFM video indexing structure and an interactive content-based retrieval strategy. This section demonstrates its application for retrieval of "video clips" from a video database of 20 h, which includes 14 Hollywood movies segmented into a total of 2,401 video clips, each of which is approximately 30 s long. Table 10.3 gives the details of the database. The iARM system is implemented to manage a centralized database using the Java 2 Enterprise Editions (J2EE), shown in Fig. 10.4. In this system, the video database is located on a single server, and the system provides user interactions through Java Server Page (JSP) interface. The requests and feedback on the client sides are implemented through JSP, which are then processed within the Java Bean on the server side.

The TFM method was applied for indexing all video clips in the database. In a separate off-line process, each video clip was indexed by a set of visual templates. The size of this set was $T_c = 2,000$. During the online process, the video search was initiated by the query submitted by the user and followed by relevance feedback. Using the same strategy as the relevance feedback technique described in [323], a new query was obtained by enhancing the relevant models and suppressing the irrelevant models from the original query [cf. Eq. (2.7)].

Table 10.3 Video database, containing 20 h of Hollywood movies

ID	Movie name	ID	Movie name
1	15 Minutes	8	Lion King
2	40 Days & 40 Nights	9	US Marshals
3	A beautiful Mind	10	Me, Myself & Irene
4	Dr. T	11	The Adventures of Pluto Nash
5	Final Fantasy	12	Romeo Must Die
6	Gladiator	13	Scooby-Doo
7	Just visiting	14	The Two Towers

Table 10.4 Average precision (%), obtained by retrieving 40 queries, measured from the top 16 retrievals, using KFVI and TFM methods with user-controlled relevance feedback, automatic relevance feedback, and semi-automatic retrieval methods

Methods		Average precision (%)
KFVI	SKF	39.22
	MKF	62.34
TFM	Initial result without RF	73.59
	User controlled-RF	90.47
	Automatic-RF	80.12
	Semi-automatic retrieval	92.03

The system was tested using 40 sample video clips chosen randomly from fourteen movies. Table 10.4 shows the retrieval results averaged over the 40 queries. From the table, it is observed that the iARM system had a very high precision of 73.6 % at the initial stage (i.e., more than 11 relevant video clips were retrieved out of the top 16 best matches). It also saw a significant improvement of 90.51 % in precision after a single feedback cycle. This implies that the TFM method is highly effective in capturing spatio-temporal information from video. This also indicates that TFM is efficient and highly adaptable, as only single user feedback was required for significant improvement.

Table 10.4 also shows the comparison between TFM and other video indexing methods that use video clustering strategies for the video content characterization. The compared methods are denoted as KFVI (key-frame based video indexing). Here, the KFVI employed video clustering approaches discussed in [320–322] for selection of the representative frames from video clips. In this way, for each video clip, frames are clustered based on frame descriptors, and frames that are close to the cluster centriods are selected as key frames. The k-mean algorithm and clustering validity method demonstrated in [321] were employed for the selection of key frames.

KFVI process began by extracting 48-bin color histogram vectors from each video frame in a given video clip. Then, it applied the clustering algorithm to the resulting histogram vectors to obtain k-means with different values of k, for $k = 1, 2, \ldots, 10$. The k-means was run multiple times for each k, and the best of these was selected based on the sum of squared errors. Finally, the Davies–Bonldin index [319] was calculated for each k, $k \in \{1, 2, \ldots, 10\}$, and the k that gave the smallest Davies–Bonldin index was chosen. In doing so, the optimum number of clusters will vary according to the cluster validity analysis of the resulting clusters. The closest frames to the clusters (one frame from each cluster) were selected as key frames, and this method is denoted as a MKF (multiple-key frame) method. For comparison, a single frame which is the closest frame to a cluster centriod was selected as a key frame, and this method is denoted as a SKF (single key frame) method. Video content similarity matching used by the SKF was obtained by comparing the descriptor vectors of the selected key frames of the query and the target videos. However, for the MKF method, similarity measures are obtained by matching multiple key frames of the query against multiple key frames in the target video clips. To be precise, let S be a similarity score. The similarity was obtained by:

$$S = \sum_{i=1}^{N} s_i \tag{10.15}$$

$$s_i = \min_{j=1,\dots,M}\{d[i,j]\} \tag{10.16}$$

where $d[i,j]$ is the distance between the i-th key-frame of the query and the j-th key-frame of the target video; N and M are the total number of key-frames of the query and target videos, respectively.

From the results, it is observed that although the SKF method can be used for retrieval of video shots, SKF is less effective in characterizing video content of video clips. The SKF result achieved 39.22 % precision. By considering multiple key frames as in the MKF method, the performance of the key-frame based video indexing method can be improved to 62.34 %. However, this result is approximately 10 % less precise than that of TFM.

In order to achieve high retrieval performance, the iARM system was implemented using the automatic and semi-automatic retrieval algorithms. The pseudo-relevance feedback using the adaptive cosine network architecture (discussed in Chap. 3) was employed. In this case, depending on the internet traffic conditions, users can submit automatic and semi-automatic queries, and the automatic query can avoid the transmission of training sample video files over the internet. Using the same set of queries as in the previous results, this system first performed an automatic retrieval for each query to adaptively improve its performance. After three iterations of signal propagation in the adaptive cosine network, the system was then assisted by users. Table 10.4 provides the summary of the retrieval results, obtained by automatic and semiautomatic methods. It is observed that the semiautomatic method was superior to the automatic method and the user interaction method. The best performance was achieved at 92.03 % precision. In addition, the moderate performance of the automatic method can be beneficial to the user when internet resources are limited.

The strength of the iARM system was evaluated against a variety of templates used by TFM for indexing video clips. Specifically, three sets of templates at $T_c = 500$, 1,000 and 1,500, were generated using a competitive learning algorithm, where T_c denotes the number of templates. These are approximately 3 %, 6 %, and 9 % of the training sample set, respectively. For each set of templates, video

Table 10.5 Average precision (%), obtained by retrieving 40 queries, using four sets of templates for video indexing

Number of templates	Average precision (%)	
	Initial result	After 1 RF
$T_c = 2,000$	73.59	90.47
$T_c = 1,500$	72.81	89.69
$T_c = 1,000$	72.50	88.13
$T_c = 500$	68.75	81.25

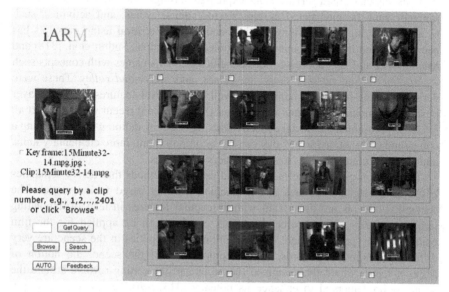

Fig. 10.4 iARM's user interface for retrieval of movie clips using the TFM method

files were indexed, and the resulting feature databases were used by the retrieval system. Table 10.5 shows the retrieval results obtained by retrieving 40 queries. It is observed that the iARM system was fairly robust compared to the deviation in the number of templates T_c. The results in the second column show the small variation in retrieval performance (i.e., 1.1 % reductions of precision) as the number of templates was reduced from 2,000 to 1,000. In this case, video matching used the non-adaptive matrix. However, the performance gap is increased to 2.3 % after relevance feedback as we had anticipated, since human interpretation has been addressed to some extent by the interactive algorithm. The results show that a set of templates with $T_c \geq 1,000$ is sufficient to model the video content in this database. This value of T_c is approximately 0.1 % of the entire video data in this collection.

10.4   Audio-Visual Fusion

When retrieving clips from a database, the user is searching not only for clips that are similar to the query in terms of the visual aspect, but also in terms of the audiovisual aspect to convey a semantic concept-based query interface. The term 'semantic concept' describes the characteristic of the desired clip derived from its distinct characteristics and expressed through audiovisual signals. The semantic may be interpreted as logical story units, events, and activities, such as airplane flying, car crashing, rioting, and so on. Retrieval using concepts has been performed in many domain applications. For example, Sudhir et al. [318] and Miyamori et al. [317] addressed the semantics of tennis games with concepts such as *baseline-rallies, passing-shots, net games,* and *server-and-volley.* These were derived by rule-based mechanisms as well as low-level features such as player position, dominant colors, and mass center [316]. In more recent works, Lay et al. [314,315] presented elemental concept indexing (ECI) by defining concepts using a compound of annotated words that can be decomposed into more elementary units, and applying grammar rules to support query operations.

This section presents the indexing and retrieval methods that derive semantics based on *perceptual* features and a machine learning based fusion model. The semantic concepts are associated with perceptual features instead of annotating terms to specify a finer perception. This interface can be applied for the film editing/making process where the perception characteristics in the scene are very difficult to express in words. In the composition of the scene, the notion of *Mise-en-scène*, where the design of the props and the setting revolve around the scene, is implemented to enhance its potency [313]. *Mise-en-scène* means "put in the scene" for almost everything including the composition itself: framing, movement of the camera and characters, lighting, set design and general visual environment, even sound as it helps elaborate the composition [312]. Such scene units are difficult to characterize with textual descriptions, while they are more easily subjected to feature extraction at the signal level. The audiovisual fusion model employing perceptual features provides a highly efficient interface to retrieve movie clips for concepts such as *Love Scene, Music Video, Fighting, Ship Crashing,* and *Dance Party.* Here these concepts are described with textual descriptions for communication with readers. However, our definitions of the semantic concepts are based on perceptual features in the video and not text descriptors.

The SVM model is adopted for fusion of audiovisual features for characterization of semantic concepts according to *perceptual features*. Although the SVM is a well-established machine learning technique [310], its application for the fusion of multimodality features has only been recently studied. A SVM-based decision fusion technique has been employed for cartridge identification [311], as well as for personal identity verification [306]. However, the SVMs have not previously been applied in decision fusion for the detection of semantic concepts in video.

10.4.1   Decision Fusion Model

Meyer et al. [309] have suggested that there are two techniques for audio-visual fusion in developing audio-visual information recognition systems: feature fusion and decision fusion. These approaches are very often referred to as early fusion and late fusion. The first approach is a simple audio-visual feature concatenation giving rise to a single data representation before the pattern matching stage. The second approach applies separate pattern matching algorithms to audio and video data and then merges the estimated likelihoods of the single-modality matching decisions. In the current application, a late fusion scheme is chosen for the following two reasons. First, visual features in the current work have a physical structure different from audio features in terms of dimensions as well as in weighting schemes. Second, based on previous studies [308] with respect to human perception, audio and visual processing are likely to be carried out independently in different modalities and combined at a very late stage. Audio contains information that is often not available in the visual signal [333]; thus, it may not be appropriate to concatenate audio and visual features into a single representation.

Figure 10.5 shows the architecture of the system which includes the fusion module and SVM. The extracted data (audio and visual) are processed by different similarity functions, d_a and d_v. The function d_a is applied to audio features, whereas the function d_v is applied to visual features. Each function, given the extracted data, will deliver similarity scores between an input sample and a model vector. These scores range between zero (accept) and one (reject). In other words, when combining two modules, the fusion algorithm processes a two-dimensional vector for which each component is a score in [0, 1] delivered by the corresponding modality expert. The SVM will combine the opinions of the different experts and give a binary decision.

Let $\mathbf{f}_a$ and $\mathbf{f}_v$ denote the feature vectors extracted from the audio and video signals, where the subscript a and v are for audio and visual, respectively. Given the video database, we can obtain a set of samples:

$$x_i = [d_{a,i}(\mathbf{f}_{a,i}, \mathbf{f}'_a) \quad d_{v,i}(\mathbf{f}_{v,i}, \mathbf{f}'_v)], \quad i = 1, 2, \ldots, N_T \tag{10.17}$$

where

$$d_{a,i} = 1 - \left\| \mathbf{f}_{a,i} - \mathbf{f}'_a \right\| \tag{10.18}$$

$$d_{v,i} = \frac{\mathbf{f}_{v,i} \cdot \mathbf{f}'_v}{\left\| \mathbf{f}_{v,i} \right\| \times \left\| \mathbf{f}'_v \right\|} \tag{10.19}$$

d_i is the function measuring the similarity between the i-th sample $\mathbf{f}_i$ and $\mathbf{f}'$ that is the feature vector of the representative sample from the positive class. $d_{a,i}$ and $d_{v,i}$ are computed from the audio and visual domain, respectively. From a given video

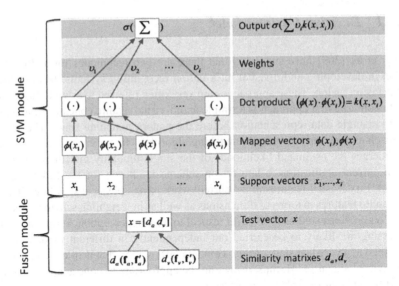

Fig. 10.5 Architecture of SVM-based late fusion method. In the fusion module, the vector x is formed by the fusion of similarity matching scores in audio and visual domains, which are respectively denoted by d_a and d_v. In the SVM, the input x and the support vector x_i are nonlinearly mapped (by ϕ) into a feature space **H**, where dot products are computed. By the use of the kernel k, there two layers are in practice computed in one single step. The results are linearly combined by weights v_i, found by solving a quadratic program. The linear combination is fed into the function $\sigma(x) = \text{sgn}(x+b)$, where b is a bias

database, a subset of samples of x_i, $i = 1,2,\ldots,N_T$ is used for training SVM to learn a specific semantic concept defined by the positive class. This is described in the following sections.

10.4.2   Support Vector Machine Learning

A mapping function $f : \chi \to \{\pm 1\}$ is estimated by the input–output training data [306, 307],

$$(x_1,y_1),\ldots,(x_i,y_i) \in \chi \times \{\pm 1\} \tag{10.20}$$

The domain χ is some nonempty set that the patterns x_i are taken from, and the y_i are the corresponding labels. It is assumed that the data were generated independently from some unknown probability distribution $P(x,y)$. The goal here is to learn a function that will correctly classify a new example (x,y), i.e., $f(x) = y$ for examples (x,y) that were also generated from $P(x,y)$. In other words, we choose y such that (x,y) is in some sense similar to the training examples. To this end, we need a similarity measure in χ, i.e.,

$$k : \chi \times \chi \to \mathbb{R} \tag{10.21}$$

$$(x, x') \mapsto k(x, x') \tag{10.22}$$

which is a function that returns a real number characterizing the similarity between x and x'. A type of similarity measure that is of particular interest is the dot product which is performed in the feature space, $\mathbf{H}$

$$k(x, x') := (\mathbf{x} \cdot \mathbf{x}') = (\phi(x) \cdot \phi(x')) \tag{10.23}$$

where the mapping function $\varphi(x)$ is applied to transfer pattern x and x' into the feature space $\mathbf{H}$, i.e.,

$$\phi : \chi \to H, \tag{10.24}$$

$$x \mapsto \mathbf{x} \tag{10.25}$$

In order to design the learning algorithm, we must come up with a class of function hyperplanes,

$$(\mathbf{w} \cdot \mathbf{x}) + b = 0 \quad \mathbf{w} \in \mathbb{R}^N, \, b \in \mathbb{R}, \tag{10.26}$$

corresponding to decision functions,

$$f(x) = \text{sgn}\left((\mathbf{w} \cdot \mathbf{x}) + b\right) \tag{10.27}$$

We can show that among all hyperplanes separating the data, there exists a unique one yielding the maximum margin of separation between the classes,

$$\max_{(\mathbf{w}, b)} \min\{\|\mathbf{x} - \mathbf{x}_i\| \, ; \, \mathbf{x} \in \mathbb{R}^N, \, (\mathbf{w} \cdot \mathbf{x}) + b = 0, \, i = 1, \ldots, m\} \tag{10.28}$$

where m is the number of data samples. This is the optimum hyperplane that has the lowest capacity. This can be constructed by solving a constrained quadratic optimization problem. The solution vector $\mathbf{w}$ has an expansion $\mathbf{w} = \sum_i v_i \mathbf{x}_i$ in terms of a subset of the training patterns, namely those whose v_i is non-zero, called *Support Vectors*. These carry all the relevant information about the classification problem; all remaining examples of the training set are irrelevant. Therefore, we may rewrite Eq. (10.27) as:

$$f(x) = \text{sgn}\left(\sum_i v_i(\mathbf{x} \cdot \mathbf{x}_i) + b\right) \tag{10.29}$$

This shows the crucial property of the algorithm that the decision function depends only on dot products between patterns. We think of the dot product space as the feature space $\mathbf{H}$. To express the formulas in terms of the input patterns lying in χ, we need to employ Eq. (10.23), which expresses the dot product of features in terms of the kernel k evaluated on input patterns,

$$k(x,x') = (\mathbf{x} \cdot \mathbf{x'}) \qquad (10.30)$$

We thus obtain decision functions of more general form,

$$f(x) = \text{sgn} \left(\sum_{i=1}^{m} v_i \cdot (\phi(x) \cdot \phi(x_i)) + b \right) \qquad (10.31)$$

$$= \text{sgn} \left(\sum_{i=1}^{m} v_i \cdot k(x,x_i) + b \right) \qquad (10.32)$$

By this definition, it is more efficient to use the kernel to obtain the dot product in $\mathbf{H}$ since $\phi(x) \cdot \phi(x_i)$ will be very expensive to compute if $\mathbf{H}$ is high-dimensional. To this end, the Gaussian radial basis function (GRBF),

$$k(x,x') = \exp(-\gamma \|\mathbf{x} - \mathbf{x'}\|^2) \qquad (10.33)$$

is utilized as a similarity measure.

As discussed in Fig. 10.5, the input x and the support vector x_i are nonlinearly mapped (by ϕ) into a feature space $\mathbf{H}$, where dot products are computed. Practically, those two layers are computed in one single step by the use of the kernel k. The results are linearly combined by weights v_i, found by solving a quadratic problem. The linear combination is fed into the function $\sigma(\cdot)$.

Figure 10.6 shows an example of a two-dimensional plot of data samples obtained from the database in the experiment. It shows a two-dimensional feature space where each sample is labeled as positive or negative according to one query concept. It can be observed that although the data is only two dimensional, the problem is not a linear separable case. The application of a non-linear GRBF kernel function is therefore more appropriate for performing nonlinear mapping for the SVM classifier, as compared to other linear functions.

10.4.3   Implementation of Support Vector Machine

To construct the optimum hyperplane [cf. Eq. (10.28)], we can solve the following optimal problem:

$$\underset{\mathbf{w},b}{\text{minimize}} \ \tfrac{1}{2} \|\mathbf{w}\|^2 \qquad (10.34)$$

$$\text{subject to } y_i \cdot ((\mathbf{w} \cdot \mathbf{x}_i) + b) \geq 1, \quad i = 1,\ldots,m \qquad (10.35)$$

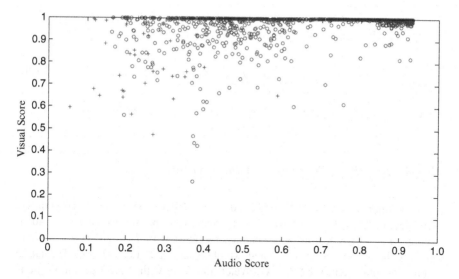

Fig. 10.6 A two-dimensional plot of data samples obtained from the database to be classified by SVM for a given query. According to the ground truth, the positive samples are marked as '*plus*' and negative samples are marked as '*circle*'

The way to solve this problem is through the Lagrangian dual. In practice, however, a separate hyperplane may not exist e.g., if a high noise level causes a large overlap of the classes. Thus, we employ a *soft margin* classifier, called C-support vector classifier (SVC) [305] for implementation in the current work. The software library for this implementation may be found in [332]. The C-SVC uses the constant $C > 0$ as the upper bound which is the only difference from the separable case [cf. Eq. (10.34)]. The technique here is to minimize the objective function,

$$\tau(\mathbf{w}, \xi) = \frac{1}{2}\|\mathbf{w}\|^2 + C\sum_{i=1}^{m} \xi_i \qquad (10.36)$$

$$\text{subject to } y_i \cdot ((\mathbf{w} \cdot \mathbf{x}_i) + b) \geq 1 - \xi_i, \ \xi_i \geq 0, \quad i = 1, \dots, m \qquad (10.37)$$

where ξ_i are slack variables. Incorporating kernels, and rewriting it in terms of Lagrange multipliers, this leads to the problem of maximizing:

$$\underset{\alpha \in \mathbb{R}^m}{\text{maximize}} \sum_{i=1}^{m} \alpha_i - \frac{1}{2} \sum_{i,j=1}^{m} \alpha_i \alpha_j y_i y_j k(x_i, x_j) \qquad (10.38)$$

$$\text{subject to } 0 \leq \alpha_i \leq C, \quad i = 1, \dots, m, \text{ and } \sum_{i=1}^{m} \alpha_i y_i = 0 \qquad (10.39)$$

where the trade-off parameter $C > 0$, and α_i, $i = 1,2,\ldots,m$ are the Lagrange multipliers. The resulting decision function can be shown to take the form:

$$f(x) = \text{sgn}\left(\sum_{i=1}^{m} \alpha_i y_i \cdot k(x,x_i) + b \right) \tag{10.40}$$

where the weight parameters v_i in Fig. 10.5 are replaced by $\alpha_i y_i$.

10.4.4   Results of Movie Clip Classification

The experimental results were conducted on a database consisting of 6,000 movie clips previously used in Sect. 10.2.5. All videos were indexed by visual and audio features. The visual feature was obtained by TFM with $T_c = 2,000$. Each video clip was described by its associated weight vector [cf. Eq. (10.14)]. The audio feature was obtained by LMM. A wavelet transform with 9-level decompositions was applied to the audio signal from each video clip. The coefficients in each high frequency subband were then characterized by the LMM. The resulting model parameters and the mean and standard deviation of the wavelet coefficients in the low-frequency subband were used to obtain feature vectors according to Eq. (10.12).

The SVM-based fusion model was applied for the classification of videos in the video database. Five semantic concepts were utilized to obtain the results. These concepts included *Fighting*, *Ship Crashing*, *Love Scene*, *Music Video*, and *Dance Party*. For each of the five concepts, the ground truth classes were obtained by manually classifying all video clips in the database. Table 10.6 shows detailed information of the data set used in the experiment. The ground truth class was used for measuring classification performance. For each concept, the system was trained using a training set of 100–250 samples randomly selected from the database according to the type of concepts. The size of the training set was approximately less than 2 % of all video clips used for testing.

In order to measure the performance of the system, three following criteria were utilized: classification accuracy, false positive rate, and false negative rate. Classification accuracy was used to measure the percentage of correct/incorrect classifications [305]. The false positive rate was the proportion of negative instances that were erroneously reported as being positive, and the false negative rate was the proportion of positive instances that were erroneously reported as negative [304].

Table 10.7 shows the experimental results obtained by the SVM-based fusion method. It can be observed that the method achieved very high accuracy, an average of more than 91 %. It should be noted that this is not a rare result. The number of negative samples was much more than the positive samples within a given class; the models can correctly classify most of the negative samples, and thus the average was high. An interesting observation was the false negative rate, since it indicated the percentage of positive samples that were correctly detected. The system had the highest false negative rate at 26.87 % for classification of the 'Ship Crashing'

Table 10.6 Ground truth and training/testing data used for video classification via the SVM-based fusion model

Type of concept	Number of instances in database	Number of movies with concept	Number of training samples (positive, negative)	Number of testing samples
Love scene	66	3	(22, 78)	6,000
Music video	41	4	(13, 87)	6,000
Fighting	413	3	(137, 163)	6,000
Ship crashing	201	1	(67, 134)	6,000
Dance party	48	1	(16, 84)	6,000

Table 10.7 Recognition rate obtained by the SVM based fusion model

Type of concept	Accuracy (%)	False positive rate (%)	False negative rate (%)
Love scene	90.97	8.91	19.70
Music video	91.03	9.03	0
Fighting	84.68	25.65	14.55
Ship crashing	91.81	7.54	26.87
Dance party	99.68	0.30	2.08
Average	*91.63*	*10.29*	*12.64*

concept. This showed, however, that 73.13 % of all relevant videos were correctly classified. Moreover, the system attained the lowest false negative rate of 0 % and 2 % for the detection of 'Music Video' and 'Dance Party,' respectively. For such concepts, we observed that the audio features extracted from video clips contributed highly to the effectiveness of the classifier. In addition, the consistency of the visual scenes in the video clips representing 'Dance Party', as well as the music in the audio enabled the classifier to achieve close to 100 % classification accuracy.

The ground truth in Table 10.6 may be used to study the generalization capabilities of the SVM-based fusion model, through examining the properties of the video test set. The table shows the number of instances of each concept in the database, and the number of different movies where each concept exists. This data shows that three of the concepts existed in more than one movie (i.e., *Love Scene, Music Video, Fighting*). From the results discussed above, given these concepts, the system can classify relevant video clips correctly, although they are from different movies. Thus, we can see that this learning system can attain generalization capabilities to some degree. Furthermore, this work aims at characterizing semantic concepts in terms of perceptual features providing the experimental database. These concepts may not be as good generalizations as the ones described by textual descriptors.

It is well known that the number of positive and negative examples should not differ much for training SVM in order to avoid classification errors. As noted from the results, positive samples were more important than negative samples for conducting effective training. Here, the performance of the classifier was studied at different settings of training data. The ground truth for the *Love Scene* concept (explained in Table 10.6) was utilized to test the SVM classifier in different training conditions. First, the number of positive samples in the training set was fixed to 22 samples (these were selected from the total of 66 samples). Then the negative samples were added to the training set one at a time and used for training. Figure 10.7 shows the recognition accuracy of the system. As we may anticipate, without negative samples included in the training set, the classifier has the highest false positive error rate. Adding more negative samples to the training set also increased the accuracy of the classifier, but with the cost of higher false negative errors.

Figure 10.7 also shows that the training size was increased to more than 2 % of the total number of samples stored in the database. When the system was allowed to learn more negative samples it produced a high false negative error rate. In order to achieve a good compromise between performance and error rates, the system required approximately 0.1 % of the total negative samples for training. In comparison, we observed from a new experiment that the system required a large number of positive samples, i.e., more than 22 % of the total positive samples, for training in order to obtain a good tradeoff between accuracy and error rate.

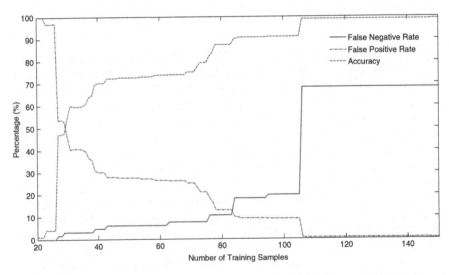

Fig. 10.7 Classification results obtained by the SVM-based decision fusion model for the "Love Scene" concept, at a different setting from the training set

10.5 Summary

The chapter focuses on the content characterization of audio and visual data, and the learning models of support vector machines for the audio-visual fusion. First, we introduce the Laplacian mixture model for audio analysis. The shape of the wavelet coefficient distribution is modeled by a low-dimensional vector of the model parameters. The index vector addresses the global characteristics of the audio content. Since videos contain mixed types of audio content, music speech, sound effects, and noise, the global characterization is effective for these types of mixed audio sources.

Video data involves both audio and visual signals to convey semantic meanings. The application of the audiovisual fusion technique provides the most accurate means of content analysis compared to methods analyzing either the visual or audio signal alone. Template frequency modeling for visual content analysis, together with the statistical technique based on the Laplacian mixture model for audio analysis capture effectively the spatio-temporal information. We demonstrate the application for characterizing semantic concepts in movie clips from a large video library. The audiovisual fusion model through a support vector machine training process can adaptively construct a decision function for classification of videos according to a given concept.

Chapter 11
Motion Database Retrieval with Application to Gesture Recognition in a Virtual Reality Dance Training System

Abstract This chapter presents gesture recognition methods and their application to a dance training system in an instructional, virtual reality (VR) setting. The proposed system is based on the unsupervised parsing of dance movement into a structured posture space using the spherical self-organizing map (SSOM). A unique feature descriptor is obtained from the gesture trajectories through posture space on the SSOM. For recognition, various methods are explored for trajectory analysis, which include sparse coding, posture occurrence, posture transition, and the hidden Markov model. Within the system, the dance sequence of a student can be segmented online and cross-referenced against a library of gestural components performed by the teacher. This facilitates the assessment of the student dance, as well as provides visual feedback for effective training.

11.1 Introduction

Recent trends toward more immersive and interactive computing come with increasing demand for more accurate tools to understand and interpret human gestural input or *gesture recognition*. Gestures are expressive, meaningful body motions involving physical movements of the fingers, hands, arms, head, face, or body with the intent of (1) conveying meaningful information or (2) interacting with the environment. In a virtual reality dance training system, the issue in recognition is the comparison of motion data captured in real-time of the trainee against the reference (trainer) data. Applied to dance training, human action recognition algorithms have been used in automated assessment of dance performance [334], visual comparison of virtual characters [335], and synthesis of dance partners [336] for various important applications. This chapter presents a method to address these issues based on two techniques: the self-organizing spherical map (SSOM) and transition analysis of the trajectory on the map.

Human gestures are temporal data; context relates to the states that have led to (or follow) the state in the present time step. Thus, the collection of states and their layout can be indicative of some meaning for gesture recognition [339, 340]. Recent studies have attempted to analyze the temporal data to see how it maps onto self-organizing maps (SOMs) [338, 341, 352]. The idea behind applying SOMs to the problem of gesture recognition is to deal with the challenge of how to effectively

© Springer International Publishing Switzerland 2014
P. Muneesawang et al., *Multimedia Database Retrieval: Technology and Applications*,
Multimedia Systems and Applications, DOI 10.1007/978-3-319-11782-9__11

parse a sequence of movements into a set of *postures*, then representing or modeling sequences of postures as a gesture. The topological map afforded by the SOM can help in this regard, as the map can be used as a basis for indexing, classification, and extraction of inherent relationships in the underlying data.

Postures are represented by a particular state of sensor values at an instant in time. For instance, Microsoft Kinect uses skeletal tracking of joint positions. Full motion capture technology used in film making and animation can also be used to describe postures, which are then mapped onto the SOM. A gesture can then be represented as a path or trajectory on the map, as traced by projecting a temporal series of postures. Each path can be used to model a type of gesture, or transitions between possible postures for a given gesture can be extracted. Unknown gestures can be recognized through a matching process (template paths) as the path of an unknown gesture is traced on the map.

Previous methods for trajectory analysis of the self-organizing maps have attempted to use the sparse code [343, 351, 352], and the posture occurrence as an analog to the bag-of word model [346, 347, 350]. These methods have some limitations in their capability for temporal information analysis, since they use only the existing of the nodes and the frequency of occurrence of the nodes (key postures) on maps. It is evident that the transitions from posture to posture (or from one form in space to next) preserve more temporal information about the dance sequence than the postures (forms in space) do themselves [340]. In order to perform trajectory analysis on the SSOM, in this Chapter, two methods for transition analysis of the SSOM trajectory are presented. The first method uses transition metric and the second method adopts the hidden Markov model (HMM) for modeling gesture on the multiple-codebook SSOM. Based on the experimental study, the newly proposed method appears to be very effective for recognizing human actions and outperforms the previous methods.

Section 11.2 will look into an architecture for a dance training system in the cave automatic virtual environment (CAVE). Section 11.3 presents the SSOM method for the construction of posture space to explore gesture trajectory. Section 11.4 presents the application of SSOM for the characterization of dance gesture. Section 11.5 presents trajectory analysis methods for gesture indexing and the construction of template matching. Section 11.6 extends these template matching methods to online recognition and gesture segmentation. Section 11.7 presents the HMMs for transition analysis of the trajectory on the multiple-codebook SSOM.

11.2   Dance Training System

The architecture of the VR dance training system is shown in Fig. 11.1, which includes four components: the motion capture, gesture recognition module, assessment and visual feedback module, and the CAVE. The CAVE has four stereoscopic projectors and four corresponding screens. Driven by a graphics cluster of five nodes, one node serves as the cluster master, while the other four drive the corresponding screens. The user wears active stereo glasses containing targets of several light refraction markers in a fixed geometry. The location and orientation of the user's eyes are traced by a six degree of freedom (6DOF) tracking system. A tracking server calculates each target's position and orientation based on images captured by tracking cameras distributed on top of the screens. The tracking data is used to determine the content to be displayed on the screens. The 3D Unity game engine and visual C# are used to implement the feedback engine, and interface with the Kinect sensor. Middle VR is used to control the graphic in the CAVE.

The goal of the system is to recognize sequences of movements, by identifying where certain target postures occur along the time-line of the performance. The recognition module extracts occurrences (phases) from the beginner's performance (a phrase is transition between identifiable postures), and then assesses them against the teachers' (ground truth) movement. Finally, the system visualizes both the teacher and student's dance sequences (or isolated movements) in a VR setting. Students participating in this process would receive feedback on the accuracy of their performance and on specific areas for which their accuracy is poor and thus in need of attention. This process is illustrated by a VR dance training system, with its various feedback protocols, as shown in Fig. 11.2.

Figure 11.3 shows the gesture recognition module that is implemented by the SSOM-based isolated gesture recognizer. The SSOM is incorporated with a template matching method (explained in Sect. 11.5) or a HMM (explained in Sect. 11.7) for gesture recognition. The sequence of frames is recorded by a standard Microsoft Kinect. Each frame contains data explaining the location of joints in 3D axes [349]. In the preprocessing block, a feature extraction module transforms the 3D positions of all joints in the captured frame to a feature vector characterizing the

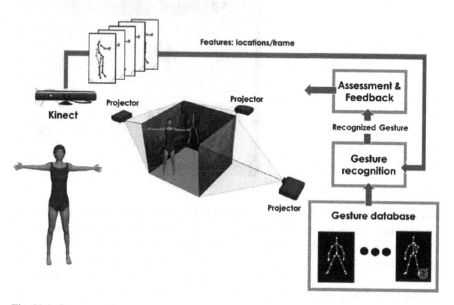

Fig. 11.1 System architecture

Fig. 11.2 Illustration of VR
dance training with feedback
protocols, including (**a**)
side-by-side feedback, (**b**)
overlay feedback, and (**c**)
score-curve feedback

frame content. The SSOM parser is performed on each frame of the gesture, thus creating the coding symbols showing a trajectory on the SSOM. The postures are characterized by a template calculated by the bag-of-word (BoW) model [350], the sparse code [351, 352], or a newly proposed method based on the posture transition matrix. For gesture recognition, the template obtained from the input gesture is compared with a set of reference templates using a matching algorithm that provides a distance score. The distance scores for all the reference templates are set to a decision rule, which provides a classification of the input gesture, and possibly an ordered (by distance) set of the best n candidates.

11.3 Spherical Self-organizing Map (SSOM)

Prior to recognition, the system discussed in Fig. 11.3 creates the gesture reference templates using a training algorithm. This is to first automatically parse samples from across the spectrum of expected dance movements, into a discrete set of postures. This is achieved using SSOM, an unsupervised clustering algorithm that reduces a large number of input data vectors to a small set of prototypical units. The SSOM enables learned postures to be allocated to, and distributed across, nodes on a predefined lattice [344, 348]. This results from the wrap-around, neighbourhood learning that occurs when the lattice forms a closed loop sphere. A useful feature of a SSOM-based approach is that the discrete space is constructed in such a way as to retain associations that exist in the original input space, i.e. postures (learned) are positioned in the map nearby to other postures that are very similar in nature. As a consequence of this topology-preserving mapping, a sequence of postures (comprised in the movement or gesture) should trace a rather smooth trajectory on the map. It is from this trajectory (sequence of key postures) that the descriptors are acquired for representing each gesture.

The map's spherical lattice is constructed by progressively sub-dividing a regular icosahedron down to a desired level (l). This results in a series of nodes uniformly arranged on a tessellated unit sphere (with uniform triangular elements). A sphere tessellated one level ($l = 1$) would result in 12 nodes, while ($l = 2$) and ($l = 3$) would each result in lattices of 42 and 162 nodes respectively. Each node on the sphere is then represented by a weight vector: $\mathbf{w}_{i,j,k} \in \mathbb{R}^D$, which models a key posture from the input space, where $\mathbf{w}_{i,j,k}$ is the weight vector of $(i, j, k)^{th}$ node. The total number of nodes represents the number of postures that can be learned by the map. In this representation, nodes are each equidistant from their immediate neighbours, with which they form a hexagonal neighbourhood.

Figure 11.4 shows a *cluster unit* of the SSOM. Each training pattern in the input space is connected to every cluster unit by a weight vector $\mathbf{w}_{i,j,k}$. Every cluster unit at (i, j, k) has a variable neighborhood ($NE_{i,j,k}$) with a decreasing radius. All the nodes that fall within the area defined by $NE_{i,j,k}$ constitute the region-of-influence of (i, j, k).

Let $\mathscr{T} = \{\mathbf{x}_i\}_{i=1}^N$ be the training set, where $\mathbf{x} \in \mathbb{R}^D$. Each vector $\mathbf{x}$ is referred to as a posture vector in a dance gesture. The learning process of the SSOM starts by initializing the weight vectors $\mathbf{w}_{i,j,k}$ with small random values distributed throughout the input space. Various steps are employed by the SSOM to topologically reorder the cluster weights on the spherical lattice, as follows [344, 348]:

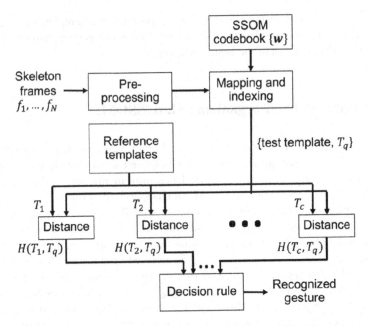

Fig. 11.3 Diagram for gesture recognition, obtained by template matching. Templates are generated by the SSOM indices

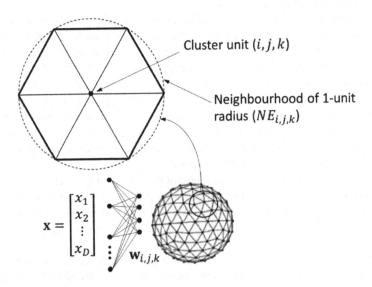

Fig. 11.4 Cluster unit of SSOM

Firstly, the input posture vector $\mathbf{x}$ is randomly selected from $\mathscr{T}$, and introduced to the SSOM. For each voxel, the best matching unit (BMU), $\mathbf{w}_{(i,j,k)^*}$ is selected, i.e.,

$$(i,j,k)^* = \arg\min\{E_{i,j,k}\} \tag{11.1}$$

where $E_{i,j,k}$ is the difference between the current input vector and the weight vectors for all cluster units,

$$E_{i,j,k} = \varphi(u_{i,j,k}) \sum_{n=1}^{D} (x_n - w_{n,i,j,k})^2 \tag{11.2}$$

x_n is the n-th component of the input vector, and $w_{n,i,j,k}$ is the weight from the n-th input, $n = 1,2,\ldots,D$, to the (i,j,k)-th node, $i = 1,2,\ldots,I$, $j = 1,2,\ldots,J$, and $k = 1,2,\ldots,K$. The $\varphi(u_{i,j,k})$ is a count-dependent non-decreasing function, used to prevent cluster under-utilization.

Secondly, information from $\mathbf{x}$ is imparted to the weights of the winning cluster unit $(i,j,k)^*$ and all the units residing within the specified neighbourhood $NE_{(i,j,k)^*}$ using,

$$\mathbf{w}_{(i,j,k)^*}^{(new)} = \mathbf{w}_{(i,j,k)^*}^{(old)} + \alpha[\mathbf{x}_n - \mathbf{w}_{(i,j,k)^*}^{(old)}] \tag{11.3}$$

where

$$\alpha = \mu(NE_{(i,j,k)^*}/NE_{initial}) \tag{11.4}$$

μ is a predefined learning rate, and $NE_{initial}$ is the initial neighborhood size in terms of the number of units.

This process of *information sharing* [i.e., Eq. (11.3)] allows the map nodes to *tune* themselves to characteristic *postures* in the input space, while forcing nearby nodes to tune to related or *adjacent* postures.

Thirdly, the same learning steps are repeated. At this point, as new input postures are presented from the training set, new BMUs compete for their representation, resulting in a locally organized distribution of key postures over nodes on the map. *Finally*, learning is terminated after a maximum number of cycles has been reached.

11.4   Characterization of Dance Gesture Using Spherical Self-organizing Map

The SSOM was applied to characterize dance gesture in a dance training system shown in Fig. 11.1 [340]. The Microsoft Kinect system provides 20 3D skeleton points to represent each player (student) in the camera's field of view. These points represent 20 joint positions of the body. In each frame, the normalized locations of all 20 joint positions were utilized to construct a feature vector, $\mathbf{x} = [\hat{x}_1 \ldots \hat{x}_i \ldots \hat{x}_{60}]^t$, where $\hat{x}_i$ is the i-th location of the joint in one of the x/y/z planes. By considering all 20 joints in the three dimensions, the dimension of $\mathbf{x}$ was 60. Here the location $\hat{x}_i$ was obtained by the normalization of its original value. This process took the hip location as the reference point and calculated all other joints relative to the hip.

Table 11.1 Isolated gesture dataset

Ballet gesture		
Label	Description	# instances (# frames)
G_1	1st position → 2nd position	8 (56–96)
G_2	2nd position → 3rd position	10 (57–77)
G_3	3rd position → 4th position	8 (59–75)
G_4	4th position → 5th position	10 (48–81)
G_5	5th position → 6th position	10 (43–80)
G_6	6th position → 1st position	10 (41–88)

Note: First position (posture 1): both arms lifted in front; second position (posture 2): both arms open; third position (posture 3): left arm in front and right arm lifted up; fourth position (posture 4): left arm open to the side and right arm lifted up; fifth position (posture 5): both arms lifted up; sixth position (posture 6): both arms put down

Table 11.1 summaries the dataset used for training the SSOM. The dataset included a set of six isolated gestures (i.e. each gesture G_1–G_6 was recorded individually, independent of any sequence of other movement/gestures). These gestures were the six basic positions of ballet dance [354]. Gesture G_1 was the dance gesture moving from the first position to the 2nd position, where the 1st position was the posture with both arms lifted in front, and the 2nd position was the posture with both arms open. All gestures G_1–G_6 are defined in Table 11.1.

In the experiments, observations are made as to how the variability in repeated gestures maps into posture space. Figure 11.5 shows a series of mappings of gesture instances (columns) per gesture type (rows). A visualization of the SSOM and associated gesture trajectories shows that even differences in frame length and duration of the gesture (variations of up to 40 % difference in frame length) do not appear to impact the consistency with which the gesture maps onto posture space. All gestures appear to trace quite characteristic and repeatable paths on the unit sphere. The start (solid blue marker) and end points (solid red marker) of the trajectories are also shown. Although gesture G_5 and G_6 are quite similar in terms of the postures traced, there is quite a clear difference in the direction of the trajectory.

It is clear from these mappings that the paths traced for different gestures are quite unique from one another, which is expected to translate into better discrimination between trajectories (and therefore, gestures). The consistency of the mapping indicates some stability in the representation of gestures, and suggests sufficient overlap should exist when generating histogram templates.

11.5   Trajectory Analysis

A posture can be represented in time series as $\mathbf{x}(t), (1 \ldots t \ldots T)$ which is a unit of a gesture element, where T is the time length of the gesture. In this way, the gesture G_i can be represented by $G_i = (\mathbf{x}_i(1), \ldots, \mathbf{x}_i(t), \ldots, \mathbf{x}_i(T))$. As shown in Fig. 11.5, each input vector $\mathbf{x}$ is quantized by the set of SSOM weight vectors. For convenience, we

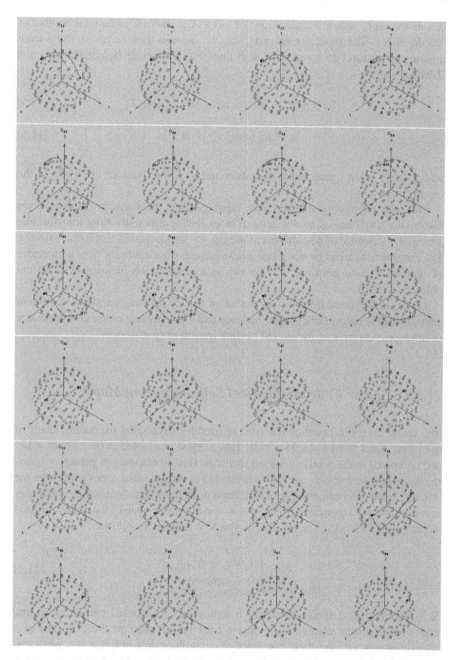

Fig. 11.5 Gesture projections: instances of gestures (*rows top-bottom*) respectively. Smooth, local sets of postures show stable, highly repeatable trajectories. *Note*: G_5 & G_6 include similar postures, with opposing trajectory paths

denote the set of weight vectors as $\mathbf{w}_c, (1 \ldots c \ldots C)$, where C is the total number of SSOM nodes. The input vectors $\mathbf{x}(t), (1 \ldots t \ldots T)$ can then be transformed from a series of postures to a series of map units based on their best matching units (BMUs), i.e.,

$$S = Q(G) = (u_1, \ldots, u_t, \ldots, u_T), t \in [1, T] \tag{11.5}$$

$$u_t = \arg\min_c(\|\mathbf{x}(t) - \mathbf{w}_c\|) \tag{11.6}$$

where $Q(G)$ is the quantization operation and u_t is the index of the BMU of the input $\mathbf{x}(t)$.

For each posture sample from an input gesture, the transformation involves finding the BMU and using this node to index the input sample. After transforming a temporal sequence of postures onto the map, an output sequence of indices results. The transformation can be described as a sequence of node indices, S, or a trajectory of individual node positions, Tr, on the spherical surface (defined in a 3D co-ordinate system).

Given the sequence or trajectory traced on the SSOM, we consider a number of alternative descriptors for a gesture instance and class: posture sparse codes, posture occurrence, posture transitions, and posture transition sparse codes.

11.5.1 Sparse Code of Spherical Self-organizing Map

The sparse code (SC) method has been utilized for structuring the coding labels of the hierarchical SOM [343, 351, 352]. This method is adopted in the current work, and compared to the newly proposed methods. During mapping of posture vectors, the weight vectors $\mathbf{w}_c, (1 \ldots c \ldots C)$ are labeled as the activated nodes if they are the winning nodes according to Eq. (11.6). Each node has a state S_c describing whether it is a winner for a gesture element or not, and the whole state of the nodes are used as the output, $SC = (S_1, \ldots, S_c, \ldots S_C)$. The S_c is defined as follows:

$$S_c = \begin{cases} 1, & \text{if } c = u_t|_{t \in [1,T]} \\ 0, & \text{otherwise} \end{cases} \tag{11.7}$$

S_c is regarded as a sparse code which represents an activated pattern of winner nodes for a gesture element. The sparse code only represents the existence of a set of postures, and not their frequency of occurrence. For instance, if a particular gesture involves a set of five postures, some of which are held for a length of time, then the sparse code will only indicate that they occurred, and won't consider the duration. This offers a time invariant measure of posture existence, and is useful when detecting gestures that may be performed at different speeds.

In Fig. 11.3, the system utilizes a reference template for recognition. Based on the SC method, a sparse code template (SCT) over the set of gesture instances for the i-th class can be computed as the reference template, i.e.,

$$SCT_i = \frac{\sum\limits_{n=1}^{N_i} SC_{i,n}}{\left| \sum\limits_{n=1}^{N_i} SC_{i,n} \right|} \tag{11.8}$$

where N_i is the number of gesture instances in the i-th gesture class, and $SC_{i,n}$ is the sparse code vector of the n-th gesture instance belonging to the i-th class.

11.5.2 Posture Occurrence

Posture occurrence (PO) is analogous to the popular bag-of-words (BOW) approach adopted for the task of pattern recognition [346, 347, 350]. In regard to the BoW approach used in information retrieval, each posture on the SSOM can be considered a unique word, while each gesture is a collection of individual words—structured according to a particular grammar (e.g. set, sequence, etc.). By aggregating the occurrence of postures in a gesture against the indexed set of nodes on the map, a histogram can be formed (over a single gesture, or set of similar gestures), thus forming a template that is used in recognition. In this method, a histogram is formed for each gesture instance n, $PO_n = [H(1), \ldots, H(c), \ldots, H(C)]^t$. The value of the c-th component is calculated by:

$$H(c) = \sum_{t=1}^{T} \delta(u(t) - c), c \in \{1, \ldots, C\} \tag{11.9}$$

where δ is the Kronecker delta function, and T is the total number of indices in the sequence of node indices S discussed in Eq. (11.5).

A reference template for the i-th gesture class can be formed by summing over the set of $PO_{i,n}$ in this class:

$$POT_i = \frac{\sum\limits_{n=1}^{N_i} PO_{i,n}}{\left| \sum\limits_{n=1}^{N_i} PO_{i,n} \right|} \tag{11.10}$$

where N_i is the number of gesture instances in the i-th gesture class and $PO_{i,n}$ is the posture occurrence vector of the n-th gesture instance belonging to the i-th class.

11.5.3 Posture Transition and Posture Transition Sparse Code

The PO and PSC methods do not consider the temporal arrangement of postures in the map. They only consider the occurrence and the frequency of the individual nodes for indexing. We observe that these methods involve making significant effort to maintain the marginal histogram of the SSOM indices (first order statistics). This fact suggests that the indexing schemes based only on first order statistics may not sufficient. Thus, a higher order statistic is employed for analysing the SSOM trajectory.

The first order statistic employed by PO and PSC captures only the properties of individual nodes, ignoring the inter-dependencies between nodes in the dataset. On the other hand, second order statistics consider the position of nodes relative to one another in the SSOM trajectory. Since the gesture contains postures which have somewhat strong correlation with their neighbour, the adoption of the second order statistics, such as covariance and co-occurrence matrix, are more appropriate for capturing the dependency between the pairs of postures from the SSOM trajectory. Based on this discussion, a feature extraction based on posture transition (PT) is obtained as follows.

Given that u_t is the index of a map unit, the function in Eq. (11.6) creates $S = (u_1, \ldots, u_t, \ldots, u_T)$—the set of indices of map units treated as a set of symbols. The u_t value of consequent points of a gesture remains the same, since consequent points are generally close in the input data space. Therefore, consequent equal values of u_t are replaced with single values which result in the following definition [338]:

$$Tr = N(S) = \{u'_1, \ldots, u'_m, \ldots, u'_M\} : M \leq T, u'_i \neq u'_{i-1}, \forall i \in [2, M], \qquad (11.11)$$

where $N(.)$ is a function that removes consecutive equal u_t value and Tr is the mapped gesture, representing the trajectory on the SSOM. With the arrangement in Eq. (11.11), the dependencies among neighboring nodes can be conveniently investigated.

The Markov random process is employed to model the trajectory. To capture the dependencies between SSOM nodes in the trajectory, the horizontal Markov empirical transition matrix [345] of the dataset in Tr is calculated. The matrix's element is given by:

$$p_h(u'_{i+1} = n | u'_i = m) = \frac{\sum\limits_{i=1}^{M-1} \delta(u'_i = m, u'_{i+1} = n)}{\sum\limits_{i=1}^{M-1} \delta(u'_i = m)} \qquad (11.12)$$

where u'_i and u'_{i+1} are a pair of neighboring node indices, M is the size of Tr, and $m, n \in \{1, \ldots, C\}$.

Table 11.2 Definition of the 30 gestures

	P_1	P_2	P_3	P_4	P_5	P_6
P_1	–	G_{12}	G_{13}	G_{14}	G_{15}	G_{16}
P_2	G_{21}	–	G_{23}	G_{24}	G_{25}	G_{26}
G_3	G_{31}	G_{32}	–	G_{34}	G_{35}	G_{36}
P_4	G_{41}	G_{42}	G_{43}	–	G_{45}	G_{46}
G_5	G_{51}	G_{52}	G_{53}	G_{54}	–	G_{56}
P_6	G_{61}	G_{62}	G_{63}	G_{64}	G_{65}	–

Note: P_i is the i-th posture. G_{ij} is the gesture created by changing from the i-th posture to the j-th posture. G_{ji} is the reversal of gesture

$$\delta(x) = \begin{cases} 1 \text{ if } x = true \\ 0 \text{ otherwise} \end{cases} \qquad (11.13)$$

Based on Eq. (11.12), the dimension of the transition matrix is $C \times C$ since the SSOM has C nodes. The *PT* feature vector is formed by arranging the elements of this matrix, $p_h, h = 1, \ldots, C^2$, into a 1-D template.

In addition, we can also obtain the posture transition sparse codes (PTSC) that are analogous to the sparse codes of postures, only differing in that they represent the existence of transitions rather than the frequency of transitions.

11.5.4   Performance Comparison

The experiments were conducted on an isolated gesture database to assess the performance of the SSOM posture space representations, gesture template definitions and matching criteria. Based on the six postures discussed previously in Table 11.1, a new set of gestures is defined, containing a total of 30 gestures and 600 instances. Table 11.2 shows a matrix describing the definitions of all gestures. In the table, given the six postures P_1–P_6, a gesture G_{ij} is formed as an isolated gesture moving from the i-th position to j-th position (i.e., moving from posture P_i to posture P_j). This definition forms the gesture set, Set I, in the upper triangle of the matrix, containing $G_{12}, \ldots, G_{16}; G_{23}, \ldots, G_{26}; G_{34}, \ldots, G_{56}$, which has a total of 15 gestures. By contrast, the gesture G_{ji} is the reversal of the gesture G_{ij}. The reversal gestures forms the gesture Set II, which contains gestures in the lower triangle of the matrix. The total number of gestures from Set I and Set II is 30 gestures.

The non-reversal gestures in Set I were firstly used. Two datasets were constructed: Teacher dataset and Student dataset. The database includes 15 isolated gestures (i.e., each gesture was recorded independently of any sequence of other movement/gestures). The structure of this dataset is summarized in Table 11.3. From the full set of Teacher gestures and Student gestures, 50 % were randomly selected and used to form gesture templates, while all 100 % were classified against these templates.

Table 11.3 Gesture database

Dataset	# Instances per gesture class		Total instances
	Teacher	Student	
Gesture Set I: G_{12}, G_{13}, G_{14}, G_{15}, G_{16}, G_{23}, G_{24}, G_{25}, G_{26}, G_{34}, G_{35}, G_{36}, G_{45}, G_{46}, G_{56}	10	10	300
Gesture Set II: G_{21}, G_{31}, G_{32}, G_{41}, G_{42}, G_{43}, G_{51}, G_{52}, G_{53}, G_{54}, G_{61}, G_{62}, G_{63}, G_{64}, G_{65}	10	10	300

Table 11.4 Gesture recognition results averaged over the 15 gestures defined in the upper triangle in Table 11.2

Testing data		Average recognition accuracy		
		L1	L2	HI
Teacher	PO	96.7	98.0	96.7
	PSC	79.3	84.0	79.3
	PT	98.7	97.3	98.7
	PTSC	87.3	92.7	87.3
Student	PO	94.0	100	94.0
	PSC	77.3	85.3	77.3
	PT	94.7	99.3	94.7
	PTSC	86.0	92.0	86.0

This system employed the SSOM configuration C2a, and was trained according to the joint position feature. In the C2a configuration, the map has the following setting: The icosahedron level is 2, the number of map nodes is 162, the number of neighborhoods is 4, and the number of epochs is 100.

Table 11.4 shows the performance of the proposed system for recognition of ballet dance performed by two persons, Teacher and Student. Here, the template matching was performed by three similarity metrics: L1 norm, L2 norm, and histogram intersection (HI). The system can attain more than 98 % recognition rate averaged over 15 classes for recognition of the Teacher dataset by using the PT template and HI for similarity matching. The PO template also gave similar recognition performance to the PT template. Moreover, the system can recognize dance from the Student dataset with 100 % accuracy by using the PO template and L2 norm for similarity matching.

Next, the two sets of gestures, Set I and Set II described in Table 11.3 were used for the experiment. This database contains 30 gestures, where each gesture G_{ij} has its corresponding reversal G_{ji}. Gesture G_{12} is described by the movement from the 1st position to the 2nd position, whereas G_{21} represents the movement from the 2nd position to the 1st position. In this case, the POs of G_{12} and G_{21} may be similar, and thus, they may be incapable for discriminating the two gestures for recognition. The PTs, on the other hand, may preserve the direction of the movement within the gestures, and they can be employed for discrimination of the reversals. This is confirmed by the results shown in Table 11.5. It can be observed from the result that the gesture template obtained by PT outperforms other indexing methods discussed. The recognition rate averaged over 30 gesture classes of the Teacher

Table 11.5 Gesture recognition results averaged over the 30 gestures defined in Table 11.2

Testing data		Average recognition accuracy		
		L1	L2	HI
Teacher	PO	77.7	74.3	77.7
	PSC	58.0	61.3	57.7
	PT	96.0	79.3	96.0
	PTSC	83.0	84.3	83.3
Student	PO	66.7	66.3	66.7
	PSC	54.7	56.0	54.7
	PT	88.3	73.3	88.3
	PTSC	79.7	83.0	76.7

These include the reversals of the gestures

dataset can reach 96 %. However, the system has a poorer performance at about 88 % for recognition of the Student dataset. This may be because the dance sequences performed by the student may be inconsistent, as compared to the teacher.

11.6 Online Gesture Recognition and Segmentation

In order to perform matching between an incoming gesture and known templates, the incoming set of postures is projected onto the SSOM to extract the unknown posture sequence $S = (u_1, \ldots, u_t, \ldots, u_T), t \in [1, T]$. This projection is conducted online as the student is performing a set of moves. The task of recognition is non-trivial, due to the differing lengths of gestures (across classes), and the differing speeds with which they may be enacted (by the student/teacher). In order to address this, an online probabilistic framework demonstrated in [352] is adopted. The standard Bayesian framework is utilised for progressively estimating an updated posterior probability $P(k|S)$ for each of the $k = 1, \ldots, K$ gesture classes. The likelihood is computed at each unit of time by considering the single posture triggered on the map, and whether or not it occurred in each gesture template. In [352], the likelihood $P(S|k)$ was computed as the ratio of the existence of the current posture in gesture class k, to the total number of different postures in class k. In the current work, the likelihood is reframed as a histogram intersection [Eq. (11.17)], between a progressively growing sequence S (inclusive of postures from time t_0 to t), which may be described as a histogram of either: PS, PO, PT or PTSC (defined in Sect. 11.5), versus the corresponding templates for each gesture class.

Let $\mathbf{h}_s$ be the input histogram for the current sample at time t, and $\mathbf{h}_k$ to be the reference template for the class k. We thus define (for time t), the posterior $P_t(k|\mathbf{h}_s)$, likelihood $P_t(\mathbf{h}_s|k)$, and prior probabilities $P_t(k)$ according to the following:

$$P_t(k|\mathbf{h}_s) = \frac{P_t(\mathbf{h}_s|k)P_t(k)}{P_t(\mathbf{h}_s)} = \frac{P_t(\mathbf{h}_s|k)P_t(k)}{\sum P_t(\mathbf{h}_s|k)P_t(k)} \qquad (11.14)$$

$$P_t(\mathbf{h}_s|k) = HI(\mathbf{h}_s, \mathbf{h}_k) \tag{11.15}$$

$$P_t(k) = \begin{cases} 1/K & \text{if } t = t_0 \\ \frac{P_{t-1}(k|\mathbf{h}_s)HI(\mathbf{h}_s,\mathbf{h}_k)}{\sum_K P_{t-1}(k|\mathbf{h}_s)HI(\mathbf{h}_s,\mathbf{h}_k)} & \text{otherwise} \end{cases} \tag{11.16}$$

$$HI(\mathbf{h}_s, \mathbf{h}_k) = 1 - \sum_i \min[h_{s,i}, h_{k,i}] \tag{11.17}$$

According to the equations above, the input sequence is allowed to accumulate postures over time t, where for each instant, the accumulated gesture is projected onto the SSOM to generate a posture sequence, which can be converted into one of the four template representations from Sect. 11.5. Likelihoods are estimated as histogram intersections, Eq. (11.17), between each reference template and that computed from the input posture sequence. A perfect intersection with a template will yield a likelihood of 1 for a given class. It is important to note that all templates are normalized, (even if calculated from a gesture sequence containing only a single posture).

As the sequence begins to resemble a gesture from the known set, it's posterior will grow, and eventually surpass a detection threshold. Upon triggering this threshold, the class k with the maximum posterior is considered detected, and the system resets the priors for all classes, and recalculates the posterior. At this point, in order to free up postures from the accumulated sequence, t_0 is set to the current time, thus the newly considered sequence grows again from this instant (flushing all past postures). This process continues, triggering new instances of detected gestures, until the end of the input sequence is reached.

In order to assess the online capability of the system to recognize and isolate gestures from a continuous dance sequence, two dataset were constructed (Table 11.6). In this dataset, all component gestures have a representation in the trained posture space. The continuous dance sequences compose of gesture G_1–G_6 as discussed previously in Table 11.1. The online recognition is applied for both the Teacher and Student, using the PO and PT descriptors respectively. The Posterior probability is captured as a trace (for each gesture class) over the duration of the dance sequence. Results for the Teacher sequence are shown in Fig. 11.6, while results for the Student sequence are shown in Fig. 11.7.

The results for the Teacher show that, for both descriptors, the posterior appears to be quite robust in estimating and switching between gestures. The maximum posterior is selected as the prediction of the gesture class at each time sample in the sequence (shown in Fig. 11.6, bottom left and right). The prediction has been able to extract and segment in an online manner, the duration of each gesture in the sequence: G_6, G_1, G_2, G_3, G_4, G_5 with some minor noise at the beginning and end of each dance. According to this result, the system can accurately recognise the dance gestures from the continuous sequence with 100 % accuracy. It is apparent that there should be a class to capture derelict cases of postures other than the learned set, otherwise the posterior will attempt to lock onto the best representation for the input (e.g. G_5 at the beginning of the sequence).

Table 11.6 Continuous gesture dataset

Ballet dance	# instances (# frames)	
Postures (gesture sequence)	Teacher	Student
Rest → 1st position → 2nd position → 3rd position → 4th position → 5th position → Rest, $(G_6, G_1, G_2, G_3, G_4, G_5)$	1 (281)	1 (273)

The results for the Student's performance are also quite satisfactory, as the person performing the movements is different from the Teacher, and more so, their ability to repeat the correct movement is somewhat limited. Nevertheless, with some minor noise, the selection of gesture class appears to follow the actual sequence (i.e., recognition accuracy of 100 %). When confusion does occur, nearby postures are selected for a relatively brief period before switching back to the correct gesture.

11.7 Trajectory Analysis on the Multicodebook SSOM Using Hidden Markov Model

The application of HMM for pattern recognition is well established [337]. The relevant work in [338] has demonstrated the application of HMM for hand gesture recognition, by learning the coding symbols of the self-organizing feature map (SOM). In the current work, the HMM is adopted and the proposed system has different aspects from the previous works. The self-organizing method is implemented with the SSOM in the current work instead of SOM, and the multicodebook is designed for the SSOM in order to minimize the vector quantization errors. It is argued that a random error in the detection of the joint's positions in the postures of gesture has an effect on the performance of the recognition stage. This error is due to the variance in input posture sequence, e.g., sensor noise, inexact repetitions, etc.

Figure 11.8 illustrates the application of HMMs and multicodebook SSOM to build the isolated gesture recognizer. There is a set of K gestures to be recognized and each gesture is modeled by a distinct HMM. The vector quantization is implemented by the multicodebooks, whereas the system in Fig. 11.3 uses a single codebook. This design is motivated by the study in [353], which suggest that it is not possible to create a universal codebook (efficient for each data class to be encoded). In addition, although a low distortion can be achieved by a large sized codebook, this leads to problems in implementing HMMs with a large number of parameters.

According to Eq. (11.5), let the SSOM indices obtained by the quantization of $\mathbf{x}$ and $\mathbf{x} + \Delta\mathbf{x}$ be respectively described by $Q(\mathbf{x}) = u$ and $Q(\mathbf{x} + \Delta\mathbf{x}) = u'$, where $\Delta\mathbf{x}$ is the random error. In the case where $\Delta\mathbf{x}$ is small, the posture coordinates with relatively small variance are mapped to the same node of the SSOM so that $u = u'$. This error will not affect the recognition since it is compensated during the SSOM clustering process. On the other hand, when $\Delta\mathbf{x} >>: u \neq u'$, the introduced error $\Delta\mathbf{x}$ will affect the trajectory Tr. The result of this error can be observed from Fig. 11.5.

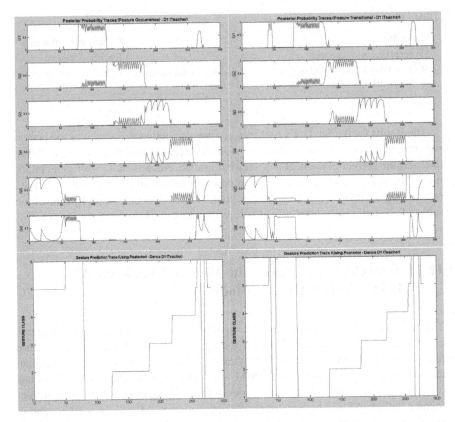

Fig. 11.6 Online recognition of Teacher dance gestures; *left top*: posterior traces based on posture occurrence; *bottom left*: class prediction trace for posture occurrence; *right top*: posterior traces based on posture transitions; *bottom right*: class prediction trace for posture transitions

Although the errors introduced by feature extraction algorithms or deviations in user performance do not influence the entire trajectory, the errors do influence the evaluation of a particular node or transition.

11.7.1 The Self-organizing Map Distortion Measurement

The structure of SSOM has various configurations, including c0, c1, c2a, c2b, c3a, and c3b; each has a different number of map nodes, from 12 to 642, respectively. These configurations constitute a map for vector quantization with a distortion, resulting from topologies and number of nodes [342]. In the current work, the SSOM is expanded to have multiple codebooks that are designed according to gesture class characteristics, instead of only one codebook.

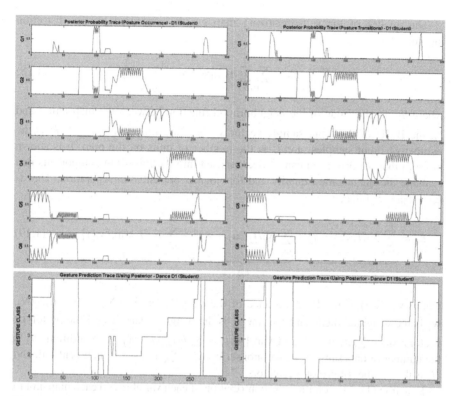

Fig. 11.7 Online recognition of Student dance D1 gestures; *left top*: posterior traces based on posture occurrence; *bottom left*: class prediction trace for posture occurrence; *right top*: posterior traces based on posture transitions; *bottom right*: class prediction trace for posture transitions

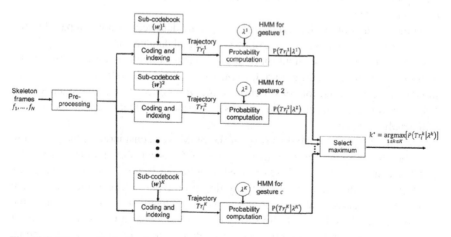

Fig. 11.8 Diagram for isolated gesture recognition using HMMs for trajectory analysis of multi-codebook SSOM

The quality of the self-organizing map can be measured by the distortion measure, E_d,

$$E_d = \sum_{i=1}^{N} \sum_{j=1}^{C} h_{b_i j} \left\| \mathbf{x}_i - \mathbf{w}_j \right\|^2 \tag{11.18}$$

where $h_{b_i j}$ is the value of the neighborhood function between the map unit j and b_i, the BMU of the input sample vector $\mathbf{x}_i$: $b_i = \arg\min_j\{\left\|\mathbf{x}_i - \mathbf{w}_j\right\|^2\}$, N is the number of input samples, and C is the number of units on the map. It is shown in [362] that the distortion can be decomposed into the following components that evaluate the quantization quality and topological presentation separation. That is $E_d = E_{qx} + E_{nb} + E_{nv}$:

$$E_d = \underbrace{\sum_{j=1}^{C} N_j H_j \mathrm{Var}\{\mathbf{x}|j\}}_{E_{qx}} + \underbrace{\sum_{j=1}^{C} N_j H_j \left\| \mathbf{n}_j - \bar{\mathbf{w}}_j \right\|}_{E_{nb}} + \underbrace{\sum_{j=1}^{C} N_j H_j \mathrm{Var}_h\{\mathbf{w}|j\}}_{E_{nv}} \tag{11.19}$$

where $\mathrm{Var}\{\mathbf{x}|j\}$ is the local variance of the data $\mathrm{Var}\{\mathbf{x}|j\} = \sum_{\mathbf{x} \in V_j} \left\| \mathbf{x} - \mathbf{n}_j \right\| / N_j$, $\bar{\mathbf{w}}_j$ is the weighted mean and $\mathrm{Var}_h\{\mathbf{w}|j\}$ is the weighted variance of the prototype vectors: $\bar{\mathbf{w}}_j = \sum_k h_{jk} \mathbf{w}_k / H_j$ and $\mathrm{Var}_h\{\mathbf{w}|j\} = \sum_k h_{jk} \left\| \mathbf{w}_k - \bar{\mathbf{w}}_j \right\|^2$. In addition, N_j is the number of data samples in Voronoi set V_j, $\mathbf{n}_j = \sum_{\mathbf{x} \in V_j} \mathbf{x} / N_j$ is their centroid, and H_j is the number of prototype vectors.

Equation (11.19) examines the contribution of each variable and each map unit to the distortion measure. The first term, E_{qx}, measures the quantization quality as the variance of the data vectors within each Voronoi set. The second terms, E_{nb} is the neighborhood bias. The last term, E_{nv}, is the neighborhood variance which measures the topological quality in terms of the closeness of prototype vectors close to each other on the map grid.

In the calculation of the variance $\mathrm{Var}\{\mathbf{x}|j\}$, the data vectors are compared to the centroid of the Voronio set, $\mathbf{n}_j$. We observe that if all data vectors $\mathbf{x}, \mathbf{x} \in V_j$ are drawn from the same class in the input space, their variance is small, and thus, reducing the overall distortion E_d. In order to reduce the sample variance, in the current work, all input data vectors used for construction of the Voronoi cells in a sub-codebook are collected from the same class. This results in Voronoi cells that include data samples with small variance.

The measurement of the distortion of the SOM was considered in the following example. Input vectors were drawn from four Gaussian distributions. A single-codebook SOM of size 2×2 was trained by all input vectors. Figure 11.9a shows the plot of all data samples and the resulting prototype vectors in the 2-D feature space. It is observed that each prototype vector converged to the centroid of the corresponding class. Figure 11.9b shows the Voronoi cells and the classification of the input vectors, obtained by the single codebook. In is observed that the sample variance in the Voronoi cells is high. In general, based on the learning procedure of the SOM, if the number of prototypes increases, more Voronoi cells are generated and lower quantization errors can be achieved. However, the size of the map also increases. In contrast, Fig. 11.10a shows the plot of the prototype vectors generated from four sub-codebooks (each sub-codebook has the size of 2×2) overlaying in the same input space. Each sub-codebook is trained separately by the input samples belonging to the same class, and the Voronoi cells with the associated members are shown in Fig. 11.10b–e. In this case, four of the 2×2 SOM produce 16 Voronoi cells if each SOM is trained separately. The variances computed on each Voronoi cell, $Var\{x|j\}$ in each sub-codebook, are less than that of the single codebook. As a result, the summation of the quantization errors [according to Eq. (11.18)] from the quantization by the sub-codebooks in Fig. 11.10b–e, is less than that of the vector quantization by the single-codebook in Fig. 11.9b, 2.4 dB.

11.7.2 The Hidden Markov Models of Gesture

As in Eq. (11.5), the transformation of the gesture G_i with the use of C-node SSOM can be expressed as $S = Q(G) = \{u_1, \ldots, u_t, \ldots, u_T\}$. This is considered as a transformation of the continuous trail to a sequence of C discrete symbols, which defines the finite states needed to build first order Markov chain models. The transformation $N(S)$ as discussed in Eq. (11.11) replaces consecutive equal values for symbols u with a single value, and outputs the trajectory Tr for the gesture G on the SSOM. This results in zeroing the self transition probability values in the Markov transition probability matrix, and thus a loss of information regarding the duration of a particular state. However, this information is not critical to gesture recognition.

A Markov model, for each of the K classes in the gesture data set, is created from the training data, i.e.,

$$\{Tr_1^k, Tr_2^k, \ldots, Tr_{N_i}^k\} \rightarrow \lambda_k \qquad (11.20)$$

where Tr_i^k is the trajectory of the i-th gesture instance in the k-th gesture class, and N is the number of instances. All $Tr_i^k, i = 1 \ldots N_i$ are obtained from the k-th sub-codebook SSOM. The sequence of the u_m' values in the trajectory Tr_i^k of the training set $\{Tr_i^k\}_{i=1}^{N_i}$, will be used for the calculation of the transition probability of the model λ_k describing class k. This results in a set of K Markov models,

$$\lambda = \{\lambda_1, \ldots, \lambda_k, \ldots, \lambda_K\} : \{Tr_1^k, Tr_2^k, \ldots, Tr_{N_i}^k\} \rightarrow \lambda_k \qquad (11.21)$$

The transformation of a gesture instance to the SSOM and the Markov model is intuitively depicted in Fig. 11.11.

In order to conduct isolated gesture recognition, the following steps are performed:

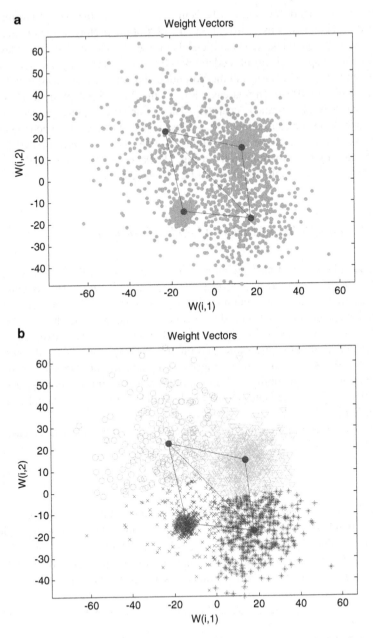

Fig. 11.9 Data clustering obtained by a single-codebook SOM of size 2×2, (**a**) the resulting prototypes and the input data, (**b**) the result obtained by the classification of input data

1. For each gesture class k, an HMM λ_k is built, i.e., the system estimates the model parameters (A, B, π) that optimize the likelihood of the training set observation vectors for the k-th gesture.
2. For each unknown gesture G_i to be recognized, the system carries out processing to measure the trajectories, $Tr_i^k = \{u_1', \ldots, u_m', \ldots, u_M'\}, k = 1, \ldots, K$, where Tr_i^k is

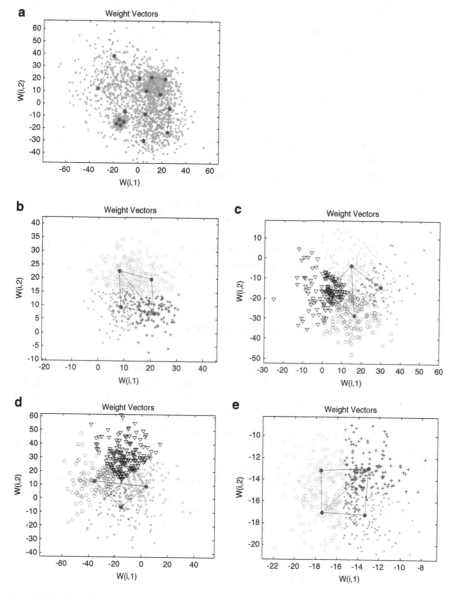

Fig. 11.10 Data clustering obtained by multicodebooks, each of size 2×2, trained separately by the data samples belonging to the same class; (**a**) the resulting prototypes of each sub-codebook overlaying in the input data; (**b–e**) the results of classification of input data in each class

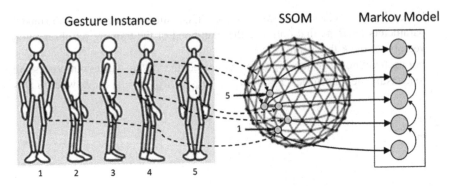

Fig. 11.11 Correspondence of postures of a gesture instance to their respective BMUs on the SSOM. These BMUs constitute the states of the Markov models

the trajectory on the k-th sub-codebook SSOM. This is followed by a calculation of model likelihoods for all possible models, $P(Tr_i^k|\lambda_k), 1 \leq k \leq K$, and followed by selecting the gesture whose model likelihood is the highest, i.e.,

$$k^* = \arg\max_{1 \leq k \leq K}[P(Tr_i^k|\lambda_k)]$$
(11.22)

where $P(Tr_i^k|\lambda_k)$ is the probability that the trajectory is generated by HMM λ_k. This probability is calculated by using the forward algorithm [355].

11.7.3   Obtaining Learning Parameters

The learning phase of HMM determines the method used to adjust the model parameters (A, B, π) to maximize the probability of the observation sequence for the given model. We can choose $\lambda = (A, B, \pi)$ such that $P(Tr|\lambda)$ is locally maximized using an iterative procedure, the Baum–Welch algorithm. We can summarize the parameters used to characterize an HMM as such: (1) N_S, the number of states in the model. The states are interconnected in such a way that any state can be reached from any other state. We denote the individual states as $S = \{S_1, S_2, \ldots, S_{N_S}\}$, and the state at time t as q_t; (2) N_O, the number of observation symbols per state. We denote the individual symbols as $V = \{v_1, v_2, \ldots, v_{N_O}\}$; (3) The state transition probability distribution is denoted by $A = \{a_{ij}\}$, and the observation symbolizing probability distribution in state j is denoted by $B = \{b_j(k)\}$. (4) The initial state distribution is denoted by $\pi = \{\pi_i\}$. Define:

$$\xi_t(i, j) = P(q_t = S_i, q_{t+1} = S_j|Tr, \lambda)$$
(11.23)

$\xi_t(i,j)$ represents the Bayesian probability of being the state S_i at time t and state S_j at time $t+1$, given the model and the observation sequence. Equation (11.23) can also be written in the form of the forward and backward variables, as:

$$\xi_t(i,j) = \frac{\alpha_t(i)a_{ij}b_j(u'_{t+1})\beta_{t+1}(j)}{P(Tr|\lambda)} \tag{11.24}$$

where α_t and β_t are the forward and backward variables, respectively. These variables can be solved inductively. The numerator term in Eq. (11.24) is just $P(q_t = S_i, q_{t+1} = S_j | Tr, \lambda)$ and the division by $P(Tr|\lambda)$ gives the desired probability measure. If $\gamma_t(i)$ is defined as the Bayesian probability of being in state S_i at time t, given the observation sequence and the model, $\gamma_t(i)$ can be related to $\xi_t(i,j)$ by summing over j, giving:

$$\gamma_t(i) = \sum_{j=1}^{N_S} \xi_t(i,j) \tag{11.25}$$

Using the above formulas, we can devise a method for re-estimation of the parameters of an HMM. A set of re-estimations from $\lambda = (A, B, \pi)$ to $\bar{\lambda} = (\bar{A}, \bar{B}, \bar{\pi})$ are:

$$\bar{a}_{ij} = \frac{\sum_{t=1}^{T-1} \xi_t(i,j)}{\sum_{t=1}^{T-1} \gamma_t(i)} \tag{11.26}$$

$$\bar{b}_i = \frac{\sum_{t \in \{t | u'_t = v_k\}} \gamma_t(i)}{\sum_{t=1}^{T} \gamma_t(i)} \tag{11.27}$$

$$\bar{\pi} = \gamma_1(i) \tag{11.28}$$

Based on Eqs. (11.25)–(11.28), if we iteratively use $\bar{\lambda}$ in place of λ and repeat the calculation of these equations, we then can improve the probability of Tr being observed from the model until some limiting point is reached.

11.7.4 Experimental Result

The HDM05 database is one of the very useful sources for testing motion analysis, synthesis and classification algorithms [356]. The proposed algorithm was applied to the HDM05 database, which contains several hours of motion capture data, including various walking and kicking motions, cartwheels, jumping jacks, grabbing and depositing motions, squatting motions, and so on. Table 11.7 shows the description of the HDM05 database. This mocap data was recorded by the optical marker-based Vicon system, shown in Fig. 11.12. A number of well-specified motion sequences were executed several times and performed by five actors. The recorded data was manually cut out to obtain suitable motion clips, which were arranged into 40 classes. Each such motion class contains various different realizations of the same type of motion, covering a broad spectrum of semantically meaningful variations.

The skeleton-based mocap file format ASF/AMC was used, which was transformed from the C3D data, the 3D trajectory of the optical markers. The ASF/AMC data comprises an explicit skeleton structure, providing information about bones, joints, and the assembly of these basic elements into a skeleton. As a pre-processing step, the joint locations were normalized by using the hip as the original location and calculating the location between the joints and the hip. The 3D locations of all joints were then used as input feature vectors.

The gesture recognition system outlined in Fig. 11.3 has been implemented and compared in terms of performance to the newly proposed system shown in Fig. 11.8.

Fig. 11.12 Optical motion capture using retro-reflective markers attached to the actor's body

Table 11.7 A list of 40 motion classes

Motion class	#	bd	bk	dg	mm	tr
cartwheelLHandStart1Reps	21	4	3	0	3	11
cartwheelLHandStart2Reps	4	0	0	0	0	4
cartwheelRHandStart1Reps	3	0	0	2	0	1
clap1Reps	17	3	3	3	5	3
clap5Reps	17	3	3	3	5	3
clapAboveHead1Reps	17	3	3	3	5	3
clapAboveHead5Reps	14	3	3	3	3	2
depositFloorR	32	6	6	6	8	6
depositHighR	28	4	6	5	6	7
depositLowR	29	4	7	6	6	6
depositMiddleR	29	4	7	5	6	7
elbowToKnee1RepsLelbowStart	27	6	6	6	2	7
elbowToKnee1RepsRelbowStart	27	6	6	6	2	7
elbowToKnee3RepsLelbowStart	13	3	3	3	1	3
elbowToKnee3RepsRelbowStart	13	3	3	3	1	3
grabFloorR	16	3	3	3	4	3
grabHighR	29	4	6	6	6	7
grabLowR	29	4	7	6	6	6
grabMiddleR	28	4	7	6	5	6
hitRHandHead	13	3	3	3	1	3
hopBothLegs1hops	36	12	9	9	3	3
hopBothLegs2hops	12	4	3	3	1	1
hopBothLegs3hops	12	4	3	3	1	1
hopLLeg1hops	41	11	9	9	3	9
hopLLeg2hops	14	4	3	3	1	3
hopLLeg3hops	14	4	3	3	1	3
hopRLeg1hops	42	12	9	9	3	9
hopRLeg2hops	14	4	3	3	1	3
hopRLeg3hops	14	4	3	3	1	3
jogLeftCircle4StepsRstart	17	2	5	3	3	4
jogLeftCircle6StepsRstart	15	1	5	2	3	4
jogOnPlaceStartAir2StepsLStart	14	3	3	2	3	3
jogOnPlaceStartAir2StepsRStart	14	3	3	2	3	3
jogOnPlaceStartAir4StepsLStart	14	3	3	2	3	3
jogOnPlaceStartFloor2StepsRStart	14	3	3	2	3	3
jogOnPlaceStartFloor4StepsRStart	14	3	3	2	3	3
jogRightCircle4StepsLstart	2	2	0	0	0	0
jogRightCircle4StepsRstart	17	2	5	3	3	4
jogRightCircle6StepsLstart	2	2	0	0	0	0
jogRightCircle6StepsRstart	12	2	5	2	3	0

The first and second column contains the name of the motion class and the total number of realizations, respectively. The third to seventh columns indicate the number of realizations for each actor separately. Here, the field actor refers to one of the five actors encoded by the initial bd (Bastian Demuth), bk (Bjorn Kruger), dg (Daniel Goldbach), mm (Meinard Muller), or tr (TidoRoder)

Table 11.8 Averaged recognition rate (%) over 40 classes, obtained by the template matching methods (PO, PSC, PT, and PTSC), compared to the HMM

Method	Similarity function	Average recognition accuracy (%)
PO	L1	41.8
	L2	41.0
	HI	41.8
PSC	L1	19.3
	L2	23.5
	HI	19.0
PT	L1	42.4
	L2	40.8
	HI	42.4
PTSC	L1	25.7
	L2	28.4
	HI	26.3
HMM		77.3

The SSOM was trained by the C1 configuration, using the following procedural parameters: icosahedron level $= 1$, map nodes $= 42$, neighborhood $= 3$, and epochs $= 200$. In order to assess the performance of the gesture template definition (i.e., PO, PSC, PT, and PTSC discussed in Sect. 11.5) and matching criteria, the system was trained using 50 % of all samples. From the full set of gesture instances, 50 % of each class were randomly selected and used to form gesture templates, while all 100 % were compared with these templates. The results are displayed in Table 11.8.

From the result, we observe that recognition performance was quite low for all scenarios. This is partly due to the complexity of the gesture movements. The sparse codes of postures appear to give lowest performance, since they considered only the existence of the postures for constructing gesture templates (each of which was a binary sparse code vector of 42 dimensions resulting from a 42-node SSOM). The PT gave a better performance than the PO method. The approach based on PT takes into account temporal information about the gesture (which is lacking in the PO vector), so it would seem reasonable that its accuracy in classification should be better.

The proposed system outlined in Fig. 11.8 was implemented. The SSOM was constructed in the same way as the previous experiment, using the C1 configuration. However, the SSOM for each gesture class was trained separately, resulting in multiple codebooks. For each class, the number of codewords in the sub-codebook was 42. For HMMs, the number of states N_S was set to 42, and the number of symbols N_O was 50. We let the number of states correspond roughly to the number of postures within the gesture. We restrict each gesture model to having the same number of states; this implies that the models will work best when they represent gestures with the same number of postures.

The system recognized the actions performed by five dancers using HMMs which were trained by 50 % of the data samples. Table 11.8 shows the recognition rate obtained by HMMs compared to others. The average for the 40 gesture classes was 77.3 %, which is significantly improved from the template matching methods (which performed at 42.4 %).

It was observed that the HMM parameters critically depended on the selection of training patterns. The performance was unstable when the number of training patterns was small. In comparison, the larger number of training patterns increased the recognition rate to: 80.5 %, 85.7 % and 89.4 % when 60 %, 70 %, and 75 % of samples were used for training, respectively. It was also observed that increasing the number of trainings [N_i in Eqs. (11.8) and (11.10)] for the template matching methods (i.e., PO, PSC, PT, and PTSC), has little effect on their recognition performance.

11.8 Summary

The first part of the chapter presents a new framework and implementation for the real-time capture, assessment and visualization of ballet dance movements performed by a student in an instructional, virtual reality (VR) setting. Using joint positional features, a spherical self-organizing map is trained to quantize over the space of postures exhibited in typical ballet formations. Projections of posture sequences onto this space are used to form gesture trajectories, used to form templates in a library of predetermined dance movements to be used as an instructional set. Two different histogram models are considered in describing a gesture trajectory specific to a given gesture class (posture occurrence and posture transitions). The histogram approach to both of the descriptors offers flexibility and generalization across instances of movement recorded from a candidate user: recognition for which, due to the natural variation of the human when repeating movements and the sensor noise introduced by the Kinect, can be a challenging task. The recognition evaluation was extended to the online case, where a dance consisting of continuous gestures is segmented online using a Bayesian formulation of the recognizer. This formulation shows much promise, effectively delineating a student's dance movement into constituent gestural units.

In the second part of the chapter, the Hidden Markov Model (HMM) method is adopted to analyze the sequential data of gesture trajectory on a spherical self-organizing map This method addresses the temporal information of human motion and aids in improving recognition accuracy. The experimental result of isolated gesture recognition using the standard motion capture database shows that the current method provides significant improvement in recognition accuracy. This recognizer will be highly important in assessing dance gestures in a completed virtual reality dance training system.

References

1. Bohn R., and Short. J.: How much information? 2009 Report on American Consumers. *University of California at San Diego, Global Information Industry Center*, (2010)
2. http://www.youtube.com/t/press_statistics, (2012)
3. http://usatoday30.usatoday.com/tech/news/2010-07-21-facebook-hits-500-million-users_N.htm, July (2014)
4. http://newsroom.fb.com/content/default.aspx?NewsAreaId=22, (2011)
5. R. Yan and W. Hsu.: Content-based and concept-based analysis for large-scaleimage/video retrieval. Proc. ACM MM, 913–914, (2009)
6. Y. Rui, T. Huang, and S. Chang.: Image retrieval: Current techniques, promising directions, and open issues. J. of visual communication and image representation, 39–62, (1999)
7. R. Datta, D. Joshi, J. Li, and J. Wang.: Image retrieval: Ideas, influences, and trends of the new age. ACM Computing Surveys (CSUR), (2008)
8. R. Baeza-Yates and B. Ribeiro-Neto.: Modern Information Retrieval, ACM Press, New York, (1999)
9. Chen, T., Yap, K. H.: Discriminative BoW Framework for Mobile Landmark Recognition. (2014)
10. Ji, R., Duan, L. Y., Chen, J., Yao, H., Yuan, J., Rui, Y., Gao, W.: Location discriminative vocabulary coding for mobile landmark search. Int. J. of Computer Vision, 96(3), 290–314, (2012)
11. Rui, Y., Hang, T. S., Mehrotra, S., Ortega, M.: A relevance feedback architecture for content-based multimedia information retrieval systems. Proc. IEEE Workshop on Content-based Access of Image and Video Libraries, 82–89 (1997)
12. Rui, Y. Huang, T.S., Mehrotra, S.: Content-based image retrieval with relevance feedback in MARS. Proc. IEEE Int. Conf. on Image Processing, Washington D.C., USA. 815–818 (1997)
13. Salton, G., McGill, M. J.: Introduction to Modern Information Retrieval. McGraw-Hill Book Company, NY. (1983)
14. Celentano, A., Sciasicio, E. D.: Feature interaction and relevance feedback analysis in image similarity evaluation. J. of Electronic Imaging, 7 308–317 (1998)
15. Müller, H., Müller, W., Marchand-Maillet, S., Pun, T., Squire, D. M.: Strategies for positive and negative relevance feedback in image retrieval. Int. Conf. on Pattern Recognition, Barcelona, Spain. 1 1043–1046 (2000)
16. Peng, J., Bhanu, B., Qing, S.: Probabilistic feature relevance learning for content-based image retrieval. Computer Vision and Image Understanding. 75 150–164 (1999)

© Springer International Publishing Switzerland 2014
P. Muneesawang et al., *Multimedia Database Retrieval: Technology and Applications*,
Multimedia Systems and Applications, DOI 10.1007/978-3-319-11782-9

17. Rui, Y., Huang, T.S., Ortega, M., Mehrotra, S.: Relevance feedback: A power tool for interactive content-based image retrieval. IEEE Trans. Circuits Syst. Video Technol. **8** 644–655 (1998)

18. Sciascio, E. Di, Mongiello, M.: DrawSearch: a tool for interactive content-based image retrieval over the net. Proc. of SPIE, **3656** 561–572 (1999)

19. Peng, J.: A multi-class relevance feedback approach to image retrieval. IEEE Int. Conf. on Image Processing, Thessaloniki, Greece **1** 46–49 (2001)

20. Wu, P., Manjunath, B. S.: Adaptive nearest neighbor search for relevance feedback in large image databases. Proc. ACM Multimedia, Ottawa, Canada (2001)

21. Aksoy, S., Haralick, R. M., Cheikh, F. A., Gabbouj, M.: A weighted distance approach to relevance feedback. IEEE Int. Conf. on Pattern Recognition, Barcelona, Spain **4** 812–815 (2000)

22. Bhanu, D., Peng, J., Qing, S.: Learning feature relevance and similarity metrics in image database. IEEE Workshop on Content-Based Access of Image and Video Libraries, CA, USA 14–18 (1998)

23. Sclaroff, S., Taycher, L., Cascia, M. La: ImageRover: A content-based image browser for the World Wide Web. Proc. IEEE Workshop on Content-based Access of Image and Video Libraries 2–9 (1997)

24. Patrice, B., Konik, H.: Texture similarity queries and relevance feedback for image retrieval. IEEE Int. Conf. on Pattern Recognition, Barcelona, Spain. **4** 55–58 (2000)

25. Choi, Y.-S., Kim, D., Krishnapuram, R.: Relevance feedback for content-based image retrieval using the choquet integral. IEEE Int. Conf. on Multimedia and Expo, New York USA. **2** 1207–1210 (2000)

26. Rui, Y., Huang, T.S.: Optimizing Learning in Image Retrieval. Proc. IEEE CVPR, **1** 236–243 (2000)

27. Ashwin, T. V., Jain, N., Ghosal, S.: Improving image retrieval performance with negative relevance feedback. IEEE Int. Conf. on Acoustics, Speech, and Signal Processing, Salt Lake City, USA. **3** 1637–1640 (2001)

28. Giacinto, G., Roli, F., Fumera, G.: Comparison and combination of adaptive query shifting and feature relevance learning for content-based image retrieval. IEEE Int. Conf. on Image Analysis and Processing, Palermo, Italy. 422–427 (2001)

29. Yoon, S. J., Park, D. K., Park, S-J., Won, C. S.: Image retrieval using a novel relevance feedback for edge histogram descriptor of MPEG-7. IEEE Int. conf. on Consumer Electronics 354–355 (2001)

30. Heisterkamp, D. R., Peng, J., Dai, H. K.: Feature relevance learning with query shifting for content-based image retrieval. IEEE Int. Conf. on Pattern Recognition, Barcelona, Spain. **4** 250–253 (2000)

31. Haykin, S.: Neural Networks: A Comprehensive Foundation, Macmillan, New York (1994)

32. Tikhonov, A. N.: On solving incorrectly posed problems and method of regularization. In Haykin, S. (eds.) Neural networks: a Comprehensive Foundation, Prentice Hall (1999)

33. Poggio, T., Girosi, F.: Networks for approximation and learning. Proceeding of the IEEE **78** 1481–1497 (1990)

34. Friedman, J. H.: Flexible metric nearest neighbor classification. Technical Report. Department of Statistics, Stanford University (1994)

35. Tahir, A., Zeytinoglu, M., Guan., L.: Application of Laplacian mixture model to image and video retrieval. IEEE Transactions on Multimedia. **9.7** 1416–1429 (2007)

36. Geversand, T., Smeulders, W. M.: PicToSeek: combining color and shape invariant features for image retrieval. IEEE Trans. on Image Processing **9** 102–119 (2000)

37. Safar, M., Shahabi, C., Sun, X.: Image Retrieval by Shape: A Comparative Study. IEEE International Conf. on Multimedia and Expo (I), New York, USA 141–144 (2000)

38. Salembier, P., Smith, J. R.: MPEG-7 multimedia descriptor schemes. IEEE Trans. on Circuits and Systems for Video Technology **11** 748–759 (2001)

39. Yap, K.-H., Kui, W.: A soft relevance framework in content-based image retrieval systems. IEEE Transactions on Circuits and Systems for Video Technology **15.12** 1557–1568 (2005)

40. Wu, K., Yap, K.-H.: An efficient radial basis function network approach for content-based image retrieval. IEEE International Conference on Acoustics, Speech, and Signal Processing **3** (2004)

41. Poggio, T., Girosi, F.: A theory of networks for approximation and leaning. Technical Report A.I. Memo No. 1140. Massachusetts Institute of Technology (1989)

42. Park, J., Sandberg, I. W.: Universal approximation using radial-basis function networks. Neural Computation **3** 246–257 (1991)

43. Broomhead, D. S., Lowe, D.: Multivariable functional interpolation and adaptive networks. Complex Syst. **2** 321–355 (1988)

44. Chen, S., Grant, P.M., Cowan, C.F.N.: Orthogonal least squares algorithm for training multi-output radial basis function networks. IEE Proc. Part F **139** 378–384 (1992)

45. Moody, J., Darken, C. J.: Fast learning in networks of locally-tuned processing units. Neural Computation **1** 281–294 (1989)

46. Chen, S., Cowan, C. F. N., Grant, P. M.: Orthogonal least squares learning algorithm for radial basis function networks. IEEE Trans. on Neural Networks **2** (1991)

47. Zhang, R., Guan, L.: A collaborative Bayesian image retrieval framework. IEEE International Conference on Acoustics, Speech and Signal Processing (2009)

48. Zhang, R., Guan, L.: Multimodal image retrieval via Bayesian information fusion. IEEE International Conference on Multimedia and Expo (2009)

49. Tong, S., Chang, E.: Support vector machine active learning for image retrieval. Proceedings of the ninth ACM international conference on Multimedia 107–118 (2001)

50. Zitnick, C.: Computing Conditional Probabilities in Large Domains by Maximizing Renyi's Quadratic Entropy. Ph.D. thesis, Carnegie Mellon University, Pittsburgh, PA (2003)

51. Rui, Y.: Efficient indexing, browsing and retrieval of image/video content. PhD Thesis, University of Illinois (1999)

52. Yan, R., Hauptmann, A., Jin, R.: Multimedia search with pseudo-relevance feedback. International Conference on Image and Video Retrieval. 238–247 (2003)

53. Yan, R., Hauptmann, A., Jin, R.: Negative pseudo-relevance feedback in contentbased video retrieval. Proceedings of the Eleventh ACM International Conference on Multimedia. 343–346 (2003)

54. Kennedy, L. S., Chang, S. F.: A reranking approach for context-based concept fusion in video indexing and retrieval. ACM International Conference on Image and Video Retrieval (Amsterdam, The Netherlands). 333–340 (2007)

55. Wu, Y., Tian, Q., Huang, T. S.: Discriminant-EM algorithm with application to image retrieval. IEEE Conference on Computer Vision and Pattern Recognition (South Carolina). 222–227 (2000)

56. Hady, M. F. A., Schwenker, F.: Semi-supervised learning. Handbook of Neural Information Processing. Berlin/Heidelberg: Springer-Verlag. 215–239 (2013)

57. Joachims, T.: Transductive inference for text classification using support vector machines. International Conference on Machine Learning (Bled, Slovenia). 200–209 (1999)

58. Wang, L., Chan, K., Zhang, Z.: Bootstrapping SVM active learning by incorporating unlabelled images for image retrieval. IEEE Computer Society Conference on Computer Vision and Pattern Recognition (Wisconsin). 629–634 (2003)

59. Rudinac, S., Larson, M., Hanjalic, A.: Exploiting visual reranking to improve pseudo-relevance feedback for spoken-content-based video retrieval. International Workshop on Image Analysis forMultimedia Interactive Services (London, UK). 17–20 (2009)

60. Carbonell, J. G., Yang, Y., Frederking, R. E., Brown, R. D., Geng, Y., Lee, D.: Translingual information retrieval: a comparative evaluation. International Joint Conference on Artificial Intelligence (Aichi, Japan) (1997)

61. Muneesawang, P., Guan, L., Automatic machine interactions for content-based image retrieval using a self-organizing tree map architecture. IEEE Transactions on Neural Network **13** 821–834 (2002)

62. Torjmen, M., Pinel-Sauvagnat, K., Boughanem, M.: Using pseudo-relevance feedback to improve image retrieval results. Workshop of the Cross-Language Evaluation Forum (Budapest, Hungary) 665–673 (2007)

63. El Demerdash, O., Kosseim, L., Bergler, S.: Image retrieval by inter-media fusion and pseudo-relevance feedback. Workshop of the Cross-Language Evaluation Forum (Aarhus, Denmark) 605–611 (2008)

64. Maillot, N., Chevallet, J. P., Valea, V., Lim, J. H.: IPAL inter-media pseudo-relevance feedback approach to Image CLEF 2006 photo retrieval. Workshop of the Cross-Language Evaluation Forum (Alicante, Spain) (2006)

65. Deselaers, T., Keysers, D., Ney, H.: Fire-flexible image retrieval engine: Image- CLEF 2004 evaluation. Multilingual Information Access for Text, Speech and Images Workshop, Springer 688–698 (2004)

66. He, R., Zhu, Y., Zhan, W.: Using local latent semantic indexing with pseudo relevance feedback in web image retrieval. International Joint Conference on INC, IMS, and IDC (Seoul, South Korea) 1354–1357 (2009)

67. El Demerdash, O., Bergler, S., Kosseim, L.: Image query expansion using semantic selectional restrictions. Workshop of the Cross-Language Evaluation Forum (Corfu, Greece) 150–156 (2009)

68. Kong, H., Guan, L.: Detection and removal of impulse noise by a neural network guided adaptive median filter. Proc. IEEE Int. Conf. on Neural Networks (Perth, Australia) 845–849 (1995)

69. Kong, H. S.: The Self-Organising Tree Map, and its Applications in Digital Image Processing. PhD Thesis, University of Sydney, Australia (1998)

70. Randall, J., Guan, L., Zhang, X., Li, W.: Investigations of the self-organizing tree map. Proc. Of Int. Conf. on Neural Information Processing, November 2 724–728 (1999)

71. Randall, J., Guan, L., Zhang, X., Li, W.: Hierarchical cluster model for perceptual image processing. Proc. IEEE Int. Conf. Acoustics, Speech, and Signal Processing 1 1041–1044 (2002)

72. Kohonen, T.: Self-organized formation of topologically correct feature maps. Biological cybernetics 43 59–69 (1982)

73. Corel Gallery Magic 65000. http://www.corel.com.Cited15Jan1999

74. Chen, Q., Petriu, E., Yang, X.: A comparative study of Fourier descriptors and Hu's seven moment invariants for image recognition. IEEE Canadian Conference on Electrical and Computer Engineering (Niagara Falls, Canada) 103–106 (2004)

75. Jarrah, K., Kyan, M., Krishnan, S., Guan, L.: Computational intelligence techniques and their applications in content-based image retrieval. IEEE International Conference on Multimedia and Expo (Toronto, Canada) 33–36 (2006)

76. Lay, J.A., Guan, L.: Image retrieval based on energy histogram of the low frequency DCT coefficients. IEEE Int. Conf. on Accoustic Speech and Signal Processing (Phoenix, USA) 3009–3012 (1999)

77. Xiong, Z., Huang, T. S.: Subband-based, memory-efficient JPEG2000 images indexing in compressed-domain. IEEE Southwest Symposium on Image Analysis and Interpretation (Santa Fe, USA) (2002)

78. Sim, D.-G., Kim, H.-K., Park, R.-H.: Fast texture description and retrieval of DCT-based compressed images. IEEE Electronic Letters 37 18–19 (2001)

79. Bhalod, J., Fahmy, G. F., Panchanathan, S.: Region based indexing in the JPEG2000 framework. Int. Workshop on Content-based Multimedia Indexing (Brescia, Italy) (2001)

80. ISO/IEC, ISO/IEC 14496-2:1999: Information technology: coding of audio-visual objects - Part 1: visual (1999)

81. ISO/IEC JTC 1/SC 29/WG 1, ISO/IEC FDIS 15444-1: information technology: JPEG 2000 image coding system: core coding system [WG 1 N 1890] (2000)

82. Said, A., Pearlman, W. A.: A new and efficient image codec based on set partitioning in hierarchical trees,. IEEE Trans. Circuits Systems Video Technol. 6 243–250 (1996)

83. Su, P.-C., Wang, H.-J. M., Kuo, C-C.J.: An integrated approach to image watermarking and JPEG-2000 compression. J. of VLSI signal processing systems for signal, image and video technology. **27** 35–53 (2001)

84. Tang, J., Zhang, W., Li, C.: An approach to compressed image retrieval based on JPEG2000 framework. Advanced Data Mining and Applications, Springer Berlin Heidelberg 391–399 (2005)

85. Do, M. N., Vertterli, M.: Wavelet-based texture retrieval using generalized Gaussian density and Kullback-Leibler distance. IEEE Trans. on Image Processing **11** 146–158 (2002)

86. Lui, C., Mandal, M. K.: Fast image indexing based on JPEG2000 packet header. Proc. Int. Workshop on Multimedia Information Retrieval (2001)

87. Ryan, T.W., Sanders, L. D., Fisher, H. D., Iverson, A. E.: Image compression by texture modeling in the wavelet domain. IEEE Trans. on Image Processing **5** 26–36 (1996)

88. Mandal, M. K., Panchanathan, S., Aboulnasr, T.: Image Indexing Using Translation and Scale-Invariant Moments and Wavelets, Storage and Retrieval for Image and Video Databases (SPIE) 380–389 (1997)

89. Karayiannis, N. B., Pai, P.-I., Zervos, N.: Image compression based on fuzzy algorithms for learning vector quantization and wavelet image decomposition. IEEE Trans. on Image processing **7** 1223–1230 (1998)

90. Muneesawang, P., Guan, L.: Multiresolution-histogram indexing for wavelet compressed images and relevant feedback learning for image retrieval. IEEE Int. Conf. on Image Processing (Vancouver, Canada) **2** 526–529 (2000)

91. Manjunath, B. S., Ma, W.Y.: Texture features for browsing and retrieval of image data,. IEEE Trans. of Pattern Analysis and Machine Intelligence **18** 837–842 (1996)

92. Manjunath, B. S., Ohm, J.R., Vasudevan, V. V., Yamada, A.: Color and Texture Descriptors. IEEE Trans. on Circuit and Systems for Video Technology **11** 703–715 (2001)

93. Media Graphics International, Photo Gallery 5,000, vol.1 CD-ROM, http://www. mediagraphics.net.Cited1November1999

94. Maand, W.Y., Manjunath, B. S.: Edge Flow: a framework for boundary detection and image segmentation,. IEEE Int. Conf. on Computer Vision and Pattern Recognition (Puerto Rico) 744–749 (1997)

95. Wong, H.-S., Guan, L.: Characterization for perceptual importance for object-based image segmentation,. IEEE Int. Conf. on Image Processing (Vancouver, Canada) 54–57 (2000)

96. Mukherjee, D., Deng, Y., Mitra, S.K.: A region-based video coder using edge Flow segmentation and hierarchical affine region matching. Proc. of SPIE **3309** (1998)

97. Muneesawang, P., Guan, L.: Image retrieval with embedded sub-class information using Gaussian mixture models,. IEEE Int. Conf. on Multimedia and Expo (Maryland, USA) **1** 769–772 (2003)

98. Naphades, M., Wang, R. R., Huang, T.: Audio-visual query and retrieval: a system that uses dynamic programming and relevance feedback. J. of Electronic Imaging 861–870 (2001)

99. Wang, R., Naphades, M., Huang, T. S.: Video retrieval and relevance feedback in the context of a post-integration model. IEEE Int. Workshop on Multimedia Signal Processing (Cannes, France) 33–38 (2001)

100. Wilkinson, R., Hingston, P.: Using the cosine measure in a neural network for document retrieval. ACM SIGIR Conf. on Research and Development in Information Retrieval (Chicago, USA) 202–210 (1991)

101. Muneesawang, P., Guan, L.: Video retrieval using an adaptive video indexing and automatic relevance feedback. IEEE Trans. on Circuits and Systems on Video Technology **15** 1032–1046 (2005)

102. Chang, S.-F., Sundaram, H.: Structural and semantic analysis of video, Int. Conf. on Multimedia and Expo (New York, USA) **2** 687–690 (2000)

103. Müller, H., Müller, W., Marchand-Maillet, S., Pun, T., Squire, D. M.: Strategies for positive and negative relevance feedback in image retrieval. Int. Conf. on Pattern Recognition, Barcelona, Spain. **1** 1043–1046 (2000)

104. Zhang, H., Smoliar, S. W., Wu, J. H.: Content-based video browsing tools. Multimedia computing and networking **2417** 389 (1995)

105. Informedia Digital Video Library Project at Carnegie Mellon University, http://www. informedia.cs.cmu.edu.Cited2001

106. Gargi, U., Kasturi, R., Strayer, S.H.: Performance characterization of video-shot-change detection methods. IEEE Trans. on Circuits and Systems for Video Technology **10** 1–13 (2000)

107. Rocchio, J.J.: Relevance feedback in information retrieval, In G. Salton, editor, The SMART Retrieval System–Experiments in Automatic Document Processing. Prentice Hall Inc., Englewood Cliffs, NJ (1971).

108. Merriam-Webster Dictionary. Merriam-Webster (2002)

109. 1st WORKSHOP ON MOBILE VISUAL SEARCH. http://scien.stanford.edu/pages/ conferences/mvs/Cited2009

110. Broder, A.: A taxonomy of web search. Proc. of ACM SIGIR, 3–10 (2002)

111. Chandrasekhar, V., Takacs, G., Chen, D., Tsai, S., Grzeszczuk, R., Girod, B.: CHoG: Compressed histogram of gradients A low bit-rate feature descriptor. IEEE Proc. CVPR, 2504–2511 (2009)

112. Chen, D., Tsai, S., Girod, B., Hsu, C., Kim, K., Singh, J.: Building book inventories using smartphones. Proc. ACM MM, 651–654 (2010)

113. Church, K., Smyth, B.: Understanding the intent behind mobile information needs. ACM Int. Conf. on Intelligent User Interfaces. 247–256 (2009)

114. Church, K., Smyth, B., Oliver, N.: Visual interfaces for improved mobile search. Workshop on Visual Interfaces to the Social and the Semantic Web (2009)

115. Csurka, G., Dance, C., Fan, L., Willamowski, J., Bray, C.: Visual categorization with bags of keypoints. Workshop on statistical learning in computer vision, Int. Conf. ECCV (2004)

116. Deng, J., Berg, A., Li, K., Fei-Fei, L.: What does classifying more than 10,000 image categories tell us? Int. Conf. ECCV, 71–84 (2010)

117. Deng, J., Dong, W., Socher, R., Li, L., Li, K., Fei-Fei, L.: Imagenet: A large-scale hierarchical image database. Proc. IEEE CVPR, 248–255 (2009)

118. Dix, A., Finlay, J., Abowd, G., Beale, R.: Human Computer Interaction (Third Edition). Prentice Hall (2004)

119. Duan, L.Y., Gao, W.: Side Discriminative Mobile Visual Search. 2nd WORKSHOP ON MOBILE VISUAL SEARCH (2011)

120. Girod, B., Chandrasekhar, V., Chen, D., Cheung, N., Grzeszczuk, R., Reznik, Y., Takacs, G., Tsai, S., Vedantham, R.: Mobile visual search. Signal Processing Magazine **28**(4), 61–76 (2011)

121. Guy, I., Jaimes, A., Agulló, P., Moore, P., Nandy, P., Nastar, C., Schinzel, H.: Will recommenders kill search?: recommender systems-an industry perspective. Proc. ACM Recommender systems, 7–12 (2010)

122. Hua, G., Tian, Q.: What can visual content analysis do for text based image search? Proc. IEEE ICME, 1480–1483 (2009)

123. Jain, R., Sinha, P.: Content Without Context is Meaningless. Proc. ACM Multimedia, pp. 1259–1268 (2010)

124. Jégou, H., Douze, M., Schmid, C.: Improving bag-of-features for large scale image search. Int. J. of Computer Vision **87**(3), 316–336 (2010)

125. Jégou, H., Douze, M., Schmid, C., Pérez, P.: Aggregating local descriptors into a compact image representation. Proc. IEEE. CVPR, 3304–3311 (2010)

126. Nister, D., Stewenius, H.: Scalable recognition with a vocabulary tree. Proc. IEEE CVPR, 2161–2168 (2006)

127. Perronnin, F., Dance, C.: Fisher kernels on visual vocabularies for image categorization. Proc. IEEE CVPR, 1–8. (2007)

128. Perronnin, F., Sánchez, J., Mensink, T.: Improving the fisher kernel for large-scale image classification. Int. Conf. on ECCV, 143–156 (2010)

129. Perronnin, F., Senchez, J., et al.: Large-scale image categorization with explicit data embedding. Proc. IEEE CVPR, 2297–2304 (2010)
130. Philbin, J., Chum, O., Isard, M., Sivic, J., Zisserman, A.: Lost in quantization: Improving particular object retrieval in large scale image databases. Proc. IEEE CVPR, 1–8 (2008)
131. Polifroni, J., Kiss, I., Adler, M.: Bootstrapping named entity extraction for the creation of mobile services. Proc. LREC, 1515–1520 (2010)
132. Robertson, S., Zaragoza, H.: The probabilistic relevance framework: BM25 and beyond. Information Retrieval 3(4), 333–389 (2009)
133. Rose, D., Levinson, D.: Understanding user goals in web search. Proc. ACM WWW, 13–19 (2004)
134. Schroth, G., Huitl, R., Chen, D., Abu-Alqumsan, M., Al-Nuaimi, A., Steinbach, E.: Mobile visual location recognition. Signal Processing Magazine, 28(4), 77–89 (2011)
135. Smith, J.: Clicking on Things. IEEE MultiMedia, 17(4), 2–3 (2010)
136. Takacs, G., Chandrasekhar, V., Gelfand, N., Xiong, Y., Chen, W., Bismpigiannis, T., Grzeszczuk, R., Pulli, K., Girod, B.: Outdoors augmented reality on mobile phone using loxel-based visual feature organization. Proc. ACM MIR, 427–434 (2008)
137. Tsai, S., Chen, D., Chandrasekhar, V., Takacs, G., Cheung, N., Vedantham, R., Grzeszczuk, R., Girod, B.: Mobile product recognition. Proc. ACM Multimedia, pp. 1587–1590 (2010)
138. Tsai, S., Chen, D., Takacs, G., Chandrasekhar, V., Singh, J., Girod, B.: Location coding for mobile image retrieval. Proc. ICST Mobile Multimedia Communications Conference, 1–7 (2009)
139. Yang, L., Geng, B., Hanjalic, A., Hua, X.: Contextual image retrieval model. Proc. the ACM Image and Video Retrieval, 406–413 (2010)
140. Yin, X., Shah, S.: Building taxonomy of web search intents for name entity queries. Proc. WWW, pp. 1001–1010 (2010)
141. Zhang, Z., Liang, X., Ganesh, A., Ma, Y.: TILT: transform invariant low-rank textures. Proc. ACCV, 314–328 (2010)
142. Zhou, X., Yu, K., Zhang, T., Huang, T.: Image classification using super-vector coding of local image descriptors. Proc. ECCV, 141–154 (2010)
143. Zhuang, J., Mei, T., Choi, S.C.H., Xu, Y.Q., Li, S.: When recommendation meets mobile: Contextual and personalized recommendation on the go. Proc. ACM Ubiquitous Computing, 153–162 Beijing, China (2011)
144. Ji, R., Duan, L. Y., Chen, J., Yao, H., Yuan, J., Rui, Y., Gao, W.: Location discriminative vocabulary coding for mobile landmark search. Int. J. of Computer Vision, 96(3), 290–314 (2012)
145. Ke, Y., Sukthankar, R.: PCA-SIFT: A more distinctive representation for local image descriptors. Proc. IEEE CVPR, 497–506 2004
146. Mikolajczyk, K., Schmid, C.: A performance evaluation of local descriptors. IEEE Trans. on Pattern Analysis and Machine Intelligence, 27(10), 1615–1630 (2005)
147. Bay, H., Tuytelaars, T., Van Gool, L.: Surf: Speeded up robust features. Int. Conf. on ECCV, 404–417 (2006)
148. Hua, G., Brown, M., Winder, S.: Discriminant embedding for local image descriptors. Int. Conf. ICCV, 1–8 (2007)
149. Nister, D., Stewenius, H.: Scalable recognition with a vocabulary tree. Proc. IEEE CVPR, 2161–2168 (2006)
150. Sivic, J., Zisserman, A.: Video Google: A text retrieval approach to object matching in videos. Proc. IEEE Computer Vision, 1470–1477 (2003)
151. Philbin, J., Chum, O., Isard, M., Sivic, J., Zisserman, A.: Object retrieval with large vocabularies and fast spatial matching. Porc. IEEE. CVPR, 1–8 (2007)
152. Schindler, G., Brown, M., Szeliski, R. City-scale location recognition. Porc. IEEE. CVPR, (2007)
153. Ji, R., Xie, X., Yao, H., Wu, Y., Ma, W. Y.: Vocabulary tree incremental indexing for scalable location recognition. Proc. IEEE ICME, 869–872 (2008)

154. Irschara, A., Zach, C., Frahm, J. M., Bischof, H.: From structure-from-motion point clouds to fast location recognition. Porc. IEEE. CVPR, 2599–2606 (2009)

155. Chen, D. M., Tsai, S. S., Chandrasekhar, V., Takacs, G., Singh, J., Girod, B.: Tree histogram coding for mobile image matching. Int. Conf. on Data Compression, 143–152, (2009)

156. Lu, L., Toyama, K., Hager, G. D.: A two level approach for scene recognition. Proc. IEEE CVPR, 688–695 (2005)

157. Knopp, J., Sivic, J., Pajdla, T. Avoiding confusing features in place recognition. Int. Conf. on ECCV, 748–761 (2010)

158. Parikh, D., Zitnick, C. L., Chen, T.: Determining patch saliency using low-level context. Int. Conf. on ECCV, 446–459 (2008)

159. Lim, J. H., Li, Y., You, Y., Chevallet, J. P.: Scene recognition with camera phones for tourist information access. Proc. IEEE ICME, 100–103 (2007)

160. Chen, T., Yap, K. H.: Discriminative BoW Framework for Mobile Landmark Recognition. (2014)

161. Harel, J., Koch, C., Perona, P.: Graph-based visual saliency. Advances in neural information processing systems, 545–552 (2006)

162. Salton, G., Buckley, C.: Term-weighting approaches in automatic text retrieval. Information processing management, 24(5), 513–523. (1988)

163. Kung, S. Y.: Kernel Methods and Machine Learning, Cambridge University Press. (2014)

164. Duda, R. O., Hart, P. E., Stork, D. G.: J. Pattern classification, John Wiley Sons. (2012)

165. Pavlidis, P., Weston, J., Cai, J., Grundy, W. N.: Gene functional classification from heterogeneous data. Int. Conf. on Computational biology, 249–255 (2001)

166. G. Gerules, S.K. Bhatia, D.E. Jackson, A survey of image processing techniques and statistics for ballistic specimens in forensic science, Sci. Justice 1–15 (2012)

167. W. Chu, L. Ma, J. Song, and T. Vorburger, An iterative image registration algorithm by optimizing similarity measurement, J.Res. Natl. Inst. Stand. Technol. 1–6 (2010)

168. T. V. Vorburger, J. Song, W. Chu, T. B. Renegar, A. Zheng, J. Yen, R. M. Thompson, R. Silver, Topography measurements for correlations of standard cartridge cases, Proc. of SPIE 7729 (2010)

169. T. V. Vorburger, J. Song, W. Chu, L. Ma, S. H. Bui, A. Zheng, T. B. Renegar, Application of cross-correlation functions, Wear 271 529–533 (2011)

170. T. J. Weller, A. Zheng, R. Thompson, F. Tulleners, Confocal microscopy analysis of breech face marks on fired cartridge cases from 10 consecutively manufactured pistol slides, J. Forensic Sci. 57(4) 912–917 (2012)

171. C. W. Therrien, Discrete Random Signals and Statistical Signal Processing, Prentice-Hall, Englewood Cliffs, New Jersey (1988)

172. B. S. Reddy and B. N. Chatterji, An FFT-based technique for translation, rotation, and scale-invariant image registration, IEEE Trans. Image Proc. 5(8) 1266–1271 (1996)

173. R. C. Gonzalez, R. E. Woods, Digital Image Processing, Prentice-Hall, New Jersey (2002).

174. J. N. Sarviya, S. Patnaik, S. Bombaywala, Image registration using log-polar transformation and phase correlation, Proc. IEEE Region 10 Conference 1–5 (2009)

175. T. Lehmann, A. Sovakar, W. Schmitt, R. Repges, A comparison of similarity measures for digital subtraction radiography, Comput. Biol. Med. 27(2) 151–167 (1997)

176. S. K. Mitra, Digital Signal Processing: A Computer Based Approach, Mc-Graw Hill, New York (2006).

177. W. Chu, J. Song, T. Vorburger, S. Ballou, Striation density for predicting the identifiability of fired bullets with automated inspection systems, J. Forensic Sci. 55(5) 1222–1226 (2010)

178. J. Canny, A computational approach to edge detection, IEEE Trans. Pattern Analysis and Machine Intelligence 8(6) 679–698 (1986)

179. Z. Geradts, J. Bijhold, R. Hermsen, Pattern recognition in a database of cartridge cases, Proc. SPIE Conf. of Investigation and Forensic Technologies 3576 (1998).

180. Wang, H., Divakaran, A., Vetro, A., Chang, S. F., Sun, H.: Survey of compressed-domain features used in audio-visual indexing and analysis. J. of Visual Communication and Image Representation, 14(2), 150–183 (2003)

181. Bao, O., Lian, M., Guan, L.: Enhancement of dissolved shot boundary detection with twin-windows amplification method. Optical Engineering, 46(12), 127004–127004 (2007)

182. Bao, O., Guan, L.: Scene change detection using DC coefficients. Proc. IEEE Image Processing, 418–421 (2002)

183. Le Gall, D.: MPEG: A video compression standard for multimedia applications. Proc. ACM Communications, 34(4), 46–58 (1991)

184. Shen, K., Delp, E. J.: A fast algorithm for video parsing using MPEG compressed sequences. Proc. IEEE Image Processing, 252–255 (1995)

185. Bao, O. K., Lay, J. A., Guan, L.: Compressed-domain video parsing using energy histograms of the lower-frequency DCT coefficients. Storage and Retrieval for Media Databases, 293–300 (2000)

186. Lelescu, D., Schonfeld, D.: Real-time scene change detection on compressed multimedia bitstream based on statistical sequential analysis. Proc. IEEE ICME, 1141–1144 (2000)

187. Shibata, Y., Chen, Z., Campbell, R. H.: A fast degradation-free algorithm for DCT block extraction in the compressed domain. Proc. IEEE ICASSP, 3185–3188 (1999)

188. Chang, S. F., Messerschmitt, D. G.: A new approach to decoding and compositing motion-compensated DCT-based images. Proc. IEEE ICASSP 421–424 (1993)

189. MSDN online, http://www.microsoft.com/

190. Gao, X., Tang, X.: Unsupervised video-shot segmentation and model-free anchorperson detection for news video story parsing. IEEE Trans. on Circuits and Systems for Video Technology, 12(9), 765–776. (2002)

191. Chaisorn, L., Chua, T. S., Lee, C. H.: The segmentation of news video into story units. Proc. IEEE ICME, 73–76 (2002)

192. Boykov, Y., Veksler, O., Zabih, R.: Fast approximate energy minimization via graph cuts. IEEE Trans. on Pattern Analysis and Machine Intelligence, 23(11), 1222–1239 (2001)

193. Boykov, Y., Funka-Lea, G.: Graph cuts and efficient ND image segmentation. Int. J. of computer vision, 70(2), 109–131. (2006)

194. Wang, C. H., Fan, X., Du, M., Elder, B., Tang, X., Guan, L.: Special Effects in Film Making with Object Based Transformations. Proc. IEEE ICME, 1519–1522 (2007)

195. Li, Y., Sun, J., Shum, H. Y.: Video object cut and paste. ACM Trans. on Graphics, Vol. 24, No. 3, 595–600 (2005)

196. Wang, J., Bhat, P., Colburn, R. A., Agrawala, M., Cohen, M. F.: Interactive video cutout. ACM Trans. on Graphics, Vol. 24, No. 3, pp. 585–594 (2005)

197. Wang, J., Xu, W., Zhu, S., Gong, Y.: Efficient video object segmentation by graph-cut. Proc. IEEE ICME, 496–499 (2007)

198. Mu, Y., Zhang, H., Wang, H., Zuo, W.: Automatic video object segmentation using graph cut. Proc. IEEE. ICIP, 371–377 (2007)

199. Gao, J., Hauptmann, A. G., Wactlar, H. D.: Combining motion segmentation with tracking for activity analysis. Inter. Conf. on Automatic Face and Gesture Recognition, 699–704 (2004)

200. Malcolm, J., Rathi, Y., Tannenbaum, A. Graph cut segmentation with nonlinear shape priors. Proc. IEEE ICIP, 360–365 (2007)

201. Dalal, N., Triggs, B.: Histograms of oriented gradients for human detection. Proc. IEEE CVPR, 886–893 (2005)

202. Hjelmås, E., Low, B. K.: Face detection: A survey. Computer vision and image understanding, 83(3), 236–274 (2001)

203. Yang, M. H., Kriegman, D., Ahuja, N.: Detecting faces in images: A survey. IEEE Trans. on Pattern Analysis and Machine Intelligence, 24(1), 34–58 (2002)

204. Chen, C., Chiang, S. P.: Detection of human faces in colour images. IEE Vision, Image and Signal Processing, Vol. 144, No. 6,384–388 (1997)

205. Govindaraju, V.: Locating human faces in photographs. Int. J. of Computer Vision, 19(2), 129–146 (1996)

206. Schneiderman, H., Kanade, T.: Probabilistic modeling of local appearance and spatial relationships for object recognition. Proc. IEEE. CVPR, 45–51 (1998)

207. Viola, P., Jones, M. J.: Robust real-time face detection. Int. J of computer vision, *57*(2), 137–154 (2004)
208. Georghiades, A. S., Belhumeur, P. N., Kriegman, D.: From few to many: Illumination cone models for face recognition under variable lighting and pose. IEEE Trans. on Pattern Analysis and Machine Intelligence, *23*(6), 643–660 (2001)
209. Ramamoorthi, R.: Analytic PCA construction for theoretical analysis of lighting variability in images of a Lambertian object. IEEE Trans. on Pattern Analysis and Machine Intelligence, *24*(10), 1322–1333 (2002)
210. Basri, R., Jacobs, D. W.: Lambertian reflectance and linear subspaces. IEEE Trans. on Pattern Analysis and Machine Intelligence, *25*(2), 218–233 (2003)
211. Yaroslavsky, L. P., Eden, M.: Fundamentals of digital optics: digital signal processing in optics and holography. Springer-Verlag New York, Inc. (1996)
212. Zheng, W., Zhou, X., Zou, C., Zhao, L.: Facial expression recognition using kernel canonical correlation analysis (KCCA). IEEE Trans. on Neural Networks, *17*(1), 233–238 (2006)
213. Christmas, W. J., Kittler, J., Koubaroulis, D., Levienaise-Obadia, B., Messer, K.: Generation of semantic cues for sports video annotation. IEEE Intl. Conf. on Image Processing, (2001).
214. Miyauchi, S., Hirano, A., Babaguchi, N., Kitahashi, T.: Collaborative multimedia analysis for detecting semantical events from broadcasted sports video. Proc. IEEE Pattern Recognition, 1009–1012 (2002)
215. Lazarescu, M., Venkatesh, S., West, G., Caelli, T.: On the automated interpretation and indexing of American football. Proc. IEEE Multimedia Computing and Systems, 802–806 (1999)
216. Nitta, N., Babaguchi, N., Kitahashi, Extracting actors, actions and events from sports video-a fundamental approach to story tracking. In Proc. IEEE Pattern Recognition, 4718–4721 (2000)
217. Xiong, Z., Radhakrishnan, R., Divakaran, A.: Generation of sports highlights using motion activity in combination with a common audio feature extraction framework. Proc. IEEE ICIP, pp. I–5 (2003)
218. Manjunath, B. S., Salembier, P., Sikora, T. (Eds.).: Introduction to MPEG-7: multimedia content description interface (Vol. 1). John Wiley Sons. (2002)
219. Fukunaga, K.: Introduction to statistical pattern recognition. Academic press. (1990)
220. N. Babaguchi, Y. Kawai, T. Kitahashi.: Event Based Indexing of Broadcasted Sports Video by Intermodal Collaboration, IEEE Trans. on Multimedia, vol. 4, 68–75 (2002)
221. Napster. http://www.napster.com/.Cited2002
222. Gnutella. http://gnutella.wego.com.Cited2002
223. Jordan Ritter, Why Gnutella Can't Scale. No, Really, http://www.darkridge.com/~jpr5/doc/gnutella.html.Cited2002
224. Corel, http://www.corel.com.Cited2001
225. H. S. Nwana.: Software Agents: An Overview, Knowledge Engineering Review, vol. 11, no. 3, 1–40 (1996)
226. Stoica I., Morris R., Karger D., Kaashoek M.F., Balakrishnan H.: Chord: A scalable peer-to-peer lookup service for internet applications. Conf. on Applications, Technologies, Architectures, and Protocols for Computer Communications, 149–160 (2001)
227. Peng C., Kim M., Zhang Z., Lei H.: VDN: Virtual machine image distribution network for cloud data centers. Proc. IEEE INFOCOM, 181–189 (2012)
228. Dikaiakos,M. D., Katsaros, D., Mehra, P., Pallis, G., Vakali, A.: Cloud computing: Distributed Internet Computing for IT and Scientific Research. IEEE Internet Computing, 13(5), 10–13 (2009)
229. Demirkan H., Delen D. Leveraging the capabilities of service-oriented decision support systems: Putting analytics and big data in cloud. Decision Support Systems, (2012)
230. Liao, J., Yang, D., Li, T., Wang, J., Qi, Q., Zhu, X.:(2014). A scalable approach for content based image retrieval in cloud datacenter. Information Systems Frontiers, 16(1), 129–141 (2014)

231. J. Sivic, A. Zisserman.: Video Google: Efficient visual search of videos. Toward Category-Level Object Recognition, 127–144, (2006)

232. J. Sivic, A. Zisserman.: Video data mining using configurations of viewpoint invariant regions. Proc. IEEE CVPR, 479–488 (2004)

233. T. Quack, V. Ferrari, L. Van Gool.: Video mining with frequent itemset configurations. Image and Video Retrieval, 360–369 (2006)

234. J. Sivic, A. Zisserman.: Efficient visual search for objects in videos. Proceedings of the IEEE, vol. 96, no. 4, 548–566 (2008)

235. J. Sivic, F. Schaffalitzky, A. Zisserman.: Object level grouping for video shots. Proc. Computer Vision-ECCV 2004, 85–98, (2004)

236. Y. Jiang, C. Ngo, and J. Yang.: Towards optimal bag-of-features for object categorization and semantic video retrieval. Proc. ACM CIVR, 501–510 (2007)

237. J. Sivic, A. Zisserman.: Efficient visual search of videos cast as text retrieval. IEEE Trans. on Pattern Analysis and Machine Intelligence, vol. 31, no. 4, 591–606 (2009)

238. A. Basharat, Y. Zhai, and M. Shah.: Content based video matching using spatiotemporal volumes. Computer Vision and Image Understanding, vol. 110, no. 3, 360–377 (2008)

239. J. Law-To, O. Buisson, V. Gouet-Brunet, N. Boujemaa.: Robust voting algorithm based on labels of behavior for video copy detection. Proc. ACM Multimedia, 835–844 (2006)

240. J. Sivic, M. Everingham, A. Zisserman.: Person spotting: video shot retrieval for face sets. Image and Video Retrieval, 592–592 (2005)

241. X. Zhou, X. Zhuang, S. Yan, S. Chang, M. Hasegawa-Johnson, T. Huang.: Sift-bag kernel for video event analysis. Proc. ACM Multimedia, 229–238 (2008)

242. D. Xu, S. Chang.: Video event recognition using kernel methods with multilevel temporal alignment. IEEE Trans. on Pattern Analysis and Machine Intelligence, vol. 30, no. 11, 1985–1997 (2008)

243. P. Xu, L. Xie, S. Chang, A. Divakaran, A. Vetro, H. Sun.: Algorithms and system for segmentation and structure analysis in soccer video. Proc. IEEE ICME, 928–931 (2001)

244. A. Ekin, A. Tekalp.: Framework for tracking and analysis of soccer video. Proc. SPIE VCIP, vol. 4671, 763–774 (2002)

245. L. Xu, Y. Li.: Video classification using spatial-temporal features and PCA. Proc. IEEE ICME. vol. 3, 485–488 (2003)

246. S. Nepal, U. Srinivasan, G. Reynolds.: Automatic detection of "Goal" segments in basketball videos. Proc. ACM MM, 261–269 (2001)

247. G. Zhu, C. Xu, Q. Huang, Y. Rui, S. Jiang, W. Gao, H. Yao.: Event tactic analysis based on broadcast sports video. IEEE Transactions on Multimedia. vol. 11, no. 1, 49–67 (2009)

248. S. Fischer, R. Lienhart, W. Effelsberg.: Automatic recognition of film genres. Proc. ACM MM. vol. 95, 295–304 (1995)

249. D. Brezeale, D. Cook.: Automatic video classification: A survey of the literature. IEEE Trans. on Systems, Man, Cybernetics, Part C: Applications and Reviews. vol. 38, no. 3, 416–430 (2008)

250. B. Truong, C. Dorai, S. Venkatesh.: Automatic genre identification for content-based video categorization. Proc. IEEE ICPR, vol. 15, 230–233 (2000)

251. S. Takagi, S. Hattori, K. Yokoyama, A. Kodate, H. Tominaga.: Sports video categorizing method using camera motion parameters. Proc. IEEE ICME, vol. 2, 461–464 (2003)

252. E. Jaser, J. Kittler, W. Christmas.: Hierarchical decision making scheme for sports video categorisation with temporal post-processing. Proc. IEEE CVPR, vol. 2, 908–913 (2004)

253. J. Wang, C. Xu, E. Chng.: Automatic sports video genre classification using pseudo-2d-hmm. Proc. ICPR, 778–781 (2006)

254. X. Yuan, W. Lai, T. Mei, X. Hua, X. Wu, S. Li.: Automatic video genre categorization using hierarchical svm. Proc. IEEE ICIP, 2905–2908 (2006)

255. R. Glasberg, S. Schmiedeke, M. Mocigemba, T. Sikora.: New Real-Time Approaches for Video-Genre-Classification Using High-Level Descriptors and a Set of Classifiers. Proc. IEEE ICSC, 120–127 (2008)

256. M. Montagnuolo, A. Messina.: Parallel neural networks for multimodal video genre classification. Journal of Multimedia Tools and Applications, vol. 41, no. 1, 125–159 (2009)

257. A. Ekin, A. M. Teklap, R. Mehrotra.: Automatic soccer video analysis and summarization. IEEE Trans. on Image Processing, vol. 12, no. 7, 796–807 (2003)

258. Y. Jiang, J. Yang, C. Ngo, A. Hauptmann.: Representations of keypoint-based semantic concept detection: A comprehensive study. IEEE Trans. on Multimedia. vol. 12, no. 1, 42–53 (2010)

259. D. Lowe.: Distinctive image features from scale-invariant keypoints. Int. J. of computer vision, vol. 60, no. 2, 91–110 (2004)

260. J. Philbin, O. Chum, M. Isard, J. Sivic, A. Zisserman.: Object retrieval with large vocabularies and fast spatial matching. Proc. IEEE CVPR, vol. 3613, 1575–1589 (2007)

261. J. Yang, Y. Jiang, A. Hauptmann, C. Ngo.: Evaluating bag-of-visual-words representations in scene classification. Proc. ACM MIR, 197–206 (2007)

262. S. Lazebnik, C. Schmid, J. Ponce.: Beyond Bags of Features: Spatial Pyramid Matching for Recognizing Natural Scene Categories. Proc. IEEE CVPR, vol. 2, 2169–2178 (2006)

263. J. Zhang, M. Marszalek, S. Lazebnik, C. Schmid.: Local features and kernels for classification of texture and object categories: A comprehensive study. Int. J. of Computer Vision. vol. 73, no. 2, 213–238 (2007)

264. J. Sivic, A. Zisserman.: Video Google: A text retrieval approach to object matching in videos. Proc. ICCV. vol. 2, 1470–1477 (2003)

265. L. Li, N. Zhang, L. Duan, Q. Huang, J. Du, L. Guan.: Automatic sports genre categorization and view-type classification over large-scale dataset. Proc. ACM MM, 653–656 (2009)

266. G. Lavee, E. Rivlin, M. Rudzsky.: Understanding video events: A survey of methods for automatic interpretation of semantic occurrences in video. IEEE Trans. on Systems, Man, Cybernetics, Part C: Applications and Reviews, vol. 39, no. 5, 489–504 (2009)

267. D. Sadlier, N. O'Connor.: Event detection in field sports video using audio-visual features and a support vector machine. IEEE Trans. on Circuits and Systems for Video Technology. vol. 15, no. 10, 1225–1233 (2005)

268. M. Xu, L. Duan, C. Xu, Q. Tian.: A fusion scheme of visual and auditory modalities for event detection in sports video. Proc. IEEE ICASSP, vol. 3, 189–192 (2003)

269. Q. Ye, Q. Huang, W. Gao, S. Jiang.: Exciting event detection in broadcast soccer video with mid-level description and incremental learning. Proc. ACM MM, 455–458 (2005)

270. L. Li, Y. Chen, W. Hu, W. Li, X. Zhang.: Recognition of Semantic Basketball Events Based on Optical Flow Patterns. Proc. ISVC, 480–488 (2009)

271. N. Babaguchi, Y. Kawai, T. Kitahashi.: Event based indexing of broadcasted sports video by intermodal collaboration. IEEE Trans. on Multimedia. vol. 4, no. 1, 68–75 (2002)

272. D. Zhang, S. Chang.: Event detection in baseball video using superimposed caption recognition. Proc. ACM MM, 315–318 (2002)

273. L. Duan, M. Xu, T. Chua, Q. Tian, C. Xu.: A mid-level representation framework for semantic sports video analysis. Proc. ACM MM, 33–44 (2003)

274. M. Tien, Y. Wang, C. Chou, K. Hsieh, W. Chu, J. Wu.: Event detection in tennis matches based on video data mining. Proc. IEEE ICME, 1477–1480 (2008)

275. Y. Zhang, C. Xu, Y. Rui, J. Wang, H. Lu.: Semantic event extraction from basketball games using multi-modal analysis. Proc. IEEE ICME, 2190–2193 (2007)

276. X. Tong, H. Lu, Q. Liu.: A three-layer event detection framework and its application in soccer video. Proc. IEEE ICME, 1551–1554 (2004)

277. T. Mei and X. Hua.: Structure and event mining in sports video with efficient mosaic. Multimedia Tools and Applications, vol. 40, no. 1, 89–110 (2008)

278. T. Wang, J. Li, Q. Diao, W. Hu, Y. Zhang, C. Dulong.: Semantic event detection using conditional random fields. Proc. IEEE CVPRW, 109–114 (2006)

279. C. Xu, Y. Zhang, G. Zhu, Y. Rui, H. Lu, Q. Huang.: Using webcast text for semantic event detection in broadcast sports video. IEEE Trans. on Multimedia, vol. 10, no. 7, 1342–1355 (2008)

280. P. Wang, Z. Liu, S. Yang.: Investigation on unsupervised clustering algorithms for video shot categorization. J. of Soft Computing-A Fusion of Foundations, Methodologies and Applications, vol. 11, no. 4, 355–360 (2007)

281. L. Zhong, C. Li, H. Li, Z. Xiong.: Unsupervised Clustering Algorithm for Video Shots Using Spectral Division. Proc. ISVC, 782–792 (2008)

282. L. Duan, M. Xu, Q. Tian.: Semantic shot classification in sports video. Proc. SPIE, 300–313 (2003)

283. X. Tong, Q. Liu, H. Lu, H. Jin.: Shot classification in sports video. Proc. ICSP. vol. 2, 1364–1367 (2004)

284. J. Wang, E. Chng, C. Xu.: Soccer replay detection using scene transition structure analysis. Proc. IEEE ICASSP, 433–437 (2005)

285. M. Kolekar and K. Palaniappan.: Semantic concept mining based on hierarchical event detection for soccer video indexing. J. of Multimedia, vol. 4, no. 5, 298–312 (2009)

286. R. Benmokhtar, B. Huet, S. Berrani.: Low-level feature fusion models for soccer scene classification. Proc. IEEE ICME, 1329–1332 (2008)

287. T. Hofmann.: Learning the similarity of documents: An information-geometric approach to document retrieval and categorization. NIPS, vol. 12, 914–920 (2000)

288. T. Hofmann.: Probabilistic latent semantic indexing. Proc. ACM SIGIR, 50–57 (1999)

289. C. Chang and C. Lin.: LIBSVM: a library for support vector machines. (2001)

290. G. Miao, G. Zhu, S. Jiang, Q. Huang, C. Xu, W. Gao.: A Real-Time Score Detection and Recognition Approach for Broadcast Basketball Video. Proc. IEEE ICME, 1691–1694 (2007)

291. J. Dai, L. Duan, X. Tong, C. Xu, Q. Tian, H. Lu, J. Jin.: Replay scene classification in soccer video using web broadcast text. Proc. IEEE ICME, 1098–1101 (2005)

292. C. Xu, J. Wang, K. Wan, Y. Li, L. Duan.: Live sports event detection based on broadcast video and web-casting text. Proc. ACM MM, 230–237 (2006)

293. A. Quattoni, S. Wang, L. Morency, M. Collins, T. Darrell, M. Csail.: Hidden-state conditional random fields. IEEE Trans. on Pattern Analysis and Machine Intelligence, vol. 29, no. 10, 1848–1852 (2007)

294. S. Wang, A. Quattoni, L. Morency, D. Demirdjian, T. Darrell.: Hidden conditional random fields for gesture recognition. Proc. IEEE CVPR, 1521–1527 (2006)

295. A. Gunawardana, M. Mahajan, A. Acero, J. Platt.: Hidden conditional random fields for phone classification. Proc. Interspeech, 1117–1120 (2005)

296. Y. Tan, D. Saur, S. Kulkarni, P. Ramadge.: Rapid estimation of camera motion from compressed video with application to video annotation. IEEE Trans. on circuits and systems for video technology. vol. 10, no. 1, 133–146 (2000)

297. L. Morency, A. Quattoni, C. Christoudias, S. Wang.: Hidden-state Conditional Random Field Library. (2008)

298. F. Sha and F. Pereira.: Shallow parsing with conditional random fields. in Proc. of HLT-NAACL, 213–220 (2003)

299. J. Lafferty, A. McCallum, F. Pereira.: Conditional random fields: Probabilistic models for segmenting and labeling sequence data. in Proc. ICML, 282–289 (2001)

300. Y. Rubner, C. Tomasi, L. Guibas.: The earth mover's distance as a metric for image retrieval. Inter. J. of Computer Vision, vol. 40, no. 2, 99–121 (2000)

301. R. Duda, P. Hart, D. Stork.: Pattern classification. Wiley-Interscience. (2001)

302. A. Jain, M. Murty, P. Flynn.: Data clustering: a review. ACM computing surveys, vol. 31, no. 3, 264–323 (1999)

303. H. Bay, T. Tuytelaars, L. Van Gool.: Surf: Speeded up robust features. Lecture notes in computer science, vol. 3951, 404–411 (2006)

304. Wikipedia, Type I and type II error http://en.wikipedia.org/wiki.Citedin2007

305. C.-C. Chang, C.-J. Lin.: Training v-support vector classifiers: Theory, algorithms, Neural Computation, Vol. 13, No. 9, 2119–2147 (2001)

306. S. Ben-Yacoub, Y. Abdeljaoued, E. Mayoraz.: Fusion of face, speech data for person identity verification, IEEE Trans. on Neural Networks, Vol. 10, No. 5, 1065–1074 (1999)

307. K. Wu, K.-H. Yap.: Fuzzy SVM for content-based image retrieval - A pseudo-label support vector machine framework. IEEE Computational Intelligence Magazine, vol.1, 10–16 (2006)

308. D.W. Massaro.: Auditory visual speech processing, European Conference on Speech Communication, Technology, Aalborg, Denmark, 1153–1156 (2001)

309. G. F. Meyer, J. B. Mulligan, S. M. Wuerger.: Continuous audio–visual digit recognition using N-best decision fusion. Inter. J. on Multi-Sensor, Multi-Source Information Fusion, Vol. 5, No. 2, 91–101 (2004)

310. C. Cortes, V. Vapnik.: Support-vector network, Machine Learning, Vol. 20, No.3, 273–297 (1995)

311. J. Zhou, L.-P. Xin, G. Rong.: Decision fusion based cartridge identification using support vector machine. Proc. IEEE Inter. Conf. on Systems, Man, Cybernetics, 2873–2877 (2000)

312. L. Manovich.: The Language of New Media, MIT Press, Cambridge, (2001)

313. D. Bordwell, K. Thompson.: Film Art: An Introduction, 7th edition, MaGraw-Hill, (2004)

314. J.A. Lay, L. Guan.: Semantic retrieval of multimedia by concept languages, IEEE Signal Processing Magazine, Vol. 23, Issue 2, 115–123 (2006)

315. J.A. Lay, L. Guan.: Retrieval for color artistry concepts, IEEE Trans. on Image Processing, Vol. 13, No. 3, 326–339 (2004)

316. M. Petkovic, W. Jonker.: Content-based video retrieval by integrating spatio-temporal, stochastic recognition of events, in: Proc. IEEE Workshop on Detection, Recognition of Events in Video, 75–82 (2001)

317. H. Miyamori, S.-I. Iisaku.: Video annotation for content-based retrieval using human behavior analysis, domain knowledge. Proc. IEEE Automatic Face, Gesture Recognition, 320–325 (2000)

318. G. Sudhir, J.C.M. Lee, A.K. Jain.: Automatic classification of tennis video for high-level content-based retrieval. Proc. IEEE Content-based Access of Image, Video Database, 81–90 (1998)

319. J. Vesanto, E. Alhoniemi.: Clustering of the self-organizing map. IEEE Trans. Neural Network, vol. 11, no. 3, 586–600 (2000)

320. H. S. Chang, S. Sull, S. U. Lee.: Efficient video indexing scheme for content-based retrieval, IEEE Trans. on Circuits, Systems for Video Technology, vo. 9, no. 8, 1269–1279 (1999)

321. C.-W. Ngo, T.-C. Pong, H.-J. Zhang.: On clustering, retrieval of video shots. Proc. ACM Multimedia, 51–60 (2001)

322. A.M. Ferman, A.M. Tekalp.: Efficient filtering, clustering methods for temporal video segmentation, visual summarization. J. of Visual Comm. and Image Rep., 9(4), 336–351 (1998)

323. G. Salton, E.A. Fox, E. Voorheers.: Advanced feedback methods in information retrieval. J. of the American Society for Information science, vol. 36, No. 3, 200–210 (1985)

324. Muneesawang, P., Guan, L.: iARM-an interactive video retrieval system. Proc. IEEE ICME, 285–288 (2004)

325. Usevitch, B. E.: A tutorial on modern lossy wavelet image compression: foundations of JPEG 2000. IEEE Signal Processing Magazine, 18(5), 22–35 (2001)

326. Jain, A. K., Duin, R. P. W., Mao, J.: Statistical pattern recognition: A review. IEEE Trans. on Pattern Analysis, Machine Intelligence, 22(1), 4–37 (2000)

327. Figueiredo, M. A., Jain, A. K.: Unsupervised selection, estimation of finite mixture models. Proc IEEE Pattern Recognition, Vol. 2, 2087–2087 (2000)

328. Crouse, M. S., Nowak, R. D., Baraniuk, R. G.: Wavelet-based statistical signal processing using hidden Markov models. IEEE Trans. on Signal Processing, 46(4), 886–902 (1998)

329. Muneesawang, P., Guan, L.: An interactive approach for CBIR using a network of radial basis functions. IEEE Trans. on Multimedia, 6(5), 703–716 (2004)

330. T. Kohonen.: Self-Organizing MAPS. 2nd edition, Springer-Verlag, (1997)

331. S. Haykin.:, Neural Networks, a Comprehensive Foundation, Prentice Hall, (1999)

332. Chang, C. C., Lin, C. J.: Library of SVMs, LIBSVM, http://www.csie.ntu.edu.tw/~cjlin/libsvm. (2008)

333. Stauffer, C.: Automated audio-visual analysis, MIT Artificial Intelligence Laboratory Memo. http://people.csail.mit.edu/stauffer/Home. (2005)

334. D. Alexiadis, P. Daras, P. Kelly, N.E. OConnor, T. Boubekeur, M.B. Moussa.: Evaluating a Dancer's Performance using Kinect-Based Skeleton Tracking. Proc. ACM Multimedia, 659–662 (2011)

335. J. Chan, H. Leung, J.K. Tang, T. Komura.: A virtual reality dance training system using motion capture technology, IEEE Trans. Learn. Technol., Vol. 4, No. 2, 187–195 (2011)

336. E. Ho, J. Chan, T. Komura, H. Leung.: Interactive Partner Control in Close Interactions for Real-Time Applications, ACM Trans. Multimedia Comput., Commun., Appl., Vol. 9, No. 3, (21)1–19 (2013)

337. L.R. Rabiner.: A Tutorial on Hidden Markov Models, Selected Applications in Speech Recognition, Proc. of the IEEE, Vol. 77, No. 2, 257–286 (1989)

338. G. Caridakis, K., Karpouzis, A., Drosopoulos, S. Kollias.: SOMM: Self organizing Markov map for gesture recognition. Pattern Recognition Letters, Vol. 31(1), 52–59 (2010)

339. Gonsales, A. O., Kyan, M.: Trajectory Analysis on Spherical Self-Organizing Maps with Application to Gesture Recognition. J. of Advances in Self-Organizing Maps, 125–134 (2013)

340. M. Kyan, G. Sun, H. Li, L. Zhong, P. Muneesawang, N. Dong, B. Elder, L. Guan.: An Approach to Ballet Dance Training through MS Kinect, Visualization in a CAVE Virtual Reality Environment. Special Issue on Visual Understanding with RGB-D Sensors. ACM Trans. on Intelligent Systems, Technology (2014)

341. Sgouropoulos, K., Stergiopoulou, E., Papamarkos, N.: A Dynamic Gesture, Posture Recognition System. J. of Intelligent Robotic Systems, 1–14 (2013)

342. Wu, Y., Takatsuka, M.: Spherical self-organizing map using efficient indexed geodesic data structure. Neural Networks, 19(6), 900–910 (2006)

343. Pierris, G., Dahl, T. S.: Compressed sparse code hierarchical SOM on learning, reproducing gestures in humanoid robots. Proc. IEEE RO-MAN 330–335 (2010)

344. Sangole A. P., Leontitis A.: Spherical self-organizing feature map: an introductory review. Inter. J. of Bifurcation, 3195–3206 (2006)

345. Fu, D., Shi, Y. Q., Zou, D., Xuan, G.: JPEG steganalysis using empirical transition matrix in block DCT domain. Inter. Workshop on Multimedia Signal Processing, (2006)

346. Yap, K. H., Li, Z., Zhang, D. J., Ng, Z. K.: Efficient mobile landmark recognition based on saliency-aware scalable vocabulary tree. Proc. ACM Multimedia, 1001–1004 (2012)

347. Guan, T., He, Y., Duan, L., Gao, J., Yang, J., Yu, J.: Efficient Bag-of-Features Generation, Compression for On-Device Mobile Visual Location Recognition. (2013)

348. Sangole, A., Knopf, K.G.: Visualization of randomly ordered numeric data sets using spherical self-organizing feature maps. Computers Graphic 27, 963–976 (2003)

349. M. Raptis, D. Kirovski, H. Hoppe.: Real-Time Classification of Dance Gestures from Skeleton Animation. Proc. of ACM Symposium on Comput. Animation, 147–156, (2011)

350. Dardas, N. H., Georganas, N. D.: Real-time hand gesture detection, recognition using bag-of-features, support vector machine techniques. IEEE Trans. on. Instrumentation, Measurement, 60(11), 3592–3607 (2011)

351. Shimada, A., Taniguchi, R. I.: Gesture recognition using sparse code of hierarchical SOM. Proc. IEEE ICPR, 1–4 (2008)

352. Kawashima, M., Shimada, A., Taniguchi, R-I.: Early recognition of gesture patterns using sparse code of self-organising map. In Advances in Self-Organizing Maps, 116–123 (2009)

353. M. Antonini, M. Barlaud, P. Mathieu, I. Daubechies.: Image Coding Using Wavelet Transform. IEEE Trans. on Image Process, Vol.1, No. 2, 205–220 (1992)

354. Noverre, J. G.: Letters on Dancing, Ballet, translated by Cyril W. Beaumont. (1830)

355. X.D. Huang, Y. Ariki, M.A. Jack.: Hidden Markov Models for Speech Recognition. Edingurgh Univ. Press, (1990)

356. M. Müller, T. Röder, M. Clausen, B. Eberhardt, B. Krüger, A. Weber.: Documentation Mocap Database HDM05. Technical report. Universität Bonn, (2007)

357. Arandjelov, O., Cipolla, R.: An illumination invariant face recognition system for access control using video. Proceedings of British Machine Vision Conference, 2004.

358. Viola, P., and Jones, M. J.: Robust real-time face detection. International journal of computer vision, 57(2), 137–154, (2004).

359. Lee, I.: Relevance Feedback for Distributed Content Based Image Retrieval. IEEE International Symposium on Computer Network and Multimedia Technology, 1–4, (2009)

360. G. Ciocca, R. Schettini: Using a relevance feedback mechanism to improve content based image retrieval, in P. Huijsmans and W. M. Smeulders editor, Visual Information and Information Systems, Springer, 105–114, (1999)

361. Lee, I., and Guan, L.: Content-based image retrieval with automated relevance feedback over distributed peer-to-peer network. IEEE Proceedings of the 2004 International Symposium on Circuits and Systems, Vol. 2, II–5, (2004).

362. Vesanto, J., Sulkava, M., and Hollmén, J.: On the decomposition of the self-organizing map distortion measure. In Proceedings of the workshop on self-organizing maps, 11–16, (2003)

Printed in the United States
By Bookmasters